# THE NEGRO IN COLONIAL
# NEW ENGLAND

LORENZO JOHNSTON GREENE

# THE NEGRO IN COLONIAL
# NEW ENGLAND

with a new preface by Benjamin Quarles

STUDIES IN AMERICAN NEGRO LIFE
*August Meier, General Editor*

ATHENEUM

*New York*

1971

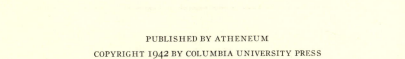

PUBLISHED BY ATHENEUM

COPYRIGHT 1942 BY COLUMBIA UNIVERSITY PRESS

PREFACE TO THE ATHENEUM EDITION COPYRIGHT © 1968 BY BENJAMIN QUARLES

ALL RIGHTS RESERVED

LIBRARY OF CONGRESS CATALOG CARD NUMBER 68-16413

MANUFACTURED IN THE UNITED STATES OF AMERICA BY

HALLIDAY LITHOGRAPH CORPORATION, HANOVER, MASSACHUSETTS

PUBLISHED IN CANADA BY MC CLELLAND & STEWART LTD.

FIRST ATHENEUM PRINTING FEBRUARY 1968

SECOND PRINTING JANUARY 1969

THIRD PRINTING NOVEMBER 1969

FOURTH PRINTING OCTOBER 1971

To My Parents
WILLIS H. AND HARRIET E. GREENE
WHOSE DEVOTION AND SACRIFICE
MADE THIS WORK POSSIBLE.

# PREFACE TO THE ATHENEUM EDITION

by Benjamin Quarles

Of the many historical works that have been given second birth by the reprint revolution of our times, few are more worthy of serious attention than Lorenzo J. Greene's *The Negro in Colonial New England, 1620–1776*. To it we are indebted for three things, if not more—for filling a gap in the literature of American colonial history, for portraying a hitherto neglected aspect of the Negro's role in our country's past and, finally, for presenting us with as fine an exhibition of the historian's craft as one could wish.

Greene's contribution to our fuller understanding of provincial America centers primarily on the African slave trade and the varied occupational role of the New England Negro. Puritan merchants, many of them from socially prominent families, found the slave trade a most lucrative commerce. They became the suppliers of slaves to British America, the triangular trade from New England to Africa to the West Indies bringing great profits to shippers in Massachusetts and Rhode Island. The trans-Atlantic trade in Negroes, as Greene makes clear, created much of the wealth and culture of Boston and Newport, stimulating art and encouraging philanthropy. The internal slave trade was small, however, in the Northern colonies, thus avoiding the heartrending scenes and callous selling techniques that one might witness in the Southern climes.

Slavery in New England was deeply rooted, being traceable as far back as 1638. In addition to the standard justifications of slavery in colonial America—the support of positive law and the existence of a chronic labor shortage—the Puritans, logically enough for theocrats, added a religious reason. Conveniently ignoring the New Testament dictum that God was no respecter of persons, the New Englanders justified Negro slavery upon Biblical grounds and the inexorable workings of Divine Providence.

Bolstered by sanctions, secular and religious, the New Englanders made the most of their heaven-sent servants. While not indispensable, slave labor proved to be most useful. Reflecting the diversified economic life of the region, a slave was likely to be put to work at whatever calling his master engaged in. A bondman in New England had to be as adept in the cabbage patch as in the cornfield, writes Greene. He had to be ready "not only to care for stock, to act as servant, repair a fence, serve on board ship, shoe a horse, print a newspaper, but even to manage his master's business."

The absence of a plantation economy kept the Negro population relatively small, numbering fewer than 17,000 out of a total of approximately 660,000 at the end of the colonial period. A somewhat thinly scattered Negro element meant that the black codes were relatively mild. Only in New England were slave marriages binding in law. Slaves could bring legal suit, their testimony being admissible against whites. The slave had some "elbow room," his status being a cross between bondage and indentured servitude. But if the New England Negro could penetrate the culture barrier, he could not scale the color line. Hence his lot was hardly enviable and if one sought to discover the built-in disadvantages of a black skin he had only to observe the problems faced by the free Negro, who, Greene points out, was probably no better off in the Puritan colonies than elsewhere.

Whether the New England slave developed a "Sambo personality," to use the provocative phrase and concept of Stanley Elkins, Greene does not tell us, for he antedates Elkins. In like fashion Greene does not enter into the more recent discussions as to which came first in colonial British America—slavery or color prejudice. But Greene's work remains a pathbreaker in one notable manner, that of viewing the Negro as an actor as well as someone acted upon, a doer on his own.

Greene furnishes us with many fresh pages on the Negro as

eighteenth-century activist. Here we meet slaves suing for their freedom, among them Abda of Hartford, Connecticut, and Jenny Slew of Ipswich, Massachusetts. We learn of Paul Cuffee, merchant and colonizer; of Lemuel Haynes, pastor of white churches; of well-to-do Abijah Prince, one of the founders of Sunderland, Vermont; of the internationally celebrated Phillis Wheatley; and of her less-known predecessor, Lucy Terry, first Negro American poet. We also meet, in lighter vein, a quartet of slave fiddlers and attend an "election" of a Negro "governor."

If much that Greene tells us is novel, he leaves no doubt as to its reliability. Greene was a close associate of the great pioneer historian of the Negro, Carter G. Woodson, an association of which the then youthful Greene was not unworthy. His documentation of this work is thorough, a feat of some magnitude in view of the scattered and fugitive nature of the source materials.

But the technical apparatus and the temperate tone do not prevent Greene's essential message from coming through. The book's organization is firm, the theme progressing logically and leaving no loose ends. If no pointed contrast is made between slavery in New England and slavery elsewhere in British America, the inferences are unmistakable. Greene writes clearly and with flashes of grace, the prosaic titles of his chapters furnishing no true index of their readability.

The translator of Tolstoy's works, Aylmer Maude, tells of a woman who said that she would like to live her life over again so that she might again have the thrill of reading *War and Peace* for the first time. Doubtless no such memorable experience awaits Greene's new readers. But they, along with a host of repeaters, may confidently expect to find in Greene a work that is both interesting and scholarly, one that makes for an enlargement of outlook and perhaps of vision.

# PREFACE

THERE is no general work on the rôle of the Negro in colonial New England. A number of articles, pamphlets, reminiscences and other accounts, dealing with certain aspects of the Negro slave trade and slavery in the separate New England colonies, or in local areas, are available, but nowhere can a comprehensive treatment of the Negro in the Puritan colonies be found. The present study is an attempt to fill this gap in the literature of American colonial history. It covers approximately one hundred and fifty years and embraces all of the New England colonies. A survey of New England's slave trade and the sale of Negroes in its slave markets is followed by a discussion of the social, political and economic repercussions of the buying and selling of slaves upon Puritan institutions.

It is difficult to express adequately the author's indebtedness to Emeritus Professor Evarts B. Greene and to Professor John A. Krout of Columbia University. Professor Greene suggested a comprehensive study of the Negro in New England, gave freely of his time and his unrivaled knowledge of the colonial period, and patiently guided the actual writing of the manuscript. Even after his retirement from active teaching in 1939, he maintained a lively interest in the study, assisting the author in securing funds to carry forward his research. Professor Krout read the manuscript several times, making detailed comments and criticisms which have been of great value. The author is also grateful to Dr. Dixon Ryan Fox, now President of Union College, in whose seminar at Columbia parts of this dissertation were originally sketched out; to Professors Harry J. Carman, Samuel McKee, Jr., Merle Curti, Arthur W. McMahon and Carter Goodrich of Columbia University for reading the manuscript and offering many helpful suggestions, and to Dr. Lawrence D. Reddick, Miss Henrietta Buckmaster, Miss Helen Boardman and Mr. Harold J. Jonas of New York City for critically reading the manuscript. The writer is indebted to many of his colleagues at Lincoln University, and especially to Mrs. Hazel Teabeau and Professor Thomas Fortune Fletcher of the English Department. Limitations of space prevent individual mention of the staffs of numerous libraries, where courteous cooperation has made research a pleasure.

The author also wishes to thank the Julius Rosenwald Fund, the General Education Board and the Association for the Study of Negro Life and History for helping to finance the study. He is similarly grateful to Mr. Harold Jonas of New York City; Dr. Ernest Bacote of Newark, New Jersey; and Mr. and Mrs. Frank Thomas of Hartford, Connecticut, who contributed toward the publication of the volume. Special thanks are due to Miss Mary Reilly, Miss Florence Bacote, Miss Miriam Stein, Mrs. Helen Scott and Professor H. Hadley Hartshorne who have assisted in preparing the manuscript for the press. Finally, the writer is deeply indebted to his wife, Dr. Thomasina Talley Greene, for her aid in checking references, and for her painstaking reading of the galley and page proofs.

For any errors and shortcomings in this volume, the author alone is responsible. He hopes that the following pages may fill a gap in the literature of colonial history. But if they do no more than point out to scholars the rich possibilities for future research in this field, his efforts will have been amply rewarded.

LORENZO J. GREENE

LINCOLN UNIVERSITY,
JEFFERSON CITY, MISSOURI,
JUNE 4, 1942.

# CONTENTS

# TABLES

# APPENDICES

# THE NEGRO IN COLONIAL
# NEW ENGLAND

# CHAPTER I
# BLACK MERCHANDISE

On August 3, 1713 the stepbrother of Benjamin Franklin advertised in the columns of the *Boston News Letter*:

> Three Negro Men and two Women to be Sold
> and to be seen at the House of Mr. Josiah
> Franklin . . . in Union Street, Boston.[1]

Josiah Franklin was a prosperous merchant,[2] who not only sold Negroes at his tavern, but also permitted other slave dealers to use his place as a show room for human chattels.[3] The sale of Negroes by Franklin should not have been surprising to the casual reader of the *News Letter* in 1713. By this time Bostonians had grown accustomed to the auctioning of slaves, for advertisements listing them for sale had become commonplace— as commonplace, in fact, as the appearance of Negroes on the bustling streets of New England towns. The manner in which this traffic began and the status of the imported blacks in the society of colonial New England is the burden of this study.

Although blacks had been sold in Boston for some time, it is not definitely known when the first Negro slaves were brought into New England.[4] Slavery, like indentured servitude, is said

1 *Boston News Letter*, August, 1713.

2 Josiah Franklin was born in Boston, August 23, 1683. For several years he carried on a thriving business at Hanover and Union Streets. James Savage, *Genealogical Dictionary of the First Settlers of New England*, 4 vols. (Boston, 1680-1867), II, 200. *The Blue Ball*, which served to identify his establishment, served equally to indicate that slaves might be bought and sold there. The building was remodelled and stood until 1858. Justin Winsor, *Memorial History of Boston*, 3 vols. (Boston, 1881), II, 273 n.; Elizabeth Donnan, *Documents Illustrative of the Slave Trade to America*, 3 vols. (Washington, 1930), III, 66.

3 In June of the same year, Franklin was displaying at his tavern, three Negro men and three Negro women owned by Messrs. Henry Dewick and William Asten. *Boston News Letter*, June 15-22, 1713.

4 *Cf.* "Queries Relating to Slavery in Massachusetts" (1795), *Massachusetts Historical Society Collections*, Fifth Series, III, 389, 391, 399.

to have existed in New England before the settlement of the Massachusetts Bay Colony in 1629 and was first identified with Massachusetts.[5] Samuel Maverick, apparently New England's first slaveholder,[6] arrived in Massachusetts in 1624[7] and, according to Palfrey, owned two Negroes before John Winthrop, who later became governor of that colony, arrived in 1630.[8] If Palfrey's statement is correct, the beginnings of New England Negro slavery would fall somewhere between 1624 and 1630.

Other authorities, however, who claim that Negro slaves were first brought to New England in 1638,[9] base their contention on a statement in John Winthrop's *Journal*, recording on December 12, 1638 the return to Boston of Captain William

5 *The History of the Colony and the Province of the Massachusetts Bay*, ed. Lawrence Shaw Mayo, 3 vols. (Cambridge, 1936), I, 374.

6 John Gorham Palfrey, *History of New England During the Stuart Dynasty*, 3 vols. (Boston, 1858-1864), II, 30 n. Palfrey says John Josselyn, an English traveller who visited New England in 1638, and who as a guest of Maverick relates the aversion of one of his slaves to forcible mating, is responsible for Maverick's being called the first slave owner in New England. "Josselyn's Account of Two Voyages to New England," *Mass. Hist. Soc. Colls.* (Boston, 1883), Third Series, III, 231; Moore, George H., *Notes on Negro Slavery in Massachusetts* (New York, 1866), p. 90, disagrees with Josselyn and Palfrey. Moore contends that had the woman been enslaved since 1629 or before, she would not have protested against forced mating. *Ibid.*, p. 9. But Moore overlooked the possibility of the woman's being a later arrival, perhaps even as late as 1638, the date of the incident. *Cf.* Emory Washburne's "Extinction of Slavery in Massachusetts", *Mass. Hist. Soc. Proceedings, 1855-1858* (Boston, 1854), III, 189; Joseph B. Felt, *Annals of Salem* (Salem, 1849), II, 414; William H. Sumner, *A History of East Boston* (Boston, 1858), p. 90.

7 Samuel Maverick (c. 1602-1676), the son of an Anglican clergyman, came to New England in 1624. He was probably identified with the colonization scheme of Sir Ferdinando Gorges. Maverick built a fortified house at Chelsea, Massachusetts, about 1625. He engaged in commerce and owned several vessels. Maverick employed both Negroes and indentured servants. *Dictionary of American Biography*, XII, 432.

8 In quoting Josselyn ("Account of Two Voyages to New England," *loc. cit.*, III, 231) Palfrey erroneously places the number of Maverick's Negroes at two, whereas Josselyn (*op. cit.*, p. 231) mentions at least three. Palfrey, *History of New England During the Stuart Dynasty*, II, 30 n.

9 Moore, *op. cit.*, p. 9; Donnan, *op. cit.*, III, 4 n.; Felt, *op. cit.*, II, 414.

Pierce in the Salem ship, *Desire*.[10] Pierce had gone to Providence and Tortugas in the West Indies with a cargo including some captive Pequod Indians, whom he had sold into slavery there. The colonists, who were in need of labor, had feared to enslave the fierce Indian warriors and ordered Pierce to dispose of them in the West Indies.[11] In exchange for his goods and chattels Pierce, according to Winthrop, brought back " salt, cotton, tobacco and Negroes . . ." [12] This statement of the Governor's is the earliest recorded account of Negro slavery in New England, evidence that led the two most painstaking investigators of New England slavery and the slave trade, George H. Moore and Elizabeth Donnan, to agree upon 1638 as the year in which Negro slaves were first brought into the section.[13] Negroes may have been enslaved before that time but earlier allusions to slavery are inferential, and even contemporaries were apparently no more certain of the facts.[14] It seems reasonable to conclude, however, that Negro slavery was introduced into New England sometime between 1624 and 1638, with the weight of evidence leaning toward the latter date. For purposes

10 Winthrop, *History of New England*, I, 260.

11 *Ibid.*, I, 148, 233-34; Moore, *op. cit.*, p. 9. In 1637, the Pequod Indians of central Connecticut, goaded to desperation by the encroachment of white settlers upon their land, attacked Wethersfield. A few months later, a combined force of Massachusetts and Connecticut militia, reinforced by their Narragansett Indian allies, fell upon the Pequod village near Mystic, Connecticut. Only a few Indians escaped the slaughter. These were sold into slavery. The women and children were enslaved in New England; the men and boys carried to the West Indies and sold into slavery. For the Pequod war, *vide* Winthrop, *op. cit.*, I, 233-234; William Bradford, " History of Plymouth Plantations," *Mass. Hist. Soc. Coll.*, Fourth Series, III, 360; William A. Hubbard, *Narrative of Indian Wars in New England*, pp. 45-48.

12 Winthrop, *op. cit.*, I, 260.

13 *Notes on Slavery in Massachusetts*, p. 9; *Documents Illustrative of The Slave Trade to America*, III, 4n. Felt also believes that Maverick's Negroes may have been purchased from the *Desire's* cargo. *Op. cit.*, II, 414.

14 *Cf.* reply of Thomas Pemberton to query of Judge Tucker of Virginia on the beginnings of slavery in Massachusetts. "Belknap Papers," *Mass. Hist. Soc. Coll.*, Fifth Series, III, 392. In 1795, Dr. John Elliot, one of the founders of the Massachusetts Historical Society was uncertain when Negro slavery was introduced in Massachusetts. *Ibid.*, p. 382.

of this study 1638 will be regarded as the year of the introduction of Negro slavery in New England.

Available data regarding the beginnings of Negro slavery are even more indefinite for the other New England colonies than for Massachusetts. Steiner tells of a Negro in Hartford, Connecticut, who was killed by his Dutch master in 1639;[15] and it is said that blacks were employed in New Haven Colony in 1644.[16] Negroes are first referred to in New Hampshire in 1645, the year in which the Massachusetts General Court ordered a Mr. Williams of Piscataqua (Portsmouth) to return to Boston a Negro stolen from Africa and purchased by him from a Massachusetts slave trader.[17] The earliest mention of Negro slavery in Rhode Island occurs in the law of 1652, which laudably, but vainly, endeavored to limit involuntary servitude to ten years.[18] As the wording of the law implies, slavery was apparently already existent in that colony at the time of the passage of the measure.[19]

It must not be assumed from the foregoing that Negroes were the only persons held in bondage in New England. Impelled by a chronic shortage of labor, the Puritans adopted the labor pattern established by the Spaniards more than one hundred years earlier.[20] Combined with Negro slavery in New Eng-

15 The owner, Gysbert Opdyck, was at that time Commissary of the Dutch fort at Hartford. Bernard Steiner, "History of Slavery in Connecticut," *Johns Hopkins University Studies in Historical and Political Science,* Eleventh Series, IX-X (Baltimore, 1896), 23 n.; Frederick Calvin Norton, " Negro Slavery in Connecticut," *Connecticut Magazine,* V, No. 6 (Hartford, 1899), p. 320.

16 Steiner, *op. cit.,* p. 20.

17 The Negro was to be sent back to Africa on the ground that he had been stolen. *Records of The Governor and Company of the Massachusetts Bay, 1642-1644* (Boston, 1835), VI, 136.

18 *Rhode Island Colonial Records,* I, 243.

19 Miss Donnan believes that Dutch traders may have sold a few slaves to Rhode Island settlers before 1652. *Op. cit.,* III, 108 n.

20 The Spaniards enslaved Indians, Negroes and white persons. In 1498, Columbus shipped 600 Indians to Spain to be sold as slaves. Sir Arthur Helps, *The Spanish Conquest in America,* 4 vols. (New York, 1900), I,

land were the several kinds of unfree labor current in that day; white,[21] Negro [32] and Indian indentured servitude,[23] Indian slavery [24] and, in occasional instances, the slavery of white people.[25] Of these servile groups the Indians, and not the Negroes, were the first to be enslaved in New England. Indian slavery dates from the Pequod War of 1637, when the victori-

113, 114. For general accounts of slavery in Spanish America, *vide* Edward G. Bourne, *Spain in America* (New York, 1904), III, 210-212, 255-260, 273; Charles Chapman, "Colonial Hispanic America," *Hispanic America Colonial and Republican* (New York, 1938), pp. 23-27, 112; Donnan, *op. cit.*, I, 16, 17.

21 White indentured servants were persons who sold themselves, or were sold, into bondage for a definite period, usually from seven to fourteen years. Indentured servitude in New England dates from the founding of Salem (about 1628). One hundred and eighty were sent over to prepare food and homes for the settlers who came over in 1629. Ulrich B. Phillips, *American Negro Slavery* (New York, 1918), p. 99; Hannah Adams, *History of New England* (Dedham, 1799), p. 27; Edward Channing, *History of The United States*, 6 vols. (New York, 1921), I, 331.

22 "Ran-away on Saturday Night last the 11th Inst. from Mr. Gershom Flagg of Woburn, a Negro Man Servant, Indentured for 7 years, named Pampeg York," *Boston Weekly News Letter*, April 15, 1742; *vide* also *Continental Journal and Weekly Advertiser*, January 31, 1782; February 21, 1782.

23 In 1776, Robert Kinsman of Plainfield, Connecticut, offered three dollars for his runaway Indian servant, James Simons. *Connecticut Gazette and Universal Intelligencer*, December 27, 1776. Lauber, *Indian Slavery in Colonial Times*, p. 295.

24 The best account of Indian slavery is in Almon Wheeler Lauber, *Indian Slavery in Colonial Times* (New York, 1913), *passim*; *vide* also files of *Boston News Letter* and other eighteenth century newspapers.

25 In 1641, William Andrews, an indentured servant, convicted of having assaulted his master, was condemned to slavery by the Massachusetts General Court. John Haslewood and Giles Player received similar sentences for theft and housebreaking. *Records of the Governor and Company of the Massachusetts Bay in New England, 1628-1641*, ed. Nathaniel B. Shurtleff (Boston, 1853), I, 246. It is probable that isolated instances of white slavery occurred throughout the colonial period. As late as 1760 a white man in Connecticut is said to have been sold into slavery in Barbados because of "notorious stealing breaking up and robbing two mills and living in a renegade manner in the wilderness." Bernard Steiner, "History of Slavery in Connecticut," *Johns Hopkins University Studies in Historical and Political Science*, Eleventh Series, IX-X (Baltimore, 1896), 23.

ous settlers themselves enslaved the captive Pequod women and children and sold the males into West Indian bondage.[26] In other words, apparently a year before the first black slaves were introduced into New England, the Indians had already been reduced to bondage. Indians, Negroes and white persons were either enslaved for life or held to service for a period of years throughout the entire colonial era.

While slavery of all types existed in colonial New England, this section became even more deeply involved in the slave trade. Puritan participation in the buying and selling of Negroes began at an early date. In this traffic, as in slavery, Massachusetts took the lead. It was the *Desire,* the Salem ship previously mentioned, that started the New England slave trade[27] and thereby laid the basis for the economic interdependence of colonial New England and the West Indies.[28] Quick to realize the almost insatiable demand in the sugar islands for Negroes,[29] who were being supplied at considerable profit by the hated Dutch,[30] the Puritan traders early began to engage in the Negro traffic.

The year 1644 was a momentous date in the history of the New England slave trade. Before that time, Massachusetts merchants had occasionally brought in Negroes from the West Indies, but in that year Boston traders attempted to import slaves directly from Africa, when an association of business men sent three ships there for gold dust and Negroes.[31] One of these vessels (probably the *Rainbow*), returned to Boston in the following year with a cargo of wine, salt, sugar and to-

26 Lauber, *op. cit.*, pp. 126, 127; Hubbard, *op. cit.*, pp. 223, 229; Moore, *op. cit.*, p. 1.

27 George Francis Dow, *Slave Ships and Slaving* (Salem, 1927), p. 268.

28 *Vide infra*, pp. 24-25.

29 Dow, *ut. supra.*

30 Donnan, *op. cit.*, I, 74-78.

31 Captain James Smith and Thomas Keyser were the moving spirits in this enterprise; other members of the group were Henry Dow, Robert Shopton, and Miles Causson. Donnan, *op. cit.*, III, 45, 45 n.

bacco,[32] having exchanged her Negroes for these products in Barbados.[33] The voyage of the *Rainbow* stimulated the entry of other Boston merchants into the African trade.[34] But the Negro traffic, although apparently lucrative, was dangerous for private traders, especially during the seventeenth century. At this time an international struggle for control was being waged on the West Coast of Africa,[35] where powerful trading combinations fought to corner the markets that supplied the slaves to the New World.[36] Chief among these organizations were the Dutch West India Company and the English Royal African Company.[37] Independent traders, however, such as the New England merchants, with their limited capital, could not compete with these monopolies which were backed by the armed forces of the competing nations. Fearing confiscation of their ships and cargo,

32 Winthrop, *op. cit.*, II, 227.

33 *Ibid.* The two other ships did not fare as well as the *Rainbow*. One was attacked by an Irish man-o-war off the Canary Islands and suffered £200 damage. The other barely escaped an attack near the Madeira Islands. *Ibid.*, p. 228.

34 In 1649, John Parrish of Boston sent the ship *Boston* to Africa. A little earlier, Henry Parkes leased half of a forty-ton ship and sent it to Africa and Barbados. Donnan, III, 9, 9n. In 1680 Sir Henry Morgan, Governor of Jamaica, reported that a New England ship (probably from Massachusetts) en route from Guinea to Nevis, laden with "Negroes, elephants teeth and gold dust had been seized at one of the French Islands." *Calendar of State Papers: Colonial, 1677-1680*, p. 630; Donnan, III, 315.

35 For the international struggle for control of the slave trade during the seventeenth century, see Bandinel, *op. cit.*, ch. iv; Donnan, I, 73-121.

36 The Royal African Company was an outgrowth of the powerful Company of Royal Adventurers Trading into Africa, which was organized in 1660. For history of this Company *vide*, George F. Zook, *The Company of Royal Adventurers Trading into Africa*. Reprinted from *Journal of Negro History*, IV (April, 1919). The Royal African Company was organized in 1672 following the collapse of the Company of Royal Adventurers. To it was granted the sole right of trading along the entire West African Coast. Ships and cargoes of independent traders violating the Company's territory were to be confiscated. The monopoly of the Royal African Company lasted until 1696, when its privileges were revoked by the British Parliament. Donnan, *op. cit.*, II, 85-86.

37 Bandinel, *loc. cit.*; Donnan, I, 73-121.

should they trespass upon the rights of these companies, daring Masachusetts traders made the much longer trip to the East Coast of Africa. By 1676 Bay Colony merchants were bringing slaves from the distant island of Madagascar.[38] Two years later John Endicott and John Saffin of Boston were selling these Negroes in Virginia.[39] In 1681 Saffin, merchant and jurist, was smuggling slaves overland through Rhode Island into Massachusetts.[40] By 1700, Boston traders were supplying the other New England colonies with Negroes.[41] In short, the New England slave trade of the seventeenth century seems to have been centered almost wholly in Massachusetts,[42] with Boston the chief, if not the only, slave port. If New Hampshire, Connecticut and Rhode Island engaged in the Negro trade before 1700, they officially denied it when questioned by the British Committee for Trade and Foreign Plantations.[43]

Although New England's share in the slave trade was small in the seventeenth century, her merchants had by 1700 laid the foundations of a lucrative commerce. They had already begun

38 So Edmund Randolph reported in his reply to the Home Government in 1676. *Historical Documents Relating to The American Colonial Church*, ed. William Stevens Perry, III, 8.

39 Helen Catterall, *Judicial Cases Concerning American Slavery and the Negro* (Washington, 1926), I, 54.

40 Donnan, *op. cit.*, III, 15-16.

41 Governor Leete of Connecticut, in his report to the Lords of the Privy Council in 1680, implied that Massachusetts merchants annually brought three or four Negroes into Connecticut from Barbados. *Public Records of the Colony of Connecticut*, May 30, 1678–June 1689 (Hartford, 1859), III, 298 (hereinafter cited as *Conn. Col. Recs.*). Gov. Cranston of Rhode Island told the British Committee for Trade and Foreign Plantations that on May 30, 1696, the Massachusetts briganteen, *Sea Flower*, had brought forty-seven slaves into Newport. *Rhode Island Colonial Records,* IV, 54.

42 Donnan, III, 4-16. Maine was included in Massachusetts. Vermont which was part of New York until 1777 had no coast line and therefore could not participate in the slave trade.

43 *Calendar of State Papers: Colonial, 1708-1709*, p. 209; *Conn. Col. Recs.,* III, 298; *Rhode Island Colonial Records*, IV, 54. (Hereinafter cited as *R. I. Col. Recs.*)

the triangular slave voyages and had learned that the West Indies offered the best market for Negroes. As comparatively few Negroes were brought to New England in the seventeenth century, the traders in these colonies made their profits as carriers rather than as exploiters of Negro labor. In 1700 there were probably not more than a thousand Negroes in all the Puritan colonies.[44]

The New England slave trade attained its greatest development in the eighteenth century.[45] Several factors stimulated its growth. The revocation by the British Parliament in 1696 of the monopoly held by the Royal African Company[46] made it possible for all Englishmen to engage legally in the slave trade. Equally important was the *Assiento* of 1713, by which England wrested from Spain the privilege of supplying 4800 Negroes a year to Spanish America for thirty years.[47] In the execution of this huge contract the participation of colonial merchants was essential.[48] Increasing demand for Negroes in the sugar islands of the British and " foreign " West Indies,[49] together with the growing employment of blacks in the tobacco and rice growing

44 According to the report of Governor Dudley of Massachusetts there were only 550 Negroes in the Colony in 1708. *Calendar State Papers: Colonial, 1708-1709*, p. 110.

45 There exists no satisfactory secondary account of the New England slave trade. For aspects of the trade, *cf.* William B. Weeden, " The Early Slave Trade in New England," *American Antiquarian Society Proceedings*, New Series, V (Worcester, 1899), p. 109; William B. Weeden, *Economic and Social History of New England*, 2 vols. (Cambridge, 1890), II, ch. 1; George Champlin Mason, *American Historical Record*, I, 312 ff.

46 *Cf.* Donnan (I, 421-429) for text. Private traders were to pay a tax of 10 percent on all European goods carried to Africa. *Ibid.*

47 The terms of the contract necessitated draining off the flower of African manhood. It was agreed that " none of the said 4,800 Negroes shall be under the age of ten years, nine parts in ten of the ... Negroes so to be furnished shall be of the age of sixteen years at least, and none of them shall exceed the age of 40 years." *Ibid.*, p. 159. For full text *vide ibid.*, pp. 158-159.

48 Mason, *op. cit.*, I, 312.

49 Donnan, I, 91; W. D. Weatherford, *The Negro from Africa to America* (New York, 1924), p. 93.

colonies of the South,[50] also furthered the growth of the New England slave trade. The British government, furthermore, encouraged and protected the traffic and vetoed every attempt of the colonists to hinder or to abolish it.[51] Increasing well-being in the colonies, and particularly in New England, gave added impetus to the slave trade. Geographic conditions also played an important role, since the New Englanders, prevented by climate and soil from reaping rich returns from agriculture, had to look elsewhere if they were to match the wealth of the landed aristocracy of the South. For this reason, the thrifty New Englanders, attracted by the prospect of far greater profits than could possibly be drawn from the land, early began to engage in commerce, the fishing industry and in the trade in Negroes.[52]

As a result of these factors the New England colonies in the eighteenth century became the greatest slave-trading section of America.[53] There came into vogue the famous triangular slave trade, with New England, Africa and the West Indies as its focal points. From New England's many ports trim, sturdy ships, built from her own forests, carried to the West Indies much needed food and other commodities, such as surplus beans, peas, hay, corn, staves, lumber, low-grade fish, horses, dairy products and a miscellaneous assortment of goods.[54] When the

50 Ulrich B. Phillips, *American Negro Slavery*, ch. iv, v.

51 *Vide* circular instructions to colonial governors in eighteenth century specifically forbidding them to assent to any law laying duties upon, or discouraging, the slave trade. For specimen of one of these circulars, *vide*, *Journal of the House of Representatives of Massachusetts, 1732-1734* (Boston, 1930), p. 23; Leonard Woods Larabee, ed., *Royal Instructions to Colonial Governors, 1670-1776*, 2 vols. (New York, 1935), II, 673-674.

52 In 1631, a year after the arrival of Governor Winthrop, Massachusetts built its first ocean-going ship, *The Blessing of the Bay*. Two years later, Boston merchants began the exportation of fish, and in 1638 they entered upon the Negro slave trade. George Dow and John Robinson, " The Sailing Ships of New England," *Marine Research Society*, Series III (Salem, 1928), p. 7.

53 Donnan, *op. cit.*, II, 405.

54 A typical cargo was that carried by the sloop *Africa*, owned by Samuel Waldo of Boston. On the first leg of a voyage to the Guinea Coast she

captains of these vessels were able to exchange their cargoes for rum, they would next proceed directly to Africa. There they bartered their rum for slaves whom they transported to the West Indies, where they disposed of them for rum, sugar, molasses and other tropical products or for bills of exchange. But there were necessary variations from this procedure. When rum was unobtainable in the islands, the Yankee captains gladly bartered their wares for sugar, cocoa, molasses or other products. The sugar and molasses were carried to New England, distilled into rum, and along with trinkets, bar iron, beads and light-colored cloth taken to Africa and exchanged for Negroes.[55] The slaves who survived the terrible ordeal of the Middle Passage—as the crossing between Africa and America was called—were sold in the West Indies for more rum, sugar and molasses, or for bills of exchange.[56]

Vital to the slave trade as well as to New England's economy were sugar, rum and molasses.[57] The distillation of millions of gallons of molasses brought from the British islands, or smuggled from the foreign West Indies, was the basis of a liquor industry of such proportions that the making of rum became New England's largest manufacturing business before the Revolution. The number of distilleries was almost incredible, with more than thirty in Rhode Island,[58] twenty-two of them in

carried to Barbados: fish, candles, wine, shoes, desks, silversmith's wares, pork, oil, staves, bricks, lead, brass, steel, iron, pewter, beads, cowries, muskets and dry goods. Donnan, III, 42 and note; cf. Mason, *American Historical Record*, I, 315; William B. Dubois, *Suppression of the Slave Trade*, p. 28 n.

55 It must not be assumed that all ships followed the same procedure. Some ships like the *Ellery* of Boston (*Boston Gazette or Weekly Advertiser*, Jan. 15, 1754) and the *Carr* of Newport (*Boston Weekly Post Boy*, July 17, 1749) sailed directly to Africa.

56 The general outlines of the triangular slave trade are well known. First hand information may be found in Donnan's *Documents* cited above, III, 42-46 and *passim*.

57 *R. I. Col. Recs., 1757-1759*, VI, 319: *American Historical Record*, I, 316; Donnan, III, 48, 203, *passim*.

58 Donnan, III, 205.

Newport,[59] and in Massachusetts sixty-three, which alone produced 2,700,000 gallons of rum in 1774.[60] Little Newburyport,
a bustling ship-building and commercial town on the Merrimac
River, had ten distilleries.[61] Of Boston's eight distilleries the
most modern one was credited with producing a large amount
of rum of remarkable cheapness.[62] Although vast quantities of
this rum were consumed at home, it was by no means all intended for domestic consumption. It was an almost indispensable article aboard fishing and whaling vessels, in lumber camps
and for the fur industry.[63] But primarily rum was linked with
the Negro trade, and immense quantities of the raw liquor were
sent to Africa and exchanged for slaves. So important was rum
on the Guinea Coast that by 1723 it had surpassed French and
Holland brandy, English gin, trinkets and dry goods as a medium of barter.[64]

Merchants spared no effort to make the slave trade as profitable as possible. Slaves and commodities were carried in small
undermanned ships with crews rarely exceeding eighteen men,[65]
while some vessels, like the *Nancy* and the *Betsy,* carried only
six.[66] According to Mason, most of the slave vessels ranged be-

59 George Champlin Mason, " The African Slave Trade in Colonial Times,"
*American Historical Record,* I, 316. (Hereinafter cited as *Amer. Hist. Rec.*)

60 Harry J. Carman and Samuel McKee, *History of the United States*
(New York, 1931), I, 135.

61 *Standard History of Essex County, Massachusetts,* ed. Dr. Henry
Wheatland (Boston, 1878), p. 318.

62 Winsor says the cost of distilling a gallon of rum was two shillings.
*Memorial History of Boston,* II, 447. *Cf.* Mason, who places the cost of
distilling a gallon of rum in the eighteenth century at as low as 5½ pence.
*Amer. Hist. Rec.,* I, 316-317.

63 Weeden, " Early African Slave Trade in New England," *loc. cit.,* p. 116.

64 *R. I. Col. Recs.,* IV, 38; *Amer. Hist. Rec.,* I, 317; Donnan, III, 135.

65 *The Gift of God* (1650) carried eighteen men; the *Mermaid* (1739)
eleven; out of 16 ships engaged in the slave trade between 1780-1790 only
one had as many as eighteen men, two had fifteen, three twelve, and three
had only seven. Donnan, III, 12, 51, 183, 337-340.

66 *Ibid.,* III, 337-340.

tween forty and fifty tons until 1750, when ships up to 200 tons were used.[67] In the early years of the trade a space three feet ten inches high was reserved between decks for the slaves,[68] but later, by reducing its dimensions to three feet three inches, additional room was made available for carrying Negroes. Men, women and children were separated by bulkheads. With only ten to thirteen inches of surface room alloted each slave [69] the Negroes, packed spoon-fashion and unable to stand, suffered cruelly on the trip to America.[70] With this extreme economy in ships and men, it is remarkable that mortality on the slave ships, great as it was, failed to reach an even higher figure.

Among the New England slave trading colonies, Massachusetts and Rhode Island ranked first,[71] with Connecticut and New Hampshire playing relatively minor roles in the traffic.[72] Boston was preeminent as the port of departure for slave ships,[73] with Newport, Rhode Island as its closest rival; [74] but Salem, New-

67 *Op. cit.*, 313. The *Fame* and *Little Becky* were of forty tons; the *Lucretia*, forty-two tons. Among the larger vessels were the *Greyhound*, one hundred fifty *tons*; and the *Susey*, one hundred thirty tons. *Ibid.*, 314; *vide* Donnan, III, *passim* for size of other vessels; *cf.* Weeden, *Economic and Social History of New England*, II, 458.

68 *Amer. Hist. Rec.*, I, 313, and note. Weeden, *ut supra*.

69 *Ibid.*, p. 313 n.

70 *Vide* Mason, *op. cit.*, p. 345; Dow, *Slave Ships and Slaving*, p. 142. For vivid first hand accounts of the slave trade, especially the " Middle Passage " in the seventeenth and eighteenth centuries, *vide* Dow, *Slave Ships and Slaving*, chs. vii, ix-xi and *passim*; Thomas Buxton, *The African Slave Trade* (London, 1840), ch. ii; Nicholas Owen, *Journal of a Slave Trader, 1746-1757*, ed. Eveline Martin (London, 1930); Donnan, *Docs.*, I-III are best of all. For pictures showing storing of Negroes aboard vessels *vide* Donnan, *Docs.*, II, plate facing p. 592.

71 For importance of Massachusetts and Rhode Island in the slave trade *vide* Donnan, *op. cit.*, III, *passim*.

72 *Conn. Col. Recs.*, III, 298; *Calendar of State Papers: Colonial, 1708-1709*, pp. 111, 209; Donnan, *op. cit.*, III, 1.

73 Elizabeth Donnan, " The New England Slave Trade after the Revolution," *New England Quarterly*, III, 260.

74 *Amer. Antiq. Soc. Proceedings*, New Series, V, 111.

buryport, Charlestown and Kittery, Massachusetts; Providence, Bristol and Jamestown, Rhode Island; Portsmouth, New Hampshire; and New London and Hartford, Connecticut all participated to a lesser extent in the Negro trade.[75] In these towns there grew up a privileged class of slave-trading merchants whose wealth was drawn largely from the Negro traffic. They enjoyed the highest social position and held public offices of the greatest trust and responsibility. The Belchers,[76] Waldos,[77] Fanueils,[78] and Cabots [79] of Boston; the Royalls [80] of

[75] For part played by these towns in the slave trade, *vide*, files of eighteenth century newspapers cited *infra* (this chapter); Donnan, *Documents*, III, *passim*; *ibid.*, " New England Slave Trade After the Revolution," *loc. cit.*, pp. 260-264.

[76] Jonathan Belcher (b. 1681, d. 1757) was a prosperous merchant of Boston and in 1730 became Governor of Massachusetts. *Lamb's Biographical Dictionary of the United States*, ed. John Howard (8 vols.), I, 256. In December 1728, Belcher and four other merchants sent the ship, *Katherine*, to Guinea. There Captain Atkinson was to exchange his cargo mostly for " good likely Negroes from 12 to 25 years of age, the greatest part to be boys." *Vide* Donnan, III, 36-38 n. for complete instructions, also *Journal of the House of Representatives of Massachusetts, 1732-1734*, p. 23 (hereinafter cited as *J. H. R. Mass.*).

[77] Cornelius Waldo, the maternal great grandfather of Ralph Waldo Emerson (*Dictionary of American Biography*, VII, 132) was a politician, land speculator, capitalist and slave-merchant. He imported miscellaneous merchandise: " Choice Irish Duck, fine Florence wine, negro slaves and Irish butter." *Ibid.*, XIX, 333. In 1734 Captain Rhodes, of Samuel Waldo's ship *Africa*, purchased on the Coast 200 Negroes, a ton of bees wax and a half ton of ivory. When Captain Rhodes lost many of the Negroes from the flux while enroute to the West Indies and then sold the remainder for unsalable cocoa, Waldo refused to pay Rhodes his bill for £1207.6.4. Rhodes sued Waldo and won a judgment of £752.56½, costs of Court, etc., *cf. New England Quarterly*, III, 136-145; and Donnan, *Documents*, III, 42-46 for Waldo's instructions to Rhodes.

[78] Andrew Fanueil was the uncle of Peter Fanueil (*Colonial Society of Massachusetts, Transactions, 1892-1894*, I, 367). At the time of his death in 1738 Andrew was one of the wealthiest men in Boston (*New England Weekly Journal*, February 14, 1738). On June 16, 1718, Fanueil was selling Negroes at his home. *Boston News Letter*, June 16, 1718. Peter Fanueil (1700-1743) was the nephew of Andrew Fanueil and at his uncle's death inherited one of the largest fortunes of the day. Part of his fortune like that of his uncle came from the slave trade. His most famous slave venture was the *Jolly Bachelor*, which was attacked by Portuguese

Charlestown; the Pepperells [81] of Kittery; and the Crownin-shields [82] of Salem, Massachusetts, were but a few of the leading slave merchants of the Bay Colony. Equally representative were the Malbones,[83] Gardners,[84] Ellerys,[85] and Champlins [86]

and Negroes on the Guinea Coast in 1742. The Captain and crew were murdered and the slaves released. His gift of Fanueil Hall to Boston was evidence of his philanthropy made possible by wealth gleaned from the slave trade. For Peter Fanueil *vide* " Publications of Colonial Society of Massachusetts," *Transactions, 1892-1894*, I, 367; *Dictionary of American Biography*, VI, 262, 263; Donnan, *Documents*, III, 52-65; D. E. Brown, *Fanueil Hall and Fanueil Hall Market* (Boston, 1901), p. 45; Winsor, *Memorial History of Boston*, II, 262-263.

79 Donnan, *Documents*, III, 66. George Cabot was an ancestor of both the late and the present Senators Henry Cabot Lodge. Charles E. Trow, *The Old Shipmaster of Salem* (New York, 1905), p. 2.

80 Isaac Royall was the brother of Jacob Royall of Charlestowne, Massachusetts. Both came from Antiqua (Donnan, *Documents*, III, 38 n.). Both were slave merchants. In 1738, Isaac offered a " group of likely Negroes from 10 to 12 years." *Weekly Rehearsal*, May 7, 1730, cited in Donnan, *ut supra*.

81 William Pepperell was one of the leading merchants of New England. He was born at Kittery Point, Maine (then Massachusetts) on June 27, 1696 and died July 6, 1759. Pepperell was deeply involved in the West India trade. Usher Parsons (*Life of Sir William Pepperell* [Boston, 1855], p. 28), says Pepperell did not participate in the slave traffic. Yet five slaves were sent him from the West Indies in 1719. *Ibid.* Whether these slaves were for Pepperell's use or were to be sold by him, neither Parsons nor Donnan (*Docs.*, III, 28) states. Of the slaves four died in transit; the other died three weeks after landing. Parsons, *ut supra*; Donnan, *ut supra*.

82 Captain George Crowninshield sent the *Polly* and *Sally* to Africa for slaves in 1788. *New England Quarterly*, III, 261.

83 The Malbone brothers—John and Godfrey—were born in Virginia, but subsequently migrated to Rhode Island. Both engaged extensively in the slave trade and the rum industry. *Dictionary of American Biography*, XII, 216. On February 21, 1737, Godfrey's schooner *Haddock* was captured with the loss of " eight slaves " and a " quantity of Gold Dust." *Boston News Letter*, February 21, 1737; cited in Donnan, *Docs.*, III, 136; *cf.* Edward Peterson, *History of Rhode Island*, p. 103; Donnan, *Docs.*, III, 131 n. Godfrey was the grandfather of Edward Greene Malbone, the famous portrait painter. *Dictionary of American Biography, ut supra*.

84 Caleb Gardner, the son of William and Mary Gardner, was born Jan. 24, 1739 and died Dec. 24, 1806. He took to the sea at an early age and rapidly rose to prominence in the commercial world. Randolph G. Adams in

of Newport; the Browns [87] of Providence, the DeWolfs [88] of

his biographical sketch of Gardner (*Dictionary of American Biography*, III, 140) merely surmised "that he was connected with the slave trade to some extent." Donnan, however (III, 337-339) shows that Gardner was part owner of the slave ships *Hope, Washington* and *Dove*, and was heavily involved in the slave trade. Gardner was prominent in public affairs and held several important offices during the American Revolution. *Dictionary of American Biography, ut supra.*

85 William Ellery was the father of the signer of the Declaration of Independence and owner of the slave ships *Amtis* and *Success.* In 1746, Ellery instructed one of his Captains to purchase in Africa "forty or fifty Negroes most of them mere Boys and Girls." Donnan, III, 138 n.; *cf.* Appleton, *Cyclopedia of American Biography*, II, 326.

86 Three Champlins—Christopher Sr., Christopher Jr., and George—carried on a flourishing trade in Negroes. Christopher Sr. (1731-1805) was a native of Charleston, South Carolina. Arriving at Newport while a boy, he later became one of the town's most prosperous merchants. For part played by Champlins in the slave trade *vide* "Commerce of Rhode Island" (ed. Gertrude Kimball), *Mass. Hist. Soc. Colls.*, Series Seven, IX, especially pp. 428-429; Donnan, *Docs.*, III, 116, 189, 266, 267.

87 The Brown family was one of the greatest mercantile families in colonial America. At least six of them, James, his brother, Obadiah, and James' four sons: Nicholas, John, Joseph and Moses, carried on one of the biggest slave-trading businesses in New England. For over fifty years this powerful family reaped large rewards from the slave trade. When James Brown sent the *Mary* to Africa in 1736, he launched Providence into the Negro traffic and laid the foundation for the Brown fortune. From this year until 1790, the Browns played a commanding role in the New England slave trade. The Browns are intricately bound up with the economic, educational, and political life of the eighteenth century. Because of their donations to Rhode Island College, the name was changed to Brown University. For the Browns, *vide.* "Letter Book of James Brown," *R. I. Hist. Soc.* (Providence, 1922), pp. x, xi; Kimball, *Providence in Colonial Times*, pp. 245-248; Weeden, *Early Rhode Island*, p. 223; Donnan, II, 83-86, 132-133, 143n., 203, 260, *passim; Dictionary of American Biography* (hereinafter cited as *D. A. B.*), III, 128-129; 141, 146-147; 148-149.

88 Anthony De Wolf came from Guadeloupe to Bristol, and there married the sister of Simon Potter, a slave merchant and privateer. Wilfred Munro, *Tales of an Old Seaport* (Princeton, 1917), p. 17. Four of their fifteen children: Charles, James, John and William became captains of vessels engaged in the slave trade. Weeden, *Early Rhode Island*, p. 190. Most famous of the brothers was James, known as "Captain Jim", who laid the basis of the family fortune. M. A. Howe, *Bristol, Rhode Island* (Cambridge, 1930), p. 62; *New England Quarterly*, III, 257. Neither state nor national pro-

Bristol, and the Robinsons [89] of Narragansett, Rhode Island.

New England merchants sold most of their slaves in the West Indies and in the southern colonies,[90] areas in which the great demand for Negroes to work the plantations resulted in high profits. Slaves, costing the equivalent of £4-£5 [91] in rum or bar iron in Africa, were sold in the West Indies in 1746 at prices ranging from £30 to £88.[92] It is not surprising, therefore, that the original destination of virtually every cargo of slaves was the sugar, or tobacco or rice colonies.

Although New England merchants were concerned chiefly with supplying the West Indian and southern markets with Negroes, they did not neglect the smaller New England market. Beginning in 1638, a limited number of Negroes was brought annually into each of the New England colonies and sold there.[93] Few details of the sale of slaves in the seventeenth century are available. There were no newspapers in the colonies at that time,[94] and there is no information on the subject to be

hibition could prevent him from continuing in the trade. In 1807, when the United States prohibited the slave trade, effective in 1808, De Wolf was still sending slaves to Charleston, S. C. Bicknell, *op. cit.*, II, 512.

89 Rowland Robinson, the son of Lt. Governor William Robinson, who owned several thousand acres of land (Updike, *op. cit.*, I, 217) amassed at least a part of his wealth from the slave trade. A cargo of twenty-eight slaves in which he had a share is reported to have arrived in such poor condition that he refused to sell them, but kept the Negroes for himself. William Davis Miller, *The Narragansett Planters* (Reprinted from Proceedings of the *American Antiquarian Society* (Worcester, 1934), p. 23.

90 Donnan, *Docs.*, III, *passim.*

91 In 1764, Captain Rogers of the firm of Vernon and Vernon bought 21 Negroes for 80 bars of iron, or an average of about 4 bars a slave. *Ibid.*, III, 202.

92 In 1746, Negroes sold for £30 to £88 in Jamaica and Barbados. In the depreciated currency of South Carolina, Negro women sold for £130 to £200 in 1755; men brought £250 to £465. The price of £100 a head at which the Vernons of Newport sold slaves to the Charleston firm of Laurens and Austen in the following year, was probably a closer approximation to normal prices. *Ibid.*, III, 116, 122, 141, 153-154, 162-163.

93 *Vide infra*, p. 17.

94 The first newspaper in the American colonies was *Public Occurrences*, published in Boston in 1690. After one issue, it was suppressed by Governor

found in the files of eighteenth century newspapers. The most valuable source is in the reports of governors or other officials to the home government. These documents are (perhaps intentionally) not very revealing, and give little more than the number of slaves brought in at a specific time, the points of shipment and the average prices paid for them.[95] In 1680 Governor Bradstreet reported to the Committee on Trade and Plantations that forty to fifty Negroes had been brought into Massachusetts from Madagascar. Most of these were women who were sold for £10, £15, and £20 apiece.[96] In the same year Governor Leete of Connecticut, in answer to queries from the Lords of the Privy Council, replied that three or four Negroes yearly were imported into the colony, and were sold for about £22 a piece.[97] Governor Cranston of Rhode Island in 1696 informed the Committee for Trade and Foreign Plantations that of forty-seven Negroes brought into Newport by a Massachusetts vessel, fourteen were sold in Rhode Island at prices ranging from £30 to £35 a head.[98] It is not definitely known, however, where the sale of Negroes took place in the seventeenth century. Sometimes Negroes, like white persons, were bought directly from the ships [99] importing them; but whether this practice was general, is uncertain.

Phipps because it allegedly reflected upon the government; the first continuous newspaper was the *Boston News Letter*. It was first printed on April 24, 1704 by John Campbell. Lyman H. Weeks and Edwin M. Bacon, *Historical Digest of the Provincial Press* (Boston, 1911), pp. 24, 34.

95 These reports were usually replies to circulars sent out to colonial governors by the home government under the names of *Heads of Inquiry*. For examples *vide Conn. Col. Recs.*, III, 293.

96 *Historical Documents Relating to the American Colonial Church*, ed. William Stevens Perry, III, 8.

97 *Conn. Col. Recs.*, III, 298.

98 *R. I. Col. Recs.*, IV, 54.

99 Governor Leete mentions the bargaining by purchasers of slaves with the "masters of vessels or merchants who imported" them. *Conn. Col. Recs.*, III, 298.

During the eighteenth century the expansion of New England industries, with a corresponding shortage of labor, as well as the phenomenal growth of the slave trade, stimulated the sale of Negroes in New England. The advent of the newspaper in 1704 [100] also proved a boon to slave merchants, by affording them the opportunity to advertise their chattels more widely. The New Englanders were the first to employ the newspaper for this purpose, and the *Boston News Letter,* the first permanent newspaper published in America, almost from its beginning on April 24, 1704, carried advertising of slaves. It listed for sale on June 1, " Two Negro Men and one Negro Woman and Child." [101]

As newspapers increased in number and circulation, slave merchants, like other business men, regularly advertised their wares. So common was the practice, that it is almost impossible to find an eighteenth century newspaper not containing such notices. Prospective Boston buyers, for example, might purchase according to their fancy: " three likely negro men and two women " from Mr. John and James Alford,[102] as " a parcel of fine negro boys and girls " from William Clark, Esq.[103] In Newport, Rhode Island, in 1740, " men women and boys " were offered for sale by Josiah Bagley; or " a parcel of likely negro men women boys and girls," might be purchased from Channing and Chaloner.[104] Connecticut and New Hampshire slave dealers advertised in a similar manner. John Bannister, a Newport merchant, was gratified to place on the Middletown,

100 Weeks and Bacon, *Historical Digest of the Provincial Press,* p. 34.

101 June 1, 12, 19, 1704; also Donnan, III, 19.

102 *Ibid.,* Oct. 20, 1718.

103 *Boston Gazette,* May 30, June 6, 1737; *vide* also *Boston Weekly News Letter,* November 13, 1741; *New England Chronicle,* April 25, 1776. For slave advertisements see files of *Boston Gazette, Boston News Letter, Boston Weekly News Letter, New England Weekly Journal, Continental Journal and Weekly Advertiser.* Miss Donnan has collected a large list of slave advertisements. *Vide op. cit.,* III, 19, 21, 25, 26, 28-29; 38-40, 50, 51, 65, 66, 67, 68.

104 Donnan, III, 133n., 143.

Connecticut market in 1752 what he considered to be the
" finest cargo of negro men, women, boys and girls " ever imported into New England.[105] In Hartford, prospective purchasers might buy "a very likely *N E G R O   B O Y*",[106] or a
" Negro man about 47 years of age." [107] New Hampshire dealers were no less active. In Portsmouth one could buy a " Negro
man about 20 years of age . . . and one Negro girl about 17
years old " ; or a " fine Negro man about 20 years of age." [108]

The source of most of these slaves cannot be definitely stated.
Negroes were brought from Africa, the West Indies, and the
southern colonies, but in what proportion is a matter of specu-
lation. The advertisements fail to give this information, although frequently describing the Negroes as " lately imported," [109] " just imported," [110] " lately arrived " [111] or " just
arrived." [112] Of 125 advertisements of slaves in newspapers examined by the author, 80 gave no indication of the source of the
supply, 19 gave the West Indies and 26 Africa as the point of
origin.[113]

It is probably true, as these figures seem to indicate, that
more Negroes were imported into New England from Africa
than from the West Indies, but nearly every cargo of slaves
brought from Africa went first to the sugar islands. Many Ne-

105 *Ibid.*, p. 144.

106 *Connecticut Courant and Weekly Intelligencer*, March 21, 1780.

107 *Ibid.*, June 9, 1778.

108 *New Hampshire Gazette and Historical Chronicle*, April 3; May 1, 1767.

109 *Boston Weekly News Letter*, November 13, 1741; *New England Weekly Journal*, October 3, 1738.

110 Donnan, *Docs.*, III, 39, 65.

111 *Boston Gazette*, May 30–June 6, 1737.

112 *Boston Weekly News Letter*, Sept. 4, 1729.

113 Seventy of these advertisements were taken at random by the writer from various eighteenth century newspapers cited herein. The remainder are from Donnan, *Docs.*, III, 4-108. A large proportion of these advertise-ments were not those of dealers, but of private persons who desired to dis-pose of their Negroes.

groes, ostensibly brought to New England from the West Indies, were sickly or "refuse" Negroes, who had been taken there first and had been found unsalable.[114] Sometimes, however, ship captains were expressly ordered to reserve some "likely" slaves for the home market,[115] but New England, as a rule, does not appear to have received prime, robust slaves. These were kept for the West Indies and plantation colonies, where they sold for higher prices.[116] New England masters could afford to buy less able-bodied Negroes, for their slaves, generally speaking, were never subjected to the exacting toil demanded of those in the West Indies.[117] Many New England Negroes, therefore, were recruited from the off-scourings of the slave ships—"refuse" persons—who sold for what they would bring.[118] Governor Dudley of Massachusetts called the attention of the Board of Trade to this situation in 1708, when he informed its members that "the Negroes . . . brought in from the West Indies, are usually the worst servants they have,"[119] which accounted for their being sold in New England. Prices indicated their quality for, according to Dudley, "they usually brought between fifteen and twenty-five pounds per head."[120]

114 In 1737, James Brown of Providence instructed his brother, Obadiah, to bring home some of the slaves he could not sell in Barbados. *Letter Book of James Brown*, p. xi.

115 William Ellery in 1746 directed Captain Hammond of his sloop *Antis* to reserve "Eight likely boys to bring home." Donnan III, 139. In 1738-39, Peter Fanueil wrote one of his agents in the West Indies asking him to send him a tractable Negro boy of 12 to 15 years old, who has had the small-pox. Winsor, *Memorial History of Boston*, II, 262.

116 *Cf. supra*, p. 31 n. for prices in West Indies and plantation colonies. For best view of prices, *vide* Donnan, *Docs.*, II, III, *passim*.

117 W. O. Blake, *The History of Slavery and the Slave Trade* (Columbus, 1857), ch. xi, *cf.* Bryan Edwards, *History of the West Indies*, II, 120-123.

118 Among them was Phillis Wheatley, the poetess, who was brought to Boston as a sickly, twelve year old, "refuse" slave girl. Benjamin Brawley, *Early Negro American Writers* (Chapel Hill, 1935), p. 31.

119 *Calendar of State Papers: Colonial, 1708-1709*, p. 110.

120 *Ibid.*

Negroes from Africa were conspicuously "played up" in the advertising columns of the newspapers. Illustrative of these advertisements are: "very likely, agreeable and healthy negro boys and girls lately imported from Guinea,"[121] and "prime young slaves" just "imported from Africa."[122] Gold Coast Negroes, because of their vigor and intelligence, were considered of highest quality in New England as well as in South Carolina and the West Indies.[123] It is not surprising, therefore, that in 1726 a dealer announced the arrival of several "choice Gold Coast Negroes,"[124] or that in 1748, Robert Hall, a Charlestown merchant, rhapsodized over "four fine likely Gold Coast Negroes" whom he had intended to sell South but later decided to offer to his fellow New Englanders.[125] In 1762 an anonymous merchant was offering "a few prime men and boy slaves from the Gold Coast."[126]

Negroes who had spent some time in the West Indies, or in the South, seem to have been found preferable to the "raw", turbulent Negroes brought directly from Africa. To New England buyers they possessed advantages over the natives, for often they had been "seasoned"; that is, they had become acclimated, were more accustomed to regular labor, could speak some English and, to some degree, were familiar with Occidental customs.[127] These qualities were especially desirable, because the New England slave, as will be indicated later, came into unusually close contact with the master's family. For this reason, men like Peter Fanueil[128] and Sir William Pepperell[129]

121 *Boston Gazette*, May 30; June 6, 1737.

122 *Vide* citations in Donnan, III, 68.

123 Bryan Edwards, *History, Civil and Commercial of the British Colonies in the West Indies*, 4 vols. (Philadelphia, 1806), II, 267-268-275.

124 Cited Donnan, III, 29.

125 *Boston Gazette or Weekly Journal*, March 22, 1748.

126 Cited Donnan, III, 68.

127 Phillips, *op. cit.*, p. 113.

128 Winsor, *Memorial History of Boston*, II, 262-3.

129 Parsons, *Life of Sir William Pepperell*, p. 28.

sometimes sent to the West Indies for slaves. Alert traders never failed to inform prospective buyers that their Negroes had been " lately imported from the West Indies " ; [130] and were therefore " fit for town or country service." [131] Other advertisements gave prominence to the fact that the " slaves could speak English," [132] had been brought up to do housework [133] or were skilled in the trades.[134]

Dealers frequently resorted to high pressure salesmanship. Black merchandise was most commonly labelled with the vague description of " likely " or " very likely." [135] Physical characteristics were prominently described. Slaves were often recommended as : " healthy," [136] " likely healthy," " strong healthy," " well-limbed," " stout," " lusty " or " lusty strong." [137] Likewise merchants frequently directed attention to the personality or to some moral quality of the slave, and often advertised their Negroes as : " agreeable," " good," " honest," or as abstaining from " strong drink." [138] At times slaves were cited as possessing a combination of desirable qualities such as " likely, agree-

130 *Boston Weekly News Letter*, Nov. 13, 1741 ; April 15, 1742.

131 *Boston News Letter*, May 5, 1718.

132 *Boston Gazette or Weekly Advertiser*, Jan. 15, 1754 ; Donnan, III, 39.

133 *New Hampshire Gazette and Historical Chronicle*, Friday, April 20, 1770 ; *Boston Gazette or Weekly Advertiser*, March 13, 1753 ; *vide* Donnan, III, 39 and *passim*.

134 Donnan, III, 66 n.

135 *Boston News Letter*, Monday, Oct. 20, 1718. Eighteenth century newspapers offer copious evidence of such descriptions. For this reason only one reference will be cited. Interested readers are referred to the files of newspapers cited herein or to Donnan III, *passim*.

136 *Ibid.*, Friday, Nov. 13, 1741.

137 *Boston News Letter and New England Chronicle*, Feb. 17, 1763 ; *Boston Gazette or Weekly Advertiser*, Jan. 15, 1754 ; *Newport Mercury*, Oct. 30 ; Dec. 11, 1784 ; *Boston News Letter*, May 19, 1718 ; Aug. 11, 1718.

138 *Boston Gazette*, May 30–June 6, 1737 ; *New England Weekly Journal*, Dec. 5, 1738 ; Nov. 7, 1738 ; *Boston Gazette and Weekly Advertiser*, Jan. 23, 1753.

able, and healthy " [139] or " strong healthy (and) ingenious." [140] Gambia and the Gold Coast denoted quality, and Negroes born there were frequently advertised as " Choice Gold Coast or Gambia Negroes." [141] Since smallpox was a common scourge among slaves and often raged with deadly virulence among the whites in colonial New England,[142] slave dealers found that their Negroes sold more easily if they had already had this disease and had become immune. In such cases the master need not fear that his bondman might contract the malady and communicate it to him or to members of his family. As a result, it was not unusual for advertisements to state that the Negro " hath had the small pox." The first notice of this nature to come to the writer's attention was one issued in 1738, but such statements may have been employed before that date.[143] If the Negro spoke English, was born in New England, or even in America, or had been in the country long enough to learn to serve efficiently the master class, his salability was also increased. Slave dealers and private individuals accordingly placed emphasis upon the fact that the Negro spoke " good English " [144] or was " born in this town," [145] " was born in the country " [146] or " has been sometime in the country." [147]

139 *Boston Gazette*, May 30–June 6, 1737.

140 *Boston Gazette or Weekly Advertiser*, June 15, 1754.

141 Bryan Edwards, *History of the West Indies*, 2 vols. (Dublin, 1793), II, 56-58. Although prizing freedom highly and enduring pain uncomplainingly, Gold Coast Negroes surpassed other Negroes in bodily vigor, courage and strength. They were also good workers. *Ibid.*, p. 59.

142 *Vide* Donnan, I, II, III, *passim*. In 1750 an epidemic of smallpox broke out in Boston. Out of 7,669 persons who contracted the disease, 569 died. *Boston Gazette or Weekly Advertiser*, Jan. 23, 1753.

143 *New England Weekly Journal*, Mar. 14, 1738. See files of this and other eighteenth century newspapers.

144 *Boston News Letter*, May 5, 1718.

145 *New England Weekly Journal*, Jan. 17, 1738.

146 *Ibid.*, Sept. 5, 19; Oct. 17, 24, 31, 1738; *Boston Gazette and Weekly Advertiser*, Jan. 15, 1754. *Vide* files of any of above newspapers cited, *passim*.

147 *Boston Weekly News Letter*, Sept. 4, 1729. *Vide* other newspapers, *passim*.

In addition to the external trade, a spirited domestic or internal slave traffic was carried on. Compared to that of the antebellum South, however, the local New England trade in Negroes was small. It was engaged in by persons who, for various reasons, such as urgent need of money, lack of employment for or dissatisfaction with their Negroes, desired to get rid of their chattels, just as one today disposes of a used automobile. The New England internal slave trade, however, lacked entirely the drama and spectacular brutality of certain phases of the Southern overland trade. Nevertheless, prospective buyers were literally bombarded with slave advertisements. One master placed on the market " a very likely young Negro girl fit for service either in town or country " ; [148] another, "A likely Negro maid aged about sixteen years fit for any service either in town or country . . . ; [149] a third, " a young Negro woman . . . who has been ten years in the country " [150] and a fourth, a " female Negro child, about seven years old," who was born in Boston.[151]

These advertisements did not diminish in number after the Revolution; rather, they seemed to increase through the stimulus of hard times and the increasing insecurity of slave property. In 1772 a Newport master offered to sell his " Negro girl about nine years old " [152] and in 1780 Dr. William Jepson of Hartford was trying to find a buyer for a " likely Negro boy." [153] In 1784, the very year that slavery was abolished in Rhode Island, a slaveholder in that state was seeking to dispose of a " likely stout Negro fellow about 23 years of Age . . . who understands the farming business exceedingly well." [154]

148 *Boston News Letter*, Nov. 24, 1726.

149 *Ibid.*, May 5, 1718.

150 *New England Weekly Journal*, March 14, 1738.

151 *Ibid.*, Jan. 17, 1738.

152 *Newport Mercury*, Aug. 24, 1772.

153 *Ibid.*, March 31, 1780.

154 *Ibid.*, Oct. 30, 1784; Dec. 11, 1784.

Throughout the eighteenth century, whites and Indians, as well as Negroes, were offered for sale.[155] A purchaser was not limited by race in his choice of a bondman, for he was free to buy a red, white or black slave. Let us assume that a Bostonian of the period had decided to buy a servant or a slave. He would naturally peruse the newspapers, where the following notice might engage his attention:

> A Lusty Indian Man-Servant, aged
> about 20 years, that speaks very
> good English, and fit for any
> service in Town or Country to be
> sold on reasonable Terms by *Mr.*
> *Jonathan Williams* over against
> the Post Office in Cornhill, Boston.[156]

If his fancy ran to a black slave, he had only to glance over the following:

> To be Sold on reasonable Terms a
> Negro Man aged about 26 years,
> and a Negro Boy aged about 14 years,
> and a Negro Woman aged about 24
> years and her child, to be seen at
> *Mr. James Pecher's* House in Salem
> Street Boston.[157]

Finally, if the prospective purchaser preferred a person of his own race, he would pay particular attention to an advertisement of this type:

> Just imported from Ireland and
> to be sold on Board the Ship
> Virtue, John Seymour, Master, now

155 The files of eighteenth century New England newspapers bound in advertisements listing members of these three groups for sale. See newspapers cited herein, *passim.*

156 *Boston News Letter*, April 1, 1717.

157 *Ibid.*, August 25, 1718.

in the Harbour of Boston, a parcel
of healthy men Servants chiefly
Tradesmen.[158]

Occasionally Negroes and whites and Negroes and Indians were sold from the same auction block. Such a scene took place in 1714, when Samuel Sewall, a prominent Boston merchant, announced the sale at his warehouse of

several Irish Maid Servants time
most of them for Five Years one
Irish Man Servant who is a good
Barber and Wiggmaker, also Four
or Five Likely Negro Boys.[159]

Five months earlier an anonymous dealer had advertised:

An Indian Boy aged about sixteen Years,
and a Negro man aged about twenty both
of them very likely and fit for any
Service, they speak very good English:
to be sold: Enquire at the Post Office
in Boston.[160]

Negroes were often sold for reasons which not only suggest a sense of humor or exasperation in the master but also shed light on the character of the slave. In 1742 a Boston owner was naively trying to dispose of a Negro " whose master vice is laziness, for which fault " alone he was to be sold.[161] Plagued by his garrulous slave, another master in 1767 wanted to sell the Negro because he had "too long a tongue."[162] Eight years later a Connecticut man sought to rid himself of a slave who expressed

158 *Boston Gazette*, Sept. 7, 14, 1741.

159 *Boston News Letter*, September 13, 1714.

160 *Ibid.*, May 3, 10, 1714.

161 The master suggested that the Negro might be more efficient " if kept employed with a master." *Boston Weekly News Letter*, April 15, 1742.

162 *Boston Gazette and Country Journal*, Sept. 4, 1767.

" too great fondness for a particular Negro wench in his old neighborhood." [163]

There were no special markets in New England where slaves might be purchased, and sales were held at any place suited to the convenience of dealers and their customers. Sometimes dealers sold black and white persons—the latter were mostly indentured servants—on board the ships which brought them.[164] Prominent Boston merchants, like Gerrish and Harris, William Clark Esq., Samuel Sewall, Alford and Alford, and Thomas Jenner of Charlestown, frequently sold their slaves from warehouses in which they were stored.[165] Others, like Bullfinch of Boston or William Pearne of Portsmouth, New Hampshire, disposed of Negroes at their stores,[166] while Josiah Franklin, step-brother of Benjamin Franklin, and William Nichols, both Boston merchants, used their taverns as auction blocks.[167] Grove Hirst, Captain Bant, John and David Jeffers, Captains Palmer and Wood, and Andrew Fanueil, also of Boston, were among the merchants who sold slaves in their homes.[168] Persons with locations that were inconvenient or not suitable for business purposes advised prospective buyers to inquire at the " post house," [169] the " post office," [170] or to " inquire . . . of the postmaster." [171] In most cases, however, such traders directed

163 *Connecticut Courant and Universal Advertiser*, Dec. 1, 1775.

164 *Boston Weekly Post Boy*, Sept. 25, 1749; *Boston News Letter*, Dec. 1, 1718; *Boston Gazette*, July 18, 1726; *New Hampshire Gazette*, Aug. 4, 1758; Donnan, III, 185.

165 *Boston Weekly News Letter*, Sept. 4, 1729; *Boston Gazette*, May 30; June 6, 1737; cited in Donnan, III, 26; *Boston News Letter*, Oct. 20, 1718; *Boston Gazette*, May 30; June 6, 1737.

166 *Boston News Letter*, Nov. 24, 1726; *New Hampshire Gazette and Historical Chronicle*, April 3, 1767.

167 *Boston News Letter*, Aug. 3, 1713; cited in Donnan, III, 25; *New England Weekly Journal*, Oct. 17, 1738.

168 Donnan, III, 25-26; *Boston News Letter*, Oct. 13, 1718.

169 *Ibid.*, Aug. 11, 1718.

170 *Ibid.*, Feb. 17; May 19, 1718.

171 *Ibid.*, June 10, 1706, cited Donnan, III, 21.

persons to " inquire of the printer." [172] A good example is the following : " To be sold, for no fault, a Negro woman that can be well recommended. Inquire of the printer." [173]

Most slave merchants dealt in miscellaneous wares and they frequently sold Negroes and whites in addition to all sorts of commodities, such as liquor, provisions and clothing. On August 11, 1718, Andrew Wyatt of the ship *Mary Anne,* advertised sundry European goods, such as " iron cordage, broadcloths . . . linen and madeira wines : also servants bound to indenture." [174] In 1738 a Boston merchant quoted : " Good Florence wine in chests, good Irish butter by the firkin [and] a likely Negro fellow; " [175] another, " two likely Negroes " along with " sundry suits of men's apparel . . . cutlery ware . . . china ware . . . feathered muffs . . . chintz . . . callamançoes " and other articles.[176] A New Hampshire merchant listed " cotton wool by the bag or smaller quantity . . . good muscovado sugar . . . choice good old rum . . . good legumvitae . . . [and] one NEGRO MAN about twenty years of age." [177] A Boston ship captain in 1749 announced the sale of " butter, beef and duck," also a group of white " men and women servants." [178]

Conclusive data on slave prices are not available. Newspaper advertisements do not give the price of the slave, but the selling price doubtless varied according to the age, sex, quality and skill of the slaves, and the bargaining power of the buyers, as well as in accordance with the fluctuations in the New England

172 *Connecticut Courant and Weekly Intelligencer*, April 20, 1779.

173 *Newport Mercury*, Aug. 10, 24, 1772.

174 *Boston News Letter*, May 11, 1718.

175 *New England Weekly Journal*, Oct. 17, 24, 1738.

176 *Ibid.*, October 24, 31, 1738.

177 *New Hampshire Gazette and Historical Chronicle*, April 3, 1767.

178 *Boston Chronicle*, Sept. 7, 1769; *Boston Weekly Post Boy*, Sept. 15; October 2, 1749.

currency.[179] The record of a slave transaction in 1652, the earliest that has come to the writer's attention, reports a Negro woman sold for £25 sterling,[180] and the inventory of the estate of Theodore Price, filed in 1672, lists a Negro at £10.[181] In 1680, the average price of a slave in Connecticut was £22,[182] while Governor Bradstreet of Massachusetts, in the same year, reported that Negroes sold for from £10 to £20.[183] In 1695, a Negro woman in Massachusetts brought £23,[184] and in 1698 a Connecticut Negro man was sold for £30.[185] From these figures it appears that the average price of slaves before 1700 was between £20 and £30. During the eighteenth century, although fluctuations in the value of the New England currency make it difficult to ascertain the real value of any commodity, slave prices were generally higher than in the previous century. In 1706, according to an anonymous anti-slavery writer, prices of Negroes ranged from £40 to £50,[186] while second-rate Negroes brought from £15 to £20 a head.[187] A Negro man sold for £50 in Suffield, Massachussetts in 1718;[188] a Negro woman for £85 in 1725-1726;[189] a boy for £25 lawful New England money in 1756;[190] and a two-year-old child for "£1 six shillings, and

179 Dewey, *Financial History of the United States* (New York, 1924), pp. 18-30.

180 *Suffolk Deeds, 1629-1697* (Boston, 1880), Liber I, p. 290.

181 *Records and Files of the Quarterly Courts of Essex County, Mass., 1672-1674* (Salem, 1916), V, 65.

182 *Conn. Col. Recs.*, III, 298.

183 Cited in Emory Washburne, "Slavery as it once prevailed in Massachusetts," *Lectures on Early History of Massachusetts* (Boston, 1869), p. 212.

184 *Massachusetts Archives: Domestic Relations, 1643-1774*, IX, 142.

185 *Connecticut Archives: Miscellaneous*, III, 23.

186 *Boston News Letter*, June 10, 1706; Donnan III, 21.

187 *Calendar of State Papers: Colonial, 1708-1709*, p. 110.

188 *Massachusetts Archives*, IX, 175.

189 "Harvard College Records," *Publications of the Colonial Society of Massachusetts* (Boston, 1935), III, 175.

190 Brown, *History of Bedford, Massachusetts* (Bedford, 1891), p. 32.

eight pence, lawful money." [191] In 1770 Dr. Joseph Warren, famous Revolutionary hero, paid £30 for a Negro boy,[192] and five years later, Henry Carver of Boston sold his eighteen or nineteen-year-old Negro boy for a mere pittance of 10 shillings.[193] George Wyllys, Secretary of the State of Connecticut, paid £30 in 1777 for a Negro woman,[194] and in Rhode Island's depreciated currency of 1770 adult slaves sold for £1100-£1200; girls for £800.[195] The average price of a slave during the eighteenth century was probably between £40 and £50 sterling, and was always much higher than that of Indian slaves.[196]

Transactions involving the sale of slaves were usually executed through regular bills of sale and were witnessed, signed and recorded just as was the sale of other property. The procedure is shown in the following document signed by Joseph Stocking of Middletown, Connecticut, in 1777, transferring his right in a Negro woman to George Wyllys:

Know all Men by these Presents that I
Joseph Stocking of Middletown in the County of
Hartford and State of Connecticut for the
Consideration of Thirty Pounds lawful Money
received to my full satisfaction of George
Wyllys Esquire of Hartford in the County aforesaid do give grant Bargain sell & convey and
deliver to the said George Wyllys Esqr his Heirs
and Assigns a certain Negro woman slave name Silvia
of the Age of twenty three years.
To have & to hold the said Negro slave
to him the said George Wyllys Esq. his Heirs

191 Temple, *History of Framingham, Massachusetts*, p. 236.

192 *Massachusetts Historical Society, Proceedings, 1875-1876* (Boston, 1876), XIV, 101.

193 *Ibid.*, pp. 257-258.

194 "Wyllys Papers," *Conn. Hist. Soc. Colls.*, XXI, 456.

195 Weeden, *Early Rhode Island*, p. 291.

196 Lauber, *op. cit.*, p. 29, shows that throughout the colonial period Negroes sold for prices ranging from two to nine times those paid for Indians.

& Assigns for and during the Term of her
Natural Life to his & their only Use benefit
& behoof.

   In Witness whereof I have hereunto set
my Hand & Seal the Second day of September Anno
Dom. 1777
         Signed Sealed & delivered
         in presence of
         JNo Smith                    JOSh Stocking
         Titus Hosmer [197]

   Negroes, like other commodities, were sold for " cash " or
" on credit," [198] and since scarcity of money made it difficult for
dealers to demand cash, installment buying was common. Newspapers frequently quoted Negroes " on reasonable terms." [199]
Occasionally the buyer was given the choice of paying for his
slave either in cash or goods. A New Hampshire master in 1767
was willing to accept " cash or good lumber " for his Negro. [200]
Sometimes a combination barter and cash sale arrangement was
effected, whereby the seller accepted part of the purchase price
in money; the balance in goods. In this fashion Joseph Lowell
of Boston bought a Negro from Benjamin Pemberton in 1695,
paying £20 in currency, the remainder in beer barrels. [201] Dr.
Joseph Warren of Boston promised to pay an additional £10 in
" potters ware " if the Negro boy whom he had purchased
proved satisfactory. [202] Prominent persons of good standing,

197 *Ibid.*, Bills of sale for slaves are numerous. For others *vide Mass.
Archives: Domestic Relations*, IX, 142; *Harvard College Records*, III, 461;
*Mass. Hist. Soc. Proceedings, 1875-1876* (Boston, 1876), XIV, 101; Samuel
Drake, *History of Middlesex County, Massachusetts*, 2 vols. (Boston, 1880),
II, 181; George Sheldon, *History of Deerfield, Massachusetts*, II, 891, 892.

198 *New England Weekly Journal*, Tuesday, October 3, 1738; *Connecticut
Gazette and Universal Intelligencer*, Friday, Dec. 27, 1776. *Cf.* files of these
and other newspapers quoted.

199 *Boston News Letter*, Nov. 3, 1718; *New England Weekly Journal*,
Oct. 3, 1738.

200 *New Hampshire Gazette and Historical Chronicle*, April 3, 1767.

201 *Massachusetts Archives: Domestic Relations, 1643-1774*, IX, 142.

202 " Wyllys Papers," *loc. cit.*, XXI, 456.

like Benjamin Wadsworth, President of Harvard College, might even be permitted to pay the first installment a month or so after the slave was delivered.[203] When Continental currency was depreciating rapidly during the Revolutionary War, some masters sought to sell their slaves " for hard money only." [204]

Colonial slave vendors, like present-day merchants, sometimes experienced difficulty in collecting the payments outstanding on their Negroes and were occasionally forced to sue in order to recover such balances. In April 1698 Mary Bedient, of Fairfield, Connecticut, was summoned to appear in Court on complaint of John Burit, and ordered to show cause why she had withheld from Burit a sum of money due on a certain Negro named Caleb Robin,[205] but the records do not indicate the outcome of the case. In the following year, Richard Blackleach of Stratford sued William Hoadley of Branford, charging that the latter had failed to pay him for " Negro Servants [and] Corne " that the plaintiff had bought from him. At the Fairfield County Court on April 26, 1699, the jury returned a verdict in favor of Blackleach, and in addition to costs of Court, Hoadley was ordered to pay the former £30.8s.[206]

Buyers of Negroes also had their complaints, for at this time the principle of *caveat emptor* prevailed. Unscrupulous persons sometimes " palmed off " unsound or sickly Negroes upon unsuspecting purchasers as " healthy " or " likely." Indignant customers then turned to the Courts for redress. In 1697 Samuel Spear of Braintree, Massachusetts, sued Ralph Rainsford of Boston on the grounds that Rainsford had sold him a lame and sickly Negro, but had claimed that he was perfectly

203 *Harvard College Records*, III, 461.

204 *Connecticut Courant and Universal Intelligencer*, Oct. 3, 1778.

205 Mary's deceased husband had acted evidently as agent for John Burit. Bedient, before his death, had deducted £21.4s out of the £30 paid for the Negro for commissions, food, lodging, dress and the like. It was for all or part of the sum withheld by Bedient that Burit sued. *Connecticut Archives: Miscellaneous*, II, 22, 23.

206 *Connecticut Archives: Court Papers, 1700-1705*, I, 373.

sound. Spear, upon finding that the Negro was crippled, demanded that Rainsford take him back. This Rainsford refused to do, contending that the Negro was in good condition when delivered, whereupon Spear brought suit. On April 6, 1697, Rainsford was summoned before the Inferior Court of Boston.[207] Although the record does not show the disposition of the action, one fact seems inescapable: this case certainly did not stop the practice. Alleging misrepresentation of a slave, Benjamin Arnold of Middletown, Connecticut, brought suit in 1761 against Theophilus Woodbridge of the same town, claiming that Woodbridge had sold him a Negro woman named Pegg, guaranteeing her to be in the best of health, although he knew at the time that she was not. The woman, Arnold discovered later, suffered from epileptic fits, which rendered her unfit for service. Arnold won the suit and the award of damages was sustained on appeal.[208] In the same year another case came before the Governor and Council, the highest court in the colony. David Leavitt of Woodbury accused Timothy Barber of Branford of deceiving him in the sale of a seventeen-year-old Negro, named Jack. According to Leavitt, Barber had assured him that the Negro was sound, but Jack shortly afterwards developed a " loathesome disease," from which he later died, and Leavitt contended that Barber had wilfully misrepresented the Negro. Barber in his own defense claimed he had previously informed the plaintiff that the Negro had shown symptoms of the disease when he first came to America, but that after treatment the slave had been well for nine years. The verdict, according to the Court, should rest upon whether the disease was " hereditary." If so, Barber was liable. The jury finally decided in the affirmative and the Superior Court awarded Leavitt £60 damages. Undismayed, Barber petitioned the Governor and Council for a new trial, but his petition was denied.[209]

---

207 *Massachusetts Archives*, IX, 143, 143a, 143b.

208 Woodbridge, feeling that he had been unfairly dealt with, appealed the case. *Connecticut Archives: Miscellaneous*, II, 50-53.

209 *Ibid.*, pp. 135-139.

So pernicious did the misrepresentation of Negroes become, that at least one effort was made to stamp out the practice by legislative action. On January 29, 1767 a " double " bill was introduced in the legislature of Massachusetts, part of which purported " to prevent frauds in the sale of Negroes," [210] but the bill failed to pass. It was read twice, failed to win a third reading and was ordered " to ly." [211] No other New England colony attempted similar action.

210 The other section aimed to provide for the support of indigent Negroes. *Mass. Archives*, IX, 450-450 back.

211 *Ibid.*

# CHAPTER II

## SOCIAL REPERCUSSIONS

THE sale of Negroes enriched not only the merchants, but some of the colonies as well. This end was achieved by the levy of a duty on all Negroes imported, a system in which Massachusetts took the lead in New England by enacting a law in 1705-6 which placed a tax of £4 on every imported Negro.[1] All slaves were to be registered at the " import office," and failure to do so carried a penalty of £8 for every Negro undeclared.[2] In 1711 Rhode Island followed with a similar enactment, imposing a duty of £3 a head and fining importers £6 a head for incoming Negroes not registered at the Naval Office.[3] Neither New Hampshire nor Connecticut placed duties upon imported blacks, principally because their slave trade was so small in comparison with that of Massachusetts and Rhode Island. When the Governor of New Hampshire was questioned by the home government in 1732, regarding the amount of impost levied upon " felons and Negroes " brought into the colony, he replied that " there never was any duties laid on either by this government." Besides, he added, so few Negroes had been brought in, " that it would not be worth the publick notice . . . to make an act concerning them." [4]

The real purpose of these duties is not clear. They probably had different meanings for different persons. Some opponents of the slave trade, like Samuel Sewall and the Boston Commit-

1 DuBois, *op. cit.*, pp. 9-15, 18-26.

2 This provision was part of an act " For the Better Preventing of a Spurious and Mixt Issue." *Acts and Resolves of the Massachusetts Bay, 1692-1704* (Boston, 1869), I, 578, 579.

3 *Charter, Acts and Laws of Rhode Island and Providence Plantations* (Digest of 1719, Providence, 1859), pp. 64-65. The Naval Officer was to receive five shillings for every Negro upon whom the duty was paid. *Ibid.*, p. 65.

4 *Provincial Papers of New Hampshire, 1722-1737* (Manchester, 1870), IV, 617.

tee of 1700, may have seen in the imposition of a duty on Negroes the ultimate abolition of the slave trade, and finally of
slavery itself.[5] But this view could not have been very wide-
spread, for the anti-slavery ranks in Massachusetts at that time
were represented almost wholly by Samuel Sewall. Racial pur-
ists, alarmed at the increasing intermixture of the races, may,
as stated in the title of the act, have hoped to prevent miscegenation. Still others, in sympathy with the preamble of the Rhode
Island Act of 1711, may have been sincerely convinced that
" the bringing in of Negroes " . . . discouraged " the importing of white servants," and that unless it were soon stopped, it
would, in time, prove " prejudicial to the inhabitants of the
colony." [6] This reason seems untenable, however, because the
number of Negroes in Rhode Island or Massachusetts at that
time could hardly have been sufficient to present much of a
handicap to incoming white labor.[7] That the Masachusetts Act,
at least, was not expressly designed for this purpose, is seen by
the fate of a bill introduced into the House of Representatives
on June 17, 1718. Entitled "An Act for Encouraging the Importation of White Male Servants and the preventing of the
Clandestine bringing in of Negroes and mulattoes," the Bill had
two readings but, probably because of the influence of powerful
slave-trading interests, it did not receive sufficient support for a
third reading, and was accordingly dropped.[8]

Whatever the purpose of these duties, they certainly did not
curtail either the slave trade or slavery. In some cases the acts

5 Sewall, in 1700, mentions a motion by a Boston Committee " to get a law
that all Importers of Negroes shall pay 40s per head to discourage their
importation." " Diary of Samuel Sewall, 1674-1729 ", *Mass. Hist. Soc. Colls.*,
Fifth Series, VI, 16.

6 *Rhode Island Charter Acts and Laws* (Digest 1719), pp. 64-65.

7 Massachusetts, according to Governor Dudley, had only 550 Negroes in
1708. *Cal. State Papers: Colonial, 1708-1709,* p. 110. In the same year Rhode
Island returned 426 Negroes. *R. I. Col. Recs.,* IV, 59.

8 *Journal of the House of Representatives of Massachusetts, 1718-1720*
(Boston, 1921), II, 25.

were defective. In other cases, the presence of slave interests in the government may have been responsible for possibilities of evasion in the laws. A loophole was provided in the Massachusetts statute by a clause permitting a Negro to remain in the colony for a year after importation, upon the owner's promise to sell him out of the colony at the expiration of that period.[9] In the event that he did so, the importer " could draw back " the entire duty of £4. Should the Negro die within six weeks after his arrival, the purchaser of the slave was permitted to recover the duty.[10] The Rhode Island law was equally futile, for it did not apply to Negroes brought directly from Africa,[11] which would seem to imply an indirect encouragement to the Guinea trade. Since non-residents (upon oath that their slaves were not for sale) might still bring in Negroes, provided that they did not tarry more than six months,[12] an opening was made for either the sale or escape of the slave before the expiration of the period.

Even if these laws had been rigidly drawn, smuggling by the slave merchants would have rendered the acts largely ineffective. It must have required in the lawmakers optimism of more than average degree to expect these merchants, who regularly flouted the mercantile regulations of the mother country, to give more than formal recognition to colonial trade laws, when such obedience meant a reduction of their profits. The laws were in fact ignored, and the merchants smuggled Negroes into Rhode Island and Massachusetts by land and by sea. In order to stop this practice, both these colonies were forced to strengthen their import laws by supplementary legislation. Rhode Island, in 1712, made all ship captains who failed to register their Negro and Indian slaves liable to imprisonment. Captains were re-

9 The owner was required to secure a statement to that effect from the naval officer. *Acts and Resolves of Mass. Bay,* I, 579.

10 *Ibid.*

11 *Rhode Island Charter Acts and Laws* (Digest 1719), p. 64.

12 *Ibid.*

quired to pay the duty before disembarking their slaves, and those who lacked ready cash were permitted to post bond, dischargeable within ten days. Should the captain refuse either to pay the duties or to post bond,[13] he was to be imprisoned until such sums were paid. The captain was also liable for a fine of £40 New England money. To facilitate the keeping of satisfactory records, the Naval Officers were to be provided with books.[14] Massachusetts resorted to more stringent measures to collect the duty, but with how much success is questionable. Supplementary legislation in 1728 compelled all masters of vessels to give upon oath a true list of their Negroes on penalty of £100,[15] and an effort was made to prevent captains from landing Negroes in adjoining provinces and smuggling them overland into Massachusetts. The law compelled all purchasers of Negroes, upon whom no duty had been paid, to register such slaves with the clerk of the town where the Negroes had been bought. Failure to do so, or to pay the duty of £4, was punishishable by a fine equal to twice the duty.[16] This act was to remain in force for ten years,[17] but continued violations called forth additional legislation in 1738, 1739, and 1742.[18] The law of 1742 reduced from twelve to six months the period during which a purchaser might draw back the duty, in event of the slave's death.[19]

13 *R. I. Col. Recs.*, IV, 131-135. Indians were included now. The duty upon them was forty shillings.

14 *Ibid.*

15 *Mass. Acts and Resolves, 1715-1741* (Boston, 1874), II, 517.

16 *Ibid.* In case of a fine, one-half was to go to the province, one-fourth to the clerk, and the other fourth to the poor of the town where the forfeiture was made.

17 *Ibid.*, p. 518.

18 *Mass. Acts and Resolves, 1715-1741*, II, 981-2; *Temporary Acts and Laws of His Majesty's Province of the Massachusetts Bay in New England* (Boston, 1742), p. 15; for manuscript of, *vide Mass. Archives, Domestic Relations*, IX, 223-225.

19 *Mass. Temporary Laws* (1742), p. 15.

Legislative interference often nullified efforts to apply the law. Persons frequently petitioned the assembly to have the duty refunded and they were sometimes successful, especially in obtaining a drawback on infant slaves or on Negroes allegedly imported for their own use. Most of the petitions submitted between 1715 and 1737 were granted. On July 22, 1715, for example, Mary Hoddall and Magdalene Beauchamp, claiming to have suffered hardships in the Tuscarora Indian Wars, in South Carolina,[20] petitioned the Massachusetts legislature to permit them to recover the duty that they had paid on eight Negroes. The House granted the petition and sent it to the Council for approval.[21] In the same year, and for identical reasons, the House granted the petitions of the Reverend Archibald Stobo that the impost on his " eleven Negro women and children be removed." [22] On July 16, 1720, the House also voted to allow Anne Tailer, a Boston widow, to draw back the duty on nine Negroes imported by her from Jamaica.[23] A more complex case was presented to the Rhode Island Assembly, when James Cranston, the colony's Naval Officer, asked for a ruling on the petition of one of the Royalls, a Massachusetts slave merchant. Royall had brought into Rhode Island forty-three Negroes upon whom he had paid the duty of £3 each. Subsequently, when he carried sixteen of the Negroes to Massachusetts, where he was forced to pay an additional duty, he appealed to Cranston, who, in turn, asked the advice of the Assembly. That body ordered that the duty on the sixteen Negroes transported to

20 The war began in North Carolina where the Indians feared their lands near the Neuse River would be taken from them for the benefit of Swiss colonists led by De Graffenreid. The Indians began the attack on September 22, 1711. Opposed by troops from North and South Carolina, they were finally beaten after a heroic resistance in 1715. Captives were sold into slavery. Edward McCrady, *History of South Carolina under the Proprietary Government, 1670-1719* (New York, 1907), pp. 496-546, *passim.*

21 *Journal H. R. of Mass., 1715-1717* (Boston, 1919), I, 52.

22 *Ibid.*, I, 48-49.

23 *Ibid.*, II, 242.

Massachusetts " be taken off and remitted." Cranston was to " collect the duty on the other twenty-nine." [24]

Not all petitioners fared so well. In 1720 the Massachusetts House of Representatives granted only part of the petition of Samuel Patishall, who prayed that the duty on four Negroes and an infant be remitted. The House refused to allow the refund on the adult Negroes, but ordered that the petition " be so far granted as that the duty on the sucking child be remitted." [25] Hugh Hall's request for a " drawback " on his Negro boy was denied in 1718,[26] and the petition of Leonard Vassal in 1722, resulted in a disagreement between the two Houses. Vassal, later one of Boston's most famous slave dealers, claimed that the Negroes were for the use of his family, and prayed that the duty be remitted. The House first granted the petition but when the Council, in concurring, added a clause reimposing the duties should Vassal sell any of the Negroes in Massachusetts, the House refused to pass the amended Bill. How Vassal ultimately fared in this case is not known, for the House, having withheld its approval, sent the bill back to the Council with the curt statement that " the House insists on their own vote." [27] The appeal of the slave merchant, Isaac Royall, for a refund of the duties on a " parcel of Negroes " whom he had imported from Antigua, likewise met with a refusal in December, 1737.[28]

The duties apparently were not sufficiently prohibitive to put an end to the slave trade. Even had they been intended for that purpose, so great were the returns from the traffic that the merchants could have paid the tax and still have realized a good profit from their sales. With Negroes selling for between £40 and £50 or more a head, when their cost price averaged between £5 and £6 apiece, neither the £3 duty imposed by Rhode Island,

24 *R. I. Col. Recs.*, IV, 454.

25 *Journal H. R. of Mass., 1718-1720*, II, 274.

26 *Ibid.*, p. 67.

27 *Ibid.*, IV, 139.

28 *Ibid.*, XV, 225.

nor the £4 levied by Massachusetts, could be considered prohibitive. Judging from the intensive efforts of Massachusetts to collect these duties through the medium of temporary laws, there is even more reason for regarding them as revenue measures. The facts fail to show any retarding influence upon the trade itself, which continued to grow until it was ruined by the Revolution.[29] The action of the Rhode Island Assembly lends further support to the view that these laws were primarily revenue measures, for in 1729, it voted to employ half of the proceeds from the duty on Negroes toward repairing and paving the streets of Newport.[30] The other half was to be used exclusively for the " support, repairing and mending the great bridges " on the mainland and on the country roads.[31]

Finally, the mother country refused to permit any encumbrance upon the slave trade, whether for regulatory or revenue purposes. Whenever it was discovered that the colonies were taxing slave imports, the British Parliament, throughout the colonial period, immediately ordered such duties repealed. As the result of Virginia's legislation in 1732,[32] circular instructions were speedily sent to all the colonial governors, forbidding them to consent to any acts levying duties upon the African trade. Of the action of Parliament in such matters, the instructions to Governor Jonathan Belcher, slave-trading Governor of Massachusetts, are typical:

> Whereas Acts have been passed in some of our
> Plantations in America for laying Duties on the
> Importation and Exportation of Negroes to the
> Discouragement of the Merchants trading thither—
> from the Coast of Africa . . . It is our Will and
> Pleasure That you do not give your Assent to or
> pass any Law imposing Duties upon Negroes imported

29 DuBois, *op. cit.*, p. 5; Donnan, III, 315, 319.

30 *R. I. Acts and Laws* (Digest 1730), p. 103.

31 *Ibid.*

32 Donnan, III, 38 n.

into Our Province of the Massachusetts Bay payable
by the Importer or upon any slaves exported that
have not been sold in Our said Province, and
continued there for the Space of Twelve Months.[33]

Pursuant to similar orders, the Rhode Island Assembly repealed
its duty on Negroes in 1732,[34] but Massachusetts, for some time,
continued to thwart the wishes of the home government by re-
course to temporary laws.[35]

Slave merchants belonged to what was then known as the
gentility. The names of many are famous in the annals of New
England, and others are intimately associated with the history
of the United States. Many were honored with private and public offices of great trust, power and responsibility. There was no
stigma attached to trading in Negroes before the Revolution,
for the slave trade was as honorable a vocation as lumbering
or fishing. Wealthy slave merchants, like the industrial captains
of the present era, were successful men—the economic, political
and social leaders of their communities—and were regarded by
their fellows as worthy of emulation.

John Campbell,[36] John Saffin,[37] and John Coleman [38] of
Boston, and Sir William Pepperell [39] of Kittery, Massachusetts,
were judges, and Campbell was for a time, also postmaster of
Boston.[40] Constant Taber [41] and Charles Collins [42] of Newport

33 *Journal H. R. of Mass., 1732-1734,* XI, 23.

34 *R. I. Col. Recs.,* IV, 471; Kimball, *Correspondence of the Colonial
Governors of Rhode Island, 1723-1775* (Boston, 1902), I, 64-73.

35 *Mass. Acts and Resolves,* II, 981-982; *Temporary Laws of the
Province of the Massachusetts Bay,* p. 15.

36 *D.A.B.,* III, 456.

37 *Colonial Society of Massachusetts, Transactions,* I, 85-86 n.

38 *Ibid.,* VI, 86-87; *D.A.B.,* IV, 312-313.

39 Parsons, *op. cit.,* p. 28; Donnan, *Docs.,* III, 28.

40 Weeks and Bacon, *op. cit.,* I, 3.

41 *N. E. Quarterly,* III, 257.

42 Donnan, III, 219.

were collectors of ports, while Caleb Gardner [43] and Peleg Clarke [44] of Newport, Moses Brown [45] and John Topham [46] of Providence and Shearjashub Bourne [47] of Bristol were members of the colonial Assembly. The highest offices in the gift of the colony—those of governor and lieutenant-governor—were held at times by slave traders. Jonathan Belcher [48] of Massachusetts and four members of the Wanton [49] family of Rhode Island held governorships, and among the lieutenant-governors were William Robinson [50] and William Ellery [51] of Rhode Island. Slave merchants like General William Whipple [52] of Portsmouth, New Hampshire, Nicholas [53] and John Brown [54] of Providence, William Vernon [55] of Newport and John Hancock [56]

43 Gardner served in the Lower House of the Rhode Island Assembly in 1777. In 1780 he was elected to the Upper House. *D.A.B.*, VII, 140.

44 *N. E. Quarterly*, III, 257.

45 *D.A.B.*, III, 147.

46 *N. E. Quarterly*, III, 257.

47 *Ibid.*

48 *Journal H. R. of Mass.* (hereinafter cited as *J. H. R. Mass.*), *1732-1734*, XI, 23; Belcher was also appointed Governor of New Jersey in 1747. *Lamb's Biographical Dictionary of the United States*, ed. John Howard, 8 vols. (Boston, 1900), I, 256.

49 Kimball, *Correspondence*, I, xxxviii-xxxix.

50 Miller, *Narragansett Planters*, p. 17.

51 Appleton, *Cyclopedia of American Biography*, II, 326.

52 Brewster, *Rambles About Portsmouth*, I, 150.

53 During the Revolution, Nicholas Brown served on the Secret Committee of the Congress and employed his ships and business connections to import clothing and munitions for the American soldiers. He also worked energetically for the ratification of the Constitution. *Vide D.A.B.*, III, 148-149.

54 John Brown (Jan. 27, 1736-Sept. 20, 1803) opposed the Stamp Act in 1765, supported the non-importation agreement of 1769-1775 and led the party which burned the *Gaspee*. He actively campaigned for the ratification of the Constitution. *Ibid.*, pp. 128-129.

55 *Cyclopedia of American Biography*, VIII, 62.

56 John Hancock was a partner of James Rowe who traded in Negroes. It is possible therefore that Hancock, one of Boston's most prominent

of Boston were prominent patriots during the Revolution. Slave dealers earned distinction in other fields also. Some were publishers like the aforementioned John Campbell [57] of Boston, founder of the first permanent newspaper in America; still others were scientists, like Joseph Brown [58] of Providence and Abraham Redwood of Newport. There were among them philanthropists, such as Peter Fanueil, the Brown brothers, noted for their bequests to Rhode Island College [59] (now Brown University) and the aforementioned Abraham Redwood, founder of the famous Redwood Library in Newport and celebrated also for his gifts to schools and colleges in Rhode Island.[60] Sir William Pepperell [61] and Sir Charles Hobby [62] were among the few colonials knighted by the mother country. After the establishment of the United States under the Constitution, at least one slave trader, Constant Taber of Newport, served as a presidential elector,[63] and two slave merchants became members of the United States Congress: John Brown of Providence, who served a term in the House of Representatives

merchants and one of the leaders of the American Revolution was at least indirectly connected with the slave trade. Abram L. Brown, *John Hancock: His Book,* p. 55 and note.

57 *D.A.B.,* III, 456.

58 Joseph Brown gained fame as a scientist and architect. He interested himself in electrical experiments, was technical adviser of the Hope Iron Furnace owned by his brother, Nicholas, and also won acclaim by observing the transit of Venus on June 3, 1769. *Ibid.,* p. 141.

59 For the philanthropy of the Browns, *vide. D.A.B.,* III, 128-129, 141, 146-149.

60 Redwood gave £500 to the Friends School in Newport and a similar amount toward the founding of the College of Rhode Island. *D.A.B.,* XV, 445. Evarts B. Greene, *Foundations of American Nationality* (New York, 1922), p. 264.

61 Pepperell married Mary Hirst, granddaughter of Samuel Sewall (slaveholder and antislaveryite), and niece of Grove Hirst, a Boston slave merchant. Parsons, *op. cit.,* p. 27.

62 Colonial Society of Massachusetts, *Transactions,* XIX, 151-152.

63 *N. E. Quarterly,* III, 257.

from 1799-1801,[64] and James DeWolfe of Bristol, Rhode Island, who in 1801 was elected to the United States Senate.[65]

That these merchants could engage in this now universally condemned traffic and still enjoy the esteem and respect of their fellow citizens shows the general acceptance of both slavery and the slave trade in colonial New England. The Puritans not only justified slavery, but gave it a triple sanction. Slavery was defended upon economic, spiritual and legal grounds.

In colonial New England, as elsewhere in the New World, there was a chronic shortage of labor.[66] When efforts to overcome this deficiency by enslaving whites and Indians seemed unavailing,[67] Negroes were regarded by many as the solution to New England's labor needs. In 1645 Emanuel Downing, brother-in-law of John Winthrop, considering Negroes essential to the well-being of the colonists, longed for a " juste warre " with the Indians by which the settlers might secure sufficient men, women and children to exchange for Negroes. The colony will never thrive, he wrote Winthrop, " untill we gett . . . a stock of slaves sufficient to doe all our business." [68] White servants, he believed, were too difficult to retain in bondage and would not work after emancipation except for " verie great wages." Downing was convinced that Negroes were less expensive than indentured servants; in fact, Negroes cost so little, he asserted, that twenty could be maintained for the cost of one white servant.[69] Antoine Court, a French Huguenot traveler who visited Boston in 1687, was so impressed by the shortage of workers that he advised prospective Huguenot emi-

64 *D.A.B.*, III, 129.

65 De Wolfe was the most notorious slave trader of the post-Revolutionary era. *N. E. Quarterly*, III, 257.

66 Weeden, *Economic and Social History of New England*, II, 449.

67 *Vide, supra*, pp. 18-20.

68 " Winthrop Papers," *Mass. Hist. Soc. Colls.*, Fourth Series (Boston, 1863), VI, 65.

69 *Ibid.*

grants to bring their own " hired help " because there was " an absolute need of them to till the land." [70] Noting the increasing use of Negroes in Boston, he warmly recommended them to his countrymen. Negroes, he added, rarely left their masters, and, even if they did, the Indians, for a small reward, would quickly return them.[71] The need for labor was still an acute problem in the eighteenth century for as late as the French and Indian War, a writer remarked that, although the population had grown recently, " labor was as dear as forty years before." He ventured the prophecy that because of the abundance of land it would be ages before labor would be cheap, for " no man will be a servant whilst he can be a master." [72]

The Puritans also justified slavery upon the highest spiritual grounds. Slavery, they maintained, was established by the law of God in Israel and, regarding themselves as the Elect of God,[73] New Englanders looked upon the enslavement of the Indians and Negroes as a sacred privilege Divine Providence was pleased to grant His chosen people.[74] Were not Negroes and Indians infidels, outside the pale of civil and spiritual rights— heathen people whose souls were doomed to eternal perdition? [75] Were they not an accursed people, the descendants of Ham or " Cham," [76] whom " it was quite proper to destroy or enslave? " [77] Upon this principle, even Roger Williams, the political and religious radical, could condone slavery. Following the

70 Cited in Nathaniel Shurtleff, *Topographical and Historical Description of Boston* (Third Edition), pp. 48-49.

71 *Ibid.*

72 Cited in Adams, *Revolutionary New England*, p. 256.

73 Moore, *op. cit.*, p. 105.

74 Cotton Mather, *The Negro Christianized* (Boston, 1706), p. 2.

75 *Mass. Hist. Soc. Colls.*, Fourth Series, VI, 218-219; Jernegan, *op. cit.*, p. 25; Wilkins Updike, *History of the Narragansett Church*, Second Edition, 3 vols. (Boston, 1907), I, 212.

76 Mather, *ut supra*.

77 Wertenbaker, *The First Americans, 1607-1690* (American Life Series). II, 231.

decimation or capture of the Pequod Indians by Massachusetts and Connecticut soldiers in 1637, Williams wrote John Winthrop, congratulating him upon God's having placed in his hands " another drove of Adams' degenerate seed." [78] From this lofty viewpoint, slavery was not an evil, but an act of mercy, whereby the soul of the slave might be brought to salvation.[79] As Samuel Dexter, a contemporary, remarked, " People in general justified the [slave] trade on the persuasion that, without some degree of acquaintance with the doctrine of the Gospel, eternal misery in another state of existence was inevitable." [80] With slavery defended upon such high grounds, even the clergy might hold slaves with an undisturbed conscience. Under this divine dispensation, not only could a devout Rhode Island elder engage in the slave trade, but he could also rejoice that " an overruling Providence had been pleased to bring to this land of freedom another cargo of benighted heathens to enjoy the blessings of a Gospel dispensation." [81] When the prominent minister and scholar, Ezra Stiles, sent a hogshead of whiskey to Africa in exchange for a slave,[82] he was but conforming to the spirit of the times. So too was the congregation of the Reverend Mr. Devotion of Suffield, Connecticut, which in 1726 voted him £20 toward the purchase of some Negroes.[83] The Puritans, as one scholar aptly states, believed that whatever suffering the Negro might experience either aboard the slave ship or in slavery was " more than offset by his fortunate delivery from a life of idolatry and savagery." [84] That Negroes were taught and even ac-

78 Williams, who had previously written Winthrop asking that the Pequod captives be used kindly and have houses and fields given them, now asked Winthrop for a little Indian boy with red upon his cheek to whom he had taken a fancy. Letter in *Mass. Hist. Soc. Colls.,* Fourth Series, VI, 218-219.

79 *Amer. Hist. Rec.,* I, 312.

80 *Mass. Hist. Soc. Colls.,* Fifth Series, III, 384.

81 *Amer. Hist. Rec.,* I, 312; *Amer. Ant. Soc., Proceedings,* New Series, V, 122.

82 Stiles, *Literary Diary,* I, 521 n.

83 Cited in Jernegan, *op. cit.,* p. 32.

84 Wertenbaker, *op. cit.,* p. 231.

cepted this doctrine is evidenced by the slave poet, Phillis Wheatley, in her autobiographical poem, *On Being Brought from Africa to America*.[85]

Finally, the New Englanders accorded slavery a legal sanction. In the Body of Liberties of 1641, Massachusetts gave slavery, as well as servitude, statutory recognition. Section 91 reads as follows:

> There shall never be any bond slaverie, villinage or Captivitie amongst us, unless it be lawfull Captives taken in just warres, and such strangers as willingly sell themselves or are sold to us. And these shall have all the liberties and Christian usages which the law of God established in Israell concerning such persons doth morally require. This exempts none from servitude who shall be Judged thereto by Authoritie.[86]

This law, which was later included in the articles of the old New England Confederation, contradicts the contention of some apologists that slavery was never legalized in New England. Historians like John Gorham Palfrey, jurists like Chief-Justice Dana, and statesmen like Charles Sumner, all labored under this illusion.[87] Yet the statute of 1641 was the first enactment legal-

85 Phillis considered it an act of mercy to have been brought from Africa. Herbert G. Renfro, *Life and Works of Phillis Wheatley* (Washington, 1916), p. 48.

86 *The Colonial Laws of Massachusetts*. Reprinted from the Edition of 1660. Sec. 91, p. 125. This law was reaffirmed in the codification of the Laws in 1649; and also in 1672. *General Laws and Liberties of the Massachusetts Colony* (Reprint, Boston, 1672), p. 10.

87 Palfrey (*History of New England,* II, p. 30 n), holds this opinion. Chief Justice Dana, instructing a jury in 1796, boldly asserted that a Negro born in Massachusetts before the Constitution of 1780 was free although born of a slave woman. Moore, *op. cit.,* p. 20. Charles Sumner, in a speech before the Senate on June 28, 1854, is said to have stated that in all her annals no person was born into slavery in Massachusetts. If they were held as such, he continued, it was not through the force of any statute law of colony or commonwealth. Cited Moore, *op. cit.,* p. 21.

izing slavery in the English colonies.[88] As such, it has been violently assailed. George H. Moore, the caustic critic of slavery in Massachusetts, maintains that the law expressly sanctioned both slavery and the slave trade, and John Hurd agrees with him.[89] Moore further asserts that the law of 1641 antedated any similar legislation in Virginia, Maryland, or South Carolina.[90] On the other hand, the measure has been eulogized by many New England writers, notably Washburne,[91] as demonstrating an early abhorence of slavery on the part of the Puritans.[92] Quincy states that the law also excluded the children of slaves from bondage.[93] The median between these conflicting attitudes is struck by Mary S. Locke. While admitting that the act was the first to legalize slavery, Miss Locke agrees with Washburne that its evident purpose was to limit that which already existed, " not to create or establish the institution." [94] The most realistic interpretation, however, is that of Edward Channing; after discussing the " pros " and " cons " of the law, Channing says: " Englishmen and English colonists of those early days had not the slightest objection to slavery as an institution. It does not seem likely, therefore, that the makers of this law intended to abolish slavery within the colonial limits; probably they only sought to reduce Biblical precepts to legal language and did not foresee the consequences of their action." [95]

88 *Ibid.*, p. 19.

89 John Codman Hurd, *Law of Freedom and Bondage*, I, 206.

90 Moore, *ut supra*.

91 For Washburne's eulogy of this act, *vide* his " Slavery As it Once Existed in Massachusetts," *loc. cit.*, pp. 201-205.

92 William Whittier in Henry Wilson, *Rise and Fall of the Slave Power in America* (Boston, 1872), I, 7. Others profess not to know whether the Act of 1641 prohibited slavery or not. *Mass. Hist. Soc. Colls.*, Fourth Series, IV, 334-335.

93 Josiah Quincy, ed., *Reports of Cases Argued and Adjudged in the Superior Court of Judicature of the Provinces of the Massachusetts Bay* (Boston, 1865), p. 29 n.

94 Locke, *op. cit.*, p. 14.

95 *History of the United States,* II, 384.

It is true that the legislation of 1641 did not establish slavery in New England, for involuntary servitude, as already indicated, had existed there since 1638.[96] The specific import of the Act of 1641 was that it bestowed legal sanction upon slavery.[97] What appeared to be the exemption of children from bondage (as implied in the statute) seems not to have been intentional but was probably the result of an oversight. Unfamiliar with slavery,[98] the Puritans apparently could not foresee in 1641 that persons born of slaves might invoke the law as legal grounds for their manumission. Such cases may actually have occurred during the period before the revision of the law in 1670.[99] At any rate, when the law was altered in the latter year, the word " strangers " was dropped. Legal slaves, henceforth, would be " lawful captives taken in just warres and *such* as willingly *selle themselves* or *are sold* (Italics mine) to us." [100] By omitting the word "strangers", Massachusetts made it possible for the children of slaves to be legally held in bondage. " This revision," says Moore, " removed the necessity for alienage or foreign birth as a qualification for slavery, and took off the prohibition against the children of slaves being ' born into legal slavery in Massachusetts.' " [101] Despite the asseverations of Quincy, Washburne, and others, who claim that " no child born into Massachusetts was ever a slave by law," [102] the conclusion of Moore seems inescapable. The traditional enslavement of Negro children after 1670 and the elaborate slave codes adopted by all the New England colonies [103] seem further to prove the legality

96 *Cf. supra*, p. 17.

97 Moore, *op. cit.*, p. 18; Locke, *op. cit.*, p. 14.

98 Tapping Reeve, *Law of Baron and Femme* (New Haven, 1816), p. 339; Hurd, *Law of Freedom and Bondage*, I, 225-226; also 179, 183.

99 Moore, *op. cit.*, p. 17.

100 *Massachusetts Records,* IV, Part II, 467; Moore, *op. cit.*, p. 16.

101 Moore, *op. cit.*, p. 17.

102 Washburne, *op. cit.*, p. 205; Quincy, *Reports*, p. 29 n; Palfrey, *op. cit.*, II, 30 n.

103 *Cf. infra*, ch. v.

of slavery in Massachusetts. Slavery was part of the cultural pattern of seventeenth and eighteenth century Massachusetts and of New England in general. The same was true of the other colonial possessions in the New World. Since most of the other Puritan colonies were usually influenced by the actions of Massachusetts,[104] their legal situation respecting slavery was similar. The case of Connecticut is typical; slavery in that colony was never established by the law, but the recognition accorded it by statute and by the Courts was such " that it may be said to have been established by law."[105]

The opinion has been general, however, that colonial Massachusetts was hostile to slavery. Says William Sumner, " slavery was repugnant to the Puritans and was regarded by them with abhorrence." [106] George Lowell Austin holds the same opinion.[107] Slavery, according to Emory Washburne, " was sustained only by force of the policy and laws of the mother country, and was abolished by the people by the very first clause in the organic law of the State." [108] The anti-slavery poet, John Greenleaf Whittier, says it was not the rigorous winters nor the stubborn soil of New England that discouraged the introduction of slavery during the first half of the seventeenth century, but rather the exalted moral qualities of the settlers themselves. Continuing, he adds: " It was the recognition of the brotherhood of man in sin, suffering and redemption, the awful responsibilities and eternal destinies of humanity, her hatred of wrong and tyranny, and her stern sense of justice, which led her to impose upon the African slave trade the terrible penalty

104 Connecticut and New Haven colonies used the Massachusetts Code of 1649 as models in preparing their legal systems. *The Colonial Laws of Massachusetts* (Reprint, Boston, 1889), p. 86.

105 *The Public Statutes (and) Laws of the State of Connecticut as Revised in May 1821* (Hartford, 1821), p. 430.

106 William Sumner, *History of East Boston* (Boston, 1858), pp. 90-91.

107 *History of Massachusetts* (Boston, 1876), p. 350.

108 " Slavery As it Once Existed in Massachusetts," *loc. cit.,* p. 194.

of the Mosaic Code." [109] Whittier's statement, however, is at variance with historical fact, for Massachusetts in the seventeenth century was, relatively speaking, as deeply concerned with slavery as was Virginia.

The alleged repugnance of Massachusetts to slavery is based upon a single incident. On a Sunday in 1645 two Massachusetts slave merchants, William Smith and Thomas Keyser, joined with London slave raiders in an attack upon an African village, killing about a hundred persons and wounding others. [110] Two Negroes, one of whom was an interpreter, were brought to Massachusetts and sold. Upon hearing of the manner in which the Negroes were acquired, the General Court of the Colony felt constrained " to register indignation against ye haynos and crying sinn of man stealing." [111] It was also voted to pass a law (which, however, never materialized) designed to prevent such occurrences in the future. In order to redress the wrong done the Negroes, the General Court decided to return them to Africa at the Colony's expense. The Court therefore ordered a Mr. Williams of Piscataqua, New Hampshire, to send back to Boston one of the Negroes whom he had purchased from Captain Smith. [112] Meanwhile Smith and Keyser were arrested, ostensibly for killing and stealing and a committee was appointed to press charges against them. Six months later (May 1647) the committee was still pondering [113] the matter. Nothing more is heard of the case, and apparently the death penalty was never imposed.

Although the action of the General Court appears to have been inspired by an abhorrence of slavery, in reality, this does not seem to have been the case. As Moore says there was prob-

109 Cited in Wilson, *op. cit.,* p. 7.

110 Winthrop, *op. cit.*, pp. 243-244. *Cf. Mass. Records*, III, 168.

111 *Massachusetts Records,* III, 168.

112 If Williams had good reason for withholding the Negro, he was to make it known immediately either in person or through his agent. Under no circumstance, however, was he to delay in returning him. *Ibid.,* 136.

113 *Ibid.,* 176, 196.

ably not a trace of anti-slavery sentiment in this gesture.[114] It was impelled rather by the Biblical injunction against man-stealing. Such an offense was a capital crime, for the Massachusetts law provided that " he that stealeth a man, and selleth him . . . he shall surely be put to death." [115] Careful reading of the records reveals that the offense of Smith and Keyser was not slavery but man-stealing.[116] Had the Negroes been lawfully acquired in exchange for rum, iron, or trinkets, probably no protest would have been made. A greater sin, in the opinion of the Puritans, was the fact that Smith and Keyser, by attacking, killing and kidnapping Negroes on Sunday, had desecrated the Sabbath.[117] Since the legal system of seventeenth-century Massachusetts was based upon the Old Testament, the action of the colony in this instance must be interpreted chiefly as strict conformity to the Biblical law and not as the introduction by Massachusetts of a new moral principle. The Puritan conscience, controlled as it was by the Biblical injunction could not but revolt against the stealing of a man, even as it would have condemned the theft of an ox, a horse, or a keg of rum. Later however, as the slave trade developed, this squeamishness over the method of obtaining Negroes disappeared,[118] and no similar case can be found in the annals of New England slavery. The slave trade, like slavery, had become a legitimate institution.

The effects of this slave trade were manifold. On the eve of the American Revolution it formed the very basis of the econ-

114 Moore, *op. cit.*, p. 31 ; *cf. Mass. Records*, II, 129. Yet, even so close a student of Negro History as Carter G. Woodson has erroneously attributed to this action evidence of an early anti-slavery sentiment in Massachusetts. Woodson, *Negro in Our History* (Edition 1928, Washington, D. C.), p. 8.

115 *Colonial Laws of Massachusetts,* ed. Whittemore. (Reprint, 1660), p. 55; *cf.* Ex. 21 : 16.

116 *Mass. Records,* II, 136, 168.

117 Winthrop, *Journal,* II, 227, 252, 253; Donnan, III, 6; also letter of Richard Saltonstall to the General Court, cited in Donnan, III, 6-7; Moore, *op. cit.*, p. 29. Cf. Ex. 2 : 8-11.

118 DuBois, *op. cit.,* p. 31.

omic life of New England:[119] about it revolved, and on it depended, most of her other industries. The vast sugar, molasses and rum trade, shipbuilding, the distilleries, a great many of the fisheries, the employment of artisans and seamen, even agriculture—all were dependent upon the slave traffic. No better statement of the importance of the Negro trade to New England's economy could be cited than the protest of her merchants against the proposed Sugar Act of 1764, which aimed to stop the smuggling of sugar and molasses as well as to raise a revenue in America. In protest the Massachusetts merchants on December, 1763, drew up an elaborate paper entitled *A Statement of the Massachusetts Trade and Fisheries*.[120] Asserting that sugar and molasses were the main ingredients of the slave trade, the merchants claimed that any duty imposed upon these articles would ruin the fisheries, cause the destruction of the rum distilleries, and destroy the slave trade. Destruction of the Negro commerce would throw 5,000 seamen out of employment and would cause almost 700 ships to rot in idleness at their wharves. Not only would it affect those immediately engaged in these industries, but its blighting effects would topple the whole dependent economic structure. Coopers, tanners, barrel makers, and even farmers would be reduced to poverty and misery, if the Act were enforced.[121] In short, the Sugar Act, by destroying the slave trade, would stop the wheels of New England industry.

Equally gloomy were the predictions of the Rhode Island merchants.[122] They visualized the ruin of about thirty distilleries, which constituted the very life blood of their trade, and the subsequent unemployment of " many hundreds of persons " who depended upon them for a livelihood. The closing of these distilleries would bankrupt many families, would ruin trade in

119 Donnan, II, xiii.

120 "Fitch Papers," *Conn. Hist. Soc. Colls.*, XVIII, 262-273.

121 *Ibid.*, pp. 263, 266, 269, 270, 271.

122 *R. I. Col. Recs.*, VI, 378-383.

general, and would permit French brandy to recapture its supremacy over rum as a medium of barter on the African Coast.[123] Besides they claimed:

> Two-thirds of our vessels will become useless, and perish upon our hands; our mechanics, and those who depend upon the merchant for employment must seek for subsistence elsewhere; and . . . a nursery of seamen, at this time consisting of twenty-two hundred, in this colony only will be in a manner destroyed; and as an end will be put to our commerce, the merchants cannot import any more British manufactures nor will the people be able to pay for those they have already received.[124]

The slave trade also helped to create a relatively large class of slave-trading merchants, like the Wantons, Channings, Waldos and Belchers, whose vested interests, as previously noted, made them the economic, political, and social leaders of their communities. While southern slaveholders like the Carrols of Maryland, the Beverlys, Washingtons, and Carters of Virginia, and the Izards, Blakes and Heywards of South Carolina,[125] derived their wealth and position from the exploitation of Negro labor, the Fanueils, Browns, Cabots, and Pepperells of New England reaped similar rewards partly from the sale of black workers.

From the Negro trade, likewise, came a great part of the wealth that afforded slave trading magnates the necessary leisure for cultural and intellectual leadership. The wealth and culture of Newport and Boston reflected to a great extent the " golden harvest " reaped from the Negro traffic.[126] In Rhode

123 *Ibid.*, p. 381.

124 *Ibid.*

125 Phillips, *American Negro Slavery*, pp. 80, 84, 95, 96.

126 Richman, *Rhode Island*, p. 114; Peterson, *History of Rhode Island and Newport in the Past*, p. 104.

Island the Botanical Garden and the Philosophical Society, later to become the Redwood Library, were both supported by the slave trader Abraham Redwood.[127] The architectural and scientific work of Joseph Brown,[128] and the stimulation given to philosophy and art by Dean Berkeley and John Smibert, philosopher and painter respectively,[129] were but additional evidences of the cultural interest made possible by the wealth amassed from the slave trade. The fortunes built up or enlarged by the slave trade, as already indicated also encouraged philanthropy. Finally, the New England slave trade helped to destroy flourishing Negro states in Africa,[130] contributed to the depopulation of that continent,[131] and introduced into New England members of an alien race who were to influence the ideals and institutions of that section throughout the colonial era.

127 Miller, *Narragansett Planters,* pp. 48-49.

128 *D.A.B.,* III, 141.

129 Miller, *op. cit.,* p. 49; *cf.* J. R. Cole, *History of Washington County, Rhode Island* (New York, 1889), p. 41.

130 The African kingdom of Ghana, the Mandingo Empire and the great Songhais Empire were but a few of the Negro states flourishing in Africa when the slave trade began. In the fifteenth and sixteenth centuries the Songhais Empire was noted for its economic, political, artistic, and literary development. For these states, *vide* Felix Dubois, *Timbuctoo the Mysterious* (New York, 1896), esp. chs. vi-xv; Maurice Delafosse, *Negroes of Africa,* ch. iii; Carter G. Woodson, *African Background Outlined* (Washington, 1936), ch. iii; Lady Lugard, *A Tropical Dependency* (London, 1905). Best of these works is Abderrahman Essadi, *Tarik-es Soudan* (1691) French translation. This is a history of the Negro kingdoms of West Africa by a scholar of the Songhais Empire written during the seventeenth century.

131 There are no exact figures on the number of Negroes taken from Africa and brought to America, but the total loss to Africa in man power must have been enormous. Woodson (*Negro in Our History,* p. 69), places the number at 50,000,000. W. E. B. Dubois (*The Negro,* p. 155) estimates the loss to be 60,000,000.

# CHAPTER III
## THE NEGRO POPULATION

SLAVES were brought into New England throughout the entire colonial period. In regard to the Negro, as well as the general population, however, accurate estimates are difficult to obtain,[1] for census taking in colonial America was very imperfect. Although the British government periodically instructed its officials to report the number of inhabitants,[2] there existed little machinery for a systematic enumeration.[3] Sometimes the colonies ignored the instructions of the mother country; at other times they gave only half-hearted compliance.[4] Even though sincere attempts might have been made to secure a trustworthy tabulation, formidable obstacles were encountered. The population was largely rural, roads were bad, and enumerators were unpaid and untrained for their work. Ignorance and superstition further handicapped the census takers,[5] as some people believed that sickness or death would follow if the people were counted.[6] Deliberate exaggerations or understatements of the figures by colonial officials, as well as the failure to specify whether the returns included Negroes and Indians, all militated

1 For the most recent and by far the most satisfactory work on the population of colonial America, including New England, *vide* the excellent statistical study by Evarts B. Greene, and Virginia D. Harrington, *American Population Before the Federal Census of 1790* (New York, 1932), p. vi.

2 Population reports were usually requested in the items listed under *Heads of Inquiry* sent at intervals to colonial governors by the British Board of Trade. For early sample of these *Heads of Inquiry* see *Conn. Col. Recs.*, III, 293.

3 Franklin Bowditch Dexter, "Estimates of Population in the American Colonies," *New Haven Historical Society Papers* (New Haven, 1918), p. 153.

4 U. S. Bureau of the Census, *A Century of Population Growth, 1790-1909*, pp. 3, 4.

5 *Ibid.*, p. 3, Dexter, *ut supra.*

6 *Documents Relative to the Colonial History of the State of New York* (Albany, 1855), V, 339.

against a reasonably reliable estimate.[7] Additional confusion resulted from the tendency to base enumeration upon houses, families, muster rolls, militia, polls, and taxables.[8] As a result, contemporary population figures cannot be accepted at face value.[9] They are only estimates, and cannot be interpreted as revealing the true situation. Furthermore, because of the irregular intervals between enumerations, no comparative picture of the Negro population is possible.

Despite these difficulties it is possible to glean from the available data some impression of the number and distribution of the Negroes in New England. Taking the section as a whole, the Negro population was comparatively small, particularly in the seventeenth century. The meagre statistics available have already been cited.[10] Certain factors, such as climate, the monopolistic restrictions on the slave trade, lack of currency, and the general poverty of the settlers, tended to keep the Negro population at a minimum. Thus, in 1700, when the total inhabitants of New England were estimated at 90,000,[11] the Negro population was probably not more than a thousand. The first general census of New England's population by race was made in 1715. At that time, there were approximately 158,000 whites and 4,150 blacks. Deliberate or unintentional errors in the figures for either date may account for the large increase. The Negro represented less than three per cent of the total inhabitants.

7 Dexter, *ut supra*. Connecticut offers a good example. At the census of 1749, the population was certified to the Board of Trade at 70,000, of whom 69,000 were whites and 1000 Negroes. Questioned concerning the authenticity of the returns, Governor Fitch sent a more reasonable estimate of the population, which " by a more careful and particular enquiry ", he found to be 128,212 whites and 3,587 blacks. *Conn. Col. Recs.*, IX, 596; X, 623.

8 To calculate the population in the terms cited above: average estimates would be militia, 5 to 1; polls, taxables, tax lists, 4 to 1; families, average size 5.7 to 6; houses, 7 to 1. Greene and Harrington, *op. cit.*, p. xxiii.

9 *Ibid.*, p. **vi.**

10 *Vide supra*, p. 23.

11 Greene and Harrington, *op. cit.*, p. 10.

Massachusetts, with 2,000 Negroes, had the largest number. Connecticut had 1,500, and Rhode Island and New Hampshire had 500 and 150 respectively.[12]

As the slave trade developed, and as wealth and population late in the eighteenth century increased, the number of slaves grew accordingly. Between 1771 and 1776, there were in New England, out of a total population of 659,446, approximately 16,034 Negroes, the largest number ever reported in that section during the colonial period.

TABLE 1

APPROXIMATE NUMBER AND PROPORTION OF NEGROES IN NEW ENGLAND
ON EVE OF REVOLUTIONARY WAR [13]

| Year | Colony | Total Population | Whites | Negroes Number | Percent |
|------|--------|------------------|--------|--------|---------|
| 1771 | Vermont ........... | 4,669 | 4,650 | 19 | .04 |
| 1775 | New Hampshire ... | 48,129 | 47,588 | 034 | 1.1 |
| 1776 | Massachusetts ...... | 349,094 | 343,845 | 5,249 | 1.8 |
| 1774 | Rhode Island ...... | 59,678 | 54,435 | 3,761 | 6.3 |
| 1774 | Connecticut ........ | 197,856 | 191,392 | 6,464 | 3.2 |
| | | 659,446 | 641,910 | 16,034 | 2.4 |

On the eve of the American Revolution Connecticut, whose slave trade was not to be compared with that of Massachusetts or Rhode Island, nevertheless had the largest number of slaves (6,464). The greater prosperity of Connecticut's inhabitants and their frugal and industrious habits were responsible for this situation. The wealth of the colony was also more equally dis-

12 Cited in *ibid.*, p. 4.

13 There is no general census of New England available for any one of these years. These figures, therefore, are composite; that is, taken over a period of five years as indicated. Vermont was included with New York. *Vide* E. B. O'Callaghan, *Documentary History of the State of New York,* I, 697; Samuel Williams, LL.D., *History of Vermont* (Walpole, 1794), p. 415; for Connecticut, *vide Conn. Col. Recs.*, XIV, 491; also pp. 485-491; for Massachusetts, *vide Journals of the Massachusetts Provincial Congress* (Boston, 1838), p. 755; for Rhode Island, *vide R. I. Col. Recs.*, VII, 253; Greene and Harrington, *op. cit.*, p. 17; *Records of the State of Vermont* (Montpelier, 1873), I, 403 n.

tributed, with few extremes of riches or poverty. While agriculture was the leading occupation, the colony had important iron, copper, shipbuilding and rum industries. New London, Hartford, New Haven, Stonington and Wethersfield were busy ports from which fishing, whaling, slave trading and general commerce were carried on. On the farm and in these industries workers were in great demand. Since few indentured servants were available, unfree workers were chiefly Negro slaves,[14] the wider distribution of wealth in that colony making it possible for more persons to own slaves than in Massachusetts and Rhode Island, where wealth was concentrated to a greater degree among merchants and landed gentry.

Rhode Island, whose total population was less than one-half that of Connecticut, had more than half as many Negroes; and no other New England colony had so large a proportion of slaves. The great slave-trading and other commercial interests of Rhode Island, together with its large rum distilleries, spermaceti works [15] and large-scale agriculture in the famous Narragansett country [16] served to increase the density of its slave population out of all proportion to that of the other New England colonies. On the eve of the Revolution the proportion of Negroes to white persons in the colony was one in fifteen; in New England as a whole, one in about forty, in Massachusetts one in fifty-five.[17]

New England's Negro population apparently remained relatively static between 1776 and 1790. When the first federal

14 Weeden, *Economic and Social History of New England,* I, 163; II, 554, 576, 651; Robert Warner, *Negroes of New Haven* (New Haven, 1940), p. 2; Charles McLean Andrews, *Connecticut's Place in Colonial History* (New Haven, 1924), p. 9.

15 Bruce Briggs, "Aaron Lopez, Colonial Merchant of Newport," *New England Quarterly,* IV, 7. Weeden, *Early Rhode Island,* pp. 222, 223, 329; ch. x.

16 Cole, *op. cit.,* pp. 40-41; Edward Channing, "The Narragansett Planters," *Johns Hopkins University Studies* in *History and Public Law,* Fourth Series, III, 6-9, 10.

17 Derived from figures cited in Table I.

census was taken in 1790, there were in New England approximately 16,822 blacks out of a total population of 1,099,206. Although the white population had grown by more than fifty per cent since 1776, the number of Negroes had increased by a little more than four per cent. The relative size of New England's Negro population in 1790 is emphasized by comparing it with that of New York State which, with 25,875 Negroes,[18] contained more than one and a half times as many blacks as the five New England states combined. After 1776, the Negroes represented a constantly diminishing ratio of the total New England population; by 1790 they made up less than two per cent of the inhabitants of that section. Rhode Island alone still maintained a fairly large proportion of Negroes, although even there the ratio of whites to blacks was sixteen to one.

TABLE 2

SHOWING NUMBER AND PROPORTION OF NEGROES IN NEW ENGLAND, BY STATE, IN 1790 [19]

|  | Total Population | White | Negroes Number | Negroes Percent |
|---|---|---|---|---|
| New England ....... | 1,009,206 | 992,384 | 16,822 | 1.7 |
| Maine .............. | 96,643 | 96,107 | 536 | 0.6 |
| New Hampshire ..... | 141,899 | 141,112 | 787 | 0.6 |
| Vermont ........... | 85,341 | 85,072 | 269 | 0.3 |
| Massachusetts ....... | 378,556 | 373,187 | 5,369 | 1.4 |
| Rhode Island ....... | 69,112 | 64,670 | 4,442 | 6.4 |
| Connecticut ......... | 237,655 | 232,236 | 5,419 | 2.3 |

The comparatively static condition of the Negro population during the Revolutionary and the " Critical Period," as shown by the census of 1790, may be explained in several ways. The Revolutionary War ruined the slave trade, and prevented the increase of the black population by importation. By 1790 all the

18 The actual increase was 788. *A Century of Population Growth, 1790-1909*, p. 22. *Vide* Greene and Harrington (citing *Heads of Families*) op. cit., pp. 9-10 where New York's Negro population is cited as 25,978.

19 *Ibid.*, Maine was still part of Massachusetts at this time.

New England states had abolished both slavery [20] and the slave trade.[21] The flight or banishment of many loyalists to Canada, or to other parts of the British Empire, carrying their slaves with them, likewise served to depress the Negro population figures.[22] Some Negroes were carried away by the British; [23] others, seeking freedom, went with the British from choice; [24] still others undoubtedly lost their lives fighting in the American army.[25] The result was a reduction of the normal rate of increase in the Negro population between 1774 and 1790.

Turning to the separate colonies, a somewhat better presentation of the growth of the Negro element, especially during the eighteenth century, may be obtained. New Hampshire at no time boasted of many slaves. Having little coast line, it was not so important commercially as Rhode Island or Massachusetts;

20 *Records of the Governor and Council of the State of Vermont*, I, 92; *New Hampshire State Papers*, IX, 896; *Acts and Resolves of Rhode Island, Feb. 1784-Dec. 1786* (Providence, n.d.), X, 6-7; *Acts and Laws of the State of Connecticut* (New London, 1784), p. 235; *Mass. Hist. Soc. Colls.*, First Series, III, 203.

21 *Papers of the New Haven Historical Society* (New Haven, 1882), III, 115; *Vermont State Papers* (Middlebury, 1823), pp. 505-506; *Acts and Resolves of Rhode Island, May 1771-Oct. 1775* (Facsimile Reprints), V, 48-50; *Acts and Laws of the State of Connecticut* (Printed by Timothy Greene (New London, n.d.), p. 234; *Acts and Laws of Mass. 1786-1787* (Reprint, Boston, 1893), pp. 615-616.

22 James H. Stark, *The Loyalists of Massachusetts* (Boston, 1910), pp. 58-62; *vide* biographical sketches, pp. 122-468.

23 *Massachusetts Laws and Resolves, 1786-1787* (Reprint, Boston, 1893), p. 954.

24 *Vide infra*, p. 146.

25 Benjamin Colwell, *Spirit of '76 in Rhode Island* (Boston, 1850), pp. 262-263; *Rhode Island Historical Tracts* (Providence, 1880) ; pp. 1-90. For Negro soldiers in other Revolutionary Armies, see " New Hampshire State Papers," *Revolutionary War Rolls* (Concord, 1886), II, 434-439; *Massachusetts Soldiers and Sailors in the War of the Revolution* (Boston, 1897), III, 10, 15, 211, 212; XII, 518, 520; Steiner, *op. cit.*, p. 26.

its slave trade and Negro population were insignificant.[26] The first Negroes were probably brought to the province in 1644,[27] but the number at the close of the seventeenth century is not known. In 1715 New Hampshire had approximately 150 blacks in a total population of 9,650 and the number apparently grew slowly until the census of 1737.[28] The largest increase seems to have taken place between 1737 and 1742, when the Negro population appears to have more than doubled, advancing from 200 to 500. The growth thereafter was slow.[29] A quarter of a century later (1767), 633 Negroes were counted,[30] but the largest number in colonial New Hampshire appears to have been in 1773, when 674 were listed. By 1790 the number of Negroes had increased to 787, at which time they constituted only six-tenths of one per cent of the total population.

Most of the Negroes in New Hampshire were concentrated in Rockingham County, in which was located the mercantile and slave trading center of Portsmouth. In 1773 almost seven-tenths of the 674 Negroes were in Rockingham County; Strafford County, with 102 Negroes, ranked second; while Hillsborough, Cheshire, and Grafton Counties had only 77, 9 and 32 blacks respectively. Portsmouth, the largest of the towns, contained the greatest number of Negroes [31] and in 1767 the town's 187 slaves comprised almost one-third of the blacks in the colony. Exeter, the only other town with an appreciable number of

26 *Vide infra*, Table 3. See also for reference notes to figures given in this paragraph.

27 *Mass. Records,* II, 136, 168.

28 The returns for Negroes show an increase of only fifty in fifteen years and no increase from 1730-1737. *Vide* Greene and Harrington, *op. cit.,* p. 71.

29 *Ibid.,* p. 71.

30 In 1775, returns were secured from less than half of the towns reported in 1767. Only 60 sent in estimates of their inhabitants in 1775, whereas 138 did so eight years earlier. *Provincial Papers of New Hampshire* (Nashua, 1873), VII, 724-781. In the census of 1786, 5 towns did not report. *Ibid.,* X, 639-689.

31 *Provincial and State Papers of New Hampshire,* X, 636; for detailed statistics *vide* Greene and Harrington, *op. cit.,* pp. 70-85.

## TABLE 3

Showing Number, Percentage, Increase and Percent Increase of
Negro Population in New Hampshire, 1767-1790

| Year | Total Population | White | Negroes | | Negro Increase | |
|---|---|---|---|---|---|---|
| | | | Number | Percent | Number | Percent |
| 1767 [a] .... | 52,700 | 52,067 | 633 | 1.2 | | |
| 1773 [b] .... | 72,092 | 71,418 | 674 | 0.9 | 41 | 6.4 |
| 1774 [c] .... | 85,000 | | | | | |
| 1775 [d] .... | 48,129 | 47,588 | 541 | | 133 | 10.9 |
| 1786 [e] .... | 95,801 | 95,452 | 349 | | | |
| 1790 [f] .... | 141,899 | 141,112 | 787 | 0.6 | 246 | 45.4 |

[a] This was the first regular census in New Hampshire. *Ibid.*, VII, 170. For enumerations in 1715, 1716, 1721, 1730, 1737, 1742, 1751, 1761, *vide* Greene and Harrington, *op. cit.*, pp. 71-72.

[b] 138 towns reported at this census. *Ibid.*, X, 636; see also pp. 625-636; *A Century of Population Growth*, pp. 150-151.

[c] The returns of this census, according to Jeremy Belknap, a contemporary author of a History of New Hampshire and one of the founders of the Massachusetts Historical Society, have not been found. *Ibid.*, p. 168.

[d] According to the enumeration schedule, the Negro returns were listed as "Negroes or slaves for life." Evidently the free Negroes were either omitted or were classed with the free whites in the total population. As noted above (note 30), only 60 towns reported their population. *Ibid.* (Nashua, 1873), VII, 724-781.

[e] At this census, the free Negroes were no doubt included with the "free inhabitants," as the 349 Negroes listed fall either under the caption of slaves or "others." *Ibid.*, X, 639-689; *A Century of Population Growth, 1790-1900*, p. 156.

[f] *A Century of Population Growth, 1790-1900*, p. 222. *Cf. Negro Population in the United States, 1790-1915*, p. 45. Here the population is given as: total inhabitants, 141,855; whites, 141,097, Negroes, 788. *Cf.* Greene and Harrington, *op. cit.*, p. 73, where population gives 630 "free" persons and 158 "slaves."

Negroes at the outbreak of the Revolutionary War, had only fifty.[32]

In comparison with New Hampshire, Massachusetts had both a larger number and a larger percentage of Negroes. Not only was the Bay Colony the richest and most powerful New England province, but next to Rhode Island it carried on the most extensive slave trade. The increase in the Negro population of Massachusetts, however, was not uniform. In 1676, according to Edward Randolph, there were " not above 200 slaves in the

32 *A Century of Population Growth, 1790-1909*, pp. 149, 150.

colony." [33] Two years later, Governor Andros reported that there were but " few slaves " and these were " proportionable with freemen." [34] In 1708 the number, according to Governor Dudley, had increased to 550.[35] The rapid expansion of the Massachusetts slave trade after 1696, together with increasing wealth, may account in part for the rise of the Negro population to 2,000 in 1715.[36] Faulty enumeration in 1708 or 1715 might have acted either to minimize or to exaggerate the number of Negroes. Twenty years later (1735), when the estimated population of the entire colony was approximately 144,000 [37] or 145,000,[38] the Negro element was reported to be 2,600, or less than two per cent of the total.[39] It reached a numerical peak in 1776, with 5,249 blacks out of a population of 349,094.[40] Negroes attained their largest proportion of the Massachusetts population, however, between 1755 and 1764,[41] a period in which they constituted 2.2 per cent of the population. The following table is illustrative.

33 Joseph B. Felt, " Statistics on Population in Massachusetts," *American Statistical Association Collections,* I, 202. It is generally admitted that Randolph's estimate of the general population of 150,000 was exaggerated. The same might apply to the Negro population. Felt, *op. cit.,* p. 141.

34 *Documents Relative to the Colonial History of New York State* (Albany, 1853), III, 263.

35 Moore, *op. cit.,* p. 50.

36 Greene and Harrington, *op. cit.,* p. 14.

37 Dexter, *op. cit.,* p. 156.

38 *A Century of Population Growth, 1790-1900,* p. 5.

39 Felt, *op. cit.,* p. 208; Greene and Harrington, *op. cit.,* p. 15.

40 *Journals of the Provincial Congress of Massachusetts in 1774 and 1775,* p. 755; *cf. A Century of Population Growth,* pp. 158-161.

41 Dr. Belknap, a contemporary of the slave era, believes that Negroes were most numerous before 1763. On the other hand, Prince Hall, an intelligent free black who was about 55 years of age in 1795, thinks that Negroes were most numerous about 1745. Chickering, *op. cit.,* p. 124 n.

## TABLE 4

APPROXIMATE NUMBER, INCREASE AND PERCENT OF INCREASE OF NEGRO
POPULATION IN MASSACHUSETTS, 1676-1790

| Year | Total Population | White | Negroes Number | Percent | Pop. Increase | % Pop. Increase |
|------|------------------|-------|--------|---------|---------------|-----------------|
| 1676 [a] .... |  |  | 200 |  |  |  |
| 1678 [b] .... |  |  | few |  |  |  |
| 1708 [c] .... |  |  | 400 |  | 200 | 100.0 |
| 1720 [d] .... |  |  | 2,000 |  |  |  |
| 1735 [e] .... | 144,000 | 141,400 | 2,600 | 1.7 | 1,600 | 400.0 |
| 1755 [f] .... | 200,000 | 195,500 | 4,500 | 2.2 | 1,900 | 70.3 |
| 1764 [g] .... | 223,841 | 218,950 | 5,235 | 2.2 | 735 | 16.3 |
| 1776 [h] .... | 349,094 | 343,845 | 5,249 | 1.5 | 14 | 0.2 |
| 1784 [i] .... | 357,510 | 353,133 | 4,377 | 1.2 | -862 | -16.4 |
| 1790 [j] .... | 378,556 | 373,187 | 5,369 | 1.4 | 992 | 22.6 |

[a] Palfrey, *op. cit.*, III, 298; Moore, *op. cit.*, pp. 48-49. For estimates not cited here *vide* Greene and Harrington, *op. cit.*, pp. 15-18.

[b] *Documents Relative to the Colonial History of the State of New York* (Albany, 1853), III, 263 (hereinafter cited as *N. Y. Col. Docs.*); Moore, p. 49.

[c] Moore, p. 50.

[d] *Ibid.*

[e] Dexter, *op. cit.*, p. 156; *cf. A Century of Population Growth, 1790-1909*, p. 5, where total population is given as 145,000; Greene and Harrington, *op. cit.*, p. 15; *cf.* Felt, *op. cit.*, p. 208; *vide Early Census Making in Massachusetts, 1643-1765*, ed. J. H. Benton, Jr. (Boston, 1905), p. 22, where total white population cited for 1728 is 120,000 persons and the Negroes at 2,000.

[f] *A Century of Population Growth*, p. 5; *cf.* Dexter, *op. cit.*, p. 157.

[g] *Century of Population Growth*, pp. 158-161. *Cf.* Greene and Harrington, *op. cit.*, p. 17, where number of blacks is listed at 5,500. Chickering (*op. cit.*, p. 112) gives number as 5,100 for 1765.

[h] *Journals of the Provincial Congress of Massachusetts in 1774 and 1775*, p. 755. (Hereinafter cited as *J.P.C.M.*)

[i] Greene and Harrington, *op. cit.*, p. 18.

[j] *Century of Population Growth*, p. 222; *cf.* U. S. Bureau of the Census, *Negro Population in the United States, 1790-1915*, p. 45, where total Negro Population is given as 5,463, 14 more than in the table. The white population is also listed as 137 more, being 373,324. Greene and Harrington (*op. cit.*, p. 119) citing U. S. Bureau of Census, *Heads of Families in Massachusetts*, pp. 9-10 cites Negroes and other free persons at 5,463.

Slaves were more evenly distributed in Massachusetts than in New Hampshire, but there was some concentration in the maritime and industrial counties of Essex, Suffolk, Bristol, and Plymouth, and in the commercial and agricultural county of

Middlesex. Much of the wealth, derived from commerce and manufacturing, centered in these districts,[42] and here the labor demand was greatest. In Suffolk County were Boston, Dorchester, Roxbury and Braintree; in Essex were Salem, Ipswich, Newbury and Gloucester—all famous for commerce, shipbuilding, fishing, whaling, or distilling. Middlesex had Cambridge, New England's educational center, and Charlestown, a flourishing port. In Bristol were Taunton and Dartmouth, and in Plymouth were Scituate, Hanover, and the town of Plymouth. In 1764 these counties possessed more than three-quarters of all the slaves in Massachusetts, Suffolk leading with 1,351 Negroes, followed by Essex with 1,070, and Middlesex with 800. Lincoln had only twenty-four and there were a few Negroes in Duke, Cumberland, York, Nantucket, Berkshire, and Worcester counties.[43]

When, at the suggestion of the Continental Congress, the census was taken in 1776, some counties appeared to have gained, and others to have lost in Negro population.[44] While the total Negro population of Massachusetts remained almost constant between 1764 and 1776,[45] the number of blacks in Berkshire County had more than doubled, with 88 Negroes in 1764 and 216 in 1776. Nantucket County showed a gain from 44 to 133; Cumberland from 95 to 162; and Lincoln from 24 to 85. Duke County with 59 at that time had the smallest Negro population. In sharp contrast to these counties, Suffolk and Essex Counties showed decreases in their Negro element. Suffolk, the heaviest loser, reported a loss of nearly fifty per cent of its Negroes, with 1,351 in 1764 and only 682 in 1776. The

42 *A Century of Population Growth*, pp. 158-161.

43 In 1764, out of 5,235 Negroes in the colony, 4,036, or 77.0 percent were in these counties. *Ibid.* Percentages derived. *Cf.* Felt, " Population ", *loc. cit.,* pp. 208-210.

44 *Vide. J. P. C. M., 1774 and 1775*, p. 755; Greene and Harrington, *op. cit.,* p. 30.

45 The increase was only fourteen. *Vide* Table 4.

decline in the number of Negro inhabitants of Essex County was much less—from 1,070 in 1764 to 1,049 in 1776.[46]

The apparent falling off in the Negro population in Suffolk County may have been the result of several factors. There may have been deliberate understatement, for the 1776 census, according to Jeremy Belknap, was unpopular.[47] Another reason may have been the exodus caused by the unsettled business conditions after the French and Indian War, which had sent thousands of people, northward, westward, and to Canada.[48] Adams estimates that between 1760 and 1774, 30,000 people left Connecticut alone, and there was migration to New Hampshire, where one hundred new towns were founded.[49] During the same period New England migrants settled seventy-four towns in Vermont and twenty in Maine. Little is known of the role played by Negroes in the westward movement, but apparently some slaves carried there by migrating families participated in pushing back the frontier and in settling western lands. Abijah Prince, a free Negro of Massachusetts is said to have been one of the original founders of Sunderland, Vermont.[50] Some Negroes eager to win their freedom, fled to the British army;[51]

46 *J. P. C. M.*, (Boston, 1838), p. 755; *cf.* Felt, *op. cit.*, p. 213.

47 Belknap was a contemporary. Cited in Dexter, *op. cit.*, p. 158 n.

48 This movement was in progress as early as 1749. The British Government encouraged it by offering free passage, provisions, muskets and ammunition to all settlers who would go to Nova Scotia in that year. A thousand were to be despatched thither, forts were to be erected and 100 cannon installed. Carpenters and other artisans were in great demand. *Boston Post Boy,* July 24, 1749; *cf.* Stark, *op. cit.*, pp. 122-168. An anonymous writer informed the Secretary of the Society for the Propagation of the Gospel in 1760 that many New Englanders were migrating to Nova Scotia. *Society for the Propagation of the Gospel, Transcripts,* Series B, I, 952 (Library of Congress, pp. 766-767). Ms. in Library of Congress, Washington, D. C. Hereinafter cited as *S. P. G. Transcripts.*

49 Adams, *Revolutionary New England,* p. 259.

50 Sheldon, *History of Deerfield, Massachusetts,* II, 899.

51 *Connecticut Gazette and the Universal Intelligencer,* April 21, 1775; Benjamin Brawley, *Social History of the American Negro* (New York, 1921), p. 53.

others joined the American forces,[52] but whatever the cause, the apparent loss in Suffolk County's Negro population was abnormally high. Nevertheless, the proportion of Negroes in Suffolk, Essex and Bristol Counties was larger than the proportion of Negroes in the entire province.[53]

Of the towns, Boston, throughout the entire colonial era, contained the largest number of Negroes; importation and natural increase sent the total from 400 in 1708 to 1,374 in 1742.[54] In that year, the town had approximately one-third of all blacks in Massachusetts, but her largest Negro population was reported in 1752. At that time there were 1,541 Negroes [55] who comprised about one-tenth of the town's population.[56] By 1755, although the number of Negroes had dwindled to 989, Boston still had the largest black population in the colony, no other town having more than 100 Negroes. In Essex County, Salem had 83; Ipswich 62; Gloucester 61, and Newbury 50; in Middlesex County, Cambridge had 56; Scituate, in Plymouth County had 43, and Kittery in York County had 35. Elsewhere, with few exceptions, the Negro population was negligible.[57] In

52 *Massachusetts Soldiers and Sailors in the War of the Revolution,* III, 15, 211, 212; XII, 518, 520; *Letters of Members of the Continental Congress,* ed. Edmund C. Burnett (5 vols. Washington, 1921) I, 217, 313; Timothy Mather Cooley, *Life of Lemuel Haynes* (New York, 1835), pp. 45-46; Benjamin and William Cutter, *History of the Town of Arlington, Massachusetts, 1635-1879* (Boston, 1880), p. 35; Walter Mazyck, *George Washington and the Negro* (Washington, 1931), chs. v-x, *passim;* Benjamin Brawley, *Social History of the American Negro,* p. 56.

53 *Cf.* Appendix, Table A.

54 Moore, *op. cit.,* p. 50.

55 *Mass. Hist. Soc. Colls.,* Third Series, I, 152; for Boston's Negro population by wards; *cf. Appendix,* Table B.

56 Lemuel Shattuck, *Report on the Census of Boston* (Boston, 1846), pp. 4, 5.

57 *Ibid., Mass. Hist. Soc. Colls.,* Second Series, III, 95-97. For list of towns and their Negro population by sex in Massachusetts in 1754-1755, *vide Appendix C. Cf.* Felt, "Population of Massachusetts," *loc. cit.,* pp. 208-216. York, Cumberland and Lincoln Counties were part of Maine. Chickering, *op. cit.,* p. 9.

1765 when Boston's population was estimated at 15,520, there were only 811 Negroes and mulattoes. Salem's Negro population had increased to 183; Ipswich had 100; an increase of 40 per cent and Cambridge 90, an increase of 62½ per cent.[58]

Ranking third in Negro population during the eighteenth century was Rhode Island. Statistics throw virtually no light on the Negro population of the province in the seventeenth century, the only official estimate being the statement of Governor Sanford to the Lords of Trade in 1680. He reported that about 200 whites and blacks were born in the colony each year.[59] For the eighteenth century, on the other hand, Rhode Island's population statistics are the best in New England. The colony manifested little of the secretiveness of Connecticut or the stubbornness of Massachusetts toward the wishes of the home government. Within seventy-five years Rhode Island took at least eight censuses.[60] In 1708, when its total population was reported as 7,181, there were 426 Negroes. Negroes were vastly more important than the indentured white servants, whom they outnumbered by almost eight to one. The following table shows the ratio of Negroes to white servants.[61]

Seven years later, the Negro population had increased slightly to 500, in a total population of 8,500. The largest increase in the number of blacks occurred between 1715 and 1755, the period of Rhode Island's greatest commercial, industrial and slave trading development. By 1730 there were approximately 1,648 Negroes in Rhode Island; 3,077 in 1749; 4,697 in 1755; 3,761 in 1774; 3,806 in 1782; and between 4,355 and 4,442 in 1790, as indicated in table 6. Significant in Rhode Island's population was the relatively large proportion of blacks, which reached its peak in 1755. In that year one out of every nine persons in the

58 Benton, *op. cit.*, Appendix; *cf.* Chickering, *op. cit.*, pp. 113-120; Felt, " Population of Mass.", *loc. cit.*, 211-213.

59 Dexter, *op. cit.*, p. 158.

60 Greene & Harrington, *op. cit.*, p. 62.

61 Dexter, *ut supra*; *cf.* Table 6, Census for 1715 omitted.

## TABLE 5
NUMBER AND DISTRIBUTION OF NEGROES IN RHODE ISLAND IN 1708 [62]

| Towns | Servants White | Negro | Total Inhabitants | Percent Negroes |
|---|---|---|---|---|
| Newport ............... | 20 | 220 | 2,203 | 9.9 |
| Providence ............. | 6 | 7 | 1,446 | .4 |
| Portsmouth ............ | 8 | 40 | 628 | 6.3 |
| Warwick .............. | 4 | 10 | 480 | 2.0 |
| Westerly .............. | 5 | 20 | 570 | 3.5 |
| New Shoreham ........ | | 6 | 208 | 2.9 |
| Kingstown ............. | | 85 | 1,200 | 7.0 |
| Jamestown ............. | 9 | 32 | 206 | 15.5 |
| Greenwich ............. | 3 | 6 | 241 | 2.9 |
| Total .............. | 56 | 426 | 7,181 | 5.9 |

colony was a Negro. This was almost three times the proportion of blacks in Connecticut where in 1761 and 1774 one out of every thirty-three persons was a Negro.[63] The proportion of Negroes in Rhode Island to whites was about one to sixteen (see Table 6).

The unusually large number of Negroes in Rhode Island late in the eighteenth century is evidence of the colony's enormous commercial activities which produced a relatively large slave-holding aristocracy. Naturally the slave trade, in which Rhode Island finally surpassed even Massachusetts, contributed largely to the increase in the colony's Negro population. The unique Narragansett Country with its large scale farming inducements also created a demand for considerable numbers of slaves.[64]

Most of Rhode Island's slaves (as in New Hampshire and Massachusetts) were concentrated in a few commercial and agricultural areas like Newport, Jamestown, Providence, South and North Kingstown, and Portsmouth. Of these Newport had the largest Negro population. In 1708 its 220 slaves constituted

62 R. I. Col. Recs., IV, 59. It should be borne in mind that Negro "slaves" were usually spoken of as servants in New England.

63 Vide infra, Table 7.

64 Channing, Narragansett Planters, p. 10.

## TABLE 6

NUMBER, PROPORTION AND INCREASE OF NEGRO POPULATION IN
RHODE ISLAND FROM 1708-1790

| Year | Total Population | White | Indian | Negroes | | | |
|---|---|---|---|---|---|---|---|
| | | | | Number | Percent | Pop. Increase | % Pop. Increase |
| 1708 [a] ...... | 7,181 | 6,755 | | 426 | 5.9 | | |
| 1730 [b] ...... | 17,935 | 16,287 | | 1,648 | 9.1 | 1,222 | 286 |
| 1749 [c] ...... | 32,773 | 28,439 | 1,257 | 3,077 | 9.3 | 1,429 | 86.7 |
| 1755 [d] ...... | 40,636 | 35,939 | | 4,697 | 11.5 | 1,620 | 52.6 |
| 1764 [e] ...... | 48,000 | | | | | | |
| 1774 [f] ...... | 59,678 | 54,435 | 1,482 | 3,761 | 6.3 | 684 | 22.2 |
| 1782 [g] ...... | 51,869 | 48,063 | | 3,806 | 7.3 | 45 | 1.1 |
| 1790 [h] ... ⎧ | 68,825 | 64,470 | | 4,355 | 6.3 | 549 | 14.4 |
| ⎩ | 69,112 | 64,670 | | 4,442 | 6.4 | 636 | 16.7 |

[a] *R. I. Col. Recs.*, IV, 59. *Cf.* Greene and Harrington, *op. cit.*, pp. 61-64 for various estimates of population for years cited in table. Where not specified, white population contains a few Indians.

[b] Edward Field, *State of Rhode Island and Providence Plantations at the End of the Century* (Boston, 1902), I, 176.

[c] *R. I. Col. Recs.*, V, 271.

[d] Greene and Harrington, *op. cit.*, p. 67.

[e] *Ibid., R. I. Col. Recs.*, VI, 379.

[f] *R. I. Col. Recs.*, VII, 253.

[g] *Records of the State of Rhode Island, 1780-1783* (Providence, 1864), IX, 653.

[h] *A Century of Population Growth, 1790-1900*, p. 222; *Negro Population in the United States, 1790-1915*, p. 45.

almost one-half of the Negroes in the province.[65] An obvious undercount in 1748-9 gave Newport only 110 blacks.[66] Between 1708 and 1755 Newport experienced a commercial and industrial expansion that was little short of phenomenal. At the height of its prosperity in 1755, the port had 1,234 blacks,[67] and the decline of its commercial prosperity during the Revolution is reflected in the smaller Negro population at the close of the conflict. In 1782, when the total number of slaves in the colony was 3,806, Newport, with 600, had only about one-sixth of the

65 Richman, *Rhode Island*, pp. 151-157. Weeden, *Early Rhode Island*, ch. v.

66 *R. I. Col. Recs.*, IV, 59. Newport had 220, or just twice that number, 30 years earlier. *Vide* Table 9.

67 Greene and Harrington, *op. cit.*, p. 67.

Negroes in Rhode Island, although they comprised about one-tenth of the town's 5,530 inhabitants.[68]

The largest concentration of slaves was in the famous Narragansett or South Country. Outstanding among the towns in this farming section were North and South Kingstown. In 1708, there were in both of these towns only 85 Negroes out of 1,200 inhabitants.[69] Thirty years later, South Kingstown was reputed to be the richest town in Rhode Island, and to have the largest percentage of slaves.[70] The Negroes, located mostly on great estates, had increased in number to 380, in a total population of only 1,978. Evidence of the massing of Negroes in this community between 1748 and 1749, is seen in the fact that one out of every five persons was a slave.[71] By 1755, so great had become the concentration of Negroes in South Kingstown that the ratio of blacks to whites was as much as one to three,[72] and only a slightly lower ratio obtained in 1782, when the proportion was about one Negro to every six white persons.[73] In 1755 only Charlestown had a higher proportion of Negroes, with 1,130 persons, of whom 712 were whites, and 418 Negroes, the latter constituting one-third of the total inhabitants.

Providence apparently did not become important as a slaveholding community until about 1748 when, with 225 blacks, it ranked second [74] to South Kingstown. By 1782, the number of Negroes in Providence had increased to 285 in an aggregate population of 4,310.[75]

68 *R. I. State Recs.*, IX, 653.

69 *Vide* Table 5.

70 Updike, *History of the Narragansett Church,* I, 207-208; *R. I. Col. Recs.*, V, 271.

71 *Ibid.*

72 Greene and Harrington, *op. cit.*, p. 67.

73 *R. I. Col. Recs.*, IX, 653.

74 *Ibid.*, V, 271.

75 *R. I. State Recs.*, IX, 653. For Negro population in Rhode Island, by towns, *cf. Appendix D.*

Connecticut, unlike Rhode Island and Massachusetts, had little active connection with the slave trade. Yet, on the eve of the Revolutionary War, Connecticut contained more Negroes than any other New England colony.[76] Contemporary census reports further show that the growth of the Negro population of Connecticut was irregular, the largest increase falling between 1749 and 1774. They also reveal the tendency of the colony to conceal from the mother country its growing importance.[77]

The colony had few slaves in the seventeenth century. In 1679 Governor William Leete of Connecticut in reply to certain inquiries from the home government, stated: " There are but fewe servants amongst us and less slaves not above 30, as we judge in the colony." [78] Thirty years later, in 1709, the Governor and Council informed the Board of Trade that there were 110 white and black servants in a total population of 4,000.[79] In 1730, the Negro population was 700, in a total enumeration of 38,000. The comparative prosperity of the colony is revealed in the fact that by 1774, the number of Negroes reached the highwater mark for colonial New England, when 6,464 were reported (see Table 7).

Between 1774 and 1790, Connecticut's Negro population had decreased by 1,045 persons or 16.1 per cent. In the latter year the Negro inhabitants, slave and free were estimated at 5,419.[80] The high mortality of slaves during the war, either because of service in the armies [81] or as a result of British raids through

76 *Vide* Table 1.

77 Dexter, *op. cit.,* p. 160.

78 *Conn. Col. Recs.,* III, 298.

79 Greene and Harrington, *op. cit.,* p. 49. The Governor must have blushed when the total number of inhabitants was reported at 4,000 for eight years earlier the total population had been certified at 30,000. *Ibid.,* p. 48.

80 *Cf.* Greene and Harrington, *op. cit.,* p. 50.

81 *Connecticut Gazette and Weekly Advertiser,* October 4, 1776; January 17, 1777; *Connecticut Gazette and Weekly Intelligencer,* March 8, 1776; *Ibid.,* April 21, 1775; Steiner, *op. cit.,* p. 26; *Conn. State Recs.,* II, 557.

## TABLE 7
NUMBER, PROPORTION, AND INCREASE OF NEGRO POPULATION
IN CONNECTICUT, 1679-1790

| Year | Total Population | White | Negroes | | | |
|------|------------------|-------|---------|---------|----------------|--------------|
| | | | Number | Percent | Pop. Increase | % Pop. Increase |
| 1679 [a] | ........ | | 30 | | | |
| 1730 [b] | ........ 38,000 | 37,300 | 700 | 1.8 | 670 | 223.3 |
| 1749 [c] | ........ 70,000 | 69,000 | 1,000 | 1.4 | 300 | 42.8 |
| 1756 [d] | ........ 131,799 | 128,212 | 3,587 | 2.7 | 2,587 | 258.7 |
| 1761 [e] | ........ 141,000 | 136,410 | 4,590 | 3.2 | 1,003 | 27.9 |
| 1774 [f] | ........ 197,856 | 191,392 | 6,464 | 3.2 | 1,874 | 40.8 |
| 1790 [g] | ........ 237,655 | 232,236 | 5,419 | 2.2 | 1,045 | 16.1 |

[a] *Conn. Col. Recs.*, III, 298.

[b] *Ibid.*, VII, 584. Increase and percentages of slaves, as well as, in some cases, the number of white inhabitants, have been derived by the author from the returns given. This applies for the entire table.

[c] *Ibid.* (Hartford, 1876), IX, 596; X, 623.

[d] There is a disparity in the returns for this year. Governor Fitch's report to the Board of Trade varies from the number given in the original census returns. According to this estimate, the total population of the colony was 130,612, of whom 126,975 were whites and 3,019 were blacks. The estimate given in the table varies from that in the footnote (*ibid.*, X, 618), because of corrected returns from Windham County. Tardy returns also may have accounted for Fitch's higher estimate. *Ibid.*, pp. 618 n., 623.

[e] *Conn. Col. Recs.*, XI, 574-575 n.

[f] *Ibid.*, XIV, 491; also pp. 485-491.

[g] *A Century of Population Growth*, p. 222; *cf. Negro Population in the United States, 1790-1915*, p. 45, where the number is given as 5,572.

the heaviest slave-holding sections of the state, may account in part for this decline. As in other colonies, some slaves may have been carried away by loyalist masters or by the British armies.[82] However, Negroes never formed more than a small proportion of Connecticut's inhabitants. In 1774, when the Negro population was greatest, only one in every thirty-three persons was a Negro and by 1790 the Negro proportion had fallen to about one in every fifty persons.[83]

The Negro population of Connecticut was more evenly distributed than in the other colonies. This feature is demonstrated

82 Elizabeth H. Schenck, *History of Fairfield* (2 vols., New York), II, 386, 397; Alexander Johnston, " Connecticut ", *American Commonwealth Series* (New York, 1881), pp. 303-304; G. H. Hollister, *A History of Connecticut* (2 vols., Hartford, 1857), II, ch. xvii.

83 *Cf.* Table 7.

clearly by a survey of the Negroes in the counties. In 1756, according to one estimate, the largest number of slaves was in Hartford County, as is shown in the table below:

TABLE 8

DISTRIBUTION OF NEGROES IN CONNECTICUT BY COUNTIES IN 1756 [84]

| County | White Population | Negroes Number | Percent | Indians |
|---|---|---|---|---|
| Hartford | 35,714 | 854 | 2.3 | |
| New London | 22,015 | 829 | 3.5 | 617 |
| New Haven | 17,955 | 226 | 1.2 | |
| Fairfield | 19,849 | 711 | 2.4 | |
| Windham | 19,669 | 345 | 1.7 | |
| Litchfield | 11,773 | 54 | 0.4 | |
| Total | 126,975 | 3,019 | 2.37 | 617 |

Closely following Hartford, was New London County with 829 slaves; Fairfield and Windham came next, while Litchfield, the most sparsely settled county, had but 54 Negroes. The two commercial counties of New London and Fairfield, had a larger proportion of Negroes than had the entire colony: New London, 3.5 per cent, and Fairfield 2.4 per cent, while the Negro proportion for the entire colony was only 2.37 per cent.

Eighteen years later in 1774, a totally different aspect was discernible. The slave population was then, 6,454. Hartford County, which had more than one fourth of Connecticut's slaves in 1756, had been displaced by New London as the leading slave county. Moreover, New London County had become the greatest slaveholding section of New England,[85] with almost twice as many Negroes as the most populous slave county of Massachusetts.[86] The 2,036 slaves in New London County constituted almost one-third of all the Negroes in the province.

84 When a correction of "one" is made for Windham county the total white population is then 126,976. As already cited, these figures are smaller both for the white and Negro inhabitants as reported by Governor Fitch in April 1756 in his replies to Heads of Inquiry from the Board of Trade. *Conn. Col. Recs.*, X, 617-618.

85 *Ibid.*, XIV, 485-491.

86 Essex County in 1776 had 1,049 Negroes. *J. P. C. M., 1774-1775*, p. 755.

Hartford and Fairfield Counties with 1,215 and 1,214 Negroes, respectively, practically tied for second place, while New Haven was next with 925. In Litchfield County, which still had the smallest Negro population, there were 440 blacks. The distribution of the population for 1774 is shown in the appended table.[87]

TABLE 9

DISTRIBUTION OF NEGRO POPULATION OF CONNECTICUT BY COUNTIES IN 1774

| County | White Population | Negro | Percent Negro |
|---|---|---|---|
| Hartford ............. | 50,679 | 1,215 | 2.3 |
| New Haven ......... | 25,896 | 925 | 3.5 |
| New London ......... | 31,542 | 2,036 | 6.4 |
| Fairfield ............. | 28,936 | 1,214 | 4.1 |
| Windham ............. | 27,494 | 634 | 2.3 |
| Litchfield ............. | 26,845 | 440 | 1.6 |
| Total ........... | 191,392 | 6,464 | 3.3 |

In regard to local distribution in 1756, Fairfield, in the county of the same name, led all the towns in Negro population with 260 blacks. Norwich, the second largest town in the colony, had 223 Negroes, and 5,317 whites, and Middletown, the metropolis of Connecticut ranked third with 218 Negroes out of a total population of 5,664. Other towns, with fairly large white and Negro population listed in the census of 1756, were Guilford and Branford in New Haven County, with 59 and 106 Negroes, respectively. Farmington, Wethersfield, and Colchester in Hartford County had 112, 109, and 84 Negroes, in the order named. In all of them except Colchester, there were seemingly larger Negro populations than in Hartford. Although one of the two capitals of the colony, Hartford in 1756 reported only 2,926 whites and 101 slaves. In New London County, the principal commercial section of Connecticut, Norwich, the largest town, stood first with 223 Negroes; Groton had 179; Stonington, 200, Lyme, 100 and Preston, 78. The largest slave-worked

87 *Conn. Col. Recs.*, XIV, 483-492. *Vide* Greene and Harrington (*op. cit.*, pp. 58-60) for comparative censuses of 1756 and 1774.

farms were also in this area.[88] In Windham County, Lebanon led with 103 Negroes, followed by Plainfield with 49. In Litchfield County, Woodbury was foremost with 49 blacks. Although towns like New Haven, Derby, and New London did not report their Negro population, there were slaves in all of them.[89]

By 1774 the three leading slave towns of Connecticut, nearly all of them commercial centers, were in New London County. The town of New London, Connecticut's chief seaport, surpassed all others with 522 Negroes; Stonington followed with 456; and Groton with 360. Stratford, in Fairfield County, was next with 354, followed by Fairfield with 319. New Haven had 273; Hartford, 150, and Middletown and Colchester, 198 and 201 Negroes respectively. Derby, which at that time included what is now Ansonia and Seymour, had 70 slaves.[90]

The Negro population of colonial New England showed a marked disproportion between the sexes with males predominating. The greater demand for male slaves and their probable greater ability to survive the voyage from Africa to America,[91] may account in part for this difference. Of 2,674 Negro slaves of sixteen years and upwards in Massachusetts in 1755, 1,500 were males and only 855 females.[92] The counties showed similar disparities: Suffolk County with 789 Negro men and 421 women had almost twice as many Negro males as females of

88 Weeden, *Economic and Social History of New England*, I, 163; William F. Davis, ed., *The New England States* (4 vols., Boston, n.d.), II, 759; George L. Clarke, *History of Connecticut* (Second edition, New York & London, 1914), pp. 189, 190.

89 *Conn. Col. Recs.*, X, 617-618.

90 *Ibid.*, XIV, 485-491. For Negro population of Connecticut by counties and towns, *cf. Appendix E*.

91 Evidence of the greater demand for males is seen in the instructions to Captain William Ellery of Newport. " By [buy] no girls and few women but prime boys and young men." Donnan, *Docs.*, III, 69.

92 In some cases the total number of slaves was given and the returns by sex omitted. The combined number of males and females therefore will not equal the total. *Mass. Hist. Soc. Colls.*, Second Series, III, 95-97.

marriageable age. Middlesex County had 215 Negro males to 123 females; Essex, 178 males to 122 females; and Hampshire County reported 56 male slaves and only 18 females.[93] A similar disproportion was evident in 1764. In that year, out of 5,235 Negroes in the colony, 3,016 were males and only 2,219 females. Every county showed a like disparity between the sexes.[94]

In nearly all the other colonies, a similar disproportion between the sexes prevailed. In 1767, male slaves outnumbered females in New Hampshire by 379 to 295;[95] in Connecticut in 1774, Negro males, 20 years of age and older, outnumbered the females of the same age group by 1,572 to 1,042. In short, 530 Negro males of marriageable age in Connecticut had no prospect of marrying within their own age group. The widest disparity was revealed in Hartford County, where 370 Negro males and only 201 females, represented an excess of 169 males. The nearest approach toward equality in numbers among the sexes was shown by Fairfield County, with only 24 Negro males in excess of the number of marriageable slave women. The excess of males over females in the Negro population of Connecticut for 1774 is shown by counties, as follows:[96]

TABLE 10

DISTRIBUTION OF NEGROES IN CONNECTICUT OVER 20 YEARS OF
AGE BY SEX AND COUNTIES IN 1774

| County | Negro Males over 20 | Negro Females over 20 | Excess Males |
|---|---|---|---|
| Hartford ......... | 370 | 201 | 169 |
| New Haven ...... | 263 | 170 | 93 |
| New London ..... | 335 | 255 | 80 |
| Fairfield ......... | 358 | 234 | 24 |
| Windham ........ | 147 | 121 | 26 |
| Litchfield ........ | 99 | 61 | 38 |
| Total ...... | 1,572 | 1,042 | 530 |

93 *Ibid.*

94 *A Century of Population Growth,* pp. 158-161. For Negro population by sex and county in Massachusetts, in 1764, *vide Appendix F,* also Benton, *op. cit., Appendix.*

95 *N. H. P. P.,* VII, 168-170. *Cf.* Greene and Harrington, *op. cit.,* p. 73.

96 *Conn. Col. Recs.,* XIV, 485-491.

Some of the towns disclosed even greater inequalities in this respect. Colchester, with 61 Negro males and 27 females over twenty years of age, showed a ratio of more than two males to every female; Farmington had three males to every female, and Chatham's ratio was seven to one. Although the larger towns tended toward a more equal distribution among the sexes, even there, the males were in excess. New Haven had 70 males and 56 female slaves over twenty; Hartford, 51 to 37; Fairfield, 91 to 66; Stratford, 108 to 70; New London, 89 to 78; Middletown, 61 to 46; and Norwich, 69 to 49.

In only a few towns were the two sexes equal in numbers. Among them were Derby, with 12 male slaves and 12 females over twenty years of age; Groton, with 42 of each sex; and Glastonbury with 13 of each sex. Litchfield had 10 Negro males and 7 Negro females of marriageable age, while Salisbury showed a similar disproportion.

By contrast, three towns in Windham County presented the unusual feature of a preponderance of female slaves over males. These were Lebanon, with 22 males and 27 females; Windham, with 15 males and 29 females, and Woodstock, with 10 males and 13 females.[97] Among the New England colonies, in Rhode Island alone were there apparently more Negro men than women. There the census in 1782 listed 1,463 Negro women, as compared with 1,343 males.[98]

The Indian population, on the other hand, showed an excess of females. Massachusetts, where in 1764 its Indian population of 1,681 consisted of 728 males and 953 females, illustrates this disparity.[99] The scarcity of Negro women, on the one hand, and of Indian men on the other, was undoubtedly a factor in the

97 *Ibid.*, pp. 485, 487.

98 Evidently the returns were not complete for the total population by sex is only 2,806, while the entire Negro population was set forth at 3,806. *R. I. Col. Recs.*, IX, 653.

99 *Century of Population Growth*, pp. 158-161.

steady amalgamation of the two races.[100] The numerical in-
equality of the sexes among the Negroes naturally made for a
shortage of slave wives, which acted to retard the growth of
the Negro population during the colonial period.[101] It stimulated
miscegenation between Negroes and other races and may likewise have encouraged sex crimes.[102]

Although whites and Indians, as will be shown later,[103] inter-
mingled with the blacks, it is impossible to determine the number of Negroes of mixed blood. Chickering, writing in 1846,
says that the Negroes of Massachusetts were a " mixed race
[and] have been for fifty years." [104] This would apply also to
most New England Negro families of today whose ancestors
have lived there for several generations. Rhode Island, in 1782
took a census of Negroes of mixed blood and it may throw
some light on earlier results of miscegenation. At that time, out
of 3,806 Negroes in the state, 464, or almost one-eighth were
mulattoes. In the towns the ratio of mulattoes to blacks varied.
Less than one-tenth of the Negro population were mulattoes in
Newport and South Kingstown, where were found the largest
number of Negroes. By contrast, almost one-fifth of the Negroes of Bristol, and more than a third of those of Warwick,
were of mixed blood. In Westerly the mulattoes actually outnumbered the blacks by 36 to 28, as indicated in the following
table.[105]

100 *Vide, infra*, ch. viii.

101 George Bancroft, *History of the United States* (Centenary Edition,
6 vols., Boston, 1876), II, 551.

102 *Cf. infra*, p. 185.

103 *Vide, infra*, pp. 198-200.

104 *Op. cit.*, p. 160.

105 *R. I. Col. Recs.*, IX, 653. For entire list of towns *vide ibid.*; Greene
and Harrington, *op. cit.*, p. 68.

## TABLE 11

NUMBER OF MULATTOES IN NEGRO POPULATION OF EIGHT RHODE
ISLAND TOWNS IN 1782

| Towns | Total Population | Negroes | Mulattoes |
|---|---|---|---|
| Newport ................. | 5,530 | 549 | 51 |
| Providence .............. | 4,310 | 252 | 33 |
| Portsmouth ............. | 1,350 | 67 | 11 |
| North Kingstown ....... | 2,328 | 188 | 22 |
| South Kingstown ....... | 2,675 | 415 | 38 |
| Westerly ............... | 1,720 | 28 | 36 |
| Bristol ................. | 1,032 | 63 | 13 |
| Warwick ............... | 2,112 | 100 | 36 |
| | 21,057 | 1,662 | 240 |

No analysis of the Negro population of colonial New England, according to slave and free status, is possible. Not until the Federal Census of 1790, was any attempt made to separate the Negroes into these categories. In that year, there were reported to be in this section 16,822 Negroes, of whom 13,059, or 77.6 per cent, were free.[106] These figures are misleading, for many of the 2,648 slaves credited to Connecticut and the 958 ascribed to Rhode Island were not actually slaves, but were in reality indentured servants. This transition had been brought out by the gradual abolition of slavery in these states in 1784.[107] Neither Vermont nor Massachusetts reported any slaves in 1790, both having abolished slavery either by constitutional provision as in Vermont, or by judicial construction, as in Massachusetts.[108] Most of New Hampshire's 787 Negroes, as indicated in Table 12, had been freed by 1790.

From the limited data available, only a small proportion of the New England families seem to have had any connection with slavery. Out of the 43,483 families in Massachusetts in

106 *A Century of Population Growth*, p. 222.

107 *R. I. Acts and Resolves*, X, 403; *Conn. Acts and Laws* (New London, 1784), p. 235; *Mass. Hist. Soc. Colls.*, First Series, III, 203.

108 *New Hampshire State Papers*, IX, 896; *Mass. Hist. Soc. Colls.*, Fifth Series, III, 403.

TABLE 12

DISTRIBUTION AND PROPORTION OF NEGROES, SLAVE AND FREE, IN
NEW ENGLAND, BY STATES IN 1790 [109]

| | Total Population | Negro Population | | | |
| | | Total | Free | Slave | Percent Free |
| --- | --- | --- | --- | --- | --- |
| New England ........ | 1,009,206 | 16,882 | 13,059 | 3,763 | 77.6 |
| Maine ........... | 96,643 | 536 | 536 | | 100.0 |
| New Hampshire .. | 141,899 | 787 | 630 | 157 | 81.1 |
| Vermont ......... | 85,341 | 269 | 269 | | 100.0 |
| Massachusetts .... | 387,556 | 5,369 | 5,369 | | 100.0 |
| Rhode Island ..... | 69,112 | 4,442 | 3,484 | 958 | 78.4 |
| Connecticut ...... | 237,655 | 5,419 | 2,771 | 2,648 | 51.1 |

1764, less than one-eighth of them owned 5,235 slaves. In 1790
only about one per cent of the 174,017 white families in New
England still held slaves. While approximately one out of every
25 families in Rhode Island was a slave-holder in 1790, in Connecticut, out of 40,876 families, only 1,556, or 3.8 per cent of
the total, still kept slaves.[110] These percentages, however, because of either outright or gradual emancipation in New England prior to 1790, do not reflect the situation as it existed during the colonial era between 1638 and 1776. Among the slaveholders reported for Connecticut were six Negro families.[111]
With the exception of a slave owned by a free Negro in Massachusetts in 1656,[112] this is the only instance of slave-holding by
Negroes in New England that has come to the writer's attention.

Any estimate of the number of slaves owned, per family,
would be conjectural. The number ranged anywhere from one
to sixty,[113] depending upon the affluence and business of the
owner. Although the average was probably about two slaves per
family, the number in the Narragansett County of Rhode Island and in Eastern Connecticut as well as in wealthy house-

109 *A Century of Population Growth*, pp. 158-161.

110 *Ibid.*

111 *Ibid.*, pp. 100, 222.

112 *S. C. R. R.*, Liber II, p. 297.

113 *Vide infra*, Slave Occupations, pp. 103, 105, 107.

holds, ran much higher.[114] The only official figures, which show
the average number of slaves per family, were made available
by the first federal census in 1790. These figures do not reveal,
however, the colonial situation, for only a small proportion of
Negroes were still held as slaves at that time. In 1790, there
were 3,763 slaves in New England, owned by 2,141 families.
This was an average of a little less than two slaves to a family.
Connecticut's 2,648 slaves belonged to 1,557 different households, giving this state virtually the same average of slaves to
a family as for New England. Rhode Island had the highest
proportion, with 958 slaves in 461 families, or an average of
about two slaves to a household.

114 *A Century of Population Growth,* pp. 100, 222.

# CHAPTER IV

## SLAVE OCCUPATIONS

THE relatively small number of Negroes in New England during the colonial period raises the question of their economic importance. The answer is to be sought in the occupational development of this section and in the extent to which Negro slaves proved adequate to its labor demands. This was an important consideration, for New England's economy was necessarily diversified. A harsh climate, unfavorable topography, and, with few exceptions, thin, stony soil, prevented large-scale agriculture, and thus precluded the amassing of wealth from the land as in the middle and southern colonies. While Virginia and Carolina planters depended upon tobacco and rice as cash crops, New England settlers raised a variety of products, chiefly vegetables, forage crops, fruits, horses, cattle and sheep. Farms, except in southern Rhode Island and eastern Connecticut, were relatively small. Even with hard labor most of the farmers eked out little more than a bare subsistence. Anything beyond this level had to come from sources other than agriculture. But these sources were not lacking. New England was blessed with abundant forests, and numerous harbors, while off its coasts were the greatest fishing grounds in the world. Recognizing these opportunities, ambitious Yankees early turned to fishing, whaling, and commerce. Shipbuilding developed and in time small manufactories, ranging from rum distilleries to iron forges sprang up. The opulence that the plantation barons obtained from their extensive domains, the enterprising New Englanders secured largely from maritime pursuits and from the slave trade.

There was a great demand for workers in these industries and laborers, skilled and unskilled, were needed for work on farms, in homes, shops, factories, shipyards, and on fishing and trading ships. Free labor was scarce and wages were high.[1] Neither white indentured servants nor Indian slaves, both of whom

1 *Vide supra*, ch. i; Jernagan, *op. cit.*, p. 196.

were employed throughout the colonial period, could supply the much needed workmen. It was primarily to furnish laborers that Negro slaves were brought into New England. They were introduced to satisfy not a specific but a general need. To meet the demands of New England's diversified economy, the slave had to be more skilled and more versatile than the average plantation Negro accustomed to the routine cultivation of a single crop. The New England slave had to be equally at home in the cabbage patch and in the cornfield; he must be prepared (as will be demonstrated) not only to care for stock, to act as servant, repair a fence, serve on board ship, shoe a horse, print a newspaper, but even to manage his master's business.[2]

The impression, nevertheless, has prevailed that because of adverse geographic and economic conditions slave labor was of little value to New England masters. This notion was expressed by several contemporary New Englanders. In 1708, for example, Governor Dudley of Massachusetts—in spite of the steady importation of Negroes into that colony—informed the British Board of Trade that the long winters kept the slaves idle during half the year.[3] Dudley further stated that the severe climate, together with the cost of clothing the slaves, so increased the cost of maintaining them, that most people preferred white indentured servants.[4] Jeremy Belknap, one of the founders of the Masachusetts Historical Society and a sincere worker in behalf of the Negroes, expressed a similar opinion in 1795. Writing to Judge Tucker of Virginia regarding slavery, Belknap said, " The winter here was always unfavorable to the African constitution. For this reason white laborers were preferable to blacks." [5] A distinguished authority on colonial history, after commenting on the rather extensive use of Negroes on the large farms in Rhode Island, concluded that the Negroes

2 *Vide infra*, pp. 103 ff.

3 *Calendar of State Papers: Colonial, 1708-1709*, p. 110.

4 *Ibid.*

5 *Mass. Hist. Soc. Colls.*, First Series, III, 199.

were of little use to the small farmers of New England.[6] More extreme is the statement of Professor Bogart, who maintains that the industrial and commercial development of New England made slavery economically unprofitable.[7] On the other hand, the mentality of the Negro, Professor Wertenbaker implies, unfitted the Negro as an efficient laborer in the diverse economy of colonial New England. Accounting for the small number of slaves in seventeenth century New England, he states: [8]

> It proved quite practicable to teach the savage African the one task which was required of him in the southern colonies, that of tending the sugar or the tobacco crops; but for the hundred and one things that the New England farm hand had to do he was entirely inadequate.

Such statements have led to the popular belief that New England slaves were used chiefly or almost entirely as house-servants. Among the authorities holding this view are such scholars as Emory Washburne,[9] Edward Eggleston,[10] John Daniel,[11] Henry Cabot Lodge,[12] and Jerome Dowd.[13]

The facts, however, do not support these conclusions. Negroes were identified with every phase of New England's economy and, as a consequence, slave labor was highly diversi-

6 Evarts B. Greene, *Foundations of American Nationality* (New York, 1922), p. 266.

7 Ernest Ludlow Bogart, *Economic History of the American People* (New York, 1936), p. 106.

8 Thomas J. Wertenbaker, *The First Americans*, p. 62.

9 "Slavery as it once prevailed in Massachusetts," *loc. cit.*, p. 215.

10 *Household History of the United States* (New York, 1901), p. 107.

11 John Daniel, *In Freedom's Birthplace: A Study of Boston Negroes* (New York, 1914), p. 6.

12 *History of the English Colonies in America* (New York, 1881), p. 442.

13 In the North says Dowd, "slave labor early disappeared from the farms and from commerce and was retained only in domestic service." *The Negro in American Life* (New York, 1926), p. 11.

fied. The very character of New England's economic development rendered inevitable a variety of slave occupations. Naturally employment of the slaves depended upon the business
of their masters, and Negroes accordingly were taught and
followed whatever calling their owners pursued, whether farming, lumbering, trading, fishing, whaling, manufacturing or
privateering.

Since colonial New England was fundamentally agricultural,
a large proportion of the slaves worked on the farms. Instead
of being employed extensively (as were the plantation blacks)
in the cultivation of staples, like tobacco, rice, and indigo,[14]
New England Negroes were used in smaller numbers in the
production of foodstuffs, forage crops, dairy products and in
the raising of livestock,[15] although flax, hemp, and tobacco,[16]
were also grown by slave labor in the New England colonies.

Contemporary newspapers offer abundant evidence regarding
the agricultural employment of New England slaves. Advertisements described Negroes: " brought up in husbandry," " fit for
town or country," " understanding the farming business exceedingly well," or as familiar " with all sorts of husbandry." [17]

How many slaves were employed at farm labor is not known.
The number of Negroes to a farm depended upon the size of
the holding, but the number could not have been large, because
New England farms were generally small and most of the
settlers were too poor to buy more than one or two slaves.[18] In

14 Phillips, *American Negro Slavery*, chaps. v-vi; *ibid., Life and Labor in
the Old South*, ch. vii; Charles Wesley, *Negro Labor*, ch. i, p. 3, especially.

15 Channing, *The Narragansett Planters*, p. 10; Andrews, *Connecticut's
Place in Colonial History*, p. 20; Miller, *Narragansett Planters*, pp. 5, 14,
20, 25, 35, 46; Updike, *op. cit.*, I, 215, 217-18.

16 *Diaries of the Reverend Timothy Walker, 1730-1782*, ed. by Joseph
B. Walker (Concord, 1889), p. 31; Miller, *op. cit.*, pp. 41-43.

17 *Boston Weekly Post Boy*, June 26, 1749; *Newport Mercury*, October
30; December 11, 1784; *Connecticut Courant and Weekly Intelligencer*,
May 23, 1780.

18 *Cf*. Governor Fitch to the Board of Trade, *Conn. Hist. Soc. Colls.*,
XVIII, 213.

Massachusetts, according to Jeremy Belknap and Robert Rantoul, three or four Negroes were employed on some of the farms.[19] On these holdings the slaves were said to have worked under conditions of comparative equality with their owners, a not unusual practice for the Puritans who extolled labor. According to Dr. Holyoke, slaves in the country towns were on the same footing as whites.[20] Madame Knight, who has left a penetrating account of her journey from Boston to New York in 1704, commented caustically upon the democratic relationships existing between the master's family and the slaves in rural Connecticut.[21] Referring to similar conditions in Massachusetts, Sheldon says: " The slaves became in a measure members of the family holding them. They worked with the father and boys in field and forest, and in the kitchen." [22]

On the more extensive farms of eastern Connecticut and in the Narragansett Country of Rhode Island the situation was different. Here considerable numbers of slaves were employed.[23] In the Narragansett Country—a narrow strip of land twenty miles long and two to four miles wide, in southern Rhode Island, a fertile soil, abundant grasses, and salt lagoons, combined with a fairly mild climate to support the greatest dairying and cattle raising community in New England.[24] The Reverend James McSparran of Narragansett, writing to the Secretary of the Society for the Propagation of the Gospel in 1727, exulted

19 " Belknap's Replies to Judge St. George Tucker " (1795), *Mass. Hist. Soc. Colls.*, First Series, III, 199; Rantoul, " Negro Slavery in Massachusetts," *loc. cit.*, p. 102.

20 Dr. Holyoke to Dr. Belknap (1795), " Belknap Papers," *Mass. Hist. Soc. Colls.*, Fifth Series, III, 302.

21 Sarah Knight, *A Journal of Madame Knight on a Journey from Boston to New York in the Year 1704* (New York, 1825), p. 40.

22 Sheldon, *op. cit.*, p. 59.

23 Channing, *The Narragansett Planters*, pp. 5, 10.

24 Rev. Andrew Burnaby, *Travels Through the Middle Settlements of North America, 1759-1760* (Third Edition, London, 1798), p. 93.

over the excellent pasturage in the Narragansett Country,[25] where horses, sheep, and cattle were raised in large numbers.[26] Upon these extensive acres developed a landed aristocracy, popularly known as the "Narragansett Planters," a group without a counterpart in New England, but possessing many of the characteristics of the manorial lords of New York or the plantation barons of the South. The Narragansett planters derived most of their wealth from dairying and stock-raising.[27] The average size of their holdings was about 300 acres,[28] but some families like the Stantons, Hazards, Champlins, Robinsons, Gardiners, and Potters owned estates of several thousand acres.[29]

These farms were profitably worked by slaves, ranging in number from five to forty.[30] Stock farming, says Channing, would have been impossible without them.[31] Most of the Negroes were engaged in dairying, for which the Narragansett section became famous.[32] Other slaves were employed in sheep raising and in growing vegetables and tobacco. One of the most profitable industries, in which chiefly slave labor was used, was the breeding of the famous horses, known as the Narragansett "pacers."[33]

25 *Society for the Propagation of the Gospel in Foreign Parts: Transcripts*, Series B, I, Part II, 837 (Library of Congress Pagination 624).

26 Weeden, *Early Rhode Island*, pp. 153, 157; Channing, *Narragansett Planters*, pp. 6-9.

27 Gertrude Kimball, *Pictures of Rhode Island in the Past* (Providence, 1900), p. 49; Updike, *op. cit.*, I, 218.

28 Updike, *op. cit.*, I, 217.

29 According to Miller, the Potter family owned 3000 acres of land by 1800; the Champlins owned 2000 acres; the Robinson held several thousand acres, one of them Andrew, purchasing 3000 acres at one time. *Op. cit.*, pp. 15-20.

30 Miller, *op. cit.*, p. 24.

31 Channing, *Narragansett Planters*, p. 10.

32 Updike, *op. cit.*, I, 217; Miller, p. 35.

33 *Cf.* Miller, *op. cit.*, pp. 25-35 for an excellent summary of the breeding of Narragansett "pacers."

Examples of the extensive and profitable employment of Negroes on Rhode Island farms are found in the records of some
of the leading families of the Narragansett Country. Governor
William Robinson, who owned a tract of land four and one
half miles long and two miles wide, was reported to have " kept
forty horses and as many slaves." Most of the Negroes worked
in his large dairy. Rowland Robinson, the younger, is said to
have owned at one time at least twenty-eight Negroes and possibly more. His father's inventory revealed only nineteen.[34]
Colonel Champlin, reputed owner of more than one thousand
acres of land possessed thirty-five horses, fifty-five cows, six
hundred to seven hundred sheep, and a " proportionate " number of slaves. James Babcock of Westerly, with two thousand
acres of land, is said to have had " horses, slaves and stock in
proportion." [35] Colonel Updike, one-time attorney for Rhode
Island, Hezekiah Babcock, and a Mr. Sewall at Point Judith
were also proprietors of extensive land holdings worked by
slave labor.[36] One of the largest of all the slave holders was
the Stanton family, whose forty slaves equalled in number the
servants of the Robinsons.[37]

A striking instance of large-scale farming by slave labor is
that of Robert Hazard of South Kingstown, Rhode Island. In
1730 he was one of the richest slave owners in New England,
and was reported, at one time to have held title to 12,000 acres
of land, part of which he converted into a large dairy farm.
Twenty-four Negro women are said to have worked in the
creamery alone. Under the task system [38] they were required to
make from twelve to twenty-four huge cakes of cheese daily.[39]

34 Miller, *op. cit.*, p. 24.

35 Updike, *op. cit.*, I, 216.

36 *Ibid.*, pp. 216-17.

37 Miller, *op. cit.*, p. 24.

38 Under the task system a certain amount of work is assigned the slave
for a given period of time. Should he complete the work earlier, the rest
of the time is his own.

39 " From my father and grandfather, I have heard that my great-grand-
father, Robert Hazard, had twelve Negro women as dairywomen, each of

Negroes tilled extensive farms in other parts of New England. Nearly every large landholder in Reading, Massachusetts, was said to have been a slaveholder.[40] Dr. Belknap, in 1795, stated that one Massachusetts farmer owned sixteen slaves.[41] The princely domain of Sir William Pepperell, which stretched from Portsmouth, New Hampshire, to Casco, Maine,[42] was cultivated partly by Negroes.[43] In eastern Connecticut, where agricultural conditions approximated those of the fertile Narragansett Country, slaves worked farms of considerable acreage. One of the largest of these holdings was the estate of Godfrey Malbone at Brooklyn. Malbone married a southern woman who as part of her dowry is said to have brought with her 50 to 60 slaves, thus apparently making Malbone the largest single slaveholder in New England.[44] In 1740 Malbone purchased from Governor Jonathan Belcher of Massachusetts 3,240 acres of land located in Windham County, Connecticut. Twenty-eight years later, he quit-claimed most of this property—then heavily mortgaged—to his sons, Godfrey and John. Besides furnishing stock for the farm, he gave them a labor force

whom had a girl to assist her, making from twelve to twenty-four cheeses a day; and since I have grown up we had one of his cheese vats of the second size; which held nearly one bushel. My father informed me that so superior was the grass in the early settlement of this country, nearly double the milk or butter and cheese gotten at present, was obtained from a cow, and that only twelve cows were allowed to each dairywoman, and her assistant, one hundred and fifty cows being about the number he generally kept." Cited in Updike, *op. cit.*, I, 218; *cf.* Miller, *op. cit.*, p. 25.

40 Samuel Drake, *History of Middlesex County, Massachusetts*, II, 279-280.

41 *Mass. Hist. Soc. Colls.*, First Series, III, 199.

42 Lodge, *op. cit.*, p. 442.

43 Parsons, *op. cit.*, p. 28.

44 John Warner Barber, *Connecticut Historical Collections* (Improved Edition, New Haven, 1838), p. 416. Colonel William Browne of Salem, Massachusetts, owned a large farm at Lyme, Connecticut, which was worked by slaves. Nine of the Negroes were confiscated during the Revolution, when Browne persisted in supporting the British cause. Steiner, *op. cit.*, p. 27.

of twenty-seven Negroes, among whom were women and children.[45]

Many slaves were also employed as house servants. In fact, they had been used as domestics from the beginning of New England slavery. In 1638, eight years after the Puritan settlement of Salem, Samuel Maverick, as indicated above, had several Negro servants on Noddles Island.[46] Fifty years later, a French traveller, Antoine Court, writing about Negro slaves in Boston, noted that " there is not a house in Boston, however small may be its means, that has not one or two [Negroes]." [47] By the eighteenth century Negro domestics were generally used. The principal families of Norwich, Connecticut, employed Negroes as house servants; [48] the same held true for Hanover [49] and Newbury, Massachusetts.[50] In the Narragansett Country no prominent household was complete without its retinue of black servants.[51] In New Haven the leading families are reported to have had the services of at least a black or two,[52] and this was true also of the prominent families of Hartford,[53]

45 Prince, Harry, Pero, Dick, Tom, Adam and Christopher, Dinah, Venus, Rose, Miriam, Jenny and Rose...and three children, Primus, Christopher, Sias, Sharper and Little Pero..." Howard W. Preston, " Godfrey Malbone's Connecticut Investment," *Rhode Island Historical Society Collections*, XVI, No. 4 (Providence, 1923), 116.

46 " Josselyn's Account of two Voyages to New England," *Massachusetts Historical Society Collections*, Third Series, III (Boston, 1833), 231.

47 Cited in Nathaniel N. Shurtleff, *Topographical and Historical Description of Boston* (Third Edition, Second Impression, Boston, 1891), pp. 46-49.

48 Frances M. Caulkins, *History of Norwich, Connecticut* (Norwich, 1845), p. 184.

49 John S. Barry, *History of Hanover, Massachusetts* (Boston, 1853), p. 175.

50 Joshua Coffin, *Sketch of Newbury*, etc. (Boston, 1845), p. 337.

51 Thomas William Bicknell, *History of Rhode Island*, 3 vols. (New York, 1920), II, 503.

52 Ezra Stiles, *Extracts from Itineraries*, etc., p. 49; *Connecticut Historical Magazine* (Hartford, 1899), V, No. 6, 320.

53 Rev. William DeLoss Love, *The Colonial History of Hartford* (Hartford, 1914), p. 184.

Waterbury,[54] Providence, Newport,[55] and Litchfield.[56] Among
the slaveholding families are some of the most famous in American history. The register of New England's aristocracy would
serve as a roll call of the Puritan slave owners.[57]

Nevertheless, most New England families had no connection
with slavery.[58] For instance, John Winthrop, first governor of
Massachusetts held no Negro slaves [59] and the revolutionary
patriots, John and Samuel Adams were very much opposed to
the system. In 1764 admirers of Samuel Adams wished to present his wife with a Negro girl, but the impecunious Adams, it
is said, refused to permit the girl to enter his house unless she
could do so as a free woman.[60] John Adams, second president
of the United States, was equally hostile to slavery. He never
owned a slave although he admitted that had he done so, he
might have saved himself considerable expense. Commenting
upon his aversion to slavery, Adams wrote in 1795:

> I have, through my whole life, held the practice of
> slavery in such abhorrence, that I have never owned a
> Negro or any other slave, though I have lived for
> many years in times when the practice was not dis-
> graceful; when the best men in my vicinity thought it
> not inconsistent with their character, and when it has
> cost me thousands of dollars for the labor and sub-

54 Henry Bronson, M. D., *History of Waterbury, Connecticut* (Waterbury,
1858), p. 322.

55 For excellent list of Rhode Island slave holders representing the most
prominent families in the state in 1778-1779, see *Rhode Island Historical
Tracts*. No. 10 (Providence, 1880), pp. 73-74.

56 Allen C. White, *History of Litchfield, Connecticut* (Litchfield, 1920),
p. 152.

57 For extended list of slaveholding New England families with Christian
names and sources, *cf. Appendix*.

58 *Vide supra*, pp. 97-98.

59 Mellin Chamberlain, *Governor Winthrop's Estate* (n. d.), pp. 140-43.

60 Wells, *Life and Public Services of Samuel Adams*, III, 187.

sistence of free men, which I might have saved by
the purchase of Negroes at times when they were
very cheap.[61]

In the many homes employing slave labor, Negro women
served as cooks, laundresses, maids, nurses and as general
household workers,[62] but they were also trained in domestic
arts. Most of the clothing worn in New England was made by
the women in their homes, therefore it was not only natural but
necessary that the mistress should teach her slaves. As a result,
many slave women helped in such household crafts as spinning,
knitting and weaving.[63] In 1759 when Mary Jennings of Windham, Connecticut, freed her woman slave Ginna, she gave her,
among other things, the wheel which the slave had probably
used in spinning.[64]

The male slaves not only performed the heavy work about
the house but also acted as cooks, coachmen, attendants, butlers,
and valets. The employment of Negro men in such capacities is
indicated by contemporary newspapers. One paper lists a boy
" who can speak French " and is " very fit for a valet;" [65] another cites a Negro man who is qualified " for any gentlemen's
service;" [66] still another commends a Negro who is " a very
good cook." [67] In most of the wealthy families of the Narragansett Country, it was said, every member had his own servant
and rarely rode unattended. Travelling in lordly fashion, mas-

61 *Works of John Adams*, ed. Charles Francis Adams, 10 vols. (Boston,
1856), X, 380.

62 *Conn. Hist. Magazine*, V, 323.

63 A Boston master offered to hire out for a term of years a " Negro
woman...that can handle her Needle well." *The Boston News Letter* for
April 21, 1718.

64 Ellen D. Larned, *History of Windham County, Connecticut*, 2 vols.
(Worcester, 1874), I, 551-52.

65 *Boston Chronicle*, Sept. 21; Oct. 12, 19, 1769; pp. 304, 334, 342.

66 *Boston Gazette or Weekly Advertiser*, Jan. 23, 1753.

67 *Boston Weekly Post Boy*, Feb. 25, 1745.

ters were usually preceded by a slave, who opened and closed gates or removed " impediments from their pathway." [68] In 1740 Joseph Burnett, an English traveller, observed this custom among the aristocrats of Boston. Says he: " When the ladies ride out to take the air, it is generally in a chaise or chair . . . and they have a Negro servant to drive them. The gentlemen ride out here as in England, some in chairs and others on horseback with their negroes to attend." [69]

Negroes were not only employed as servants and field workers in New England but, contrary to popular opinion,[70] they were actively engaged as laborers in its various industries. As shipbuilding, lumbering, iron forges, rope-walks, cooperage plants, distilleries, and other businesses increased in size and number, especially during the eighteenth century, the demand for workers became more acute. Help was also needed for the blacksmith shop, the carpenter shop, the tannery and the printing press. Before the factory era, most of these industries were carried on by a single master craftsman with a few apprentices or helpers, but an adequate supply of white labor was not always available. For this reason rising Yankee capitalists were forced to train and to employ Negro slaves in their business. Some of the slaves worked at unskilled tasks or performed such menial jobs as those of helpers, porters, errand boys, teamsters and ditch diggers.[71] Many New England slaves, however, were employed as skilled workers, because during the entire colonial period the supply of artisans was so limited in all the colonies that Negroes were everywhere taught the trades. There was no

68 Updike, *op. cit.*, I, 226.

69 G. L. Kittredge, *The Old Farmer and His Almanac* (Cambridge, 1920), p. 286.

70 *Vide supra*, pp. 101-102.

71 *Connecticut Courant and Weekly Advertiser*, May 23, 1780; Benjamin Hobart, *History of Abingdon, Massachusetts* (Boston, 1866), pp. 254-255; " Diary of Samuel Sewall," *loc. cit.*, VI, 66; " Diary of Edward Augustus Holyoke, 1760-1800," *Holyoke Diaries, 1709-1800*, ed. George Francis Dow (Salem, 1911), p. 43; " Diary of Mrs. Mary Vial Holyoke, 1760-1800," *Holyoke Diaries, ut supra*, p. 116.

color line in colonial industry. New England Negroes, therefore, (like those in the other colonies)[72] were prominently associated with every aspect of the industrial life of their section.
With their masters to protect them from the competition of
white laborers, Negro slaves secured a type of job much higher
than that available to black workers in the same section today.

The employment of Negroes as artisans apparently began
soon after they were first brought into New England; for in
1661, less than a quarter of a century after slavery was introduced into Massachusetts, one Thomas Dean of Boston was
employing a Negro as a cooper. Negroes probably had been
working at the trades even earlier. Prior to that year the Boston
Town Meeting had passed a law—perhaps inspired by the attitude of white mechanics—forbidding the use of Negroes in the
crafts. In violation of this statute, Dean employed his slave at
the barrel-making trade. On the fifth of September the town
fathers, after duly considering the matter, gave Dean nine days
in which to stop employing the Negro. For the future, Dean
was enjoined from using his slave not only as a cooper, but
also in " any other manufacture or science ", on pain of a fine
of twenty shillings for every day he continued so to employ the
Negro.[73] This is the only evidence, so far uncovered by the
writer, showing the Puritan attempt, by legal means, to prevent
Negroes from competing with white mechanics in the skilled
trades.[74]

This ordinance, however, did not stop the use of Negroes as
artisans. Throughout the entire period, especially in the eighteenth century, Negroes held an important place in New Eng-

72 Jernegan, *Laboring and Dependent Classes*, ch. i; Samuel McKee, Jr.,
*Labor in Colonial New York, 1667-1776* (New York, 1935), p. 126.

73 *Boston Records, 1661-1701*, p. 5.

74 Similar attempts were made to restrict the employment of Negroes—
slave and free—in the South by white workmen. Jernegan, *op. cit.*, pp. 20-21.
These efforts continued unsuccessfully throughout the antebellum period.
W. E. B. DuBois, " The Negro Artisan," *Atlanta University Publication*,
No. 7 (Atlanta, 1902), p. 15; Lorenzo J. Greene, and Carter G. Woodson,
*The Negro Wage Earner* (Washington, 1930), pp. 15-17.

land industry. Here, as in the South, the master class simply overrode the opposition of white mechanics, and used their slaves in whatever trade was necessary to their business. The helplessness of the white worker was later translated into a sullen hatred of the slaves. This hostility of white labor toward the Negro slaves, according to John Adams, had great influence in abolishing slavery in New England.[75] In spite of such opposition, however, slaves continued to work as bakers, ship carpenters, coopers, printers, blacksmiths, tailors, sawyers, house carpenters, and printers so long as slavery was in force. Rantoul says that in Massachusetts, ship carpenters, anchor makers and rope makers employed a large number of slaves.[76] Skilled occupations of slaves are frequently alluded to in newspaper advertisements. One paper offered for sale a " good house carpenter and joyner . . . on reasonable terms; "[77] another recommended a slave who had worked for " five or six years at the cooper's business;"[78] a third advertised " a stout able-bodied Negro man, who has had considerable experience at the ship carpenter's trade,"[79] and a fourth offered a young " Negro taylor who works well at the trade."[80]

Additional light upon employments of skilled Negroes is shed by other advertisements. One cited a Negro skilled in the baking

[75] "Argument might have some weight in the abolition of slavery in Massachusetts, but the real cause was the multiplication of labouring white people, who would no longer suffer the rich to employ these sable rivals so much to their injury. The common people would not suffer the labor, by which alone they could obtain a subsistence, to be done by slaves. If the gentlemen had been permitted by law to hold slaves, the common white people would have put the slaves to death, and their masters too, perhaps." John Adams to Jeremy Belknap (1795), " Belknap Papers," *Mass. Hist. Soc. Colls.*, Fifth Series, III, 402.

[76] *Op. cit.*, p. 102.

[77] *Boston News Letter*, March 10, 1718.

[78] *Boston Chronicle*, July 11, 18, 1768, p. 274.

[79] *Boston Gazette or Weekly Advertiser*, April 9, 16, 1754.

[80] *Ibid.*, January 22, 29; February 12, 1754.

of " ship bread;" [81] another " a Negro blacksmith who makes anchors;" a third, a Negro ropemaker; and a fourth a Negro " who has been for many years used to the distilling business." [82] A Negro runaway was described as a cooper by trade;[83] another as one who worked at the trade " of bloomer." The public was warned that he would " probably seek employment in that business." [84]

In order to maintain the supply of slave mechanics, Negro boys were apprenticed to the trades [85] and some of them seem to have become very proficient in their work. For example, a slave carpenter is said to have finished handsomely the parlor of Richard Hart of Portsmouth, New Hampshire.[86] The pressman of the first newspaper printed in New Hampshire was a Negro slave, named Prince Fowle; [87] and the Negro of John Campbell, publisher of the *Boston News Letter,* probably aided in printing the first permanent newspaper in the English colonies.[88] Negro slave mechanics also helped build the Jewish Synagogue at Newport, Rhode Island.[89]

In the great maritime industries of New England slaves were also employed on the fishing, whaling and trading ships.[90] Not even the privateers were without Negro workers.[91] Werten-

81 *Conn. Courant and Weekly Intelligencer,* April 20, 1779.

82 *Boston News Letter,* August 4, 1718.

83 Cited in Johnston, " Slavery in Rhode Island," *loc. cit.,* p. 28.

84 Alain C. White, compiler, " The History of the Town of Litchfield, Connecticut," *Litchfield Historical Society* (Litchfield, 1920), p. 152.

85 *Boston Gazette or Weekly Advertiser,* February 12, 19, 26; March 5, 1754; *Boston Gazette and County Journal,* Sept. 14, 1767.

86 Brewster, *op. cit.,* I, 208.

87 *Ibid.,* I, 208-209.

88 Weeks and Bacon, *op. cit.,* p. 59.

89 Andrews, *Colonial Folkways,* p. 199.

90 Johnson, " Slavery in Rhode Island," *loc. cit.,* p. 127; *Mass. Archives,* IX, 149, 186; *E. C. C. R., 1680-1683,* VIII, 297; *cf.* newspapers cited below.

91 Howard Chapin, *Rhode Island Soldiers and Sailors, 1755-1762* (Providence, 1918), pp. 23, 29; *Rhode Island Privateers, 1739-1748,* pp. 23, 34, 49.

baker, nevertheless, asserts that white fishermen had nothing to
fear from the competition of the blacks, because Negroes could
not endure the hardships of fishing. He also contends that Negroes proved a failure as sailors.[92] This opinion hardly coincides
with the facts, for from the seventeenth century on, Negroes
were employed on all sorts of New England vessels. As early
as 1682 a Negro belonging to Peter Cross of Massachusetts,
had so demonstrated his ability as a seaman, that he was managing his master's sloop at sea.[93] Newspapers occasionally advertised a Negro as " a very good sailor." [94] Reports of accidents
on board ships further testify to the maritime employment, if
not to the skill, of the slaves. In 1724 a Negro on board a Boston vessel was killed by the fall of a sailyard; [95] in 1754, a Negro boatman was drowned when a " lighter " sank off the
Massachusetts coast,[96] and in 1768, among the crew that per-
ished in a storm off the coast was Captain Patterson of Boston
and his Negro man.[97] Negroes not only served aboard the fishing vessels of Marblehead, Massachusetts, but even found employment on slave ships.[98]

The fitness of Negroes for such work is further attested by
the fact that they actually were solicited for service aboard
ships, and in some instances ship captains hired slaves as seamen. In 1702 Captain Halsey of Boston employed Toney, the
slave of Samuel Lynde of the same town, as cook aboard his
vessel.[99] A year later John Mico of Boston hired out his slave

92 Wertenbaker, *op. cit.*, p. 62.

93 *E. C. C. R.*, VIII, 297.

94 *Ibid.*, Jan. 15, 1754.

95 *New England Weekly Journal*, April 24, 1724.

96 *Boston Gazette or Weekly Post Advertiser*, Jan. 29, 1754.

97 *Boston Chronicle*, December 19, 1768.

98 *Ibid.*, Jan. 11, 1770; on one occasion, a Negro sailor saved the entire
crew from death by giving a timely warning as the slaves rose in rebellion
aboard the ship. Donnan, II, 374-75.

99 *Mass. Archives*, IX, 149.

Jeffrey, as a seaman to Captain Samuel White.[100] Fugitive Negroes, like the notorious Arthur [101] or Crispus Attucks, later a victim in the Boston Massacre, sometimes found employment on trading ships.[102] Prince Hall, founder of Negro Masonry, in the United States, served as a steward on a vessel plying between Boston and England.[103] So great was the need of crews to man the sailing vessels of New England that shipmasters often encouraged Negroes to run away to sea.[104] All too frequently captains whose vessels were undermanned impressed slaves into service aboard their ships.[105] So serious did this practice become that all the New England colonies found it necessary to enact legislation, forbidding captains to take slaves and servants aboard their vessels without permission.[106] The penalties were sometimes severe as in the case of Captain John Moffatt of Boston, fined fifty pounds in 1724 for carrying a Negro to Portugal in violation of this law.[107]

Negroes were also engaged as workers in the important whaling industry. For instance, Paul Cuffee, who later became merchant, philanthropist, and colonizer, began his career aboard a whaler bound for Mexico and the West Indies.[108] In some

100 *Ibid., Domestic Relations, 1643-1774*, IX, 157. Mico expressly admonished White to take as good care of the Negro as if Jeffrey were his own property.

101 *The Life and Dying Speech of Arthur, a Negro Man Who Was Executed at Worcester, Oct. 20, 1768, For a Rape Committed on the Body of Deborah Metcalf.* Broadside in Library of American Antiquarian Society, Worcester, Mass. *Vide infra*, ch. vi.

102 Temple, *History of Framingham, Massachusetts*, p. 255.

103 Johnston, " Slavery in Rhode Island," *loc. cit.*, p. 127.

104 For legislation to stop this practice, *vide infra*, pp. 128-138.

105 *Mass. Archives*, IX, 185.

106 *Colonial Laws of Massachusetts* (Reprinted from Edition of 1672 with Supplements through 1686, Boston, 1890), p. 281; *Conn. Col. Recs., 1689-1706*, IV, 40; *Rhode Island Charter Acts and Laws* (Digest, 1719), pp. 70-71.

107 *Mass. Archives*, IX, 186.

108 *Memoir of Paul Cuffee: A Man of Color*, ed. W. Alexander (London, 1819), p. 7; *Journal of Negro History*, VIII, 156.

cases nearly half of the whaling crew were Negroes. As late as 1807 it was reported that the larger whaleships carried " twenty-one men, of whom nine are commonly blacks;—the smaller—sixteen men; of whom seven are blacks." The crew of the whaler, *Lion,* in that year carried three officers, eight white men, a boy and nine Negroes.[109] During the colonial struggles and the American Revolution, Negroes, both slave and free, served in various capacities on privateers and public ships of war.[110] Not only were Negroes actively engaged in New England's maritime industries, but according to Johnston, they made excellent seamen.[111]

The wide variety and quality of occupational opportunities proved a valuable training school for the slaves. By demonstrating a marked interest and ability in discharging their masters' affairs, some Negroes were rewarded with positions of trust and responsibility. Attention has already been directed to the slave who had charge of his master's vessel.[112] In 1679 Mingo, the hired slave of Miles Foster of Boston, managed a warehouse owned by Roger Darby,[113] and Prince, the slave of Colonel Joseph Buckminster of Framingham, Massachusetts, superintended a large farm for his master.[114] Sharper, the slave of Colonel Enoch Brown of Middleboro, was probably an itinerant peddler in 1775 for in that year James Bowdoin informed Josiah Quincy that Sharper was travelling " on a trading jour-

109 *Mass. Hist. Soc. Colls.,* Second Series, III, 29.

110 *Vide infra,* pp. 188-190.

111 Johnston, *op. cit.,* p. 127.

112 *Vide supra,* p. 115.

113 During the terrible fire in Boston, of August 7, the warehouse was destroyed. Darby brought suit against John and Mary Dutch, alleging that during the excitement, attendant upon the fire, they had stolen certain goods from the building. The case was tried before the Quarterly Court, held at Ipswich, Massachusetts, in May 1680. Lucretia Derby (spelling varies) testified, in part, that her goods had been " left in good condition to be taken on board by Mingo, Miles Foster's Negro who had charge of the warehouse." *E. C. C. R.,* VII, 368.

114 Temple, *op. cit.,* p. 237.

ney to Dartmouth, and the neighboring towns." [115] Lemuel Haynes, indentured servant of Deacon David Rose of Granville, Massachusetts, did most of the buying for his master.[116] Mesheck, the slave of Colonel Hinsdale of Deerfield, Massachusetts, operated for his owner at Deerfield a store located opposite the house of George Sheldon, the town's historian.[117] Another slave had unusual responsibility as the manager of a menagerie whose attraction was a lion, recently brought from Africa and advertised by the *Boston News Letter* as follows:

> All Persons having the Curiosity of seeing the Noble
> and Royal Beast the Lyon, never one before seen in
> America, may see him at the House of Capt. *Arthur Savage*
> near Mr. Coleman's Church, Boston, before he is transported.[118]

Some Negroes served as apprentices to physicians and even as doctors. In an era when ministers, magistrates, innkeepers, grocers, barbers, and even butchers were physicians or surgeons, Negroes and Indians who apparently had some knowledge of roots and herbs set up as medical practitioners and, according to Alice Earle, were patronized by the community. A case in point was a Connecticut Negro, Primus, who, as apprentice to his master, helped the doctor in his surgery and in his practice of medicine. When the doctor died, Primus is said to have begun the practice of medicine on his own account, is reported to have become "extraordinarily successful throughout the county," and as Mrs. Earle adds, "even his master's patients

115 "The Bowdoin and Temple Papers," *Massachusetts Historical Society Collections*, Sixth Series, IV (Boston, 1897), 393-394.

116 Timothy M. Cooley, *Life and Character of Lemuel Haynes* (New York, 1839), p. 31.

117 Sheldon, *op. cit.*, p. 51.

118 The slave had apparently been involved in arguments with patrons while caring for his master's interests, therefore, in order to avoid disputes, all persons, entering the gate were advised to pay him six pence apiece. April 7, 1718.

did not disdain to employ the black successor, wishing no doubt their wonted bolus and draught." [119]

Not only was Negro labor in New England used in specific tasks, but many Negroes fell into the category of " Jack of all trades," that is, they were able to turn their hands to several different kinds of work. Nowhere did the Negro show greater adaptability to the labor needs of New England than in this capacity, for the " handy " man was almost indispensable to Yankee masters, especially on the farm. The slave, then, who was equally adept at tilling the soil, shoeing a horse, chopping wood or repairing a fence, was extremely valuable to his master. Negro women who could cook, spin, sew, milk, preserve fruit, make maple sugar and, if necessary take a turn in the field were similarly esteemed. The very nature of New England's complex economy, together with the ever present labor shortage, made it necessary for the slave or servant, like the master, to be able to do more than one thing. Indeed it is probable that most of the New England slaves actually belonged in this class. On this point, newspapers are illuminating. A slave might be advertised as skilled in " all sorts of household work, used to the cooper's business and a very good sailor;" [120] another as fit for either skilled labor or " country work;" [121] a third as " capable of doing all sorts of house work and has likewise been used to the printing business," [122] and a fourth, as one " that can do any sort of work in doors or out, [and] can work at the ship carpenters trade." [123] Negro women described as " fit for any service either in town or country," [124] or " finely accomp-

119 Earle, *Customs and Fashions*, pp. 356-358; *vide* Perry Miller and Thomas H. Johnson, *The Puritans* (New York, 1938), pp. 386-387.

120 *Boston Gazette and Weekly Advertiser*, Jan. 15, 1754.

121 *Ibid.*, February 12, 1754.

122 *Continental Journal and Weekly Advertiser*, May 15, 1777.

123 *Boston Gazette and Weekly Advertiser*, Jan. 29, 1754.

124 *Boston News Letter*, May 5, 1718.

lished for any sort of household business," [125] or " skilled in all household arts and especially talented in needle work," [126] were exceedingly valuable for the New England household.

It was not necessary to own slaves in order to use their services, for persons who needed labor could occasionally hire Negroes. Masters who did not have enough work for their slaves to do, and who did not wish to support them in idleness, often hired them out in an effort to realize something from their investments.[127] Newspaper advertisements reflect this situation: a Boston master offered to hire out a " Negro woman about 30 years of age capable of any household work, and can be well recommended;" [128] another a Negro girl " fit to attend family;" a Negro man who " plays well on the violin," and a Negro man " fit for town or country work." [129] The labor market was evidently saturated for this particular type of individual for the last advertisement appeared in three consecutive weekly issues.[130] The hiring out of slaves seems to have been a general practice. As early as 1694 Judge John Saffin of Boston rented his slave, Adam to Thomas Shepard, promising the slave his freedom at the end of seven years.[131] Attention has already been directed to the subsequent hiring out of slaves as seamen [132] and mechanics.[133] When a slave was rented, master and renter entered into a formal contract, specifying the length of service,

125 *New England Weekly Journal*, October 17, 1738.

126 *Boston News Letter*, April 21, 1718.

127 For this practice in colonial New York *vide* McKee, *op. cit.*, pp. 129-30. Hiring out of slaves was also a common practice in the South during the entire slavery period. In one instance a South Carolina master permitted his son to hire out twelve slaves for $1200 a year, giving him half of it to pay for his schooling. Frederic Bancroft, *Slave Trading in the Old South* (Baltimore, 1931), p. 146 n. *Vide ibid.*, pp. 146-64 for discussion of this practice in the South.

128 *Boston Gazette and Weekly Advertiser*, Feb. 26, 1754.

129 *Ibid.*, January 22, 1754.

130 *Ibid.*, January 29; February 12, 1754.

131 *Mass. Archives*, IX, 153.

132 *Ibid.*, pp. 149, 157.

133 *Vide supra*, p. 119.

nature of employment,' and compensation which the master
should receive for the hire of his slave. Thus in 1702 when
Samuel Lynde of Boston hired out his Negro to serve as cook
aboard a privateer during Queen Anne's War (1702-1713),
Lynde was to be paid one full share of the prizes taken by the
ship:

I, John Halsey of Boston in New England Marriner, Commander
of the Briggantine Adventure a private Man of warr Doe hereby acknowledge that the day of the date thereof I have
listed and received on board s$^d$ Briggantine, as one of her
Company, a Young Negroe Man, named Toney belonging to
Samuel Lynde of s$^d$ Boston M$^r$cht [merchant].   And I the said
Commander Doe by these presente Covenant with the s$^d$
Samuell Lynde his Exect$^s$ [Executors] and Adm$^{ts}$ [Adminis-
trators] That the said Toney shall be Entitled unto one
full and whole share of all prizes plunder which the
s$^d$ private Mann of Warr and Company, Shall take upon their
Expedition as much as any able Saylor on board not being
an officer; the s$^d$ Toney performing the duty and business
of a Cooke on board.   And further That I will at the
s$^d$ Briggantines returne to her Commission port restore the
s$^d$ Toney to his Master the s$^d$ Sam$^{ll}$ Lynde (Excepting
Mortality & Enemys) and will then be accomptable and pay
unto him or his Assignes what shall be due and belong to
s$^d$ Toney as his share . . . as witness my hand and Seal this
twenty fourth day of September Anno dm Seventeen hundred
and two.

               *Signed Sealed and Delivered*
               In the presence of us
                         Daniel Allen
                         Jn Valentine
                         John Halsey [134]

Rarely is the price of rented slaves given. In 1676, a Massachusetts slave was hired out at the rate of five and a half pounds

[134] The signature of Samuel Lynde does not appear. *Mass. Archives*, IX,
149.

a year. In this instance, the master, Jonathan Corwin, experienced difficulty in collecting for the hire of his slave. In June 1680 Corwin, of Massachusetts, sued Elizabeth Gibbs and John Wing of the same colony for £22. Corwin charged that the defendants owed him that amount for the four years' service of his Negro man " Zanckey." In defense Wing contended that it had cost more than that sum for medical care during the slave's illness. But the Court awarded damages to Corwin.[135] Whether this case set a precedent for holding the renter of the slave responsible for the latter's health, while in his service, is not definitely known.

Instead of hiring out unemployed slaves, New England owners frequently offered them for sale. This practice was followed increasingly during the depression following the French and Indian War with its unsettled economic conditions attendant upon the quarrel between the colonies and England, just before the outbreak of the Revolution. Unable to find employment for their slaves, masters sought to salvage something from their investment by selling them. For this reason Negroes were frequently sold for " lack of employment." A Boston master offered for sale " a likely strong, healthy Negro girl about 19 years of age, fit for either town or country service, indoors or without, sold for nothing but want of employ ";[136] a New Hampshire owner would sell for " cash or short credit a likely NEGRO MAN, about thirty years of age, well built and fit for any sort of labour also a NEGRO GIRL, about 18 years of age . . . both sold for want of employment"[137] and a Connecticut owner advertised a " likely Negro wench, healthy and strong and used to all kinds of household work together with her male child about 4 years old.—The above wench is sold for no fault, the owner at present having no employ for her."[138]

135 The slave had been ill with the smallpox and the French pox. *E. C. C. R., 1678-1680*, XII, 394-395.

136 *Boston Gazette and Weekly Advertiser*, Feb. 26, 1754.

137 *New Hampshire Gazette and Historical Chronicle*, April 20, 1770.

138 *Connecticut Gazette and Universal Intelligencer*, November 22, 1776.

Fortunately for these masters a demand sometimes existed for their surplus labor. Persons who needed extra workers used the newspaper columns to make known their desire to buy or rent slaves. Sometimes they preferred white indentured servants;[139] at other times, Negroes. One man wanted to buy a " Negro fellow " from " 24 to 30 years of age with his wife that can be well recommended";[140] another, wanted " a strong hearty Negro wench,"[141] and a third advertised for " a likely well bred Negro boy from 10 to 15 years old."[142]

From the evidence cited showing the employment of Negroes in various fields it seems evident, despite frequent assertions to the contrary, that Negroes were a valuable and essential part of New England's labor supply and that they unquestionably played a role in the commercial and industrial development of that section.

139 *New Hampshire Gazette and Historical Chronicle*, Jan. 9, 1767; also *ibid.*, April 3, 1767.

140 *Boston Weekly Post Boy*, June 26, 1749.

141 *New England Chronicle and Universal Advertiser*, Dec. 13, 1776.

142 *Continental Journal and Weekly Advertiser*, Feb. 27, 1777. For other instances see files of newspapers cited.

# CHAPTER V

# MACHINERY OF CONTROL

THE successful employment of Negro slaves in New England required sundry laws for their control, for as the number of Negroes increased, their felonies and misdemeanors grew accordingly, and this acted as a spur to special legislation. Laws were necessary to indicate what constituted a crime for Negroes, to prescribe punishments, and to adjust penalties to fit an impecunious class of bondmen. Not only must the master be protected in his property (which the slave represented), but he must also be safeguarded against insurrections on the part of his property. Legal proscription must preserve the yawning economic, social and political chasm between the ruling class and the slaves, by prohibiting intermarriage between them. Out of this necessity evolved a body of legislation, commonly known as slave codes, laws not peculiar to New England, for every slave-holding colony in the New World found it necessary to enact such legislation. Slave codes were not the outgrowth of conscious planning but developed from local attempts to meet certain emergencies as they arose.[1] Barbados was the first English colony to place restrictive legislation upon the slaves. Her black code of 1644[2] served as a model for the early slave statutes of Virginia (1661), Maryland (1663), and South Carolina (1702). Although in the main New England's slave control was apparently based upon the foregoing enactments, in some respects that region led the way.

Slave legislation was forced upon the Puritan colonies shortly after the introduction of slavery. Since chattel slavery was un-

1 This characteristic is discernible in the preambles of the laws. *Vide, R. I. Col. Recs.*, VI, 64-65; *Conn. Acts and Charters* (1729), p. 870; *Acts and Resolves of the Massachusetts Bay, 1742-1756*, II, 647-648.

2 Phillips, *American Negro Slavery*, p. 490; Virginia's slave code was begun in 1661. James Ballagh, *History of Slavery in Virginia*, p. 34; George M. Stroud, *Sketch of the Laws Relating to Slavery in the Several States* (Philadelphia, 1827), p. 2. *Vide* also *ibid.*, pp. 2-3, 11; Phillips, *op. cit.*, p. 492.

known to Englishmen when America was colonized,[3] no legal status could immediately be assigned to Negroes as slaves.[4] The first Negroes brought to Virginia seem to have been indentured servants,[5] and the same was probably true of the slaves first brought to New England. For a while there was virtually no difference between Negro slavery and indentured servitude. Slavery, if it could be called such, at first existed only by custom, and positive law was needed to make it a legal institution. Massachusetts was the first colony to take this step.[6] When called upon to decide who should be considered slaves, the Bay Colony legislature boldly legalized perpetual servitude,[7] and in 1641, twenty years before any similar pronouncement by a continental English colony, Massachusetts had ordained the legal enslavement of Indians, whites and Negroes.[8] This law, as previously stated, was subsequently adopted by the New England Confederation, which consisted of the united colonies of Massachusetts, Connecticut and Plymouth.[9] Faced with the same problem in 1652, Rhode Island, which was not a member of the New England Confederation, distinguished itself when the Commissioners of Providence Plantations passed a law limiting involuntary servitude to ten years.[10] Negroes and white persons under fourteen years of age were to serve their masters until they were twenty-four, when they were to be freed and owners who refused to emancipate their slaves or who attempted to sell them into slavery elsewhere were punishable by a fine of

3 Tapping Reeve, *Law of Baron and Femme* (New Haven, 1816), p. 339; Hurd, *Law of Freedom and Bondage,* I, 225-226.

4 Hurd, *ut. supra;* also pp. 179, 183.

5 Ballagh, *History of Slavery in Virginia*, p. 28; Donnan, III, 1.

6 *Vide supra*, p. 63 ff.

7 *Colonial Laws of Mass.* (1660), p. 125; *Vide supra*, p. 63.

8 Virginia's law legalizing slavery was not passed until 1661. Ballagh, *op. cit.*, p. 34.

9 *Colonial Laws of Massachusetts* (Reprint, Boston, 1889), p. 86; *cf.* *supra*, p. 63 and note.

10 *R. I. Col. Recs.*, I, 248; *vide supra*, p. 18.

£40.[11] Although some Negroes probably won their freedom
through the application of this legislation, the law later was
generally disregarded.

The Massachusetts law of 1641 did not determine the status
of the children of slaves. When this question arose in 1670, the
Massachusetts legislature (as indicated elsewhere) promptly revised the earlier statute and made it legally possible for the children of slaves to be sold into bondage.[12] By the common law of
England, which prevailed in the colonies, children held the same
status as the father (*partuus sequitur patrem*). In essence, the
child was free or slave, depending upon the condition of the
father.[13]

From the point of view of the master, the common law was
economically detrimental. Should one of his slave women bear
a child by a freeman, be he white, Indian, or Negro, the master
would lose not only the potential wealth that the child represented, but also the labor of his slave during and immediately
after her confinement. Virginia was the first colony to legislate
upon the problem: in 1662 the Assembly enacted a statute in-
voking the Roman Law regarding slavery: *partuus sequitur
ventrem*.[14] Thereafter the child followed the condition of the
mother. Although none of the New England colonies effected
the change legally, custom and tradition achieved the same end.

The question of colonial defense also inspired New England
slave legislation. The ever-present Indian danger and the
French menace in Canada made military preparedness impera-
tive and during the early years every adult male was urgently
needed to protect the settlements. Therefore, in May 1652 all
" Negers and Indians " who lived with or were servants of the
English in Massachusetts were compelled to undergo military
training.[15] Negroes probably served in the militia of Connecticut

11 *Ibid.*
12 *Mass. Records*, IV, Part II, 467; *vide supra*, p. 65.
13 Stroud, *op. cit.,* p. 11.
14 Ballagh, *op. cit.,* p. 43.
15 *Mass. Records, 1644-1657*, III, 268.

until 1660,[16] but before the end of the seventeenth century Negroes and Indians were specifically barred from the militia in New England. Massachusetts took the lead by excluding all Negroes and Indians, even those " servants to the English " from military duty in 1656.[17] This drastic action was probably motivated by the colonists' fear of Indian-Negro uprisings. As a result of an insurrection of this nature which took place at Hartford in 1657,[18] Connecticut passed a law three years later exempting all Negroes and Indians from military duty.[19] Massachusetts, in 1693, again ruled that all Negroes and Indians, along with " members of the council, the representatives . . . secretary, justices of the peace, president, fellows, students and servants of Harvard College," ministers, school masters, and a few others were to be excused from military training.[20] Throughout the remainder of the colonial period, Negro and Indian slaves were legally excluded from the militia. In 1723, when the Massachusetts legislature appropriated funds for strengthening Castle William, the main defense of Boston harbor, apprehension over the possible treachery of slaves, was clearly apparent in the clause that prohibited any " Indian, Negro or Mulatto to be enlisted or retained there except [as] a servant of the captain."[21] Connecticut's militia act of 1715 again barred Negroes [22] and, in 1784, long after the immediate Indian danger had passed, and notwithstanding the service of Negroes in the Revolutionary armies, the state still barred them from militia duty.[23] The military proscription of the Negro, first imposed

16 *Conn. Col. Recs.*, I, 349.

17 *Mass. Records*, III, 397; IV, Part I, 257.

18 " Wyllys Papers," *Conn. Hist. Soc. Colls.*, XXI, 137-138; *vide infra*, p. 160.

19 *Conn. Col. Recs., ut. supra.*

20 *Acts and Resolves of the Massachusetts Bay, 1692-1714*, I, 130. Hereinafter cited as *Mass. A. and R.*

21 *J. H. R. of Mass., 1723-1724*, V, 105-106, 210.

22 *Conn. Acts and Laws* (New London, 1729), p. 78.

23 *Acts and Laws of the State of Connecticut* (New London, 1786), pp. 38, 188, 233.

against him through fear of retaliation during the colonial period, still persists in modified form to the present time. Although his services have always been used in time of war, he alone, of all the groups comprising the American population, has been compelled to fight for the right to fight.

The foregoing acts were but forerunners of the actual slave codes that began about 1680 and continued in process of development almost until the end of the colonial period. In essence, slave statutes attempted to deal with such things as running away, drunkenness, theft, destruction of public property, prevention of riots and insurrections, curtailment of the slaves' freedom of locomotion, and prevention of any defamation or assault upon a white person. The laws also dealt with the care of indigent and superannuated slaves, and set forth conditions under which slaves might be freed. The slave codes of the New England colonies, which are similar in intent and wording, often applied to Indian slaves and indentured servants as well as to Negroes, and occasionally to free white minors.

The earliest of these laws attempted to protect slave property. Negroes and white servants apparently had been carried away, or had been escaping, aboard vessels sailing from the New England colonies. Massachusetts, which was the first to legislate against this practice, passed a law on October 13, 1680, prohibiting the master of any " ship, sloop, ketch, or vessel ", of more than twelve tons from entertaining on board any servant or Negro or from sailing out of any port of the colony with such persons on board without a permit from the governor or his appointee. Violations carried a penalty of twenty pounds; should the slave or servant be injured, the fine was to be doubled.[24]

Ten years later, Connecticut followed with a more comprehensive law, by the terms of which all Negro and Indian servants were forbidden to wander beyond the town limits, or

24 *Mass. Col. Laws. Reprinted from Edition of 1672 with Supplements through 1686* (Boston, 1890), p. 281.

places where they belonged, without a ticket or a pass either from some authority or from their masters. Bondmen disobeying this decree would be deemed runaways, and every inhabitant was enjoined to take them up and return them to their masters, who would pay the accrued charges. All ferrymen were forbidden to allow such persons to cross on their ferries under pain of a fine of twenty shillings.[25] In 1715 the law was revised to include Indian servants and other servants—presumably white.[26] Rhode Island in 1714 found it necessary to pass similar legislation,[27] for her Negro and mulatto slaves often ran away under pretense of being sent on errands for their masters, and were transported by the ferries out of the colony. The law of 1714 forbade all ferrymen under penalty of twenty shillings to " carry convey or transport any slave or slaves " across any ferry out of the colony, without a certificate from their master or mistress, or some regularly constituted person. Rhode Island's law was more severe than that of Connecticut or Massachusetts upon the abettor of the runaway, for in addition to the fine, the ferryman was to pay all costs and charges sustained by the master, incident to the loss of the slave. If damages did not exceed forty shillings, any two justices of the peace might render judgment; where damages were in excess of this amount, the master might recover by action of trespass in the General Court of Trials. The intrenched position of the slaveholder is clearly seen in this law, for all public officers of the colony and all citizens as well were charged with arresting, securing the slave, and notifying his master.[28] But the law was powerless to prevent the carrying away of Negroes by privateersmen and other vessels. Newport is said to have had sixty privateers in active

25 *Conn. Col. Recs., 1689-1706,* IV, 40.

26 *Conn. Acts and Charters* (New London, 1729), p. 87.

27 *R. I. Charter Acts and Laws* (1719 Digest), pp. 70-71.

28 Any person securing a runaway slave might recover charges from the master. *Ibid.*

service during the French and Indian War, and evidently their captains had no scruples against accepting or even kidnaping Negro slaves in order to complete their crews, for Negroes actually served in several capacities aboard many of them.[29] In order to stop the abduction of Negroes, a law of 1757 imposed a crushing fine of £500 upon any commander of a man-of-war or master of a merchant ship who should knowingly carry any slave or slaves out of the colony.[30] The fine was to be recovered by the colonial treasurer " by bill, plaint, or information " in any court of record in the colony. Owners might bring suits for damages against offenders,[31] and should a master suspect that his slave was aboard a vessel, upon application to the ship's captain, he was to be permitted to search the ship in the presence of one or more substantial witnesses. Refusal by the captain was to be accepted as full proof that the slave, with the captain's knowledge, was actually aboard the vessel.[32]

Another set of laws was directed against theft, a common offense. Sometimes Negroes were induced to steal from their masters by white persons, who either bought or received the stolen goods. Massachusetts, by a law of 1693, pioneered in an effort to break up this practice. All persons were prohibited from buying or receiving any goods from Negro, Indian, or mulatto servants, if there was the slightest suspicion that the articles were stolen. All persons violating this law were to restore to the owner in specie the value of the merchandise, if unaltered, double the value if the goods were not recovered, and for the offense of theft, Indian, Negro, and mulatto servants, or slaves were to be whipped, not exceeding twenty lashes.[33] The law, when it failed to produce the desired effect, was

29 Chapin, *Rhode Island Soldiers and Sailors,* pp. 23, 29.

30 *R. I. Col. Recs., 1757-1769,* VI, 64-65.

31 *Ibid.*

32 *Ibid.*

33 *Mass. A. and R., 1692-1714* (Boston, 1869), p. 156.

strengthened in 1698. Under the revised legislation, receivers of stolen goods were not only still required to make restitution, as in the act of 1690, but, if unable to do so, they were to be publicly whipped with no more than twenty stripes, although offenders might escape the whipping if they rendered satisfaction by service.[34] Penalties for the slave were also increased. Negroes and Indians were to be punished with twenty stripes as formerly, and were to be further prosecuted, unless the stolen property was recovered.[35] The Connecticut law of 1708, while almost identical with that of Massachusetts, was even harsher. If the white person who received the stolen goods was unable to return double the value of the purloined articles, he was to be whipped. The slave, upon conviction, was not only required to return the goods but was also to be whipped " not exceeding thirtie stripes." [36] The New Hampshire law of 1714 embodied the features of Connecticut's statute, with the exception that the slave was to receive a maximum of only twenty lashes. However, the slave would be further prosecuted unless the goods had been stolen from his master.[37] Rhode Island's law regarding theft was the most severe of all. Any Indian or Negro slave accused of stealing was to be tried by the assistants or justices of the peace in the town where the offense was committed. These officers were fully empowered to sentence the slave upon conviction to be whipped with fifteen stripes on the naked back at the public whipping post, or even to banishment from the colony. With the exception of death, banishment was the most terrible punishment that could be meted out to the slave, for it usually meant deliverance into the merciless type of slavery practised on the sugar plantations of the West Indies. Masters of such convicted slaves, however, upon posting bond,

34 *Ibid.*, p. 325.

35 *Ibid.*

36 *Conn. Col. Recs., Oct. 1706-Oct. 1716*, V., 52.

37 *Acts and Laws of His Majesty's Province of New Hampshire in New England* (Portsmouth, 1771), pp. 39-40.

might appeal the case to the General Court, or to the General Courts of Trial and General Gaol Delivery within the province.[38]

There were other laws designed to prevent conspiracies and other disturbances of the peace; these were often inspired by reports that slaves had committed, during the night, many " disorders, insolencies, and burglaries." [39] Connecticut, in her law of 1690 dealing with runaways, had already forbidden Negroes and Indians to be on the streets after nine o'clock.[40] Massachusetts followed in 1703 with a law by which all Indian, Negro, and mulatto slaves were forbidden to be abroad after nine o'clock at night, or to be absent from their master's house, unless upon some errand for their respective owners.[41] Any slave or slaves, unable to give a good account of their business, might be taken up by any person and brought to the nearest justice of the peace, or might be imprisoned in the common jail, watchhouse, or constable house, until the following morning. They were then to be brought before a justice of the peace, who might order such slaves to a house of correction where they would be whipped with ten stripes and then dismissed, unless charged with other crimes.[42] Where there was no house of correction the slaves were to be publicly whipped by the constable. All Negroes who misbehaved or created disturbances were to be subject to the same penalty.[43] Rhode Island followed with an act in the same year, which, although it embodied features identical with those of the Massachusetts law, imposed the severer penalty of fifteen stripes.[44] Before punishment was

38 *R. I. Charter and Laws* (Digest, 1719), pp. 101-102; cf. *R. I. Acts and Laws, 1636-1705* (Providence, 1705), p. 58.

39 *Mass. A. and R., 1692-1714,* I, 535.

40 *Conn. Col. Recs.,* IV, 40.

41 *Mass. A. and R., 1692-1714,* I, 535.

42 *Ibid.,* p. 536.

43 *Ibid.*

44 *R. I. Col. Recs.,* III, 492.

inflicted, however, the Negro was first to be tried and convicted by a justice of the peace. The law was more sweeping in its scope than were earlier statutes of this kind, for it applied to free Negroes and Indians as well as to slaves.[45] It also gave wide discretionary power to the constable in regard to punishment, for he might apply more than fifteen lashes if, in his judgment, the " incorrigible behavior " of the slaves required it.[46] The New Hampshire measure, which was copied almost verbatim from that of Massachusetts, provided a penalty of ten stripes.[47] All of these laws were amended during the eighteenth century. By a law of 1723, Connecticut added costs of court to the penalty of twenty lashes, unless the master redeemed his slave by paying a fine, not exceeding twenty shillings.[48]

There was further legislation to keep the slaves from disturbing the peace. In Massachusetts, nocturnal disorders created by Negroes became so annoying that a group of wealthy Roxbury slave-holders, among whom were Edward Ruggles, John Holbrook, James Jarvis, Ebenezer Don and others, petitioned the legislature in 1723 for a law to restrain them.[49] In response to this petition the House of Representatives, on June 7, 1723, appointed a committee to consider means for the better " regulating Indians, Negroes and Molattoes," [50] and on July 17 the Committee brought in a bill under the grandiloquent title : " An act for the better regulating Indians, Negroes, and Mullatoes, and preventing many mischievous practices which the Indians, Negroes and Mulattoes have of late in a most audacious manner to the great disturbance and grievous damage of his Majesties good subjects, more especially in the town of Boston

45 *Ibid.*

46 *Ibid.*

47 *N. H. Acts and Laws* (Portsmouth, 1771), p. 52.

48 *Conn. Col. Recs.*, VI, 390; *Conn. Acts and Laws* (Revision 1750), p. 230.

49 Winsor, *Memorial History of Boston,* II, 355.

50 *J. H. R. of Mass., 1723-1724,* V, 18-19.

addicted themselves to." [51] The bill was passed by the House [52] but did not receive sufficient support for a third reading in the Council.[53] Elisha Cooke, chairman of the Committee and sponsor of the bill, thereupon asked leave to introduce another bill. Permission was granted and another bill, having the same purport as the former but with a shorter title, was introduced into the House on December 4, 1723.[54] It was read, sent to a committee for amendment, brought back to the House, where it received three readings, and was there finally lost.[55]

Nocturnal street disorders still continued. Street lamps were broken or extinguished, other public property was destroyed, and the lives and property of pedestrians were endangered. Finally, Massachusetts in 1753 enacted a law punishing any free person guilty of such crimes with a fine of five pounds and costs of prosecution for the first offense; [56] for the second violation, the fine was to be doubled and, should the offender fail to pay the fine within six months, he was to suffer six months' imprisonment. The act further provided that any " Negro, Indian or Molatto servant or servants who shall between the setting of the sun and the rising thereof," deliberately break, remove, or extinguish street lights, upon conviction shall be publicly whipped with ten stripes for the first offense. For the second and succeeding convictions, the penalty was twenty stripes.[57] In the same year Negroes and whites were accused of disturbing the peace by parading the streets, building bonfires, " carrying pageants and other shews " and insulting and abusing pedestrians with " horrid profanity, impiety and gross immoralities."

51 Ibid., p. 36.

52 Ibid., pp. 36, 43, 48.

53 Ibid., p. 114.

54 Ibid., p. 145.

55 Ibid., p. 292.

56 For law see Mass. A. and R., 1742-1756, III, 645-646.

57 Ibid.

They were further charged with extorting money and with being responsible for the death of a pedestrian who was killed during one of these riotous outbreaks.[58] To stop these disturbances there was enacted in 1753 a law providing that, should more than three persons, " disguised or armed with pageants or weapons of any sort," parade the streets or lanes of any town in the province and exact money or anything of value from the people, said persons were to be fined forty shillings and to be imprisoned for one month. Negroes were to be whipped with ten stripes at the discretion of the justice of the peace.[59] To prevent arson Negroes were also forbidden to build bonfires, or to set fire to any combustible materials in the streets or lanes within ten rods of any house or building, under pain of the same penalty.[60]

Stringent laws were passed to keep liquor from the slaves. In order to safeguard the master class not only Negro slaves, but also white indentured servants and Indian slaves, came under this prohibition. Again Massachusetts set the example for the other New England colonies. In 1693 the Bay Colony forbade any licensed " innholder, taverner, common victualler, or retailer " to allow any apprentice, servant or Negro, except by special permission of their owners, to drink in their houses, under penalty of ten shillings for every offense.[61] Ten years later Connecticut enacted a similar but more comprehensive law than the Massachusetts statute, for it applied to the sons of freemen as well as to apprentices, indentured servants, and Negroes. Violators were to be punished by a fine of ten shillings, or corporal punishment of not less than ten nor more than fifteen stripes, at the discretion of the justice of the peace.[62] New Hampshire in 1715 passed a similar law which

58 *Vide* law in *ibid.*, pp. 647, 648.

59 *Ibid.*

60 This law was to remain in force for **three years.** *Ibid.*

61 *Ibid., 1692-1714,* I, 154.

62 *Conn. Col. Recs.,* IV, 437-438.

carried with it the same penalty as the earlier Massachusetts statute from which it was undoubtedly taken.[63] In Rhode Island, which had the largest proportion of Negroes,[64] legislation regarding this offense was, as in other cases, comparatively severe. By a law of 1750 all persons were forbidden to " sell, truck, barter, or exchange," liquor of any kind with any Indian, mulatto, or Negro servant or slave.[65] Not even cider could be sold to them. Violations carried the heavy fine of thirty pounds for each offense. The law encouraged spying, for one-half of the fine was to go to the informer, the other half to the town in which the offense was committed.[66] A little later Massachusetts, unable to stop this practice, enacted a more stringent law, which applied to free minors as well as to slaves. Violations were punishable by a fine of four pounds and, as in Rhode Island, one-third was to go to the informer, the remainder to the collector of excise.[67]

Fearful lest the entertaining of servants and slaves in private homes might lead to theft, plots, or other disturbances by the bondmen, housekeepers were forbidden by law to entertain them. In 1703-04 Rhode Island prohibited all householders from entertaining any Negro or Indian servant in their homes after nine o'clock at night, without the permission of the master of such servants, under penalty of four shillings for each offense,[68] the fine to be used for the benefit of the town. A more sweeping act was passed in 1750. By this law, any housekeeper who violated the above act or who permitted any slave or servant to enjoy " dancing, gaming or any other diversion whatever " in his house, was to be fined fifty pounds, or suffer im-

63 *New Hampshire Acts and Laws* (Portsmouth, 1771), p. 57.

64 *Cf. supra*, pp. 85-86.

65 *R. I. Acts and Laws, 1745-1752* (Newport, 1752), pp. 92-93.

66 " Old Tenor " was a colonial currency. *Ibid.*

67 *Mass. Acts and Laws, 1757-1768*, IV, 204, 308, 497.

68 *R. I. Acts and Laws, 1636-1705*, p. 38; *R. I. Acts and Laws* (Digest, 1730), pp. 50-51; *R. I. Col. Recs.*, III, 492-493.

prisonment for one month.[69] The law bore especially hard upon free Indians, Negroes, and mulattoes. If found guilty of entertaining slaves, they were no longer to be permitted to keep house, but were to be dispossessed.[70] In addition, they were to lose their freedom for the space of a year, during which time they were to be bound out to service,[71] the wages accruing from their labors to be used for the benefit of the town wherein the offense was committed.[72] Connecticut's law of 1723 was milder, for the head of a family entertaining Indian or Negro slaves after nine o'clock at night was to forfeit twenty shillings, half of which was to go to the complainer, the other half to the town treasury.[73] For the same violation in New Hampshire, the host was to be fined twenty shillings; the slave to be whipped with ten stripes.[74]

Laws also forbade Negroes to strike or to defame a white person. This was an extremely drastic law, for by an enactment of December, 1705-06 any Negro or mulatto who dared to strike a white person in Massachusetts was to be severely whipped at the discretion of the justices before whom the offender was convicted.[75] But the Connecticut law of 1708 exceeded in severity the Massachusetts statute. After citing the frequent turbulence and quarrels between the slaves and white persons, the law provided a penalty of not more than thirty stripes for any Negro who disturbed the peace, or who attempted to strike a white person.[76] Of all these laws the harshest was the statute against defamation of a white person. By Connecticut's law of 1730 any Negro, Indian, or mulatto slave

69 *R. I. Acts and Laws, 1745-1752*, p. 93.

70 *Ibid.*

71 *Ibid.*

72 *Ibid.*

73 *Conn. Acts and Laws* (New London, 1786), p. 234.

74 *New Hampshire Acts and Laws* (Edition 1771), p. 52.

75 *Mass. A. and R., 1692-1714*, I, 578.

76 *Conn. Acts and Laws* (New London, 1729), p. 138.

who uttered or published, about any white person, words which would be actionable if uttered by a free white was, upon conviction before any one assistant or justice of the peace, to be whipped with forty lashes. The severity of the law, however, was tempered by a clause that permitted the slave to make any plea, or to submit the same evidence in defense or justification of his act, as might any free person being sued on a similar charge.[77]

Although most of these laws were passed in the interest of the master class, occasionally their purpose was for the benefit of the towns or even in the interest of the slaves. Many masters, after their slaves had become old and useless in their service, set them at liberty, as they would a worn-out horse, with the result that they became public charges and a burden to the towns.[78] In order to save the towns this expense, all masters were required to support their former slaves should they come to want. The first colony to take such action was Connecticut, where a law of 1702 made the master or his heirs, executors, or administrators legally responsible for the upkeep of indigent Negroes, should they come to want after liberation.[79] In the following year, Massachusetts passed a more specific law. No master might emancipate a slave without first posting a bond of fifty pounds, and no slave was to be regarded as free unless the bond had been posted. Should the slave come to want, he was to be cared for by his former owner, although the selectmen of the towns reserved the right to put the slave out to service at any time.[80] Following the example of Massachusetts, Rhode Island, in 1729, required every master to post a bond of one hundred pounds as guarantee that his slave, after emancipation, would not become a public charge either " through sick-

---

[77] *Conn. Col. Recs.*, V, 52-53.

[78] See preamble of *Connecticut Law of 1702. Conn. Col. Recs., 1689-1706,* IV, 375.

[79] This law was to remain in force for one year. *Ibid.,* pp. 375-376.

[80] *Mass. A. and R.,* I, 520.

ness, lameness " or any other cause.[81] As in Massachusetts, no slave would be deemed free unless the bond had been posted. In case the slave became destitute, he was to be supported by his former mistress or master, but as in Connecticut, the former slave, at the discretion of the justices of the peace or wardens of the town, might be put out to service.[82] Since many masters continued to shift to the towns the responsibility of caring for their freedmen, Connecticut in 1711 revised her earlier law and made it incumbent upon the master to support his former slave. If he failed to do so, the selectmen of the town were to care for the slave and recover the costs from the owners, their heirs, executors, or administrators.[83]

Some laws tended to improve the lot of the slaves. All masters were forbidden to work their servants on Sunday, unless it was absolutely necessary. On the other hand, the Puritans' strict observance of the Sabbath would not permit the slaves to engage in any " game, sport play, or recreation " on Sunday.[84] A much more important law, sponsored by the mother country in 1686, provided the death penalty for any master who wilfully killed his servant or slave.[85] Enforcement of the law, however, was left to the colonial courts.

Unique among the laws controlling the slaves was the Massachusetts statute of 1705-1706, which forbade marriages and illicit sex relationships between Negroes and white persons.[86] Although race intermixture, as will be shown later, was common in all the New England colonies, Massachusetts alone in this section resorted to legal means to stop it.[87]

81 *R. I. Col. Recs.*, IV, 415-416.

82 *Conn. Acts and Charters* (New London, 1729), p. 164.

83 *Ibid.*

84 *R. I. Acts and Charters* (1719), p. 32.

85 *Documents Relative to the Colonial History of the State of New York* (Albany, 1853), III, 547; *cf.* Reeve, *Law of Baron and Femme*, p. 340.

86 *Mass. A. and R.*, I, 578; *vide infra*, pp. 208-209.

87 *Ibid.*

Harsh as some of the general laws for the control of slave labor undoubtedly were, they were often supplemented by even more drastic local regulation, especially in districts where there were heavy concentrations of Negroes. In colonial times, as today, whether in the North or the South, the severity of proscriptive legislation against Negroes was determined by the density of the Negro population. The oppressive character of these regulations reflected the gravity of the threat inherent in a large number of Negroes in a given locality to the continued dominance of the master class. Nowhere was the slave menace more formidable, or the restrictive legislation so onerous, as in Boston and in South Kingstown, Rhode Island.[88]

In 1742, when Boston had about one-third of the slave population of Massachusetts,[89] the town's supplementary legislation bore more heavily upon the Negroes than did that enacted for the colony as a whole. Apprehension over Negro-Indian uprisings is clearly apparent in the local slave ordinances. In 1723, Negro, Indian, and mulatto slaves, it is recorded, were forbidden to remain on Boston Common after sunset, even though they had their masters' permission to visit the Common.[90] A law of July, 1728, stopped all Negro, Indian, and mulatto servants or slaves from buying provisions from country people, either in the market or elsewhere, because white persons had complained that buying by the slaves drove up prices. The law, however, permitted the slave to direct the seller to his master or mistress who, if so inclined, might make such purchases.[91] Any slave convicted of breaking this law was to be fined five shillings.[92] Because of quarrelling, fighting, and other disturbances of the peace by Negroes, servants, and free

88 *Vide infra*, p. 142.

89 *Vide supra*, p. 84.

90 Robert Means Lawrence, *New England Colonial Life* (Cambridge, 1927), p. 97.

91 *Boston Town Records, 1700-1728*, p. 275.

92 *Ibid.*, p. 223. This penalty was imposed by a law of June 24, 1728. *Ibid.*

white youths, a drastic law passed by the town fathers in 1728 provided that no Indian, Negro, or mulatto might carry a stick or cane, either by day or night, which might " be fit for quarrelling or fighting or any other thing of that nature." The penalty for the first offense was a fine of ten shillings, but if the stick or cane bore iron rings, a nail or a spear point on the ends, the fine was to be doubled.[93] In order to reduce theft and to stop the meeting and conferring of Indians and Negroes, as well as to prevent damage to the inhabitants of the town, a Boston law of May, 1746, prohibited all Negroes, Indians, and mulattoes from keeping " any hogs or swine whatever " within the limits of the town, without the consent of their masters. Any person who rented ground to any Negro, Indian, or mulatto for a sty or even permitted him to keep a hog on his land, was, upon conviction, to be fined twenty shillings. The slave might be corrected (presumably by whipping) before any justice of the peace.[94] Negro, Indian and mulatto servants, moreover, could not stroll unnecessarily about the streets, lanes or Commons on Sunday.[95] Nor were they permitted to be on the streets after nine o'clock at night on any day of the week. The penalty was five shillings, payable by either master, mistress or slave.[96] Slaves were expressly forbidden to roam the streets during the church services,[97] but the laws evidently were not rigorously enforced, for in 1757 it was enacted that if any Negro, Indian, or mulatto slave violated the town laws of Boston, he was to be fined or whipped. Punishment was not to exceed twenty nor to be less than five stripes, depending upon the nature and aggravation of the offense.[98]

93 *Ibid.*, p. 224. Lame and decrepit persons were excepted from the injunction against carrying sticks or canes. *Ibid.*

94 *Ibid., 1742-1757,* pp. 96-97.

95 *Ibid.*, p. 326.

96 *Ibid.*

97 *Ibid.*, p. 315.

98 *Ibid.*, pp. 319, 330-331.

Even more severe were the local slave ordinances of South Kingstown, Rhode Island. In this rich Narragansett town where, in 1755, one out of every three persons was a Negro,[99] repressive by-laws supplemented the already harsh Rhode Island slave code. So fearful of slave insurrections was the ruling class that in 1718 a law was enacted providing that if any Negro slave were caught in the house or cottage of a free Negro, both were to be whipped.[100] Eight years later, Indians and Negroes were forbidden to hold social gatherings out-of-doors.[101] Increase in the Negro population toward 1750 brought in its wake a tightening of slave-control measures. In addition to the Rhode Island law prohibiting the sale of liquor to slaves, the South Kingstown planters decreed that not even cider could be sold to a slave;[102] in fact, nothing could be sold to a slave without his master's permission.[103] A Negro could not own a pig, cow, or stock of any kind in South Kingstown under penalty of thirty-one lashes.[104] Finally, any Negro convicted of theft might be whipped or banished at the discretion of two justices of the peace.[105]

Oppressive as were these controls in New England, they were much milder than similar codes governing Negroes in New York and in the tobacco colonies. In New York after 1705 any slave found travelling alone forty miles from Albany was upon conviction to be put to death.[106] In colonial Virginia, runaway slaves found abroad at night were to be dismembered.[107]

99 *Vide supra*, p. 88.

100 Channing, *Narragansett Planters*, p. 11.

101 *Ibid.*

102 *Ibid.*

103 *Ibid.*

104 *Ibid.*, pp. 11-12.

105 The slave might appeal if he furnished bonds to prosecute it. *Ibid.*, p. 11.

106 *New York Colonial Laws*, I, 582.

107 Henry Walter Hening, *Statutes at Large of Virginia*, IV, 132.

If a slave struck a white person in South Carolina he was to be severely whipped for the first offense; for the second offense he was to have his nose slit and be branded in the face; for the third offense he was to suffer death.[108] Further, in both colonial Virginia and South Carolina, the killing of a slave by the master, as the result of punishment or dismemberment, was not a crime punishable at law.[109] Compared to these methods of slave control, those of New England were mild indeed.

108 David J. McCord, *Statutes at Large of South Carolina*, VIII, 343.

109 Hening, *op. cit.*, III, 33; McCord, *op. cit.*, VIII, 345.

# CHAPTER VI
# CRIMES AND PUNISHMENT

NOTWITHSTANDING their elaborate machinery for regulating the Negroes in New England, Puritan attempts to control slave labor often broke down. The effectiveness of the slave codes was weakened in several ways. In the first place, the laws do not seem to have been rigorously enforced.[1] Secondly, the popular conception of the natural docility of the Negroes under bondage proved as mythical in New England as in other parts of slave-holding America.[2] Neither the Negro nor his Indian and white fellow-bondmen remained passive in their bondage. Chafing under the yoke of slavery, the Negro frequently sought and took advantage of any opportunity either to gain his freedom or to avenge himself upon those who had enslaved him. As a result, the records are strewn with a large number of misdemeanors and crimes of the slaves directed against the master class. Thirdly, certain controls either broke down entirely or were partly removed in times of emergency. This was particularly true in regard to the ban on Negroes' bearing arms. Although they were denied the right to enter the militia in peace time, during the stress of war prohibitions were removed, and Negroes, as will be shown later, fought as soldiers, sailors, and marines in all the colonial wars and in the Revolution as well.[3] Lastly, the effectiveness of slave regulation was reduced simply because Negro slaves, like other bondmen, often would not adjust themselves to their debased condition.

Despite the stringent and oftentimes brutal efforts of the Puritans to insure conformity to their social, political and re-

1 Samuel Sewall, "Selling of Joseph," *Mass. Hist. Soc. Colls.,* Fifth Series, VI, 18. Masters sometimes pleaded for the mitigation of sentences imposed upon their Negroes. Sometimes whites did not press serious charges against Negroes. *Vide infra,* this chapter.

2 Helen T. Catterall, editor, *Judicial Cases Concerning American Slavery and the Negro* (Washington, 1926), I, 154.

3 *Vide infra,* pp. 187-190.

ligious institutions, contemporary court records are filled with criminal cases involving all classes and races.[4] That the legal control of slave labor was only partly effective is evident from the number and variety of crimes perpetrated by Negroes, crimes which the slave codes were intended to prevent.

The most common offense of the slaves was running away. So prevalent was this practice, that almost every eighteenth-century newspaper until the end of the Revolutionary era carried advertisements for fugitive slaves.[5] Not only Negroes, but white and Indian runaways were thus cited, and rewards of varying amounts were offered for the return of the fugitives. In 1718 a Rhode Island master advertised for his Negro runaway as follows:

> Ran away from his Master Charles Dickinson of Boston-neck in Kingstown, in Narragansett in Rhode Island Colony, a Negro man aged about 25 years, who had on him a new homespun weastcoat and breeches of the same [cloth] with shoes and stockings on, and an old black torn hat: Who shall take up said Negro and convey him to his Master above said, or advise him so that he may have him again shall be fully paid for the same.[6]

Similar advertisements appeared until the end of the Revolutionary era. In 1738, for example, the Reverend Samuel Allis, of Somers, New Hampshire, offered three pounds reward for his runaway man, Coffe;[7] in 1749, Samuel Johnson of Kittery, Massachusetts, offered " a reasonable reward and . . . all neces-

4 Cf. *Records and Files of the Quarterly Courts of Essex County, Massachusetts.* 8 vols. *passim; Records of the Court of Assistants of the Massachusetts Bay, 1630-1692,* 3 vols., *passim*; and other court records cited herein.

5 The files of eighteenth-century newspapers, such as the *Boston News Letter, the Boston Gazette, the Connecticut Gazette and Universal Intelligencer* and others contain hundreds of these advertisements.

6 *Boston News Letter,* April 21; May 19, 1718.

7 *New England Weekly Journal,* Oct. 10, 17, 1738.

sary charges" for the return of his fugitive Negro;[8] in 1768, John Whiting of New London promised a reward of five dollars for the return of his slave, Peter;[9] and as late as 1784, a Newport, Rhode Island slave-holder advertised for his Negro girl, Violet, who had run away, wearing "a cinnamon colour'd tow-cloth jacket and petticoat".[10]

During the Revolution, many slaves fled to the British, hoping thereby to gain their freedom. A Colchester, Connecticut, slave is supposed to have joined the British in 1776,[11] and in the same year three Negroes are reported to have escaped to British vessels lying off New Haven,[12] while a number of Newport Negroes also took refuge with the British fleet. Several runaways were later recaptured by Admiral Esek Hopkins.[13]

Some of these Negro fugitives, like runaway whites, carried with them part of their master's wardrobe or other valuables. Coffe, slave of the aforementioned Reverend Allis, carried away with him "his master's gun of several pounds value," and also several pounds in money.[14] A slave belonging to Edward Garfield of Waltham, Massachusetts, provided for his comfort and amusement by taking with him a supply of his master's clothes and a "good violin."[15] Tite, a Hartford fugitive, also carried away a violin.[16] The master of another runaway minimized a similar loss by explaining that the thief was a "miserable performer." A white indentured servant took away with him among other things "two silver spoons marked J.W.E."[17]

8 *Boston Weekly Post Boy,* September 18, 25; October 2, 9, 16, 1749.

9 *New London Gazette,* December 2, 1768.

10 *Newport Mercury,* October 30, 1784.

11 *Connecticut Gazette,* June 7, 1776.

12 *Ibid.,* April 12, 1776.

13 *New England Chronicle,* April 25, 1776.

14 Whether the money belonged to him is not clear. *New England Weekly Journal,* Tuesday, October 10, 17, 1738.

15 *Continental Journal and Weekly Advertiser,* May 8, 1777.

16 *Connecticut Courant and Weekly Intelligencer,* Tuesday, Aug. 3, 1779.

17 *Continental Journal and Weekly Advertiser,* Oct. 30, 1777.

The rewards offered for fugitives varied according to the valuation placed on them by their owner, but the real amount of the reward (because of currency fluctuations) was rarely constant. In 1738 a Boston master first promised four shillings [18] for his slave's return but, evidently realizing that this amount was not sufficient, he later increased it to five pounds. In 1749, several masters offered " £10 old Tenor " for the recovery of their Negroes; [19] and another in 1769 offered £ 5 for the return of his Negro man.[20] A New Hampshire owner in 1767 promised four dollars for the recovery of his three indentured servants, one of whom had run off with a schooner.[21] Four years later a reward of two dollars was offered by Daniel Brewster of Portsmouth for the apprehension of his runaway servant.[22] On the other hand, Malcolm McNeil of Boston in 1749 promised a reward of £20 for the return of his white indentured tailor.[23] Although in terms of the depreciated currency of the Revolution some rewards offered seemed unusually large, their actual values were less than in the colonial period. During the seventies and eighties, sums of fifty,[24] one hundred,[25] three hundred,[26] and even five hundred dollars [27] in almost worthless Continental money were offered for the return of Negro runaways. On the other hand, some rewards were so trivial, that they seem to indicate a waning in the value of Ne-

18 *New England Weekly Journal,* January 31, 1738.

19 *Boston Weekly Post Boy,* September 25; October 16, 17, 1749; *Ibid.,* August 14, 1749.

20 *Boston Chronicle,* June 22, 1769.

21 *New Hampshire Gazette and Historical Chronicle,* Nov. 20, 1767.

22 *Ibid.*

23 *Boston Weekly Post Boy,* Oct. 16, 1749.

24 *Continental Journal and Weekly Advertiser,* Oct. 30, 1777.

25 *Ibid.,* August 19, 26, 1779.

26 *Connecticut Courant and Weekly Intelligencer,* August 22, 29; September 3, 1780.

27 *Continental Journal and Weekly Advertiser,* May 24, 1781.

gro labor, the inability of the owner to pay more for the recovery of his property, or perhaps a growing fear, in view of the rising abolitionist sentiment in New England, that property in Negroes was rapidly becoming insecure.[28] By way of illustration: in 1775 a Connecticut master promised ten dollars reward for the recovery of his thirty-four-year-old Negro man;[29] in 1775, Timothy Penny, of Roxbury, Massachusetts, offered the same sum in Revolutionary currency for his fugitive slave woman;[30] in the previous year, a Boston owner had promised as little as four dollars reward for his thirty-seven-year-old Negro woman.[31] The nadir in this respect was reached by a Dr. John Cobbett of Boston, who in 1777, offered four pence for the return of his twenty-year-old Negro, Felix.[32]

In addition to descriptions of, and rewards for, fugitive Negroes, the newspapers introduced a feature which was later to become prominent in the advertising for runaways in the antebellum South: a stereotyped picture of a fugitive Negro in a short skirt, carrying a bundle on his head and a stick in his hand. The first newspaper to introduce this practice seems to have been the *New London Gazette,* in 1768. It was in this graphic manner that John Whiting advertised in its columns for his runaway, Peter.[33] The subsequent use of this device by New England masters, however, seems to have been rare. Unfortu-

28 Efforts to abolish slavery in New England began in earnest with the Revolutionary era. Many persons began to consider slavery inconsistent with the natural rights of man, inherent in the Revolutionary philosophy. In New England the struggle for independence became merged with the anti-slavery movement. *Vide* Nathaniel Niles *Two Discourses on Liberty* (Newburyport, 1774), pp. 31-37; Nathaniel Appleton, *Considerations on Slavery in a Letter to a Friend* (Boston, 1767), *passim;* Alice Baldwin, *The New England Clergy and the American Revolution* (Durham, 1928), p. 128; Locke, *Anti-Slavery in America,* pp. 40, 48, 60, 63, 69.

29 *Connecticut Courant and Universal Intelligencer,* Nov. 17, 1775.

30 *Continental Journal and Weekly Advertiser,* Sept. 25, 1777.

31 *Ibid.,* Sept. 19, 1776.

32 *Ibid.,* March 12, 1777.

33 *New London Gazette,* December 2, 1768.

nately there are no estimates of the number of runaway slaves, but probably hundreds absconded.[34]

Just how many of these fugitives were caught is not known. Many doubtless made good their escape; others were returned to bondage. For example, a Negro belonging to Sir William Pepperell, escaped and fled to the West Indies, but was arrested and returned to his master.[35] A Connecticut runaway was captured at Lyme, in the same state, in 1776, and confined in the New London jail, where his owner, upon paying the charges might recover him.[36] Later in the same year Richard Pitkin of Hartford, captured two Negroes who had escaped from their masters in Little Rest, Connecticut. They had run away two years before, and during the period of their freedom had been employed at sea.[37] At least one fugitive preferred death to re-enslavement; a runaway from Coventry, Rhode Island, realizing that his capture was imminent, is said to have " cut his own throat and soon after expired." [38]

Although attempting to escape was not a serious crime, and was usually punished by flogging,[39] Negroes committed many other offenses, both petty and serious. They seem to have been guilty of the same infractions as were the whites, and their crimes were many and varied. Incomplete records often fail to reveal definitely the nature of these infractions. The earliest appearance of a Negro in a New England Court seems to have been in 1641-42, when Mincarry, " a Blackmore," was brought before the Massachusetts Court of Assistants presided over by Governor John Winthrop.[40] For his unnamed offense, Mincarry

---

34 From scattered newspaper files, the author has collected more than one hundred cases of fugitive slaves.

35 Donnan, *op. cit.*, III, 28.

36 *Connecticut Gazette and Universal Intelligencer,* April 17, 1776.

37 *Ibid.,* June 21, 1776.

38 *Boston Chronicle,* March 26, 1770.

39 *Cf. supra,* p. 128 ff.

40 *Records of the Court of Assistants of the Massachusetts Bay, 1630-1692,* II, 118 (Hereinafter cited as *R. C. A.*).

was " admonished and dismissed." [41] At a town meeting in 1672, Samuel Reeps of Providence refused to secure the release of his Negro slave, who had been arrested for an unstated offense.[42] Seven years later, a warrant was issued for Joseph, the " mulatto" slave of a Massachusetts master.[43] This significantly is the first use of the word " mulatto " in the Massachusetts Court Records and it appears to indicate legal recognition of the results of racial crossing.

Of the specifically named crimes committed by Negroes, stealing and breach of the peace were perhaps the most common. For the latter misdemeanor a mulatto was brought before the Salem Quarterly Court on June 3, 1680; [44] but cases of theft were much more frequent. Sometimes the Negroes acted upon their own initiative; at other times white persons encouraged them to steal. In 1672, Silvanus Wano (note the surname), a slave belonging to Deacon William Parks of Boston, convicted of stealing money from his master, was sentenced to pay the latter £20 in currency, to be whipped with twenty stripes, pay costs of Court, and to be confined to jail until the sentence was executed.[45] Wano was a " repeater," for just four years earlier he had been punished for stealing his master's horse.[46] One night in 1741, five Boston Negroes stole a long boat belonging to a Mr. Salmon and tried to escape to St. Augustine, Florida. Next morning they were captured in Barnstable Bay and committed to jail.[47] In the Ipswich (Massachusetts) Court in March, 1673,

41 *Ibid.*

42 *Early Records of the Town of Providence,* VII, 227.

43 The charge was not given. *Records and Files of the Quarterly Courts of Essex County, Massachusetts, 1678-1680,* VII, 326 (hereinafter cited as E. C. C. R.).

44 *E. C. C. R., 1678-1680,* VII, 425.

45 How Wano was to secure £20 is a mystery. "Records of the Suffolk County Courts, 1671-1680," *Publications of the Colonial Society of Massachusetts* (Boston, 1833), XXIX, Part 1, p. 113. (Hereinafter cited as S. C. C. R.).

46 *Ibid.*

47 They were Spanish Negroes. *Boston Gazette,* Sept. 28; Oct. 5, 1741.

Peter Leycros, Jonas Gregory, and Symon Word were fined £5 for receiving five gallons of wine stolen by a Negro from his master,[48] and four years later, George Major of the same town was fined, branded and bound for good behavior for stealing meat and other provisions from John Knight. Major and his wife were further accused of receiving stolen goods from Knight's Negro boy. On several occasions, according to the boy, Major and his wife had persuaded him to steal powder, wool, meal and sugar from his owner.[49] In 1680, at the January term of the Essex County Court, Hannah, a Boston Negro, was convicted of stealing a box of surgical instruments, valued at £7, from Daniel Stone. Though Hannah claimed the goods were entrusted to her by a white man to be handed over to one Mary Rittum, Hannah was convicted, found guilty, and sentenced to be whipped with ten stripes. She was also to pay ten pounds to Stone in addition to Court costs. For receiving the stolen goods, Mary Rittum was fined forty shillings, twenty to be paid to the court, and twenty to Stone. With three white men acting as her bondsmen for the sum of £30, Hannah appealed the case, asking that the fine be remitted, but Governor Bradstreet upheld the verdict of the County Court.[50] Two years later, Benedict Pulsipher of Ipswich, convicted of stealing sugar, wine and biscuits from a sloop owned partly by Stephen Cross, was sentenced to be whipped and to pay half the treble cost of the goods. Pulsipher's father, who petitioned the Court to release his son from the sentence, contending that the Negro in charge of the vessel had influenced his son to steal, attributed his son's theft to feeble-mindedness, alleging in support of his statement that after four years of schooling, his son could not even learn " his letters." [51]

48 *E. C. C. R., 1672-1674*, V, 141.

49 *Ibid., 1675-1678*, VI, 253, 255.

50 For this case, see *S. C. C. R., 1671-1680*, XXX, Part, II, pp. 1153-1157.

51 *E. C. C. R., 1680-1683*, VIII, 297-298.

The pilfering of these Negroes, however, pales into insignificance before the crimes of Johnson Green,[52] whose record of minor thefts reads like the story of the life of a petty eighteenth-century Jesse James. Born of a Negro father and an Irish mother, Johnson committed an amazing series of thefts, until he was finally arrested, convicted, and hanged " for the atrocious crime of burglary " at Worcester on August 17, 1786. Green's account of his crimes was taken down by a reporter who visited him in the Worcester jail the day before he was hanged. Beginning his criminal career at twelve years of age when he stole " four cakes of gingerbread and six biscuits out of a horse cart," Green continued to steal until his execution at the age of twenty-nine.

Evidently a confirmed thief, for his pilferings covered a wide range of articles, including food, money, clothing, and liquor, Green did not confine his activities to any one state, but spread them over New York, Massachusetts, and Rhode Island. While a member of the American Army, stationed at West Point, in 1781, he and two other soldiers broke open a suttler's " markee " and stole " three cheeses, one small firkin of butter, and some chocolate." For this offense he received one hundred stripes. Undeterred, however, he committed robberies in 1783 at Easton and Bridgewater, Massachusetts. Transferring his activities to Rhode Island in 1784, he stole goods to the value of forty dollars at Providence, " thirty weight of salt pork " from a cellar in Patuxet Bridge, " a pair of trousers, three pairs of stockings, and a shirt " out of a washtub at Patuxet, and " a leg of mutton " from Colonel George Leonard at Norton. Then he returned to Massachusetts. After a series of thefts there he went back to Providence, where he was caught, imprisoned in 1786, and later returned to the Worcester jail. In Worcester he was convicted of burglary and sentenced to be hanged. Like most

52 The Life and Confession of Johnson Green Who is to be Executed this day, August 17, 1786, for the *Atrocious Crime of Burglary Together* with his *Dying Words*. (Broadside in the Library of the American Antiquarian Society, Worcester, Mass.).

thieves, Green profited little from his burglaries. When asked what became of the goods he had stolen, he answered: " some . . . I have used myself—some I have sold—some have been taken from me—some I have hid where I could not find them again, and others I have given to lewd women who induced me to steal for their maintenance." He died, exhorting others to eschew his evil ways.[53]

Negroes, like whites, were accused of witchcraft during the celebrated witches' purge that swept over Salem in the late seventeenth century. On July 2, 1692, Candy, the Negro slave of " Marguerett " Hawks of Salem, was arrested, charged with having " wickedly malliciously and felloniously " practiced her arts of sorcery upon one Ann Putnam of the same town.[54] Because of Candy's witchery, the said Ann was alleged to have been " afflicted, consumed, wasted, pined and tormented." [55] During the trial the terror-stricken Candy is said to have accused her mistress, who, equally terrified, confessed in order to save herself.[56] The jury in the slave's case, however, returned a verdict of " not guilty ", and Candy was acquitted.[57] A few months before, Mary Black, the slave of Nathaniel Putnam of Salem, along with Edmund Bishop and his wife, were imprisoned on similar charges.[58] Mary's examination on April 22 illustrates the flimsy evidence and crowd hysteria that was general during the witchcraft trials and which sent several innocent persons to their death. Mary stoutly denied that she was a witch or that she had ever harmed anyone.[59] During her trial her inquisitor asked the spectators whether Mary hurt them, and several replied in the affirmative. Asked why she did so, the

53 Ibid.

54 Mass. Archives, CXXXV, 30, Document 31.

55 Ibid.

56 Felt, Annals of Salem, II, 476.

57 Mass. Archives, CXXXV, p. 30, Document 31 (Reverse).

58 Felt, ut supra; cf. Charles Osgood and H. M. Batchelder, Historical Sketch of Salem (Salem, 1879), p. 26.

59 Mass. Archives, CXXXV, 18. Document 20.

slave denied that she harmed anyone. Mary was wearing a neck cloth which was fastened with a pin. She was ordered to remove the pin and fasten the neck cloth again. As she did so several persons cried out that they had been pricked: [60] " Mary Walcott was pricked in the arm " until it bled; "Abigail Williams was pricked in the stomack and Mary Lewis was prick't in the foot." Because of the hysterics of these women, Mary was committed to jail,[61] but her ultimate fate is unknown.

Negroes were frequently guilty of incendiarism. Some of these acts were probably accidents, but many of them seem to have been deliberately perpetrated by slaves, apparently as a protest against their enslavement. Negroes set fire to ships, warehouses, and other buildings, but their main attention apparently was centered upon the homes of their masters. In 1681 Maria, the slave of Joshua Lamb of Roxbury, and Jack, belonging to Samuel Wolcott of Weathersfield, Massachusetts, were convicted of setting fire to the homes of their respective masters. The sentences meted out to them were barbaric: Maria was sentenced to be burned to death; Jack was to be hanged, then burned " to ashes " in the same fire with her.[62] James Pemberton, another Negro convicted of being an accomplice of Maria, was sentenced to banishment " out of the country." [63] Several years later, a Negro girl attempted to blow up the house of her Boston master, William Thomas, by dropping a live coal in a cask of gunpowder. The resulting blast shattered the house

---

60 *Ibid.*

61 *Ibid.*

62 *R. C. A., 1630-1692*, I, 198, 199; *cf. Colonial Society of Massachusetts, Transactions, 1899-1900* (Boston, 1904), VI, 324-326. Although the Mosaic Code which formed the basis of the Massachusetts legal system in the seventeenth century, demanded " a burning for a burning," it is doubtful whether white persons accused of the same offense would have been so punished. *Col. Laws of Mass.* (1672), Reprint, p. 52. According to Cotton Mather, " Burning for Burning was required by the Word of the glorious God Fulfilled by His hand." " Diary," *loc. cit.*, Seventh Series, VIII, Part II, 686 n.

63 *R. C. A., 1630-1692*, I, 197, 198.

and seriously injured the girl. No one else was hurt.[64] In 1738 a group of Boston Negroes accidentally set fire to a warehouse during a night frolic. Seeing the building ablaze, they threw away their food and fled. Only by dint of hard work were the flames prevented from destroying an entire row of warehouses.[65] Much more disastrous was the burning of a brig commanded by Captain Malbone, near Newport in 1767. As the craft, heavily laden with rum and other Jamaica products, neared Newport, a Negro boy, mistaking a rum hogshead for a water keg, accidentally set fire to the ship when a lighted candle he was carrying came in contact with a bucket of rum. In the resulting conflagration five persons were burned to death and the ship and its entire cargo to the value of £6000 sterling was destroyed.[66]

In addition to arson, Negroes wreaked vengeance upon their masters in other ways. In one instance, a slave mutilated his master's son. The crime occurred in Middletown, Connecticut, where Barney, a Negro belonging to Jonathan Allyn of that town, emasculated the latter's son.[67] Barney was indicted for the offense before the Superior Court at Hartford, but, although he pleaded guilty, the Court could not sentence him, for there existed no law covering such a crime. The Court then appealed to the Legislature for advice as to what punishment should be meted out to the Negro.[68] Equally dismayed, the Legislature (since it could not pass an ex-post facto law) [69] vaguely admonished the Court to " proceed and cause such punishment to be inflicted on . . . Barney according to their best

64 *Boston Weekly Post Boy,* June 26, 1749.

65 *New England Weekly Journal,* January 17, 1738.

66 *New Hampshire Gazette and Historical Chronicle,* September 4, 11, 25, 1767.

67 *Conn. Archives.*: *Crimes and Misdemeanors, 1737-1755,* IV, 67.

68 *Ibid.*

69 Samuel Peters, *A General History of Connecticut* (London, 1781), 83-88.

skill and judgment." [70] The Court, thereupon, is said to have invoked the Jewish law of an " eye for an eye and tooth for a tooth." The Negro is reported to have suffered accordingly.[71]

Slaves also attempted or actually committed murder. Not infrequently these crimes were directed against the master or members of his family. For wounding his master with a knife and pointing a gun loaded with iron slugs at him, Nicholas, the slave of John Roy of Charlestown, was sentenced, in 1677-78, to be whipped with twenty-nine stripes, to pay Court costs and to be jailed until his master should sell him out of the country.[72] In the following year a general alarm was sent throughout Essex County for a Negro who had attempted to murder a white woman. The Negro had been imprisoned but had escaped " with a great chain about one of his legs." [73] In 1689, New Hampshire petitioned the Governor and Council of Massachusetts asking what disposition should be made of a Negro murderer being held in irons there.[74] For attempting to kill his mistress by putting " ratsbane " (an arsenic compound) in her milk, Caesar, belonging to Josiah Walcott of Salem, was sentenced in 1695 to be whipped with ten stripes and to pay costs of the Court;[75] on May 16, 1752, a young Boston Negro was executed for poisoning an infant and sixteen years later, a Negro of Sherburne, Massachusetts, applied to a doctor for some " ratsbane " to poison a white man who had struck him.[76] Slaves occasionally murdered one another. Edward Holyoke noted in

70 *Conn. Archives, ut. supra.*

71 Peters, *op. cit.,* p. 84.

72 *S. C. C. R., 1671-1680,* XXX, Part II, 884. The charges of Court as well as fines fell upon the master. He also had to bear the cost of maintaining his Negro while in jail. *Ibid.*

73 *E. C. C. R., 1678-1680,* VII, 421.

74 New Hampshire was at that time a part of the Dominion of New England. *Provincial Papers of New Hampshire, 1686-1727* (Manchester, 1868), II, Part I, 40.

75 Felt, *op. cit.,* II, 460.

76 *Boston Chronicle,* June 6, 1768.

his diary for March 34, 1747, that Will, a mulatto, shot and instantly killed a Negro named Cato, belonging to John Denny of Boston.[77] In 1772 three Negroes were arrested in Newport for the alleged poisoning of a Negro slave woman.[78]

Sex crimes were numerous in colonial New England, and Negroes as well as whites were often severely punished for their commission. Rape was common among both blacks and whites. Two outstanding cases, which occurred in Boston in 1674, not only illustrate this point but also reveal the practical evolution of criminal law in colonial New England. At the April term of the Court of Assistants, Patrick Jennison, white, was convicted of criminally assaulting an eight-year-old girl.[79] Although rape was a capital crime, the Court was unable to sentence him because the law applied only to girls ten years of age and over. The question of Jennison's punishment, therefore, was referred to the deputies.[80]

In the meantime, following this case, the law was evidently revised for six months later, Basto, a slave belonging to Robert Cox, of Boston, was sentenced to be hanged for raping the three-year-old daughter of his master.[81] Three years later, John, a Boston Negro, accused of pulling one Sarah Phillips off her horse and attempting to assault her, was sentenced to be whipped severely with thirty-nine lashes and to be sold out of the country.[82] For attempted rape upon the wife of John Rice, another Boston Negro named Bristol was sentenced (on April 7, 1721) to be severely whipped with thirty-nine stripes on two succeeding Thursdays. Bristol's master interceded for him, however, and petitioned the legislature for mitigation of the

77 *Diary of Edward Augustus Holyoke, 1709-1756*, edited by George Francis Dow (Salem, 1911), p. 42.

78 *Newport Mercury*, Monday, Dec. 7, 1742.

79 *R. C. A., 1630-1692*, I, 199.

80 *Ibid.*

81 *Ibid.,* p. 74.

82 He was also to pay five pounds to his intended victim and costs of Court as well. ' S. C. C. R.", *loc. cit.*, XXX, 1067.

slave's sentence, claiming he had already beaten Bristol more severely than the Court had ordered. He further stated that he intended to sell the Negro out of the province and feared that the sentence, if executed, would not only render Bristol more incorrigible, but would make him less salable, and this would be to the master's great disadvantage.[83] At Hartford, a Negro belonging to a New York master, criminally assaulted the wife of Ephraim Andrews of New Hartford. Andrews petitioned the Legislature for damages to the sum of £415 but that body, on October 1, 1743, awarded the wife only £30 in colonial currency.[84] Cuff, a New Haven Negro sentenced to death for raping a white woman, petitioned the Assembly on May 14, 1749, to change his sentence to anything but death.[85] A Negro convicted of rape was sentenced to death at Worcester, Massachusetts, in 1768, while a white man for attempting the same crime was sentenced to sit on the gallows.[86]

The most unusual case, however, was that of the Negro Arthur, who was executed at Worcester, on October 20, 1768, for criminally assaulting Deborah Metcalf, a white woman.[87] Arthur (if his confession taken down in prison two days before his execution can be believed) was a notorious criminal whose malefactions would make good material for a novelist. Like the aforementioned Johnson Green, his crime career began early. At the age of fourteen, although kindly treated by his master, Richard Godfrey, of Taunton, Massachusetts, he was " so un-

83 *Mass. Archives: Domestic Relations, 1643-1774*, IX, 178-179.

84 *Connecticut Archives: Crimes and Misdemeanors, 1737-1755*, IV, 71, 73.

85 The outcome is unknown. *Ibid.*, pp. 118, 119.

86 *Boston Chronicle,* Oct: 3, 10, 24, 1768. Sitting on the gallows, sometimes with a rope around the neck, was a frequent punishment for attempted crimes or other offenses. For other cases of rape, *vide* Daniel Wadsworth, *Diary of the Rev. Daniel Wadsworth,* edited by George Leon Walker (Hartford, 1899), pp. 196, 120, 121.

87 *The Life and Dying Speech of Arthur, a Negro Man Who Was Executed at Worcester, Oct. 20, 1768, For a Rape Committed on the body of one Deborah Metcalf.* (Broadside in Library of American Antiquarian Society, Worcester, Massachusetts).

happy " in his bondage that he ran away. Then followed a life of theft, drunkenness and licentiousness. He shipped on a whaler from Nantucket, but returned to rob a store, and to escape from prison after having been arrested and confined. After spending three years at sea, Arthur came back and committed so many offenses that his master determined to get rid of him. Sold to different masters in Massachusetts, he continued to lead a life of debauchery and crime among white, Indian, and Negro women. On one occasion he assaulted a white woman whom he met at a corn-husking at Little Cambridge, Massachusetts. Pursued to Boston by the enraged husband, Arthur engaged in a fight with him and coming off the victor, set out for Cambridge, committing a series of burglaries en route. His master, hearing of his plight, arranged to place him aboard a vessel bound for Maryland. But when the vessel did not arrive at the stated time, Arthur set forth upon new depredations, which finally ended with his raping Deborah Metcalf, a white widow. Mrs. Metcalf informed Arthur's master of the crime, but offered to settle the matter for a cash consideration, provided he would sell Arthur out of the country. To this arrangement the master agreed but, on the way to Albany, they met the sheriff with a warrant for the Negro. Arthur escaped by stealing the sheriff's horse.[88] On the following day he was arrested and jailed in Worcester, but again escaped and continued his robberies until his capture on September 17, 1763. At Worcester he was tried and found guilty of rape, but prayed for " benefit of clergy " which, after a year's consideration, was denied him. On October 20, 1764, Arthur, at the age of twenty-one was hanged, thus bringing to an end a crime career that stopped short only of murder. He apparently expressed the hope that his fate would prove a warning to all persons, and died, admonishing the slaves " to avoid desertion from their masters, drunkenness and lewdness."[89]

88 *Ibid.*

89 *Ibid.*

In addition to sex crimes Negroes, by occasional plots to win their freedom by force, kept the colonists fearful of general insurrections. With a hostile Indian population, the New Englanders, like the other settlers, were apprehensive lest these two exploited groups combine to gain their liberty. Reports of slave uprisings in the West Indies and the other colonies, especially those in nearby New York,[90] served to increase this tension.

Insurrections, or rumors of them, began early. In 1663, Elinor Howell, of Hartford, asked the General Court of Connecticut for damages of £100 because of an uprising by Negroes and Indians six years earlier, during which her house and many others had been destroyed. The Court awarded her £12.[91] In 1690, citizens of Newbury, Massachusetts, became panic-stricken over the arrest of Isaac Morrill, who was charged with inciting an insurrection among the Negroes and Indians. Morrill, a native of New Jersey, was reported to have encouraged Negro and Indian slaves to leave their masters and to join him, promising them " that the English would be cut off " and the Negroes would be freed. Morrill, however, was arrested and sent to Ipswich for trial. There he confessed his intention to seize a vessel at Newbury and escape to Canada. From that point he planned to lead a detachment of French and Indians in an attack upon the frontier in which he would " save none but the Indians and Negroes." Among those implicated in the plot were James, the Negro slave of Robert Dole, and Joseph, the Indian slave of a Mr. Moody, both of Newbury.[92] Although the number of Negroes in Newbury could not have been large in 1680, any rumor or suggestion of intrigue between the Negroes and Indians was almost certain to cause a wave of excitement and fear. In 1738

90 The most serious of these alarms in New York occurred in 1741. *Vide* Daniel Horsemanden, Esq., *The New York Conspiracy or a History of the Negro Plot* (New York, 1810).

91 " Wyllys Papers," *Conn. Hist. Soc. Colls.* (Hartford, 1924), XXI, 137-138. The Indians for their share in the revolt, were fined £800. *Ibid.*

92 Joshua Coffin, *A Sketch of the History of Newbury and Newburyport, Massachusetts* (Boston, 1845), pp. 153-154.

a panic was precipitated in Nantucket upon the disclosure of a supposedly formidable plot by Indians to destroy the town. The Indians, according to one of their number, planned to burn the town at night, destroying only the English.[93] Investigation, however, revealed that the plot was nothing more than a false rumor, which had been circulated by a drunken Indian woman.[94] Three years later a conspiracy by Negroes to burn Charlestown, Massachusetts, was brought to light. The principals were a Negro boatswain, belonging to John Garnier, and Kate, the slave of Francis Varambaut. They first set fire to the house of a Mrs. Snowden " with a malicious and evil intent of burning down the town." [95] Kate was arrested and convicted of the crime on the testimony of an old Negro woman, who happened to be alone in the house when the act was committed. For a long time, Kate steadfastly maintained that she had had no accomplices but being condemned to death and promised a pardon if she would divulge the names of those implicated with her, she accused the boatswain. After much prevarication during which he accused several Negroes, the boatswain finally confessed that he and Kate alone were to blame. Sentenced to death, he made no further confession but died, it was said, " like an impudent hardened wretch." Slavery had so hardened the boatswain against white persons that he is said to have " looked upon every white man as his declared enemy." [96] Boston was terrorized in 1723 by a series of fires " purposely set by ye Negroes " which caused such great fear that the Reverend Joseph Sewall preached a special sermon and emergency laws were passed severely punishing all Negroes caught in the vicinity of a fire.[97]

93 *New England Weekly Journal,* October 10, 1738.

94 *Ibid.,* October 17, 1738.

95 *Boston Gazette,* September 28; October 5, 1741.

96 *Ibid.*

97 Extra watch and the militia were called to keep slaves in order when a fire broke out. Later the town decreed all Indian, Negro and mulatto servants or slaves must remain indoors during fires. Joshua Coffin, *An Account of Some of the Principal Slave Insurrections* (New York, 1860), p. 12.

During the troubles with Great Britain, wild rumors of Negro insurrections were current. Reports were circulated by some persons that the British soldiers were actually inciting the slaves to revolt against their masters. Such a rumor alarmed New London, Connecticut, in 1768, when " a person of probity " was reported to have heard three British officers remark that " if the Negroes were made freemen, they should be sufficient to subdue those damn'd Rascals [the colonists]." A writer in the *New London Gazette,* ironically commented that this action and " others of a like nature " were but specimens of Lord Hillsborough's lenient and persuasive methods " to bring back his Majesty's misled subjects to a sense of their duty." [98] Whether the rumor was true or merely radical propaganda to inflame the people against Great Britain cannot be ascertained, but it did serve to heighten the general fear of a slave revolt. In January 1768, when Bostonians were reading of slave insurrections in Virginia of the previous Fall in which several whites had been killed,[99] rumors spread of a Negro uprising in Boston, instigated by a British officer, Captain Wilson. Apprised of these reports, the selectmen of the town, including John Hancock, Joshua Henshaw, and Samuel Pemberton, lodged a formal complaint against Wilson with the justices of the peace of Suffolk County. They specifically charged that on the night of October 28 Wilson, a captain of the Fifty-ninth regiment of Foot, had " in the sight and hearing of divers persons," uttered many abusive epithets about the townspeople. He was further accused of inciting the slaves to rise up and " cut their masters' throats," promising the Negroes their freedom and some of their masters' property if they did so. Wilson, who, it was alleged, pictured the British soldiers as the deliverers of the blacks from slavery, is also reported to have told them, " now that the soldiers are come the Negroes shall be free " and the " Liberty Boys, their oppressors, shall be slaves." The complainants demanded that

98 *New London Gazette,* December 2, 1768.

99 *Boston Chronicle,* January 18, 1768.

Wilson be arrested and dealt with according to the law. So panic-stricken did the people become over a possible uprising of the slaves, that regulations governing Negroes were rigidly enforced, and the town watch was ordered to arrest all Negroes absent from their masters' house at unseasonable hours of the night.[100] Wilson was arrested and bound for trial but, owing to a maneuver by the Attorney General, the indictment was quashed. Shortly afterwards, Wilson left the province.[101]

Four years later a mulatto, George Stewart, was convicted of having participated in a riot at Gloucester, Massachusetts, and was sentenced to sit for an hour on the gallows at Salem, with a rope around his neck and then to be whipped with twenty stripes.[102] Abigail Adams, the wife of John Adams, reports another conspiracy that was discovered in Boston in September, 1774. The details, she wrote her husband, were kept secret, adding " What steps they will take in consequence of it I know not." Mrs. Adams, who had never owned a Negro, closed by saying she wished sincerely " there was not a slave in the province." [103] In 1775 reports of another threatening Negro uprising came from Framingham, Massachusetts. According to Temple, when the Minutemen marched to Lexington at the outbreak of the American Revolution, a rumor was started among the people of Framingham that the " Negroes were coming to massacre them all." Fearful of the slaves' vengeance, and still nursing memories of Indian atrocities, the women, left alone, are said to have " brought axes, pitchforks, and clubs, into the house, and securely bolted doors and passed the day and night in anxious suspense." [104] But the uprising never came for the Negroes of Framingham were loyal to the colonists.[105] As the

100 *Ibid.*

101 Moore, *op. cit.,* p. 129; Drake, *op. cit.,* I, 754.

102 Felt, *op. cit.,* p. 462.

103 *Letters of Mrs. Adams,* edited by Charles Francis Adams (Boston, 1841), II, 24.

104 Temple, *History of Framingham,* p. 275.

105 *Ibid.*

Revolution progressed, the patriots tried to intensify feeling against the British by reminding the people of their attempts to persuade the slaves to revolt and kill their masters. In a series of thirty-six items entitled " *Remember,*" addressed to the American people, in a Connecticut newspaper on April 5, 1776 was the following exhortation: " Remember the bribing of negro slaves to assassinate their masters." [106]

While these actual or rumored insurrections compared neither in violence nor in hysteria with Negro uprising in the West Indies and plantation colonies, or even in nearby New York, they served to show the restiveness of the Negro under bondage, his continued efforts to gain his freedom, and the fear engendered in the master class because of the terrible vengeance that their bondmen might wreak upon them. They were further indicative of the fact that, however mild the system of slavery, the Negro, like the whites and Indians, constantly yearned for and even took violent means to gain his liberty.

While Negroes committed crimes against the master class, the latter were also guilty of offenses against the slaves. An incomplete list of crimes against Negroes would include abduction, selling of free Negroes into slavery, false accusation, adultery,[107] rape and mutilation. In May, 1695 Abraham Samuels of Boston was placed under bond of one hundred pounds for his appearance on the first Tuesday of July at the Inferior Court of Common Pleas. He was specifically charged with having kidnaped, in the previous year, a Negro belonging to John Papine, of St. Christopher.[108] In 1725 John Moffat of Kittery, Massachusetts, commander of a fishing vessel, was convicted of abducting a Negro belonging to Richard Treavitt of Marblehead and carrying him on a voyage to Portugal, without the permission of his master.[109] In defense Moffat denied any knowledge

106 *Connecticut Courant,* Friday, April 5, 1776.

107 *Vide infra,* pp. 206-207.

108 *Mass. Archives,* IX, 137.

109 *Ibid.: Domestic Relations,* pp. 182-184; 187-195.

of the slave's presence aboard the ship until the second day out, when the Negro was found hiding under wood in the forecastle. Before sailing, he added, his ship had been carefully searched for stowaways, both by townspeople and by his crew, including himself. Moffat also claimed that he would have returned the Negro to Plymouth, whence he had started, but the wind being fair he could not turn back. Efforts to induce other captains to return the Negro from Oporto also failed because they sailed before he was aware of their departure. Asked why he had not returned the slave to his master upon arriving at Lynn, Moffat replied that as soon as the ship docked the Negro deserted, otherwise he would have placed him in jail. As Moffat was undoubtedly guilty, the Court fined him £50 which was awarded to Treavitt.[110]

In other cases unscrupulous persons sold free Negroes into slavery. In 1772 Nathan Simmons of Haverhill, Massachusetts, sold two free Negro children and their Indian mother to Jonathan Chadwick of the same town. The mother, Priscilla, who was married to a Negro named Jupiter, sued Chadwick for her freedom. The case was tried at Newbury where the Court decided that the sale was illegal.[111]

Sex crimes against Negroes, as will be shown later, were numerous.[112] There is reported at least one instance of the mutilation of a Negro by a white person. In 1718, according to the *Boston News Letter,* a white man discovering a Negro and a white woman on a road near New London, Connecticut, whipped out a knife and emasculated him. This punishment, according to the report, should serve as a warning " for all Negroes—meddling for the future, with any white women, lest they fare with the like treatment." [113]

110 *Ibid.*

111 Chadwick appealed. *Essex Institute Historical Collections* (Salem, 1865), VII, 73.

112 *Vide infra,* p. 203 ff.

113 March 3, 1718.

Sometimes Negroes were deliberately accused of crimes that they had not committed. In colonial times, as at present, a Negro might be falsely charged by a white woman with rape, a grave offense, punishable by death. In 1757 Hannah Beebe of Lyme, Connecticut, accused Bristo, a Negro belonging to the Reverend George Beckwith, of having assaulted her. On this charge, Bristo was tried before the New London Court, found guilty, and sentenced to death. Later Hannah, conscience-stricken, told Justice Ely that her mother had sworn falsely in testifying that the marks on her body were the result of the Negro's attack upon her. Hannah also confessed that one Thomas Lazier had persuaded her to accuse Bristo, although she knew that the slave was innocent. The testimony of witnesses brought out further details of the case. It developed that Hannah's father and mother had instigated the false charge against Bristo, in the hope of extorting money from Beckwith. Two witnesses testified to this effect, one Sarah Sandus even charging that Hannah had told her that the minister would give her £700-800 to save Bristo. Another witness swore that Hannah also hoped to receive money from the Court as balm for her damaged character. Supporting this testimony was William Brockway, who testified that the girl's father, within the hearing of Brockway's wife, had asked whether the Court would not grant his daughter a considerable sum of money in the event Bristo was convicted. To this Brockway replied that, if it did not, the Court " would not do her justice." With this array of evidence Beckwith on January 20, 1757, petitioned the General Assembly for the release of his slave and Governor Thomas Fitch, convinced that the Negro had been the victim of a vicious plot, ordered the sentence suspended. The Assembly later ordered him set free, but the records do not show what punishment, if any, was imposed on Hannah and her parents.[114]

114 *Connecticut Archives: Misdemeanors and Crimes, 1756-1773*, pp. 47-53.

# CHAPTER VII
## THE SLAVE BEFORE THE LAW

THE Negro slaves of New England occupied a dual status: they were considered both as property and as persons before the law. The lines were not rigidly drawn between these two categories, however, largely because of the peculiar religio-social philosophy of the Puritans regarding slavery. Migrating to America with the avowed purpose of founding a Bible Commonwealth in the New World, seventeenth century New Englanders modelled many of their institutions on the pattern outlined in the Old Testament.[1] Especially was this true in regard to slavery. In the law legalizing slavery in 1641, the Massachusetts legislature expressly stated that the slave should " have all the liberties and Christian usages which the law of God established in Israel doth morally require." [2]

The law, in practice, went far toward bettering the legal position of the New England slave. The slavery of the Old Testament was patriarchal, with two recognizable classes of bondmen. One group of slaves, Jews, commonly referred to as " servants," were to serve their masters for six years, after which they were to go free, unless they voluntarily chose to remain with their masters.[3] The Jewish slave was in reality " a poor brother," who had lost his liberty but not his civil rights.[4] In essence the Jewish slave was part of the master's family.[5]

1 A splendid example of this is the code of laws prepared by Nathaniel Ward. *Vide Colonial Laws of Massachusetts* (Reprinted from Edition of 1672), pp. 14-16; *Conn. Acts and Laws*, pp. 12-13.

2 *Colonial Laws of Mass.*, p. 53.

3 Ex. 21:2-6; Isaac Mendelsohn, *Legal Aspects of Slavery in Babylonia, Assyria, and Palestine, 3000-500 B. C.* (Williamsport, Pa., 1932), p. 49; Salo Baron, *A Social and Religious History of the Jews*, 3 vols. (New York, 1937), I, 59, *cf.* Cobb (*Law of Slavery*, p. xxxix) who says that the Jewish slave was freed at the end of the seventh year.

4 Cobb, *op. cit.*, p. xxxix, says the Jewish slave might acquire property. Paul's servant Tiba is said to have owned twenty slaves. *Ibid.*

5 Mendelsohn, *op. cit.*, p. 49.

The second class of slaves were non-Jewish—Gentiles or
"strangers"—who were sold to the Jews. These were "bondservants" or slaves for life.[6] Although their lot was more difficult, bondservants were protected by the Mosaic Law from extreme mistreatment. Should their yoke become unbearable, they
might run away, and later legislation even forbade the return
of the fugitive to his master.[7] The bondmen were considered
members of the master's family and were to be "brought to
God" by their owners.[8]

Neither of these forms of bondage was adopted without
change by the Puritans. They apparently developed a slave system under which the status of bondman was something between
that of the Jewish "servant" and the Gentile "slave." As such
the Negro was considered a part of the Puritan family[9] and,
in keeping with the custom of the Hebraic family, was usually
referred to as *servant,* rarely as "slave."[10] In accordance with
the Jewish conception of slavery, especially in the seventeenth
century, many slaves were freed after six years of faithful
service.[11]

The net result was to make New England slavery a curious
blending of servitude and bondage. Under this system the slave
assumed a more or less indeterminate status, varying between
that of person and that of property. At times this arrangement
proved embarrassing for the master and advantageous for the
slave, for many Negroes took advantage of the looseness of
their legal bonds to appeal to the Courts for their freedom.[12]

6 *Ibid.,* p. 7.

7 Baron, *op. cit.,* I, 59.

8 Even the bondservants or "strangers" bought by the Jewish masters
were to be circumcized. Lev. 17:10, 11, 12, 13, 27.

9 *Vide infra,* pp. 191, 219, 276 ff.

10 *Early Records of Providence,* IV, 71-72; IX, 153; *Mass. Archives,*
IX, 154, 154a; *Vide infra,* ch. viii.

11 *Vide infra,* p. 291.

12 *Vide infra,* p. 182 ff.

Evidence of the indefinite status of the New England slaves may be seen in an analysis of the Negroes as property and as persons.

In several respects slaves in New England were considered personal property. As such, they were assessed as taxable estate like other goods and chattels. For a time in Massachusetts, however, slaves—both Negro and Indian—were regarded alternately as polls and as personalty. At first Negro slaves, if taxed at all, seem to have been rated as polls. In the law of 1646, when a tax of 1s 8d was levied upon all male persons above sixteen years of age, servants and children " as take not wages " were to be paid for by their masters.[13] By 1675 slaves had evidently come to be rated as property in Massachusetts, for in the taxable estate of Paul White of Newbury was a Negro, assessable at 3s 4d.[14] With the exception of the assessment of 1694, slaves continued to be regarded as personal estate.[15] Two years earlier Massachusetts had given recognition to this status when in raising taxes for the purpose of strengthening the defenses of Boston harbor, Negro, Indian, and mulatto slaves were placed in the same category as horses, sheep and swine.[16] Cows and horses, four years old and over, were assessed at thirty shillings, and able-bodied " Negro mulatto and Indian servants, fourteen years old and over," were assessed at the rate of twenty pounds estate for males, and fourteen pounds estate for females.[17]

13 *Colonial Laws of Massachusetts.* Reprinted from Edition of 1672. (Boston, 1887), p. 24. An interesting feature of this poll tax was its being levied according to ability to pay. Butchers, bakers, other skilled laborers and "artists" were assessed higher rates than workingmen and laborers. *Ibid.*, pp. 23-24.

14 *E. C. C. R., 1675-1678*, VI, 225; *cf.* Moore, *Notes*, p. 62; "Social and Industrial Condition of the Negro in Massachusetts," *Thirty Fourth Annual Report of the Bureau of Statistics and Labor* (Boston, 1904), p. 222.

15 In 1694 all Indian, Negro and mulatto slaves and servants, male as well as female, above sixteen years were to be assessed at 12s. per poll. *Mass. Acts and Laws, 1692-1714*, I, 167.

16 *Mass. A. and R., 1692-1714*, I, 213, 214.

17 *Ibid.*, p. 214.

Slaves were similarly assessable in later years. In 1696, the assessors of the various towns of Massachusetts, upon receiving warrants requiring them to levy certain specified rates on all taxable polls, were specifically instructed to appraise "all Indian, mulatto and Negro servants as other personal estate." [18] Later in the same year and in 1697, like instructions were issued.[19] In 1698 came two other acts specifically classifying slaves as property. One provided not only that all Negro, Indian, and mulatto slaves be reckoned as other personal estate, but that their value be determined "according to the sound judgment and discretion of the assessors." In addition, the legislature levied a tax of one penny in the pound on all slaves above the age of fourteen.[20]

Similar instructions were issued in succeeding years [21] but the directions given to the assessors by a Massachusetts law of 1707 made a sweeping distinction between Negro, Indian and mulatto slaves, and servants of the same races. All slaves were to be taxed as other personal estate at one shilling in the pound; each male slave over fourteen years to be valued at £20; each female slave over fourteen years at £15. But all Negro, mulatto and Indian male servants were to be appraised as polls, not as personal estate.[22]

In the other New England colonies, however, slaves seem to have been classified regularly as personalty. On May 10, 1727 a committee submitted to the New Hampshire House of Representatives a plan for reapportioning taxes among the several towns and parishes of the province. Polls sixteen years and upwards were to be assessed at 100 pence; [23] slaves between the

18 *Ibid.*, p. 240.

19 *Ibid.*, pp. 278, 302.

20 *Ibid.*, pp. 337, 359, 386.

21 *Ibid.*, pp. 483, 495, 551, 610, 710.

22 Allowances were to be made for the age or infirmity of the slave. *Mass. Acts and Laws, 1692-1714*, I, 615.

23 *Provincial Papers of New Hampshire, 1722-1737* (Manchester, 1870); hereinafter cited as *N.H.P.Ps.*

ages of sixteen and forty years of age were to be taxed *ad valorem*. Here, as in Massachusetts, Negro and Indian slaves were classed with domestic animals, for oxen and horses were assessed at £4; cows at £2 :10. Sheep, however, were untaxed in order to encourage the production of wool.[24]

Because of complaints that both real and personal property had been assessed unfairly throughout the province, the Assembly on June 1, 1728, passed a new tax bill by which assessments on horses, oxen and cows were reduced, and an average valuation of £20 per head was placed on every male Negro, Indian and mulatto slave.[25] The revised valuation of domestic animals, Indian and Negro slaves read:[26]

Each ox .......................................... £3 : — : —
Each cow ......................................... £2 : — : —
Each horse ....................................... £3 : — : —
Each hog ......................................... £ : 10 : —
Each Negro Mulatto and Indian Slave being male .. £20: — : —

Negro and Indian males were thus given an assessed valuation of more than six times that of an ox or a horse, and ten times that of a cow.

It was this inclusion of Negroes and Indians in the tax lists along with domestic animals that moved humanitarians like Judge Samuel Sewall and the Reverend John Eliot[27] to protest against slavery, and led Sewall at the time when Massachusetts was contemplating a revision of its tax list in 1706, to attempt, albeit vainly, " to prevent Indians and Negroes being rated with horses and hogs." [28] Negroes continued to be included in this category until slavery was abolished; and in New Hampshire all " Indian, Negro and mulatto slaves " and servants of both

24 *Ibid.*

25 *Ibid.*, 304-305.

26 *Ibid.*

27 " Diary of Samuel Sewall," *Mass. Hist. Soc. Colls.*, Fifth Series, VII. 87; Cotton Mather, *Life of John Eliot*, pp. 101-102; " Diary of Cotton Mather," *Mass. Hist. Soc. Colls.*, Seventh Series, VIII, Part II, pp. 384, 769.

28 *Diary, ut supra.*

sexes were in 1753 returned as rateable property.[29] In 1761 Rhode Island slaves were included in this category along with houses, wharves, factories, windmills, and money at interest.[30] As late as February, 1780 " male negro & mulatto slaves from 16 to 45 years of age " in New Hampshire were taxed at ten shillings each and female slaves between the same ages at " 5 shillings each." [31] This practice only ended with the abolition of slavery; in fact, it was not until five years after the emancipation of the slaves in New Hampshire that the legislature finally abolished the practice of considering Negroes as personalty.[32] Moreover, it was as personal property that Negroes were bought, sold and transferred and formal bills of sale were generally executed to effect transfer of title to the slave.[33]

As property, moreover, slaves could be seized or sold to satisfy legal claims brought against either themselves or against their masters. For example, a case of seizure occurred in Salem, Massachusetts in 1670. On October 26 of that year, Will Hollingsworth secured a writ of attachment against Michael Powell, Jr., claiming that Powell had failed to return certain goods and money placed in his custody. Upon serving the warrant Edward Grove, constable of Salem, attached Powell's Negro boy, " Seasar," as the " proper goods of the said Powell." [34] Another case involved Dr. Zabdiel Boyleston of Boston. Boyleston had

---

29 *N.H.P.Ps.* (Manchester 1872), VI, 175.

30 *Itineraries of Ezra Stiles*, ed. Franklin B. Dexter (New Haven, 1916), p. 23.

31 *N.H.P.Ps.*, VIII, 849.

32 *Ibid.*, IX, 897. Indian slavery having been abolished, Indians were no longer characterized as personal property. *Ibid.*

33 *Vide supra*, ch. 1; It has been said that in Massachusetts no bill of sale or deed was needed to acquire property in a Negro, that the slave might pass from one person to another like any other chattel, upon delivery. Moore, *op. cit.*, p. 26 n., citing *Mass. Reports*, XVI, 110. This opinion, however, cannot rest upon facts, for the records show that the bill of sale was the accepted manner of acquiring property in a slave. *Vide supra*, p. 45 ff.

34 *E.C.C.R., 1667-1671*, IV, 233.

treated Mary Lyon, a white woman, who had been seriously wounded by a Negro. When he was unable to collect from the woman for his services, Boyleston, in 1706, petitioned the legislature to sell the Negro and give him the proceeds up to £56.6s. The Negro had been sentenced to be whipped, but Boyleston insisted that he be sold. In response, the legislature appointed a committee to consider the matter,[35] but the result of their deliberations is not known. In 1672, when John Keene and his wife Hannah sued Thomas Blighe of Boston for the return of their Negro boy whom Blighe had detained, the jury found for Keene. Blighe was ordered not only to return the Negro but to pay £30 damages as well.[36]

More significant was a similar case that occurred in Providence, Rhode Island. Here a slave named Cuff, belonging to Thomas Borden of Portsmouth, Rhode Island, was convicted of trespass against Comfort Taylor, a widow of Little Compton, Massachusetts. At a court of equity held at Providence on the second Tuesday in October, 1743, the plaintiff was awarded a judgment of £200 and costs against Cuff. But Comfort, realizing that the slave could not discharge the judgment, and also recognizing that in the event of Cuff's imprisonment she would lose the damages awarded by the Court, petitioned the General Assembly to empower the sheriff to sell the Negro. While admitting some doubt as to the right of the sheriff so to dispose of Cuff, Comfort contended that the sheriff " ought to have power to do so, because the Negro is not free, but a private property." The plaintiff, therefore, prayed that the sheriff " be empowered to sell him as other personal estate, taken by execution, to satisfy debts." Swayed by Comfort's plea, the Assembly granted the petition and voted that " the sheriff of the said

35 *Mass. Archives: Domestic Relations, 1643-1774*, IX, 161. The records do not give the name of the Negro or his master. *Ibid.*

36 *S.C.C.R., 1671-1680*, XXIX, Part I, 159.

county of Newport . . . be and he is hereby fully empowered to sell said negro Cuff as other personal estate." [37]

Slaves were reckoned as property in legal documents also. In wills and inventories of estates, Negroes were listed in the same manner as bedsteads, china ware, guns, money, and horses. In his will of 1653 Captain Keayne of Chelsea, Massachusetts mentioned " a Negro maide and a Scott " who were inventoried with his country estate, along with two Negroes and a " child negro " at Boston.[38] The inventory of the property of Theodore Price, which was assessed at £240 in 1672, included a Negro rated at £10.[39] Jonathan Whipple of Providence left a Negro boy valued at £47.[40] In addition to a library of 190 volumes and 349 pamphlets, the Reverend John Williams, of Deerfield, Massachusetts, left aprons, spoons, six cows, including a " weak backed " cow . . . " the mulatto boy Meseek and the black boy Kedar," appraised at £80 apiece.[41] Among the worldly goods left by John Stoughton of Boston were " a stone house, 5 bbl. [barrels] of stinking beife, 3 pairs of linen drawers, one Negro man named John & one Negro boy named Peter." [42] In his will of March 11, 1762, Robert Hazard of Newport disposed of six Negroes as follows:

> I give to my beloved wife *Sarah,* my mulatto woman called Lydia, also four cows, . . ." . . . also the use of my mulatto man Newport . . . to my daughter Sarah . . . two feather beds . . . one bay mare . . . also my negro woman Bell or Isabel; . . . to my son *Jonathan,* my mulatto man Newport,

---

37 Comfort evidently received little for her efforts, for the Assembly voted that after the " fine of £20 be paid into the general treasury, and all other charges deducted out of the price of [the] said negro," the remainder be applied to satisfying the judgment. *R.I.Col. Recs.,* V, 72-73.

38 Mellen Chamberlain, *Documentary History of Chelsea, 1624-1824* (2 vols.), I, 663.

39 *E. C. C. R., 1672-1674,* V, 65.

40 *Early Records of Providence: Will Book,* No. 2, XVI, 192.

41 Sheldon, *History of Deerfield,* I, 465-466.

42 *E. C. C. R., 1671-1680,* XXIX, Part I, 47.

. . . also mulatto boy *Dick* . . . .; to wife Sarah, negro child, Phillis . . . to daughter *Sarah,* negro child Phebe.[43]

Reckoned as movable goods, slaves escheated to the town, if the master died without heirs. Upon the death of John Mathewson, on September 18, 1716, his Negro slave woman passed to the town of Providence.[44] Four years later the former woman slave of one John Angell became the property of the town in the same manner.[45] Upon the death of the wealthy William Crawford of Providence, his widow, Sarah being adjudged incapable of managing his property,[46] his entire estate—valued at more than £3531—including three Negroes, appraised at £120—reverted to the town.[47] Ordinarily these Negroes were sold with other goods for the benefit of the community.

Not until the eve of open hostilities with Great Britain were Negroes, who thus became the town's property, given their freedom. In 1774 Jacob Shoemaker of Providence, dying intestate, left among other property six Negroes, four of whom were infants. The town, sensible of its own struggle for liberty, could not with consistency, it is said, sell these slaves again into bondage. In town meeting, therefore, it was voted " unbecoming to the character of freemen to enslave the said negroes." The town further agreed to " give up all claim of right or property . . . in the said negroes." The adult Negroes were to be placed under the care of the town council, and the children bound out to service.[48]

Like horses, carriages, or other personal property, slaves were often sold with the estate of the deceased. Notices of such sales frequently appeared in colonial newspapers and attracted no

43 Updike, *op. cit.*, I, 527-528.

44 The total estate was appraised at " £253—03—0." *Early Records of the Town of Providence: Will Book*, No. 2, XVI, 10-11.

45 July 27, 1720; *ibid.*, p. 163.

46 *Ibid.*, p. 156.

47 *Ibid.*, p. 154.

48 William R. Staples, *Annals of the Town of Providence* (Providence, 1843), pp. 236-237.

more attention at the time than do similar sales today of auto-
mobiles or radios. The following advertisement, which appeared
in three consecutive weekly issues of a Boston newspaper in
1757, offers a good illustration: [49]

> To be Sold at the public Vendue on Thursday the 23d Instant,
> at the House where the late Mr. *Henry Darrell,* deceas'd,
> dwelt, the Household Furniture and Goods of said Deceased,
> consisting of Feather Beds, Bedsteads, Chairs, Tables, Desks,
> Brass and Copper Ware, 2 Turkey Carpets, a parcel of Iron-
> mongery and Tin Ware, sundry Pieces of Plate, Men's Ap-
> parel, and a Collection of Books; also a Negro Man and
> Woman, and a Horse and Chaise.

A similar sale which took place near Rye, New Hampshire,
in April, 1767, was advertised in a New Hampshire newspaper
as follows: [50]

> TO BE SOLD at Public Vendue on Tuesday the 22nd of
> April Instant, at Two O'clock Afternoon at the House where
> the late Mr. *Thomas Beck* lived, in the road leading to Rye,
> near Mr. John Langdon's . . . ONE yoke of OXEN, several
> steers; Cows; Sheep; 1 good Horse; several Calves; with
> sundry other Things, Wearing Apparel, &c. ALSO
> A likely Negro GIRL

When John Salmon of Boston died, his property, including
seven slaves, was sold to the highest bidder by Captain Robert
Stone at the Royal Exchange Tavern in King Street. Exactly
at noon on Thursday, March 28, 1754, the auctioneer placed on
the block " thirteen truck-horses "; and at 3 o'clock in the
afternoon " six negro men and one Negro girl." [51]

[49] *Boston Gazette or Weekly Advertiser,* May 7, 14, 21, 1757.

[50] *New Hampshire Gazette and Historical Chronicle,* April 3, 1767.

[51] *Boston Gazette and Weekly Advertiser,* March 19, 1754. Customers
were later notified on Tuesday, April 16, that the same auctioneer would sell
" two thousand 800 gallons of New England Rum ". *Ibid.,* April 16, 1754.

Though in general regarded as property, slaves in some instances were recognized as persons. As such, they were accorded certain legal rights commonly associated with freemen. As a person, the New England slave had a right to life;[52] in short, says Reeve, the slave had the same right to life as had the apprentice. Where either this law or custom prevailed the Puritan master then had no legal control over the life of his slave: if a master killed his slave he was answerable as if he had killed a freeman.[53] Although a master might reasonably and moderately correct and chastise his servant or slave,[54] the deliberate murder of his bondman was a capital crime.[55] On this point, Thomas Hutchinson, Chief Justice and later Governor of Massachusetts is very explicit. Writing to Lord Hillsborough in 1771, he says, " Slavery by the Provincial laws gives no right to the life of the servant; and a slave here is considered as a servant would be who had bound himself for a period of years exceeding the ordinary term of human life . . ."[56] In New England, the right of the slave to life was far different than in the southern colonies where, as previously set forth, the killing of a slave by his master in course of punishment was not a crime.[57]

Slaves, as persons, might also acquire, receive, hold, and transfer property. According to Reeve, a slave could hold property as devisee or legatee. Thus the slave had the same right to property as had the apprentice. Should a master take away such property the slave might sue him through his *prochein ami*.[58]

52 Quincy, *Reports*, p. 31 n., Reeve, *op. cit.*, p. 340; *New York Colonial Documents*, III, 547; *Acts and Laws of His Majesty's Province of New Hampshire* (Portsmouth, 1771), p. 101; cf. *Correspondence Concerning Moore's Notes on Slavery in Massachusetts*, p. 7.

53 *Op. cit.*, p. 340.

54 Swift, *op. cit.*, I, 221; *Mass. Reports*, IV, Part I, 127.

55 *Laws of New Hampshire, ut supra*; Reeve, *op. cit.*, p. 340; Quincy, *op. cit.*, p. 31 n.

56 Cited in Quincy, *ut supra*.

57 *Vide supra*, p. 143; *infra*, p. 234 n.

58 *Op. cit.*, pp. 340-341; *vide* also Quincy, *Reports*, p. 31 n.

There are on record several examples of this right of the slave to hold property. In 1653 Captain Keayne of Boston left £5 to his three Negroes,[59] and twenty-nine years later Richard Hutchenson of Massachusetts left to his black servant, Peter,[60] five acres of land. The will, dated January 19, 1679, three years before the death of the master, specified that the land was to descend to the heirs of Peter but was, in the event Peter died without issue, to revert to Hutchenson's executor and his heirs.[61] This document would seem to indicate that not only had precedents been established for the ownership of property among slaves, but also for the descent of such property to their children.

Additional support for this view is afforded by a bill of sale, in which one Ephraim Carpenter sold to Frank, the Negro " servant " of Silas Carpenter of Providence, a certain tract of land for seven pounds. The deed, drawn in 1694, records that Ephraim Carpenter " relinquishes to the said Negro and his heirs [62]

> all that Right of land wch [which] is mine or that doth any wayes belong unto me with out the line by the Towne of Providence Called Ye Seven mile line . . . all of which said Right or shier of land aforesaid for & in Consideration of Seven pounds Sterling in hand already well & truly payd unto

59 *Mass. Records*, III, 268.

60 Since slaves were usually called servants in New England, it is quite likely that Peter was a slave.

61 " I give unto Black Peter my servant five acres of land lying by & adjoining to ye land above expressed to him and his heirs, or if he have no heires then It shall return to my executor his heires and assignes." *E.C.C.R., 1680-1683*, VIII, 434 n.

62 *Early Records of Providence*, V, 278-279. By the Rhode Island Law of 1652, Frank should have been a servant since bondage in that colony was limited to ten years. The law, however, was never effectively observed, therefore Frank may have been a slave, although listed as a servant. *Vide R. I. Col. Recs.*, I, 243. " In Oct. 1707, Lieut. John Hawley, administrator to the estate of John Negro, was granted power by the General Court to sell £10 worth of this land, it appearing . . . that he owed that amount more than his moveables would pay." Steiner, *op. cit.*, p. 17.

me by the sd frank negro I do sell and pass over from me my heirs Executors Administrators & Assignes unto the aforesaid frank Nigro his heirs Executors Administrators & Assignes to have & to hold the said Right or shier of land & be for the only proper use and behoof of the said ffrank Nigro his Heirs Exsecutors, Administrators & Assignes forever . . .

More than half a century later, the Reverend Matthias Plant of Newbury, Massachusetts, gave his slave girl, Lucy, all but seventeen acres of a plot of land owned by him in Almsbury, New Hampshire. Lucy was also to be given her freedom at the death of Plant's widow.[63] Several years earlier, Joshua Bagley, Sr., of the same town, who already had given his Negro servant [slave], Robert, several lots of land, further stipulated that the slave was not to be sold but was to serve his widow until her death, after which time he was to be free.[64]

As further proof of their personality, slaves enjoyed virtually the same rights in the New England courts as did freemen. Slaves could offer testimony either for or against white persons even in cases not involving Negroes. This was quite different from the situation in the colonial South or even in New York [65] where Negroes were expressly forbidden to give evidence against a white person. There they could act as witnesses only for or against one another.[66] Typical was the attitude of Virginia where a law of 1732 prohibited all Negroes, slave or free, from giving evidence, except at a trial of a slave for a capital crime.[67] No such law appears to have been passed in New England. Significant, too, was the fact that the wife of a slave was not allowed to testify against him.[68]

63 Providing the girl served her mistress faithfully until the latter died. *Vide* original bequest in Cuvier, *History of Newbury*, p. 255. Mrs. Plant freed Lucy and Robin in 1753. *Ibid.*

64 *Ibid.*, p. 254.

65 *N. Y. Col. Laws*, I, 598.

66 Hurd, *op. cit.*, II, 82.

67 Hening, *Statutes at Large of Virginia*, IV, 327.

68 Quincey, *Reports*, p. 30 n.

Many examples of Negro testimony before New England courts are available. As early as 1663 a Negro woman gave evidence in the paternity case of *Taylor* vs. *White*,[69] but ten years later, when Erasmus James brought suit for debt against Richard Smith, the legality of slave testimony was questioned. The case came before the term of the Salem Quarterly Court for February, 1673, when a decision was rendered in favor of the plaintiff. Smith appealed the case on the ground that the bill bore no date, and that action was begun merely for the purpose of picking a quarrel with him. He also objected to what he claimed was the legal testimony of a Negro slave owned by Mary Rowland. Replying, James contended that the bill was a memorandum, and in response to Smith's allegation that the slave's testimony was unlawful, James asserted that the Negro was of such a " carriage and knowledge that her testimony had been accepted several times before ". In testifying, the Negro girl—about sixteen years of age—had corroborated James' statement. According to her, six or seven months earlier James' wife, Mary, had made for Smith " four shirts " and " three pairs of drawers " which cost between four and three shillings apiece. James claimed that Smith had not paid this bill, but at the June term of court, 1673, judgment was reversed in favor of Smith.[70]

This verdict, however, did not bar slaves from future testimony against whites in the courts of New England. Six years later a Negro named Wonn played a prominent role before the Salem Quarterly Court in the criminal indictment against Bridget Oliver for witchcraft. This was a grave offense, for witchcraft was punishable by death. Wonn, who belonged to one John Ingerson, told such a " convincing " story concerning Bridget's power of sorcery that his testimony was partly responsible for her indictment. Wonn first accused Bridget of bewitching his horses, testifying that about a month earlier he had just

69 *E.C.C.R., 1662-1667*, III, 101; *cf. infra*, p. 204.

70 *E.C.C.R., 1672-1674*, V, 179-180.

loaded a sled with wood and had gone a certain distance when, finding it necessary to return to the woods, " his horses started and snorted as if they were frightened and would not go forward but ran down into the swamp up to their bellies." Only with a considerable effort, the slave continued, was he able to get the horses out of the swamp. Witnesses were sure that the horses were bewitched. About a week later, when Wonn went to the barn to feed the horse and cow, he experienced another miraculous happening. On his second trip he saw Bridget sitting " upon the beam with an egg in her hand." He picked up a pitch-fork to strike her, but she vanished. Asked to identify the person he had seen Wonn asserted, " it was the shape of saide Bridget as shee now stands before the court." Bridget continued to plague him, for Wonn further testified that while at dinner :[71]

> I saw two black catts : & wee haveing one blacke cat of our owne & no more I said how came two black catts heare, & before my words were well out of my mouth felt three sore gripes or pinches on my side that made me crye out, & I had very much paine there and soreness for halfe an hower after.

Mainly as a result of Wonn's testimony, Bridget Oliver was ordered to appear for trial before the Court of Assistants in Boston, where the court ruled that she should be held in bail pending her trial. She posted bond.[72] Besides showing the slave's competency to testify against whites in New England, Wonn's testimony further demonstrates the flimsy evidence upon which innocent persons were condemned to death during Salem's witchcraft frenzy.

By the eighteenth century, the testimony of slaves seems to have been generally accepted in New England courts. A most illuminating case is recorded in Connecticut in 1739. In May of that year Samuel and Silence Chapman, executors of the last will and testament of the late Simon Chapman of Windsor,

71 *Ibid.*, VII, 329-330.
72 *Ibid.*, p. 329.

appealed to the General Court for a retrial in the case of *Chapman* vs. *Anderson*. This action had been tried in April, 1739 before the Hartford County Court where John Anderson was awarded a judgment against the Chapmans in the sum of more than £44.[73] Upon the appeal the Chapmans contended that during the trial they had been " deprived of a principal witness . . . one Abraham, a negro servant." They further prayed that the " said Abraham be admitted as a lawful witness, with any other evidence " that they might adduce, and the Court granted the petitioners a new trial before the County Court to be held at Hartford on June 3, 1739.[74]

Slaves were also allowed to sue before the courts of New England. Reeve says that a master was as liable to be sued for beating, wounding or for moderate chastisement of a slave as he would be if he had thus treated his apprentice.[75] The slave, as already indicated, might sue either on his own motion or through his *prochein ami*.

There were also many suits for trespass, and through these Negroes often won their freedom.[76] One of the earliest of such actions was that of *Abda* vs. *Richards*. Abda, a mulatto slave belonging to Thomas Richards of Hartford, Connecticut, was the bastard son of a Negro woman and a white man. In 1702 Abda ran away and went to live with Captain Wadsworth of the same town. Richards sued Wadsworth for the recovery of his property. Abda then lodged a countersuit for damages against his master for having detained him in bondage for a year, claiming that because of his white blood there could be no legal grounds for his enslavement. On the basis of this contention Abda was declared a freeman by the Inferior Court of Common Pleas held at Hartford in 1704. The master was sentenced to pay the slave £12 damages in addition to costs of

73 £ 38, 16s, 8d. York money and " £ 2s 3d Costs " in the currency of the colony. *Conn. Col. Recs.*, VIII, 246.

74 *Ibid.*

75 Reeve *op. cit.*, p. 340.

76 *Vide infra*, pp. 295-297.

court. Richards appealed the case to the General Assembly, the highest court in the colony. Largely through the persuasive logic of the Reverend Gurdon Saltonstall, ancestor of the present governor of Massachusetts (1941), the decision of the lower court was reversed, and Abda was returned to his master. Saltonstall successfully convinced the court, that despite Abda's white blood, the child had the same status as the mother. Although Saltonstall admitted that there was no law specifically providing for the enslavement of mulattoes, he added that the custom of enslaving them had the same force as law. This case was extremely important because it set a legal precedent for holding mulattoes in bondage.[77] Almost as famous was the case of Adam, the slave of Judge Saffin of Boston. When Saffin refused to liberate the slave as he had agreed, Adam sued his master in 1701 and finally won his freedom, but only after a sharply-contested, two-year struggle in the Massachusetts courts.[78]

The liberal sentiment which marked the eve of the American Revolution further encouraged slaves to seek their liberty by bringing suits against their masters. When Caesar, a slave belonging to Richard Greenleaf of Newburyport, sued his owner in 1773 for fifty pounds for unlawfully detaining him in slavery, the court awarded him his freedom and damages of eighteen pounds and costs.[79] A year later a slave of Caleb Dodge of Beverly, Massachusetts, won a similar suit for freedom in the Essex County Court, the tribunal holding that no legal justification existed for retaining a man in bondage for life.[80] Most

77 For this case vide Conn. Archives: Miscellaneous, 1662-1789, First Series, II, 10 - 21d. For general account vide Steiner, op. cit., p. 17.

78 This case will be treated at length under the Free Negro. Cf. Mass. Archives, IX, 152-153; Mass. Hist. Soc. Proceedings, VII, 161-165; Collections of the same Society, Fifth Series, VI, 16-20; Moore, op. cit., pp. 251-256. The best account of this case is contained in Publications of the Colonial Society of Massachusetts, 1892-1894 (Boston, 1895), pp. 87-112, wherein Mr. Abner Goodell has presented new evidence in the case from manuscript records.

79 Coffin, Sketch of Newbury, p. 241; Moore, Notes, p. 118.

80 Moore, op. cit., p. 119.

celebrated of all was the *Walker* vs. *Jennison* case which was decided at Worcester, Massachusetts in 1783. The victory won by Walker against his master finally resulted in the emancipation of the slaves in Massachusetts.[81]

That the slave enjoyed the right of appeal is evident from the foregoing citations. In the cases of *Abda* vs. *Richards,* *Adam* vs. *Saffin, and Walker* vs. *Jennison,* for example, the slaves carried their appeals to the highest courts of Connecticut and Massachusetts.[82]

The slave could make a contract and, once the agreement was formally made, the master was as firmly bound as if he had contracted with a freeman.[83] There are numerous instances of this right of the slave. For example, in 1694 the above named John Saffin and his slave, Adam, entered into a formal agreement whereby Adam was to receive his freedom after six more years of faithful service.[84] A similar contract was drawn up in 1699 between William Hawkins of Providence, Rhode Island, and his slave, Jack.[85] During the American Revolution Isaac Smith of Boston formally agreed to free his slave, Scipio Dalton, provided that the latter served him for two years after the date of the contract to which Dalton signed his name.[86] Slaves who were unable to affix their signature entered their mark upon the document. Such contracts, as will be shown later, were an avenue by which many slaves secured their freedom.[87]

There is much evidence in support of the proposition that, as persons, the slaves in New England enjoyed the same judicial procedure and protection in criminal cases as did white persons.

---

81 *Mass. Hist. Soc. Colls.*, Fourth Series, IV, 336-339; Moore, *op. cit.,* pp. 211-215.

82 *Vide supra.*

83 *Vide infra*, pp. 291, 295 ff.

84 *Mass. Archives*, IX, 153.

85 *Early Records of Providence*, IV, 71-72.

86 Ms. in Library of Massachusetts Historical Society, Boston.

87 *Vide infra*, p. 291.

For example, they had the right of trial by jury, and before trial they must be regularly indicted for crimes in the same manner as free white malefactors. As early as 1668 a Negro named Frank was hailed before the Boston Court of Assistants on a charge of *conspiracy*. The specific bill accused him of aiding and abetting one John Pottell (jailed for the murder of a ship's cook) to escape from prison. The grand jury, however, refused to return an indictment against the slave, stating that " wee the Grand Jurie doe not find frank negro: guilty of the fact unto this bill of inditement." [88] In 1677, a jury sitting in the same courtroom, found Jack, the slave of John Faireweather of Boston, *not guilty* of the charge of bestiality.[89] By contrast, the Reverend Daniel Wadsworth reported that a grand jury sitting at Hartford, Connecticut on September 19, 1743, returned true bills of indictment against three Negroes accused of murder.[90]

Slaves indicted for criminal offenses seem to have possessed the same right as freemen to pass upon their trial jurors. This practice is illustrated in the case of Robin, a Negro slave belonging to Andrew Gardner of Muddy River, Massachusetts, who was indicted for manslaughter. When arraigned before the Court of Assistants on December 24, 1691 Robin pleaded not guilty. A jury was thereupon impaneled and, according to the record, " the prisoner making no challenge against any of them they were sworn for his tryal." [91] The verdict in this case was *guilty*.[92]

These slave trials seem to have been held with as much gravity and formality as were those of freemen. A case in point is that of Edward Thomas, one of the jurors chosen to try Robin.

[88] The Bill was signed by " Hugh Mason with the consent of the rest ... " *E.C.C.R., 1630-1692*, III, 194.

[89] *R.C.A.*, I, 74.

[90] *Diary of Reverend Daniel Wadsworth, 1737-1747*, ed. George Leon Walker (Hartford, 1899), p. 104.

[91] *R.C.A.*, I, 304-305.

[92] *Ibid.*, pp. 304, 305, 321.

For failing to appear when called " at the impanelling of a jury to pass upon Robin," Thomas was fined five shillings.[93] Neither slaves nor free Negroes appear to have served as jurors in New England.

A regular inquest was held when a slave met with violent or unnatural death. One of the earliest recorded instances occurred in Essex County, Massachusetts in 1662, when a coroner's jury, consisting of twelve men,[94] returned a verdict of suicide in the death of John, a Negro belonging to one Henry Bartholomew. The Negro had been found shot to death in October, 1661 [95] and the jury reported to the September term of the Salem Quarterly Court that they had

> Viewed the place wheare the negroe was found lying & a gun lying by him, & heard the relation of severall witnesses, that were called, before he was quite dead, & viewing his body & finding where the shot went into one [on] his leaft side, & came ptly through about his shoulder blad behind, and being all agreed in our apprehentions, doe Judg according to our best apprehention, that he did willingly contrive & was ye only acter in his owne death by shooting of ye sayd Gun into his own body.[96]

Nineteen years later another coroner's jury held an inquest over the body of a Negro belonging to George March of Salem. Finding no wound and, learning that he had left his master almost a week before his death, the jury concluded that the " want of suitable refreshment, hunger and cold had been the cause of his death." [97]

93 *Ibid.*, p. 305.

94 John Browne, Richard Prince, Walter Price, John Gedney, Dani'l Rumbel, John Gardner, William Woodcocke, Nicholas Potter, Thomas (Cromwell?), Joseph Gardner, Robert Gray and Hilliard Veren. *E.C.C.R., 1656-1667*, II, 421.

95 *Ibid.*

96 " Sworn, 23: 10: 1661 before Wm. Hathorne." Verdict accepted in Sept. 1662. *Ibid.*

97 *Ibid.*, VIII, 59.

Finally, slaves, as persons, served as soldiers, sailors, and marines in the armed forces of colonial New England. Although, as heretofore pointed out, Negroes were legally barred from militia duty [98] during peace time, under the stress of war the Puritans disregarded such proscriptions and admitted Negroes into their armies. The first mention of a Negro soldier was in 1690, exactly eighty-five years before the outbreak of the Revolution. In that year a slave was killed while serving aboard an English ship,[99] and the Massachusetts legislature paid the master £20 [100] as compensation for the loss of his property. In 1713 a New Hampshire master was paid £4.6s for the services of his slave who had fought at Fort William Henry in New York.[101] Three years later, Nero, belonging to the Reverend Mr. Swift of Framingham, Massachusetts served as trumpeter in Captain Isaac Clark's company of that town.[102]

In the wars of the eighteenth century, Negroes fought in larger numbers. For King George's War (1742-1748) the militia rolls of Rhode Island,[103] Connecticut [104] and New Hampshire [105] show from one to three Negroes in the companies of these colonies. In Captain Elisha Hall's company of New London, Connecticut, were two Negroes, Adam and Charles, the former having been the first man of the entire company to enlist.[106] Among the 101 members of Captain Thomas Cheyney's company of Massachusetts, which was raised for the expedition against Canada in 1747, were three Negroes, Will, Cuffee and Samuel.[107]

98 *Vide supra*, p. 126 ff.
99 *Mass. A. and R.*, VII, Appendix II, p. 169.
100 *Ibid.*
101 *Provincial Papers of New Hampshire, 1722-1737*, VIII, 442.
102 *Temple, History of Framingham, Massachusetts*, p. 236.
103 *R. I. Hist. Soc. Publications*, New Series, III, 244-245.
104 "Law Papers, 1747-1750," III, *Conn. Hist. Soc. Colls.*, XV, 158-159.
105 "Revolutionary Rolls," I, *New Hampshire State Papers*, XIV, 18.
106 "Law Papers," *loc. cit.*, pp. 151-154.
107 *R. I. Hist. Soc., Publications, ut supra.*

Greater efforts were put forth by Negro soldiers in the French and Indian War (1756-1763). With the French and Indians, under the able leadership of Montcalm, ravaging their borders, the colonies adjoining Canada needed every available man for military duty. This need was felt particularly in Massachusetts and Connecticut which, with New York, bore the brunt of the struggle. The British requisition system of obtaining recruits for the colonial militia broke down,[108] and many towns were unable to furnish their quota of white men. Recruiting officers, therefore, gladly admitted Negroes and Indians, slave as well as free, into the colonial ranks. Little Deerfield, Massachusetts, alone had four Negroes in its quota.[109] In the militia of Providence, Rhode Island, Negroes bearing such names as James, Sambo, Caesar and Benjamin Negro, were conspicuous.[110]

On sea, as well as on land, Negroes fought in the colonial wars. Black men served aboard colonial war vessels as cooks, sailors and marines. In 1697 a slave, who had been pressed into service, died aboard a British warship and his mistress, Ruth Knile, was granted £20 by the Massachusetts legislature as compensation for her loss.[111] Most of the Negroes served on privateers, armed merchantmen, whose owners secured letters of marque authorizing them to carry on warfare against the enemy on the high seas. All the New England colonies fitted out privateers, which scoured the ocean, capturing or sinking hostile merchant vessels.[112] Rhode Island was especially famous for privateers, Newport alone sending out more than sixty such

108 Troops were raised for colonial wars by the mother country's requiring each colony to furnish a number of men in relation to the population. The colony then made a similar levy upon each town.

109 Sheldon, *Negro Slavery in Deerfield*, p. 53.

110 " Nine Muster Rolls of Rhode Island Troops During the Old French War and Captain Rice's Journal," *Society of Colonial Wars in the State of Rhode Island* (Providence, 1915), pp. 10-11.

111 *Mass. A. and R.*, VII, Appendix, II, 169; *cf. Mass. Archives*, LXI, 357.

112 Howard Chapin, *Rhode Island Privateers*, pp. 12, 15.

ships during the French and Indian War.[113] Negroes probably
served on all of them. As early as 1704 Toney, the slave of
Samuel Lynde, of Boston, shipped as cook aboard a private
man-of-war.[114] Both black and white crews fought on privateers
like the *Virgin Queen*,[115] *Invincible Shepherd*[116] (1740), the
*Revenge*[117] (1742), the *Providence*[118] and the *George*.[119] Of a
complement of thirty-seven hands who made up the crew of the
*Revenge,* five were Negroes.[120]

From the foregoing, it is evident that long before the American Revolution, Negroes had served in both branches of colonial defense, fighting in mixed regiments or crews.[121] If any
difference in treatment occurred because of their color, the records consulted do not reveal it. For their services, Negroes apparently received the same wages as did the white soldiers.[122]
and privateers were paid a full share of the prize money,[123] but
the slave soldier had to give all or half of his wages to his

113 Kimball, *Correspondence of the Colonial Governors of Rhode Island,*
p. xxxvii.

114 *Mass. Archives: Domestic Relations, 1643-1774,* IX, 149.

115 Chapin, *Rhode Island Privateers, 1739-1748* (Providence, 1926), p. 23.

116 *Ibid.,* p. 49.

117 *Ibid.,* p. 34.

118 Howard Chapin, *Rhode Island Soldiers and Sailors, 1755-1762,* p. 36.

119 *Ibid.,* p. 29.

120 Chapin, *Rhode Island Privateers,* p. 34.

121 *Vide Muster Rolls* cited above.

122 Samuel Sambo, obviously a Negro, served 72 days in 1746 and his
whole wages amounted to £1. 16s; William Taylor (white) who served 76
days received £1. 18. For 305 days service Caesar Noxit, who appears to
be a Negro was paid £7. 12s. 6d. Peter Gardner (white) for 315 days service
got £7. 17s. 6d.. "Three Muster Rolls of Rhode Island, 1746," *Soc. of the
Colonial Wars in Rhode Island and Providence Plantations* (Providence,
1915), Rolls 2 and 3.

123 *Mass. Archives,* LXI, 357; *ibid., Domestic Relations, 1643-1774,* IX,
149. This seems to have been the case even on board Spanish privateers
where in 1745 a mulatto named Limena aboard the privateersman Nuestra
Senora de los Deblores y Animas drew "an equall share with the White-
men." John Franklin Jameson, *Privateering and Privacy in Colonial America*
(New York, 1923), p. 310.

master. Negroes like the aforementioned Toney,[124] Caesar, Sambo, and Benjamin Negro turned over their wages to their respective owners,[125] while slaves like James Sambo, Peter Chese and James Underwood, who either had more liberal owners or had enlisted for them, kept half of their wages and gave the remainder to their masters.[126]

The New England Negroes played their greatest military role in the American Revolution. When Paul Revere and William Dawes aroused the Massachusetts countryside on that memorable night of April 18, 1775, they called Negro as well as white Minutemen to the defense of American liberties. Along with Colonel Parker, Colonel John Nixon, Captain Simon Edgehill, Warren and Prescott, went the Negroes Peter Salem of Framingham,[127] Job Potomea and Isaiah Barjonah of Stoneham, Cuff Whitemore of Cambridge,[128] Prince of Brookline,[129] and Pompey of Braintree.[130] On the next day embattled whites and Negroes gathered on Lexington Common and struck the first blow for American independence. All of these Negroes joined the Minutemen before April 18, 1775, Lemuel Haynes of Connecticut enlisting as early as 1774.[131] In all it is recorded that some 3,000 Negroes fought in the American ranks during the Revolution.[132]

124 Toney's master, Col. John Lane, wrote Harrison Gray, treasurer of Massachusetts, directing him to give to Moses Abbott, the bearer of the letter, "all the wages" due him for the services of his "Negro man toney more." Brown, *History of Bedford, Mass.*, p. 31.

125 Sambo's pay of £116. 16s. was collected by D. Wall, who was either his master or the latter's representative. "Nine Muster Rolls of R. I.," etc., *loc. cit.*, p. 23. Benjamin Smith collected Benjamin's wages, £184. 3s. 9d.

126 *Ibid.*, p. 10; *cf.* pp. 20, 24, 25.

127 Temple, *History of Framingham, Mass.*, p. 278.

128 Benjamin and William Cutter, *History of the Town of Arlington, Massachusetts* (Boston, 1880), p. 35.

129 *Massachusetts Soldiers and Sailors of the Revolutionary War*, XII, 788.

130 *Ibid.*, p. 520.

131 Timothy Cooley, *Life of Lemuel Haynes* (New York, 1835), pp. 45-46.

132 Brawley, *Short History of the American Negro*, p. 29.

# CHAPTER VIII

# THE SLAVE FAMILY

THE personality of the New England slaves is also revealed by their marital relationships. As members of the Puritan family, they assimilated the manners and customs of their masters. This process was accelerated by the peculiar nature of the domestic institutions of colonial New England. Among the Puritans, the family was the fundamental unit, economically and socially, and preservation of its integrity was of paramount importance for it served as the chief means of perpetuating Puritan ideals and culture.[1] Much of the responsibility for insuring the stability of the family fell upon the male head. The father, in accordance with Hebraic tradition, exercised considerable control over everyone who dwelt under his roof—whether wife, minor children, servants or slaves.[2] Supplementing the paternal authority, as well as protecting the family from demoralizing influences, were the pronouncements of the Puritan legal code. Offenses against parental authority were capital crimes. Sons who rebelled against their fathers and children who cursed or struck their parents were to be put to death. Adultery, rape, sodomy and bestiality were also capital crimes.[3] Premarital sexual relationships were not to be tolerated and offenders were hunted down and severely punished.[4]

Marriage was rigidly controlled. In an endeavor to rid them-

1 Calhoun, *Social History of the American Family*, I, 82; Robert Warner, *Negroes of New Haven: A Social Study* (New Haven, 1940), p. 5. For excellent summary of colonial New England family, *vide* George Elliot Howard, *History of Matrimonial Institutions*, 3 vols. (Chicago and London, 1904), II, ch. xii.

2 *Earle, Fashions and Customs in Colonial New England*, pp. 14, 98; Warner, *op. cit.*, pp. 5-6, *cf.* Richard B. Morris, *Studies in the History of American Law* (New York, 1930), pp. 127, 128-129.

3 *Acts and Laws of His Majesties Colony of Connecticut* (1702), pp. 12-13; *Colonial Laws of Mass.* (Reprint, 1672), pp. 14-16.

4 *Vide infra*, p. 202 ff.

selves of Popish and Anglican influence the Puritans decreed
that marriage was a civil contract.[5] The Founding Fathers
recognized no scriptural warrant for the performance of marriage by clergymen: marriage was concerned with business and
property and was therefore the proper function of the magistrate and not of the minister. For this reason up to 1686
clergymen were forbidden to perform the wedding ceremony in
New England.[6] Mutual consent of both parties was required before the marriage could take place.[7] Furthermore, all the New
England colonies required that wedding banns be read either at
three public meetings or be posted in a public place at least fourteen days before the wedding.[8] These regulations applied to black
as well as white persons, slaves as well as freemen. As a member
of such a community the Negro was forced to revise the ideas,
attitudes, and practices regarding marriage and sex relationships which he had brought from Africa, and to adopt those of
the master class.

As a result, instead of the loose sexual relations generally
characteristic of the plantation Negroes,[9] New England slaves
were compelled to marry in the manner prescribed for the general population.[10] Once married, moreover, they were expected

5 Calhoun, *op. cit.*, I, 60; Felt, *Ecclesiastical History of New England*, I,
244; Joseph Kirk Folsom, *The Family: Its Sociology and Social Psychiatry*
(New York and London, 1934), p. 151.

6 In 1685 a Huguenot clergyman was brought into Court charged with having performed a wedding ceremony in Boston. He promised to stop, broke
his word and later went to New York. Calhoun, *op. cit.*, I, 61; *cf.* Earle,
*Customs and Fashions*, pp. 70-71.

7 Calhoun, *op. cit.*, I, 59.

8 The intentions and the names of the contracting parties were read by
the town clerk, deacon, or the minister, at either of these foregatherings,
and a notice of the same placed on the church door or on a " publishing
post." Howard, *op. cit.*, II, 145, 147; Earle, *Customs and Fashions*, p. 70.

9 E. Franklin Frazier, *The Negro Family in the United States* (Chicago,
1940), ch. ii, esp. pp. 24-27.

10 Calhoun says that common-law marriages among slaves seem to have
been valid in New England. *Op. cit.*, I, 65. Quincy further states that by the

—as were free white persons—to observe the sanctity of the nuptial tie. The Puritans could not with consistency deny marriage to their slaves, for the Negroes were constant witnesses of the stringent efforts made by the master class to punish immorality. To withhold marriage from the slaves would have been demoralizing to the master's household for the New England Negroes came into unusually close contact with the master's family and ordinarily lived in the same house with their owner. Furthermore, the general laws regulating marriage and sex relations could be easily applied to Negroes, because they not only constituted a small minority of the population, but were largely concentrated in the towns.

Marriages among the blacks, accordingly, were duly solemnized and recorded in the same manner as those of white persons. The social relations leading to marriage of the principals, however, are rarely revealed. Courtship must have been brief, for masters were disinclined to permit slaves to neglect their tasks. It was comparatively simple, however, when both Negroes belonged to the same master, as in the case of Caesar and Fidella, the slaves of Judge Lynde.[11] Then the pleasantries of lovemaking might be intermixed with the daily chores, or an hour or two of courtship might be enjoyed in the kitchen at the end of the day's work. If the slaves belonged to different masters, the man might receive permission to call upon the woman after working hours. In that case, she would perhaps entertain him in the kitchen. The time for courtship was limited, for the slave, who had no written pass from his owner, would be

Superior Court of Judicature of Massachusetts in 1758 the child of a female slave (who had not been married by any of the forms prescribed by the laws of this land [Massachusetts]) by another slave who had kept her company with her master's consent was not a bastard. *Reports*, p. 30 n.; Moore, *op. cit.,* p. 58. In view of the many cases of Negroes who were punished for "fornication" and "bastardy" neither Calhoun's nor Quincy's statement can be accepted as reflective of the general situation. Nor has any law been found to substantiate either claim, *vide*, ch. v; *cf.* Howard, *op. cit.,* II, 224-226.

11 They were married in Boston on Nov. 23, 1710. "Twenty-Eighth Report of the Record Commissioners," *Boston Marriages, 1700-1751* (Boston, 1898), XXVIII, 29.

whipped if caught on the streets after nine o'clock at night.[12] Should the master refuse to permit his Negro to visit a slave woman, or should the owner of the woman object to the slave's coming to his house, the lovers might meet clandestinely.[13] Other opportunities for social intercourse, at which such a union might originate, could be found in casual meetings at church,[14] at school,[15] or at one of the slave festivals, especially at the "Governor's" election and subsequent reception.[16] "Bundling" or "tarrying," in which a couple went to bed with their clothes on, was a common feature of courtship in colonial New England, but the records do not reveal whether this practice was followed by the slaves.[17]

Even after the slave had won the affections of the lady of his choice, and had gotten the consent of both masters, he might not marry immediately. He still must comply with the law regarding wedding banns.[18] Compulsory publication of the intention to marry, as indicated above, was required of everyone, regardless of race or condition. In accordance therewith, on November 16, 1700, " Semit Negro and & Jane Negro " published their banns, as required, two weeks before their nuptials; " Charles Negro & Peggee Negro," who were married August

12 *Mass. A. and R., 1692-1714*, p. 535; *Conn. Col. Recs.* (Hartford, 1872), pp. 390-391; *Acts and Laws of His Majesty's Province of New Hampshire* (Portsmouth, 1771), p. 52 (hereinafter cited as *N. H. Acts and Laws*), *R. I. Col. Recs.* (Providence, 1858), III, 492.

13 *E.C.C.R.*, VIII, 141.

14 C. F. Pasco, *Two Hundred Years of the S.P.G.* (London, 1901), p. 47.

15 Updike, *op. cit.*, III, 90; "Diary of Cotton Mather," *Mass. Hist. Soc. Colls.*, VIII, Part II, 442, 448.

16 Frances M. Caulkins, *History of Norwich, Connecticut* (Norwich, 1845), 185; Felt, *Annals of Salem*, II, 419-420; Updike, *op. cit.*, I, 213-214; *vide infra*, p. 249 ff.

17 For this custom, *vide* Dana Doten, *The Art of Bundling* (1938); Earle, *Customs and Fashions*, pp. 62-63.

18 Joseph B. Felt, *Ecclesiastical History of New England*, I, 387; *Mass. A. and R.*, I, 6.

3, 1710, did likewise, as did " Lewise Negro & Martha Negro " before their marriage on January 18, of the same year.[19]

The preliminaries once observed, marriages of New England slaves were duly solemnized and recorded along with those of white persons. Contemporary documents contain a large number of such records. As early as 1659 two former slaves, Moninah and Mungaley, were living legally as man and wife in Salem [20] and there is a record of John Cram and Lucretia, his wife, Negro slaves of Governor Theophilus Eaton of New Haven, having been united in marriage.[21]

Marriage being regarded as a civil contract, slaves as well as free white persons up to 1686 were married by magistrates; by either magistrates or clergymen after that date.[22] In 1700 ' Bastien, Negro Servant to John Wait and June Lake, Negro Servant to Mr. Thair," were married by Samuel Sewall, the famous diarist. On December 20, 1722 Will and Pegg, belonging respectively, to John Webb and Richard Dowse of Boston, were joined in wedlock by Mr. John Webb.[23] On May 1, 1750, the Reverend John Checkley of Providence performed the marriage ceremony for two Negro slaves,[24] and on October 24, 1776, the Reverend Chauncey Whittlesey of New Haven officiated at the wedding of Charles and Rhoda, Negro servants of Samuel Thacher.[25]

Where such marriages took place between slaves of different masters, the question as to the future support of the wife and children naturally arose. Solution of this problem, in at least one instance, illustrates the patriarchal conception of slavery in

19 *Boston Marriages*, 1700-1751, XXVIII, 29.

20 *E.C.C.R., 1656-1662* (Salem, 1912), III, 183.

21 *Connecticut Magazine*, V, No. 6, p. 323.

22 Calhoun, *op. cit.*, I, 63.

23 *Boston Marriages, 1700-1751*, XXVIII, 2.

24 " John Checkley, or the Evolution of Religious Toleration in Massachusetts Bay," *Prince Society Publications*, ed. Rev. Edmund F. Slater (Boston, 1897), II, 216.

25 " Early Connecticut Marriages," *Bureau of American Ancestry*, ed. Frederick C. Bailey (New Haven, 1896-1906), II, 216.

New England. Faced with a dilemma when their slaves were about to marry in 1700, John Waite and Debora Thair of Boston sought the advice of Judge Samuel Sewall. Waite's Negro man, Sebastian, had proposed marriage to Mrs. Thair's Negro woman, June, and both masters were anxious to settle the question regarding the support of the woman before the banns were published. Mrs. Thair insisted that Waite allow Sebastian one day out of every six for the support of his intended wife and family. To this proposal Waite objected, but offered instead to give Sebastian five pounds a year toward the support of his family, besides furnishing Sebastian with food and clothing. When neither master appeared satisfied with the other's proposal, Sewall persuaded Mrs. Thair to accept Waite's arrangement.[26] The banns of the slaves were then published and the marriage, as indicated, was solemnized.[27]

These marriages not only united slave men and women, but also free Negroes and slaves. Sometimes marriages were contracted between free men and slave women. The master gained from the arrangement, for the children became his property. On March 7, 1755, Lancaster Hill, a free Negro, and Margaret, the Negro servant of Silvester Gardiner, were married at Boston. Seven months later Homer, a free Negro, and Katherine, belonging to Thomas Coverly, became man and wife.[28] On June 8, 1758, Pompy Blackman, a free Negro, and Patience, the servant of Mr. Nathaniel Bethune, were married.[29]

Sometimes free Negroes bought and married slave women. Abner, a slave belonging to John and Luke Wright of Wethersfield, Connecticut, who was given his freedom in 1777, four years later purchased his wife Zepporah for £40.[30] A more revealing example is that of Scipio, a free Negro of Boston, who

26 "Diary of Samuel Sewall," loc. cit., VI, 22.

27 Boston Marriages, 1700-1751, p. 2.

28 Ibid., 1752-1809, p. 16.

29 Ibid., p. 29.

30 Henry R. Stiles, The History of Ancient Windsor, Connecticut, 2 vols., (New York, 1904), I, 701.

in 1724 paid £50 for his fiancee, Margaret. The bill of sale read: [31]

> Whereas Scipio, of Boston aforesaid, Free Negro Man and Laborer, purposes Marriage to Margaret, the Negro Woman Servant of the said Dorcas Marshall . . . that the said Intended Marriage may take Effect, and that the said Scipio may Enjoy the said Margaret without any Interruption . . . She is duly sold with her apparel for Fifty Pounds.

The couple were subsequently married on December 9, 1724.[32]

Free Negro women frequently married slave men. The fact that the children resulting from such unions were free [33] gave an incentive, other than mutual attraction to such marriages. Contemporary records show many such unions: London, Negro servant to Mrs. Hepsiba Howard, and Kate, a free Negro, on January 16, 1756; [34] Will, the property of Samuel Ellison, and Hagar, a free Negro, on August 24, 1758,[35] and Cudjoe Borden, a slave, and Elizabeth, a free Negro, who were united in marriage by the Reverend Ezra Stiles of Newport on January 2, 1776.[36]

In addition to these unions, there were marriages of free Negroes whose nuptials were duly inscribed upon the records. As early as July 5, 1701 Cotton Mather performed a marriage

31 Cited in Moore, *op. cit.*, p. 57 n.

32 " Scipio Negro Late Servt to Grove Hirst Esqr. and Margaret Negro Late Servt. to Mr. Dorcas Marshall: Dec. 9, 1724." *Boston Marriages, 1700-1751*, p. 161.

33 Children followed the status of the mother. Hurd, *op. cit.*, I, 231-232. Judge Reeve even claims that if a slave married a free woman with his master's consent he became free because his master had allowed him to contract a relation incompatible with the state of slavery. By his consent the master is held to have agreed to abandon his right to him as a slave, *op. cit.*, p. 341. Reeve may have been theoretically correct in his view but not one case of a slave receiving his freedom on such grounds has come to the writer's attention.

34 *Boston Marriages, 1752-1809* (Boston, 1903), XXX, 18.

35 *Ibid.*, p. 29.

36 *Literary Diary of Ezra Stiles*, ed. Franklin B. Dexter, I, 658; *Boston Marriages, 1752-1807*, p. 29.

between two free Negroes of Boston, Joseph and " Marea."
A little later, Sambo and Elinor, free Negroes, were married
by Samuel Sewall.[37] On November 5, 1753, Phoebe, a mulatto
of Westerly, Rhode Island, and Joshua of Charlestowne in the
same colony were married by Joseph Crandall, Justice of the
Peace.[38] In New Haven on June 12, 1777, the Reverend
Chauncey Whittlesey married two free Negroes, Pomp and
Leah.[39]

Negroes not only married among themselves but considerable
intermixture went on between Negroes and other racial groups,
especially between Indians and Negroes. It was said that many
Indian slaves in Connecticut had gradually lost their racial iden-
tity by intermarriage with Negroes.[40] In Rhode Island, according to Weeden, " marriages between negroes and Indians were
common," [41] while in Duke County, Massachusetts, the Indians
were reported to be " much intermixed with white and negro
blood." [42] At Gay Head, in the same colony, an investigation
showed that of 142 Indians only nine men were racially pure;
' the rest are largely intermixed, chiefly with negroes." [43] Of
the 327 members of the Marshpee tribe in the same colony in
1771, " 14 of them were negroes, married to Indians." [44]

The process of amalgamation sometimes resulted from the
union of red and black slaves, as in the marriage of " Roben
Wood negro servant to Peter Buell and Judah Pallon, Indian
servant to N. Buell " in Coventry, Connecticut, on January 20,
1729-30.[45] Scipio, a mulatto slave, and Hannah, an Indian

37 *Ibid., 1700-1751*, p. 5.

38 " Marriages of Charlestowne, Rhode Island," *Narragansett Historical
Register*, ed. James Arnold (Hamilton, 1882-1883), I, 266, 271.

39 *Early Conn. Marriages*, I, 14.

40 Steiner, *op. cit.*, p. 11.

41 *Early Rhode Island*, p. 310.

42 *Mass. Hist. Soc. Colls.*, Second Series, III, 93.

43 *Ibid.*, p. 95.

44 *Journal of Negro History* (Washington, 1920), V, 50.

45 Susan Whitney Dimock, *Births, Marriages, Baptisms and Deaths in
Coventry, Connecticut, 1711-1844* (New York, 1847), p. 170.

woman, were joined in wedlock in New London by the Reverend Eliphalet Adams in 1718,[46] and Adam Allen in 1761 and Ebedmelick in 1764, both of whom were Negro slaves, married Indian women in Plymouth, Massachusetts.[47]

In other cases, Negro slaves married free Indian women, as illustrated by an advertisement that appeared in the *Boston Weekly Post Boy* in 1741, in which a Rhode Island master offered a reward of five pounds for his mulatto slave, who had run off with his (the Negro's) Indian wife.[48] Salem Poor, a Negro, who was later cited for his gallantry during the American Revolution, also married a half-breed Indian woman.[49]

Intermarriage also occurred between free Negroes and free Indians. Scipio of New London, Connecticut, married Hannah, an Indian woman of the same town in August 1718 [50] and in 1715, the Selectmen of Boston ordered an Indian woman, whose husband was a mulatto, to leave the town.[51] On July 7, 1746, Cuffee Slocum, who had recently been manumitted by his master, John Slocum of Dartmouth, Massachusetts, took as his wife, Ruth Moses, an Indian girl of the same city.[52] One of the sons of this union was Paul Cuffee (the name of Slocum having been dropped by him about 1778),[53] the famous merchant, whaling captain and colonizer.[54] He, too, was married to an Indian girl, Alice Pequit of Dartmouth.[55]

Occasionally the blood of three different races was blended in these marriages. Weeden relates a Rhode Island marriage in

---

46 *Early Conn. Marriages,* II, 10.

47 *Plymouth Church Records, 1620-1854,* XXIII, 492-493.

48 *Boston Weekly Post Boy,* Sept. 14, 1741.

49 *Standard History of Essex County,* ed. Dr. Henry Wheatland, p. 237.

50 *Early Conn. Marriages,* II, 10.

51 "Report of Record Commissioners of Boston," *Selectmen's Records, 1701-1751* (Boston, 1884), XI, 226.

52 *Journal of Negro History* (Washington, 1923), VIII, 154.

53 *Ibid.,* p. 155.

54 *Ibid.,* p. 156, *et seq.*

55 *Ibid.,* p. 159.

which white, black, and red strains were united. Thomas Walously, says Weeden, "was a mustee or at least an octoroon," who later married an Indian woman.[56] The same was true of Crispus Attucks, an early hero of the American Revolution[57] and of Lewis, a Rhode Island Negro of mixed Negro and Indian blood, who married a white woman, named Mary Matthews.[58]

Miscegenation between the Indians and Negroes was brought about by several factors. In the first place, there were no legal obstacles to the amalgamation of these two subject races.[59] Moreover, the lowly status assigned to both groups by a master class of whites served to abolish social differences between them, and to draw them more closely together in a spirit and common brotherhood of suffering. Nor did the Indian seem to evince any disinclination to mate with the Negro. Furthermore, the scarcity of Negro women of marriageable age in New England encouraged Negro men to look upon Indian women as possible wives.[60] Not having enough women of their own, and sometimes barred either by law or sentiment from intermarriage with white persons, the Negroes united freely with Indians.[61] Evidences of such intermixture are patent even today in many New England Negro families.

An analysis of Negro and Indian marriages reveals several significant sidelights. Among the most outstanding is the general absence of surnames among the Negroes. Notable exceptions occurred in the cases of James Nash and Sarah Marion, who were married on December 7, 1710,[62] and John Humphrey

56 *Early Rhode Island*, p. 310.

57 Temple, *op. cit.*, p. 255.

58 "Marriages of Charlestowne, R. I.," *loc. cit.*, I, 268-269.

59 Indian and Negroes were grouped together in the slave codes of all the New England Provinces. *Vide supra*, ch. v.

60 *Vide supra*, p. 93 ff.

61 *Journal of Negro History*, V, 47-48, 56-57; *Mass. Hist. Soc. Colls.*, Second Series, III, 94; Daniel, *op. cit.*, pp. 3-4.

62 *Boston Marriages, 1700-1751*, p. 28.

and Lidiah Kitteradge, whose banns were published on January 22, 1724.[63] But in the majority of instances the Christian name alone is given, followed by the word " Negro." Records of such marriages as that of " Robin Negro and Kate," " Titus Negro and Nell Negro," " Josiah Negro and Jane Negro," " Mingo Negro and Maria Negro " are numerous.[64] Surnames did not become common for Negroes until after slavery had been abolished in New England.

The records further show that the Puritans regarded these slave marriages with as much gravity as they did those of free persons, for they were performed by some of the most distinguished members of the clergy and of the bench. Among the ministers are to be found such famous names as Cotton Mather, Benjamin Coleman, Benjamin Wadsworth, Thomas Bridge, Thomas Cheeves, Samuel Williard, John Webb, Samuel Stillman, and Joseph Sewall of Massachusetts;[65] Ezra Stiles, Chauncey Whittlesey, Eliphalet Adams of Connecticut;[66] and John Checkley of Rhode Island.[67]

Not only was there intermarriage between the subject races, but blacks sometimes married members of the master class. Unions between whites and blacks, however, seem to have been much less frequent than those between Negroes and Indians. According to contemporary testimony, miscegenation between whites and Negroes occurred chiefly between black men and white women. Such was the view of Samuel Dexter, a prominent Boston merchant, benefactor of Harvard College, and a member of the Massachusetts legislature. Writing to Dr. Jeremy Belknap in 1795 he stated: " Intermarriages between whites and blacks are very rare, oftener between black men and white

63 *Ibid.*, p. 161.

64 *Ibid.*, p. 13.

65 *Boston Marriages, 1700-1751*, XXVIII, 3, 5, 28, 29, 31, 108 and *passim*; XXX, 15, 16, 45, 90 and *passim*.

66 Stiles *Literary Diary*, I, 658; *Early Conn. Marriages*, pp. 1, 10, 12, 13, 14.

67 Slater, " John Checkley," *loc. cit.*, II, 216.

women than on the contrary." [68] Whether this was true in general of such marriages cannot be definitely determined, but the record of several marriages between white women and black men lends support to Dexter's statement. Lemuel Haynes, noted below as the first Negro to preach regularly to a white congregation in America, not only was the son of a white woman and a full-blooded pure African,[69] but Haynes himself married a white woman,[70] as did also Festus, the son of Abijah Prince of Sunderland, Vermont.[71] Similar marriages were also performed in Rhode Island.[72] In Connecticut, racial crossing apparently took place with some frequency. Records of marriages between Negroes, and of Negroes with Indians, usually designate the race or racial mixture of the contracting parties by such words as " Indian," " Negro," " free Negro," " mulatto," or " mustee." Where such identification is lacking, as in cases like " Ben," a free Negro, with Jenny, servant to Mr. Isaacs, or Isborn, a free Negro, " with Mindivell widow," it is possible that one of the parties to the marriage was white.[73]

There was much sexual promiscuity among all races and classes in colonial New England, and no matter how carefully the authorities—civil and religious—strove to maintain proper sexual relationships, court records abound with cases of immorality.[74] Hundreds of malefactors were haled before the courts charged with fornication, bastardy, or both. Many of these persons were Negroes, both slave and free, all of whom were subject to the general laws governing sex relationships. Bondage

---

68 *Mass. Hist. Soc. Colls.*, Fifth Series, III, 386.

69 Cooley, *op. cit.*, p. 28.

70 *Ibid.*, p. 70.

71 Sheldon, *History of Deerfield, Massachusetts*, II, 900.

72 " Marriages of Charlestowne Rhode Island," I, 268, 269.

73 *Early Connecticut Marriages*, I, 7, 8.

74 For numerous instances of fornication and rape by whites *vide Essex County Court Records*, VIII, 15, 43, 47, 87, 97, 99, 100, 104, 140, 145-146, 181, 228, 237, 241, 274, 275, 279, 289, 298, 299, 302, 367, 368, 371, 372, 375-377, 389, 422, 424, 440; *cf. ibid.*, I-VII, *passim*; S.C.C.R. *passim*.

gave no sexual license to the New England slave. He was as liable to arrest and punishment for gratifying his sex appetite outside of marriage as was the free white person. Many cases can be cited in support of this statement. As early as 1660 Juggy, the slave woman of Captain White of Newbury, Massachusetts, was sentenced to be whipped for fornication.[75] Sixteen years later, Grace, the slave of Richard Dole of Ipswich, was sentenced to be whipped and pay a fine for having an illegitimate child.[76] David and Judith were whipped for fornication in 1678,[77] and two years later Hagar and Toney received similar sentences for the same offense.[78]

Sexual promiscuity not only went on among the slaves, but much illicit intercourse took place between Negroes and whites. Such relationships were not confined to any particular class of whites, for both free and bound males of the master group sought and enjoyed the intimate favors of slave women. In seeking the causes for such associations in the antebellum South, Frazier raises several pertinent questions which are applicable on a smaller scale to New England. He inquires:

> In view of the relations of superordination and subordination between the two races, how far did these associations originate in mere physical compulsion? How far did the women of the subordinate race surrender themselves because they were subject to the authority of the master race? Or was the prestige of the white race sufficient to insure compliance on the part of the mulatto women, both slave and free? How far was mutual attraction responsible for acquiescence on the part of the woman?[79]

No doubt all these factors entered into the extra-legal sexual relationships between white men and Negro women in colonial

---

75 *E.C.C.R.*, II, 247.

76 *Ibid.*, V, 316, 411.

77 *Ibid.*, VIII, 141.

78 *Ibid.*, VII, 411.

79 Frazier, *Negro Family in the United States*, p. 65.

New England but the records examined, unfortunately, shed no light on this point.

Nevertheless, miscegenation between the master class and slave women was common. According to Weeden, " illicit intercourse between white men and colored women in Rhode Island marked a numerous progeny." [80] The same was true of Massachusetts where the court records abound in cases of " fornication " or " bastardy." [81] In 1663, Walter Taylor was formally accused of being the father of a child, born out of wedlock to the slave of Captain White of Hampton, Massachusetts. Taylor then sued White for defamation, asserting that the charge caused him " to be reproached and derided up and down the country." Although the slave maintained in Court that Taylor was the child's father and there was the corroborating testimony of a white woman, the Court declined to convict Taylor. Instead, it tacitly recognized his guilt by fining him forty shillings for commencing " a vexatious suit " against Captain White.[82] Sixteen years later, when Kathalina, a Boston slave, named Lofton Loney as the father of her bastard child, the court again refused to fasten the paternity of a Negro child upon a white man. Lofton, strongly protesting his innocence, was acquitted. Upon the double charge of fornication and bastardy, Kathalina was sentenced to be whipped with fifteen stripes and to be fined forty shillings.[83] A similar case involved Miriam, the slave woman of John Pynchon, Jr., of Massachusetts. Miriam accused an Englishman named Cornish of being the child's father. Cornish evidently made good his escape, but Miriam paid the usual penalty of a whipping and a fine.[84] White women, charged with the same offense, were similarly dealt with.[85]

80 Weeden, *Early Rhode Island*, p. 310.

81 See *E.C.C.R.*, *passim*; *S.C.C.R.*, *passim*, *R.C.A.*; *passim*.

82 *E.C.C.R.*, *1662-1667*, III, 101.

83 *S.C.C.R.*, *1671-1680*, XXX, Part II, 1164.

84 *Ibid.*, XXX, Part II, 809.

85 In a case involving white persons in Massachusetts, Martha Stanton, charged with fornication and having a bastard child in 1672-73, accused

Although the courts in none of the foregoing cases actually designated a white man as the father of a slave woman's child, numerous instances exist of such declarations where evidence seemed to substantiate the Negro's accusation. In a court held at Salisbury, Massachusetts, in April 1675, John Clarke was branded as the " reputed father of the bastard child of Bess, the negro of Robert Smart, according to the law." [86] In 1672 not only did a Massachusetts Court convict Christopher Mason, a white indentured servant, of the paternity of a child born to a slave woman, but also sentenced him to be whipped with twenty stripes and ordered him to pay costs of Court.[87] William Rane, charged with a similar offense eight years later, was not only fined but ordered to pay three shillings a week to the master of the slave woman toward the support of the child.[88]

In some paternity cases no mention is made of the father either by the accused or by the court. For example, Dina the slave of Benjamin Roffe of Newbury, Massachusetts,[89] Maria, Simon Lynde's Negro woman,[90] and Grace, the slave of William Coleman,[91] both of Boston, were convicted of having illegitimate children and sentenced to be whipped. Who were the unnamed fathers of these children? The masters?

Thomas Trott as the father. But Trott denied the charge so stoutly he was released. Martha was convicted and sentenced to be whipped with fifteen stripes and pay costs of Court. *Ibid.*, XXIX, Part I, 222. Francis Bacon paid a similar penalty in 1674. *Ibid.*, p. 487. Sarah Buckminster, a widow, received a like punishment in the same year. *Ibid.*, p. 442.

86 *E.C.C.R.*, VI, 23.

87 *S.C.C.R.*, XIX, Part I, 185, 232. The convicted white man was Christopher Mason; the woman, Bess, the slave of Joseph Rock. Bess also received twenty stripes. *Ibid.*

88 This case came before the Salem Quarterly Court of Massachusetts for June 1680. *E.C.C.R.*, *1678-1680*, VII, 410.

89 This case occurred in 1676. The woman had the alternative of paying a fine. *E.C.C.R.*, *1675-1678*, VI, 138.

90 *S.C.C.R.*, *1671-1686*, XXX, Part II, 809.

91 *Ibid.*, p. 841.

Paternity cases were common among the unfree groups, whether black, white, or red. The lowly condition of these persons, the community of feeling engendered among them as a result of their common bondage, their close association throughout hours of labor, together with the probable proximity of their sleeping quarters, all made for sexual freedom among them. About 1672, Jasper, an Indian slave, was whipped and fined for having an illegitimate child by Joan, a Negro slave woman. Both Jasper and Joan were owned by the same master.[92] Occasionally, members of two different races shared the same slave woman. In 1678-79 Robert Corbet, a white servant, George, a Negro slave, and Maria, a Negro woman, all belonging to Stephen French, were sentenced by the Suffolk County Court of Massachusetts to be whipped with twenty lashes and to pay costs of Court. Both Corbet and George had been adjudged guilty of " fornication " with Maria.[93]

Miscegenation between white and black was also often furthered by adultery. Because of this charge, several white families and at least one Negro family were broken up. On September 27, 1750, Nicholas Brown of Westfield, Massachusetts, appealed to the General Court for a divorce from his wife, Agnes. Brown charged his wife with having had sexual relationships with several Negroes, and he specifically accused her of being the mother of a mulatto child by a Negro slave named Primus. On February 8, 1751, the legislature, lending a receptive ear to Brown's plea, granted him a divorce and declared him free to marry again.[94] In October of the same year the legislature dissolved the marriage of Ralph and Lois Way of Hadley, Massachusetts, on the ground that Lois had borne a bastard son by a Negro slave named Boston.[95] Charging her

92 The case was tried before the Suffolk County Court of Massachusetts for January 1672-73. *S.C.C.R.*, XXX, Part II, 233.

93 *Ibid.*, p. 991.

94 *Massachusetts Archives: Domestic Relations, 1643-1774*, IX, 349-352a.

95 *Ibid.*, IX, 359-364a.

husband Benjamin with adultery, desertion, and bigamy, and also with being the father of a mulatto child by a Negro girl, Sarah Foster applied for a divorce in 1755. The legislature ordered Foster to appear before its Board on the first Wednesday of the next session and to show cause why Sarah's petition should not be granted.[96]

In 1742 a slave named Boston petitioned for a divorce from his wife, Hagar. In his appeal to the General Court of Massachusetts, on April 15, 1742, Boston charged that Hagar " not having the fear of God before her eyes and being instigated by a white man has been guilty of the detestable sin of adultery and during the time of intermarriage was delivered of a mulatto bastard child begotten on her body." [97] According to witnesses Hagar claimed that William Kelley, a white soldier, was the child's father.[98] After duly considering the petition, the legislature granted Boston a divorce.[99]

Ridicule, fines, divorce, and corporal punishment failed to stop the interbreeding of Negroes and whites. These devices were as powerless to prevent miscegenation in New England as were the more severe penalties in the colonial South.[100] Proof of this failure was seen in the increasing number of mulattoes. As their numbers multiplied, they became a legal problem, and before the end of the seventeenth century, they were classified separately in the laws governing slaves. Massachusetts first applied this distinction in 1693;[101] Connecticut followed in 1704.[102] Rhode Island [103] and New Hampshire did so in 1714.[104] There-

96 *Ibid.*, IX, 393-394.

97 Massachusetts Archives, IX, 248.

98 *Ibid.*, pp. 249, 250.

99 *Ibid.*, p. 248.

100 *Maryland Archives, January 1637/38—September, 1664*, I, 533-534; Hurd, *op. cit.*, I, 240, 249, 250, 251 n.; 252-253. *Vide Journal of Negro History*, III, 341-346.

101 *Mass. A. and R.*, I, 156.

102 *Conn. Col. Recs.*, IV, 40.

103 *R. I. Acts, Laws and Charters* (Digest, 1710), p. 70.

104 *N. H. Acts and Laws* (Portsmouth, 1771), pp. 38-40.

after slaves were usually referred to either as " Indians," " Negroes," or " mulattoes." The legal designation of these mixed breeds by the term " mulatto," " molato," " molatto " or " malatto " persisted until the extinction of slavery in New England.

The increasing number of mulattoes, through intermarriage and illicit relationships, soon caused alarm among Puritan advocates of racial purity and white domination. Sensing a deterioration of slavery, if the barriers between master and slaves were dissolved in the equalitarian crucible of sexual intimacy, they sought to stop racial crossing by statute. Precedent had already been established by Virginia and Maryland (1664) both of which had passed harsh laws outlawing intermarriage between whites and blacks.[105] Massachusetts, however, was the only New England colony to take such action. In December, 1705-06, the legislature enacted a stringent law for the " better preventing of a spurious and mix't issue." The first section of the act was designed to stop promiscuous sex relations between Negro men and white women. It provided that " if any negro or molatto man shall commit fornication with an English woman, or a woman of any other Christian nation " in Massachusetts, both were to be severely whipped by order of the justices of assize, or the court of general sessions of the peace within the county where the offense was committed. The man to be " sold out of the province " within six months after conviction and during the interim was to be confined to jail at his master's charge. The woman was to support the child, if any at her own expense. If unable to do so, she was to be bound out to service for as long a period as the justices should deem necessary for the child's maintenance.[106] The second section prohibited all white men—Englishmen and other Christians—from promiscuous relations with Negro or mulatto women. Upon conviction, both were to be severely whipped. The man was to be fined five pounds which was to be used for the support of the government. He was also to be responsible for the care of any children that

105 *Maryland and Archives, January 1637/38—September 1664*, I, 533-534.
106 *Mass. A. and R.*, I, 578.

might result from the association.[107] The woman was to be sold
out of the province. Aside from the death penalty, banishment
was the most severe punishment that could be imposed upon
New England slaves, who were terrified by the ruthless type of
slavery practiced in the West Indies.[108] Another section of the
law forbade marriages between whites and blacks. No English
or Scottish subject, nor any other Christian, might contract
marriage with a Negro or mulatto. Any one performing such
a ceremony was to be fined fifty pounds, one half to go to the
government, the other half to the informer. The fine was recov-
erable in any court of record in the colony either by " bill, plaint
or information." In order to remove all possible grounds for
mixed marriages, section five of the act expressly forbade the
master to deny marriage to his Negro with one of his own
race.[109]

In practice the law did not have the desired effect. In the first
place it did not annul the marriage once it had taken place, a
fact significantly stressed by Judge James Winthrop in his reply
to Dr. Jeremy Belknap in 1795.[110] Nor did it effectively check
promiscuity between the races, for economic considerations on
the part of the master overrode concern for morality and even
racial integrity. In case his slave violated the law, the owner
would not only lose his services for six months but would also
have to bear the cost of the Negro's imprisonment. The master
was also saddled with costs of court for the prosecution of his
slave. In view of his potential loss, the owner could hardly be
expected to inform against his chattel. Furthermore, since the
master, upon the slave's conviction, faced the total loss of his
property without compensation, he often tended to overlook, or
to conceal as long as possible, such violations of the law. Thus
Samuel Sewall noted that many masters in order to save their

107 *Ibid.*

108 W. O. Blake, *History of Slavery and the Slave Trade* (Columbus,
1857), pp. 214, 215, 246, 258-259.

109 *Mass. A. and R., ut supra.*

110 *Mass. Hist. Soc. Colls.*, Fifth Series, III, 390.

property, actually connived at the illicit relationships of their slaves, "lest they should be obliged to find them wives or pay their fines."[111]

Neither legal prohibition in Massachusetts, nor sentiment, if any, in the other colonies apparently prevented the intermixing of whites and blacks. The futility of this effort is shown by the large proportion of mulattoes in the colonies toward the close of the Revolutionary period. Especially was this true in Rhode Island. In 1782, there were 51,869 inhabitants in the entire state. Of these, 3,806 or 7.3 per cent were Negroes who, in turn, were divided into 464 mulattoes and 2,342 blacks. The mulattoes comprised almost one-eighth of the Negro population of the state. The towns showed varying proportions: in that year almost one-tenth of the Negroes of Newport were mulattoes; in Portsmouth, about one-sixth, and more than one-third in Bristol and Warwick showed mixed blood. In Westerly, the mulattoes actually outnumbered the blacks, 36 to 28.[112] Whether slaves of mixed blood received more privileges than the pure Negro, or were assigned to more desirable types of work, such as frequently occurred in the antebellum South,[113] cannot be stated with authority. In essence, blacks and mulattoes, because of New England's peculiar economic system, seem to have been on the same footing.

In addition to illicit sexual relationships, the slave family was subject to other disruptive influences, apart from those operative upon the domestic relationships of free white persons. Marital associations were necessarily irregular and unstable. The very character of slavery made such a condition inevitable. Slaves, as stated above, assumed no surname upon marriage. The psychological and emotional bond of unity which the marriage ceremony was intended to impart could hardly have been

111 Sewall, "Selling of Joseph," *Mass. Hist. Soc. Colls.*, Fifth Series, VI, 18.

112 *R. I. State Recs., 1780-1783*, IX, 653.

113 See E. Franklin Frazier, "The Negro Slave Family," *Journal of Negro History*, XV, 208-211.

experienced by the slaves. For example, when Caesar and Dinah,[114] married, they—like many of their fellow bondmen—left the wedding ceremony not as Mr. and Mrs. Jones or Smith, but just as they had presented themselves; as Caesar " negro " and Dinah " negro." They still remained the property of their respective masters and were still subject to their authority. Whatever the wishes or desires of the slaves, those of the owner must have priority. The sanction of parental rights and duties, in the last analysis, lay not in the slave mother and father but in the master. Especially where slaves belonged to different owners, marriage did little more than legalize sexual intimacy. This characteristic of slave marriages was so apparent to the Reverend Samuel Phillips of Andover, Massachusetts, that when uniting slaves in wedlock, he pronounced them " licensed to be conversant and familiar together as husband and wife." [114a]

Economic considerations might result in the breakup of the slave family at any time. Although the Puritans went to the greatest lengths to safeguard the integrity of their own families, they were unable or unwilling to extend the same protection to the slave family.[115] Puritan love of money proved stronger than respect for domestic ties. As a result, Palfrey notwithstanding,[116] slave families might be broken up at any time, husband and wife might be sold or given to masters in different localities. Typical was the dissolution of the slave family owned by the Reverend John Swift of Framingham, Massachusetts. When the minister died in 1743, the family of Nero and Dido —who had been married twelve years—was broken up: Nero was given to Ebenezer Robie, Swift's son-in-law, who lived in Sudbury; Dido and her daughter were bequeathed to Mrs. Swift who continued to reside at Framingham. Even at her

114 " Early Connecticut Marriages," *loc. cit.*, I, 29.

114a Cited in Howard, *op. cit.*, II, 225-226.

115 Calhoun, *op. cit.*, I, 80.

116 Palfrey says that the slave mother and father were never separated in New England. *History of New England*, II, 30 n.

death, the slave family was not to be reunited, for Dido and her daughter were to be given to the widow's daughter-in-law.[117]

Not only death of the master, but also the profit motive, often broke up the slave family. The slave mother and her young children were sometimes regarded as a unit, and mother and children were separated from husband and father and sold.[118] Contemporary newspapers offer abundant evidence on this point. One advertisement quoted a " likely Negro wench, about 22 years old and a child about four years old . . ."; [119] another, a " likely Negro woman with a likely male child, 10 months old; " [120] and a third, "A Negro woman age about 24 years, and her child, a girl about five years." [121] Occasionally a master would offer to sell mother and child separately, as is illustrated by a Boston advertisement in 1782, which listed for sale a Negro woman, nineteen years old and her infant of six months to be sold either " together or apart." [122]

The slave family was also disrupted by the sale of the children. Offspring of slaves became the property of the woman's owner and as such were economic assets in the possession of the master. They were sometimes taken from their parents and sold with as little restraint as one would sell a calf, pig, or colt. For example, one newspaper offered for sale a " child about four years old; " another a " female Negro child about 13 or 14 years of age," and a third, a " likely Negro girl about 13 or 14 years of age." [123] In one instance even an infant was sold when

117 Temple, op. cit., p. 236.

118 Frazier found that in the antebellum South the Negro mother and her young children were generally treated as a group. The Negro Family in the United States, p. 57.

119 New England Weekly Journal, Feb. 21, 1738.

120 New England Chronicle, April 25, 1776.

121 Boston News Letter, Aug. 25, 1718.

122 Boston News Letter, May 1, 1732.

123 New England Weekly Journal, Jan. 17, Feb. 21, 1738; April 18, 1728.

in 1738, Ezekiel Chase of Newbury, Massachusetts, sold to John Merrill, for forty pounds, his " Negro boy Titus about one year and a half old." [124]

Disruption of the slave family sometimes resulted from the giving away of Negro children like puppies or kittens, after the mother had weaned them. Again it was a matter of business. If the master felt unable to support an additional slave or if, especially during the hard times of the Revolutionary period, he did not have work for the child to do, he was only too willing, if no buyer appeared, to give the child away. Hence, such advertisements as: " a fine Negro child of a good healthy breed to be given away—enquire of the printer; " [125] or " a fine healthy female child to be given away." [126] In one instance arrangements were made for the disposal of the child before it was born. Thus a Boston master advertised: "A Negro child soon expected of a good breed, may be owned by any person inclining to take it away." So eager was the master to be relieved of the child that he offered a sum of money to anyone who would accept it.[127]

Far more terrible than the selling of slave children by the master was the deliberate murder of their infants by slave mothers. Infanticide was resorted to mainly by women who had borne illegitimate children. Bastardy usually carried the penalty of a fine and from ten to twenty lashes well laid on. Frantically seeking to evade such punishment by concealing the evidence of their crime, slave and white women alike sometimes killed their offspring and thus laid themselves liable to the more dreaded charge of infanticide, a crime punishable by death. It would be interesting to know how far the murder of their infants by slave women can be interpreted as a protest against slavery. At any rate a number of slave women were arraigned for bastardy and murder. Occasionally, as in the case of a Negro in Tiver-

124 Coffin, *Sketch of Newbury*, p. 337.

125 *Boston Weekly News Letter*, June 26, 1760.

126 *Boston Gazette or Weekly Advertiser*, June 25, 1754.

127 *Continental Journal*, December 21, 1780.

ton,[128] Rhode Island, they were acquitted. When found guilty, however, they were sometimes brutally whipped, more often sentenced to death. In the case of Anna, the slave of Rebeckah Lynde of Charlestown, Massachusetts, a savage penalty was exacted. For the murder of her child she was sentenced to stand on the gallows for an hour with a rope about her neck, the other end fastened to the gallows. She was then to be tied to the tail of a cart and whipped with thirty stripes from the gallows to the prison. After being jailed for a month, she was " then to be conveyed by the marshall Generall to Charlestowne," where she was to be again whipped. After this ordeal and upon paying costs of court and imprisonment, Anna was to be released.[129] More frequently, slave women so accused were upon conviction sentenced to death. Such was the fate of Jenny, a Boston slave, who was sentenced to die in 1767; [130] and of Kate, a Hartford Negro, found guilty of the same crime.[131]

Negro women were not the only sufferers on this score. White women, bond and free, were similarly dealt with. In 1682, Elizabeth Payne [132] and in 1678, Cordin Drabston of Boston were acquitted of " bastardy " but whipped for fornication.[133] Less fortunate was Elizabeth Emmerson of Haverhill, Massachusetts, who was sentenced to death in 1691, for murdering her two illegitimate offspring.[134]

Other factors making for demoralization of the slave family in the South, such as forcible mating and the breeding of slaves for market, were rare in New England. Although newspapers

128 *Newport Mercury*, March 15, 1773.

129 *R. C. A. 1630-1692*, I, 29-30.

130 *Boston Gazette and County Journal*, March 16, 1767.

131 Kate was sentenced to death on September 12, 1743. The Reverend Wadsworth of Hartford who had attended all the sessions of the case and had prayed with Kate, recorded it in his diary. Wadsworth, *Diary, 1737-1747*, pp. 100, 106.

132 *R.C.A., 1630-1692*, I, 228.

133 *Ibid.*, pp. 125-126.

134 *Ibid.*, p. 357.

often quoted Negroes " of a good breed," only two instances of compulsory mating and breeding have been found there. As early as 1639 Samuel Maverick of Noddle's Island, Massachusetts, is said to have tried to mate a former African queen with one of his Negro men. According to Josselyn, an English traveller, who was visiting Maverick at the time: [135]

> The second of October, (1639) about 9 of the clock in the morning, Mr. Mavericks Negro woman came to my chamber window, and in her own Countrey language and tune sang her very loud and shrill, going out to her, she used a great deal of respect towards me, and willingly would have expressed her grief in English; but I apprehended it by her countenance and deportment, whereupon I repaired to my host, to learn of him the cause, and intreat him in her behalf, for that I understood before, that she had been a Queen in her own Countrey, and observed a very humble and dutiful garb used towards her by another Negro who was her maid. Mr. Maverick was desirious to have a breed of Negroes, and therefore seeing she would not yield by persuasions to company with a Negro young man he had in his house, he commanded him, wil'd she nill'd she, to go to bed with her, which was no sooner done, but she kicked him out again, this she took in high disdain beyond her slavery and this was the cause of her grief.

The second instance relates to a slave owner of Hanover, Massachusetts, who is said to have bred slaves for the market.[136] Neither of these cases is improbable for, as repeatedly stated, Negroes who had assimilated the customs and manners of New England were preferred to " unseasoned " blacks brought direct from Africa or even from the West Indies.[137]

[135] Josselyn probably meant that she had been a queen in Africa. " Josselyn's Account of Two Voyages to New England," *Mass. Hist. Soc. Colls.*, III, 231.

[136] Barry, *History of Hanover*, p. 175.

[137] See such phrases as " born in this country," " born in this countay," etc. *New England Weekly Journal*, September 5, 1738; *vide supra*, p. 38.

New England slave women were not generally valued for their breeding qualities. Indeed, rapid slave breeding seems not to have been regarded with favor by the owners. No advertisements so far have been found that played up the breeding proclivity of slave women. Just the opposite situation prevailed in the South, where a continued demand for slave labor, especially after the invention of the cotton gin, placed a premium upon rapid child-bearing by Negro women. Girls were often expected to become mothers at fifteen; [138] and forcible mating was common. In New England, however, no economic sanction existed for such a rapid multiplication of slaves. The economy of this section could absorb only a certain number of Negroes. Once the saturation point was reached the increase would only encumber the master's household, thereby entailing additional outlay with slight prospect of future return. Consideration for the slave family, therefore, broke down in the face of economic interest, and masters who could not profitably employ the offspring of their slaves either sold or gave them away. Since prolific breeding by slave women in New England was unprofitable and a burden to the master, Negroes were occasionally sold merely because they bred too fast. Thus the *Continental Journal* advertised for sale a Negro girl who " has been used to a farmer's kitchen and dairy, and is not known to have any failing but being with child which is the only cause of her being sold." [139]

What was the reaction of the slave parents to the break-up of their families? On this score the records for the most part are silent, but in a petition presented to the Massachusetts legislature by a group of Boston Negroes in 1773, there is voiced

138 It is not possible to make any accurate statement concerning the age at which most New England slave women became mothers. Breeding propensities were not played up in advertisements. However, in the quotations of slaves for sale it is possible to say that many were mothers at the age of eighteen. See *New England Weekly Journal*, Tuesday, February 21, 1738. For excellent account of this in the South in refutation of the thesis set forth by U. B. Phillips (*American Negro Slavery*, pp. 360-362), see Frederic Bancroft, *Slave Trading in the Old South* (Baltimore, 1931), pp. 26, 67-87; *passim*.

139 Cited Moore, *op. cit.*, p. 209.

an impassioned statement of the effect of slavery upon the Negro family. After appealing for their freedom as a natural right,
the slaves lamented the destruction of their domestic ties. Said
the petitioners in part:

> The endearing ties of husband and wife we are strangers to
> for we are no longer man and wife than our masters or
> mestesses [mistresses] thinks proper . . . Our children are
> also taken from us by force and sent many miles from us
> wear [where] we seldom or ever see them again there to be
> made slaves of for Life which sometimes is vere [very] short
> by Reson of Being dragged from their mothers Breest
> [breast]. How can a slave perform the duties of a husband
> to a wife or parent to his child?   How can a husband leave
> master and work and cleave to his wife? How can the wife
> submit themselves to there [their] husbands in all things?
> How can the child obey thear parents in all things? [140]

This appeal, like others, fell upon unsympathetic ears in the
legislature. Almost a quarter of a century was to pass before
the Negroes in New England were to develop family institutions free from the disruptive influences of slavery.

[140] The entire petition may be found in *Mass. Hist. Soc. Colls.*, Fifth
Series, III, 432-433.

# CHAPTER IX
## MASTER AND SLAVE

SLAVERY was considerably milder in New England than elsewhere in colonial America. Negroes were brutally treated in the West Indies and in parts of South America, areas where absentee ownership, industrialized slavery with its emphasis upon profit, the overwhelming proportion of blacks to whites, and the masters' constant fear of Negro uprisings, all made for harsher treatment of the slaves. Notorious for brutality toward their Negroes were the Dutch; rivalling them were the Portuguese and the French. In the plantation colonies of English America slaves were often flogged, mutilated and tortured and the killing of a slave by the master in the colonial South was not a crime punishable at law.[1]

Contrasted with this type of bondage, slavery in New England was comparatively humane. This condition was the result, in part, of the nature of New England's economy which could not absorb large numbers of slaves. In no sense did the economic welfare of colonial New England depend wholly upon slave labor. Psychologically, New England masters did not live in terror of Negro uprisings to the same degree as did the planters in the West Indies, Brazil, or in the colonial South. As a result they were not compelled to hold their slaves in such abject servitude as did the slave owners of South Carolina, where the Negroes greatly outnumbered the whites. On the eve of the American Revolution only one person in fifty was a Ne-

1 For the cruelty of Dutch masters in Guiana and Surinam, during this period *vide,* Sir Harry Johnston, *The Negro in the New World* (New York, 1910), pp. 113-120; for the Portuguese, *vide* Arthur Ramos, *The Negro in Brazil* (Washington, 1939), pp. 20-23; Johnston, *op. cit.,* p. 94; *Journal of Negro History,* XIV, 315 ff; for the French in Haiti *vide* Lothrop Stoddard, *The French Revolution in San Domingo* (Boston, 1914), ch. v; Johnston, *op. cit.,* p. 140; for the plantation South, *vide* Henry Waller Hening, *Statutes at Large of Virginia, 1711-1736* (Richmond, 1814), IV, 128, 132, 133; David J. McCord, *Statutes at Large of South Carolina* (Charleston, 1840), VII, 343-345; Carter G. Woodson, *The Negro in Our History,* p. 225.

gro in New England; in South Carolina two out of three persons were Negroes.[2] The more intimate association of masters and slaves in New England, necessitated by the diversity of New England's economic life, also made for kinder treatment of the slaves. Religion, as already pointed out, played an important role. The fact that the New Englanders regarded the slaves as persons divinely committed to their stewardship[3] developed a patriarchal conception of slavery, which along with other factors, went far to mitigate the unhappy condition of their bondmen. Congregational ministers and magistrates like John Eliot,[4] Cotton Mather,[5] Ezra Stiles,[6] Edward Holyoke,[7] and Samuel Sewall,[8] who wielded a powerful influence in shaping the thought of colonial New England, helped through precept and example to foster this benign paternalism. No better spokesman for this viewpoint could be cited than the erudite Cotton Mather who wrote:

> I would always remember, that my servants are in some sence my children, and by taking care that they want nothing which may be good for them, I would make them as my children; and so far as the methods of instituting piety in the mind which I use with my children, may be properly and prudently used with my servants, they shall be partakers in them—Nor will I leave them ignorant of anything, wherein I may instruct them to be useful to their generation.[9]

2 For convenient summary of Negro and white population on the eve of the Revolution, *vide,* Greene and Harrington, *op. cit.,* pp. 6-7.

3 By no one is this attitude better expressed than by Cotton Mather (*The Negro Christianized,* p. 4), who reminded the Puritans that "the Negroes may be the Elect of God placed in their hands by Divine Providence."

4 Cotton Mather, *Life of John Eliot,* p. 109.

5 "Diary," *Mass. Hist. Soc. Colls.,* Seventh Series, VIII, Part II, 384.

6 *Literary Diary of Ezra Stiles,* I, 25, 39, 90, 213.

7 "Diary of Reverend Edward Holyoke, 1709-1768," *Holyoke Diaries, 1709-1856,* pp. 17, 18, 21-22, 23.

8 "Diary of Samuel Sewall," *loc. cit.,* VII, 296, 394.

9 "Diary" in *Mass. Hist. Soc. Colls.,* Seventh Series, VIII, Part II, 384.

Mather not only treated his own slaves kindly but also expressed concern about slaves in general. He formed a Negro Society, which met in his home, and wrote pamphlets advocating the Christianization and humane treatment of the slaves. In November, 1716 he wrote to Thomas Prince, asking whether the African slaves were " treated according to the rules of humanity." Mather also was anxious to know whether the Negroes were regarded as " those that are of one blood with us " . . . who " have immortal souls in them and are not mere beasts of burden." [10]

Emulating their leaders, many masters manifested similar consideration for their slaves. Before his death Deacon Clark of Waterbury, Connecticut, arranged for his slave, Mingo, to choose with which of his master's sons he preferred to live. After staying with Thomas for a while, Mingo is said to have objected to his new master's keeping a tavern, and soon afterwards left him and went to live with the other son, Timothy.[11] Partridge Thatcher of New Milford, Connecticut, liberated all of his slaves during his lifetime, and is said to have treated them " with a kindness enough to put to shame the reproaches of all the abolitionists of New England." [12] So kindly had Benjamin Isaacs of Norwalk, Connecticut, used his slaves that when the British raided Norwalk, during the American Revolution, the Negroes are said to have saved their masters' house from destruction.[13] The Negro slave of the famous Brown brothers of Providence is reported to have been on such inti-

10 *Ibid.,* p. 687.

11 Henry Bronson, *History of Waterbury* (Waterbury, 1858), p. 323.

12 Thatcher freed his Negro slave, Sibly, at the time of her marriage. *Two Centuries of New Milford, Connecticut.* Prepared by the Historical Committee, Various Citizens of New Milford and the Editorial Department of the Grafton Press (New York, 1907), pp. 102-103.

13 National Society of the Daughters of the American Revolution, *The Colonial and Revolutionary Homes of Wilton, Norwalk,* etc. (Norwalk, 1901), p. 45.

mate terms with the family that he called them by their nick-
names—Nickie, Josie, Johnnie and Mosie.[14]

John Hancock and Colonel Henry Bromfield both formed
strong attachments for their slaves. When Bromfield purchased
an estate in Cambridge and retired to it soon after the opening
of the Revolution, he took with him his favorite Negro slave,
Othello, or " Thurlo " as he was better known. Despite the close
relationship existing between the two, the slave is said to have
regarded his master's seclusion as a sort of punishment, and one
day was said to have been overheard, addressing an unruly cow
in this fashion: " You are cross, you are ugly; you'll have to
eat alone same as Massa does." When the slave died in 1813 a
stone tablet, bearing the following inscription marked his
grave:[15]

OTHELLO

THE FAITHFUL FRIEND OF HENRY BROMFIELD
CAME FROM AFRICA ABOUT 1760
DIED 1813 AGED ABOUT 73.

Newport, the slave of Ezra Stiles, was so attached to him that
when Stiles freed him and moved to Providence, Newport followed his former master and reentered the family as a hired
man.[16]

Indicative also of the kind treatment of the slaves was the
permission occasionally granted to Negroes to buy things on
credit. The slave of Nathaniel Ames, for example, was allowed
in 1751 to buy on Ames' account, goods to the sum of £3.4s.[17]
Pomp, the slave of Ebenezer Wells of Deerfield, Massachusetts,
is said to have had a personal account at the store of Elijah
Williams in the same town. Other slaves exercised the same

14 Augustine Jones, ' Moses Brown," *Rhode Island Historical Society
Papers* (Providence, 1892), pp. 6, 7.

15 Abram English Brown, *John Hancock: His Book* (Boston, 1898), pp.
111-112.

16 Mathews, " Hired Man and Help," *Colonial Society of Massachusetts
Transactions, 1897-1898,* V, 238.

17 *Diary of Dr. Nathaniel Ames, 1752-1822,* ed. Charles Warren (Cambridge, 1932), p. 22.

privilege. Their purchases, Sheldon says, were mostly jack-knives, brass shoe buckles, and powder.[18] Where they were personally responsible for their accounts, Deerfield slaves usually discharged them either by cash or by payment in fox skins. Evidently the slaves honored the confidence of the storekeepers, for Sheldon says " I do not recall one [account] that is not balanced and square." [19]

The slaves also seem to have been well fed. Except in households where large numbers of slaves were owned, Negroes probably were given the same food as the family in which they served, for in many cases slaves even ate at the same table with their masters. Hawthorne says that in middle class families the slaves had their places at the table; [20] one Negro testified that he was bewitched while sitting at dinner; [21] and Cuffee, another slave, received his freedom while at the dinner table with his master's family.[22] Contemporary testimony indicates that in this respect Negroes, particularly in rural sections, were almost on the same plane as their masters' family.[23] From no one did this practice receive greater criticism than from Madam Knight, who travelled through Connecticut in 1704. Complaining of this great familiarity between the slaves and their masters, she criticized the farmers as " too indulgent . . . to their slaves; suffering too great familiarity from them, permitting you to sit at table and eat with them (as they say to save time), and into the dish goes the black hoof as freely as the white hand." [24]

18 Sheldon, *History of Deerfield*, II, 893-894.

19 *Ibid., Negro History in Old Deerfield*, p. 53. (In Schomburg Collection, New York Public Library).

20 Cited Calhoun, *Social History of the American Family*, I, 82; Moore, *op. cit.*, p. 33.

21 *E. C. C. R., 1678-1680*, VII, 329.

22 *Journal of Negro History*, VIII, 154.

23 Jeremy Belknap in *Mass. Hist. Soc. Colls.*, Fifth Series III, 302.

24 *Journal of Madame Knight On A Journey from Boston to New York in the year 1704* (New York, 1825), p. 40; *ibid.* (Boston, 1920), pp. 37-38.

The slaves apparently were well housed and their quarters did not differ much from the accommodations afforded servants today. In general, slave lodgings depended upon the number of Negroes owned by a household.[25] Where there were only a few slaves, they usually lived in the masters' house.[26] Sometimes they even slept on the same floor;[27] more frequently, however, they occupied an extra story above the main floor;[28] often they slept in the garret.[29] Occasionally the Negro quarters were in the cellar as in the case of the slaves of Benjamin Isaacs of Norwalk, Connecticut.[30] Where several slaves were owned by a family the Negroes, like those on the Southern plantations, usually lived in out-buildings behind the mansion house. This arrangement was followed not only in the Narragansett Country and eastern Connecticut[31] where relatively large numbers of slaves were employed, but also in town families such as that of Isaac Royall. Here the slave huts were located at the side of the Royall mansion.[32]

In one instance a slave was reported to have been as comfortably housed as his master. While visiting Marblehead, Massachusetts, in 1704 Dr. Alexander Hamilton was told by his host that his valise was in the slave's room. Desiring to see what the slave's quarters were like, Hamilton decided to get the bag himself and upon entering the room, he relates it was " a most spacious one furnished *a la mode de Cabaret,* with tables, chairs, a fine feather bed with quilted counterpane, white calico canopy

25 Samuel Batchelder, " Colonel Henry Vassal and His Wife Penelope," *Cambridge Historical Society Publications,* X, 63.

26 *Boston Gazette,* Sept. 28; Oct. 5, 1741.

27 *Ibid.*

28 Batchelder, *op. cit.,* p. 63.

29 Updike, *op. cit.,* I, 208-209; *Boston Weekly Post Boy,* June 26, 1749.

30 *The Colonial and Revolutionary Homes of Wilton, Norwalk,* etc., p. 92.

31 Updike, *op. cit.,* I, 208-209.

32 Batchelder, *op. cit.,* p. 63.

or tester, and curtains, every way adapted for a gentleman of his degree and complexion." [33]

If the testimony of newspaper advertisements may be accepted, slaves were apparently well clothed in New England. Thus when Shubal, a slave belonging to Lemuel Sturtevant of Halifax, Massachusetts, ran away in May, 1754, he wore " a felt hatt . . . a strait bodied or mixed colour'd great coat with pewter buttons, a striped jacket without sleeves, white woolen shirt, his breeches the same with his coat [and] light colour'd blue stockings." [34] Jack had on a "*red* mill baize jacket, the sleeves newer than the body, nankeen waistcoat and breeches, (and) white worsted stockings." [35] Caesar, another fugitive, was arrayed in " a froost and trowsers, check shirt no stockings and an old pair shoes; " [36] and when Primus ran away from his Durham (New Hampshire) master he was attired in " a blue serge coat, a gray lapell'd jacket lin'd with red baise, a pair of deerskin breeches of light color, a bever hat, and a pair of blue yarn stockings." [37]

Although these slaves ran away during warm weather, similar advertisements tend to show that in winter they were apparently clad warmly enough to withstand the rigors of the New England climate. Warm clothing was necessary, if for no other reason than to protect the master's investment, if the slave brought from the tropics was to survive the severe New England climate. A March fugitive wore a " grey bear-skin double-breasted jackett, with large white metal buttons, and striped under ditto, long striped trousers, with leather breeches under them, [and] a sailors dutch cap." [38] Constant fled in the dead of

33 *Dr. Alexander Hamilton's Itineraries Being a Narrative of a Journey from Annapolis, Md. Through Del., Pa., N. Y., N. J., Conn., R. I., Mass. and N. H. from May to September, 1704.* ed. Albert B. Hart (St. Louis, 1907), p. 145.

34 *Boston Gazette or Weekly Advertiser,* May 21, 1754.

35 *New England Chronicle,* May 9, 1716.

36 *Boston Weekly News Letter,* Aug. 4, 1768.

37 *Boston News Letter,* August 4, 1768.

38 *Boston Chronicle,* March 25, 1769, p. 100.

winter dressed in " a blue pea jacket: a pair of buck skin breeches, a pair of large flowered brass buckles, [and a] check sirt [shirt] ;" [39] another January runaway was clad in a " brownish coloured drugget coat, a blue jacket, a spreckled woolen shirt, old yarn stockings, and a pretty good hat." [40]

The same newspapers also seem to reveal that the Negroes were dressed as well as, or occasionally better than, indentured servants. Perhaps this was due to the master's knowledge that the indentured servant was more inured to the climate than were the Negro slaves. For example, a white servant, running away in June, wore a " white shirt and long jacket," [41] while another who fled in February, had on " an old fustian coat, tore in the elbows, a woolen shirt, collar lined with white cotton a brown waistcoat, leather apron, blew pair of leggins, a pair of old leather breeches [and] a pair of old shoes." [42] On the other hand, an Irish servant, who fled from Massachusetts was better dressed. He was attired in " a brown holland jacket, a new dark colour'd coat, double breasted, fac'd with green, which has a large cape, a pair of black skin breeches, bluish yarn stockings [and] a brown wigg." [43]

Despite the fact that the slaves apparently were well fed, housed, and clothed in New England, illness was common among them. The change from the tropics to the damp, cold environment of New England caused much sickness from respiratory and other ailments during the period of adjustment. The treatment of sick slaves naturally varied, according to their owners, but in the main they seem to have been well cared for. This was true even in the Narragansett Country, where the largest numbers of slaves were employed.[44] Ailing Negroes ap-

39 *Boston Gazette or Weekly Advertiser*, Jan. 28, 1755.

40 *New England Weekly Journal*, Jan. 31 ; Feb. 14, 21, 1738.

41 *Boston Gazette*, May 30, June 6, 1737.

42 *Boston Chronicle*, Feb. 5-8; Feb. 8-12; Feb. 19-22; Feb. 22-26; March 5-8, 1770.

43 *Boston Weekly Post Boy*, Sept. 1741.

44 Miller, *op. cit.*, pp. 23-24.

parently received the same attention from their owners as did other members of the family. Occasionally the slaves were attended by the family physician, and in exceptional cases they were given the services of a nurse as well as those of a doctor.[45] So favored was the hired slave mentioned above, who was successively stricken with the smallpox and the " French pox." [46] Sometimes the cost of caring for sick slaves bore heavily upon the owners. For services rendered to two Negro slaves and a servant girl of Benjamin Gibbs of Essex County, Massachusetts, in 1675-76, Dr. John Toton presented the master with a bill for six pounds, ten shillings.[47] Owners like Mrs. Mary Holyoke of Cambridge, and the Reverend Joseph Greene of Salem, manifested much tenderness toward their sick slaves [48] and Samuel Sewall prayed at the bedside of his sick slave, Boston.[49] Neighbors also occasionally visited sick slaves, as noted by the Reverend Joseph Greene, who, on April 3, 1708, mentioned in his diary that " Captain Dran and his wife and sister came here to see our sick slave, Flora." [50] White midwives usually attended slave women at childbirth; one midwife, a Mrs. Turner of Newport, told Ezra Stiles that between 1746 and 1762 she had delivered two hundred and eighty-four Negro children.[51]

Slaves suffering from contagious diseases such as the smallpox were often accorded the same treatment as whites. After

45 *S. C. C. R., 1671-1680,* XXX, 649-650; *E. C. C. R., 1678-1680,* VII, 394-395.

46 *Vide supra,* p. 122 and note.

47 *S. C. C. R.,* XXX, 649-650.

48 The sole item recorded in the diary of Mrs. Holyoke for Oct. 16, 1763 was " Cato sick with the mumps." *Diary of Mrs. Mary Vial Holyoke, 1760-1800,* p. 60; " Diary of the Rev. Joseph Greene of Salem Village, 1700-1715," *Essex Institute Collections* (Salem, 1866-1870), p. 79.

49 " Diary," *loc. cit.,* VII, 394.

50 " Diary of the Rev. Joseph Greene of Salem Village, 1700-1715," *loc. cit.,* p. 79.

51 *Itineraries of Ezra Stiles,* ed. Franklin B. Dexter, p. 29.

the introduction of inoculation, first used by Dr. Zabdiel Boyleston of Boston to check the ravages of smallpox in 1721, Negroes as well as whites were frequently immunized against the
disease.[52] Boyleston's six-year-old son and his Negro man,
thirty-six, and a Negro boy, two and a half years old, were used
for the experiment.[53] During the great epidemic of 1752 Deacon
John Tudor, one of the overseers for the poor of Boston, reported that 1970 whites and 139 blacks had been inoculated.
The results were gratifying for in the third ward where he
served, Tudor reported that 120 whites and five blacks had been
inoculated and "not one died."[54] Slaves suffering from smallpox were sometimes confined to the same hospitals as whites,
as is shown by a case in Boston in 1769. According to the
*Boston Chronicle*:

> On Thursday last a Negro woman servant of Mr. Wingfield
> near Wings Lane, and on Friday following Capt. Parker,
> lately arrived from Philadelphia, had eruptions of the small
> pox and were both immediately removed to the hospital. Red
> flags are kept out and guards continued at the above mentioned
> places for the safety of the inhabitants.[55]

Occasionally, however, masters paid scant attention to sick
slaves. A case in point was the treatment of Caesar, the slave
of Mary Wells and Timothy Childs of Deerfield, Massachusetts. A veteran of the French Wars, he was found lying "sick
unto death" in an old unheated shack where he had been left
by his master. According to an eye witness the Negro had little
covering, "not even a bed of straw under him" and "nothing
. . . [under] his body but an empty bed tick."[56]

52 During the smallpox epidemic in Charlestowne, Massachusetts between
May and December 1752, 307 whites and 47 Negroes were inoculated. *Boston
Gazette or Weekly Advertiser*, Tuesday, March 13, 1753.

53 Drake, *History and Antiquities of Boston*, II, 562.

54 *Deacon Tudor's Diary, 1732-1793*, ed. William Tudor (Boston, 1896),
pp. 7-8.

55 July 31, 1769.

56 Sheldon, *op. cit.*, p. 53.

The care of indigent, aged, or infirm slaves was similar to that given to other dependents. They were to be cared for by their masters or, in the event of the owner's death, by the administrators of the latter's estates, or else the towns made provision and charged the costs to the owner or to his estate. Otherwise, the slaves became town charges.[57] This was the case in Muddy River, Massachusetts, where, in 1723, the town voted to grant " two pounds ten shillings " to buy clothing for a destitute Negro woman.[58]

Occasionally destitute slaves suffered, while the town [59] attempted to shift responsibility for their care either to another town or to the legislature, or because legal involvements prevented the administrator from securing the necessary funds from the estate to provide for his charges. Illustrative of the former, was the petition of the town of Uxbridge, Massachusetts which, in 1766, petitioned the General Court to relieve it of the care of two aged and infirm Negroes. The slaves had formerly been owned by the Reverend Nathan Webb who sold them to a certain John Alden, but the latter finding the Negroes of no use to him, moved away, leaving the slaves destitute. The legislature refused the request of Uxbridge and the Negroes were again thrown back upon the town for support.[60] In the same year Peter Charndon, executor of the estate of the late Nathaniel Cunningham of Boston, petitioned the legislature for the right to sell part of the estate, in order to indemnify the town of Cambridge for the support of two Negroes who formerly belonged to Cunningham. Charndon explained that all available funds belonging to the estate had been expended, and that the town of Cambridge refused further support for the Negroes,

57 *Cf.*, pp. 138-139.

58 *Muddy River and Brookline Records, 1634-1838* (Boston, 1875), p. 124.

59 Attempts by one town to shift the burden of supporting indigent former slaves caused many lawsuits between the towns where the Negroes had resided. *Cf.* Nathan Dane, *Abridgement and Digest of American Law* (8 vols.), II, 411-413.

60 *Mass. Archives: Domestic Relations, 1643-1774,* IX, 448-450.

until it had been compensated for the money already spent in their behalf. Whether the legislature granted Charndon's request is not known.[61]

Notwithstanding comparatively favorable living conditions, slave mortality was apparently heavy. High death rates were common for all classes and races during this period, so high, in fact, that in Boston deaths exceeded baptisms [62] for fourteen of the twenty-one years between 1731 and 1752. The heaviest mortality among the slaves was caused by smallpox, measles, respiratory ailments, rheumatism, and mumps.[63] Incomplete vital statistics show that in a single year (December 31, 1769 to December 1, 1770), seventy-nine Negroes died in Boston,[64] while over the same period 404 whites died. In one week three whites and two Negroes were buried in Charlestown, Massachusetts, and over a similar period five whites and five blacks died in Boston.[65] Statistics covering a period of thirteen years reveal the deaths of 2,175 whites and 501 Negroes in Newport. For this period the average number of deaths for white persons was approximately 167; for Negroes about 38.[66] Because of insufficient data, per capita death rates cannot be computed. Boston, which began recording vital statistics in 1704, had 11,780 deaths between 1701 and 1730, of which 9,941 were whites and 1,839 blacks. Between 1731-1752 a similar proportion in the mortality between the races was evident.

Negro and white mortality, according to statistics, fluctuated considerably. Epidemics of smallpox, measles, and fevers frequently scourged colonial New England, causing marked upward surges in the death rate. In 1721, as a result of smallpox,

61 *Ibid.*, pp. 451-452.

62 *Boston Gazette or Weekly Advertiser*, Jan. 23, 1753, *cf.* Appendix.

63 *Ibid., Diary of Mrs. Mary Vial Holyoke*, p. 60; *E. C. C. R.*, VII, 394-395.

64 *Essex Gazette*, Jan. 1-8, 1771.

65 *Boston Gazette or Weekly Advertiser*, April 9, 1754.

66 Between 1760-1772. *Newport Mercury*, January 11, 1773. Averages mine.

the total deaths were more than treble those for 1720. White mortality increased from 261 to 968, while that of Negroes rose from 68 to 134, or more than double that of the preceding year. Smallpox and measles in 1729 and 1730, "epidemical fever" from 1745-1747, and smallpox again in 1752, caused similar variations upward in the death rates of both whites and blacks.[67] The relatively high death rate naturally tended to reduce somewhat the efficiency of slave labor.[68]

There are few records of the punishments inflicted upon slaves by their masters, for even the newspapers throw little light upon the beating or mutilation of slaves. Advertisements for Southern fugitives often called attention to scars or marks borne by the runaways, which not only served as means of identification but also offered mute testimony to their treatment. Rarely, however, do such instances appear in the newspapers of New England. Occasionally notices specified that the runaway "hath been branded in the forehead with the letter B and hath his right ear cut."[69] Another slave had lost "part of his great toe;"[70] a third bore "a scar on his chin," and a fourth had "the top of two [of] his fingers froze off."[71]

Notwithstanding the scanty testimony afforded by the newspapers, both servants and slaves were sometimes brutally beaten in New England. Whippings were common in the colonial period. The New Englanders particularly did not believe in "sparing the rod." Children, scholars, students, soldiers, sailors and other grown-ups were privately and publicly flogged.[72] Ac-

---

67 *Boston Gazette and Weekly Advertiser*, January 23, 1753. *Vide Appendix* for comparative tables for these years.

68 *Ibid., vide* files of newspapers quoted, for additional information on vital statistics.

69 The Negro would hardly have been branded by his latest master because the owner's name was Read. Not even the cut on the Negro's ear can be directly attributable to Read for it may have been received from a former master, possibly in the West Indies. *Ibid.,* August 14, 1749.

70 *Boston Chronicle,* June 22, 1769, p. 200.

71 *Boston Weekly Post Boy,* Sept. 25; Oct. 16, 1749.

72 Earle, *Customs and Fashions in Old New England,* pp. 33-35, 102.

cording to Robert Means Lawrence, " full grown persons also were whaled privately and publicly including unruly slaves who had committed some misdemeanor and wives who failed to keep their husbands good natured." [73] With flogging of free people so common, naturally servants and slaves were not spared.

Indentured servants were often subjected to merciless whippings. In fact, they frequently appear to have been treated worse in this respect, than the slaves.[74] Was it because of the character of the servants, many of whom were described as lazy, unruly, dishonest and vicious? Or was it because the master realized that if he killed or maimed his servant, either through overwork, beating, or otherwise, he would suffer only the loss of the servant's labor for a period of time, whereas if he so treated his slave he would not only be deprived of the Negro's labor, and potential offspring but might lose his property as well. Self-interest, therefore, may have prompted some masters to act more humanely toward their slaves than toward their white indentured servants. Whatever the reason, court records offer abundant testimony to the cruel usage of indentured servants.[75] For example, Joan Sinflow, the Irish servant of Thomas Maule, testified that her master beat her so severely with a horsewhip, that she spat blood for a fortnight.[76] In 1652 another master, John Betts of Cambridge, Massachusetts beat his servant, Robert Knight, to death with " a great plough staffe." [77] In only the latter case was even a fine imposed.[78] For flogging his servant unmercifully and " hanging him up by the heels as butchers do

73 *The Not Quite Puritans* (Boston, 1928), p. 202.

74 Earle, *op. cit.*, pp. 97-104.

75 Masters were frequently haled before the Courts by their indentured servants on charges of excessive cruelty. *E. C. C. R., 1680-1683*, VIII, 11, 184, 222, 225, 296, 302, 314, 315, 317, 411; I-VII, *passim; R. C. A.*, II-III, *passim.*

76 *E.C.C.R.*, 222-223.

77 *R. C. A.*, III, 24-25.

78 *Ibid.*

beasts for the slaughter," Phillip Fowler was sentenced merely to pay costs of court.[79]

Although there are fewer instances in the court records of the flogging of slaves, Negroes were sometimes cruelly beaten. Nicholas Letchmer of New London, Connecticut, was arrested on a charge of brutally whipping his slave, Zino. The town is said to have been so stirred up over the incident that when Letchmer was tried, the courthouse could not accommodate the crowd.[80] In 1695 Nathaniel Cane of Maine Province beat to death his slave woman Rachel.[81] Twenty-four years later a Massachusetts master flogged his slave so unmercifully that he died.[82] Sometime later a Connecticut master, bitten on the thumb while beating his slave, died of lockjaw.[83] Ministers also beat their slaves, as in the case of the Reverend McSparran of Narragansett who whipped Maroca for bearing two illegitimate children. He later stripped, tied and whipped Hannibal, because the slave had stayed out all night. When McSparran finished, his " poor passionate dear " [wife], thinking Hannibal had not been sufficiently corrected, seized the whip and added a lash or two.[84] Even the Quakers, generally known for their kindness to the slaves, were not free from this charge. But the Quakers were the first to register an organized protest against such severities and they led in taking drastic measures against guilty members of their own group. In 1711 the Rhode Island Friends dropped a woman from their Society because of her inhuman

79 E. C. C. R., 1680-1682, VIII, 302-303. In 1682, a Massachusetts court took William Saunders from his master " on account of great abuse by beating."

80 Lawrence, The Not Quite Puritans, p. 203.

81 Correspondence Concerning Moore's Notes on Slavery in Massachusetts (New York, 1866), p. 7 n.

82 Ibid., pp. 1-3.

83 Frances Caulkins, History of Norwich, Connecticut (Norwich, 1845), p. 329; Steiner, op. cit., p. 21.

84 Weeden, Early Rhode Island, p. 150.

treatment of a slave.[85] The same organization, in 1770, disowned another woman for beating her slave so ruthlessly that he died shortly afterwards. This denial read:

> Whereas a woman Friend hath given over to hardness of heart to such a degree she hath been not only consenting but encouraging the unmerciful whipping or beating of her negro man servant, he being stript naked, and hanged up by the hands in his masters house, and then beating him, or whipping him so unmercifully . . . that it was in some measure the occasion of his death that followed soon after, the which we do account is not only unchristian but inhuman for which cause we find ourselves concerned to testify to the world that we utterly disown all such actions and especially the Friend above mentioned.[86]

Reports of the barbarous treatment of slaves and servants reached England during the seventeenth century, and the mother country made an effort to curb these brutalities. In 1686 the Board of Trade and Plantations authorized Sir Edmund Andros, newly appointed governor of the Dominion of New England, to stop the excessive flogging of servants, and to make the wilful killing of Indian and Negro slaves a capital offense. Andros was expressly directed to have a law passed " for the restraining of inhuman severity which by ill masters or overseers may be used towards the christian servants or slaves," to provide that the " willful killing of Indians and Negroes be punished with death," and to impose a " fitt penalty for the maiming of them." [87] New Hampshire was probably the only New England colony to frame such a law. By an enactment of May 13, 1718, any master convicted of maiming or

85 Rufus Jones, *The Quakers in the American Colonies* (London, 1911), pp. 156-157 n.

86 *Ibid.*, p. 156 n. Quakers were not the only ones guilty of such floggings, but they were active in ferreting out these instances and in punishing publicly the perpetrators.

87 *Documents Relative to the Colonial History of the State of New York* (Albany, 1853), III, 547.

otherwise cruelly maltreating his servant was not only required to free him, but also to compensate him as the court might adjudge.[88] Section two expressly provided the death penalty for any person or persons " who shall willfully kill his Indian or negro servant or servants . . ." [89]

Although the killing of a slave or servant thus became a capital offense, there is no record that any New England master ever paid the death penalty for such a crime.[90] In a test case that arose in May 1695 the court did not interpret the killing of a slave as a capital offense. Nathaniel Cane (mentioned above) was tried and convicted before the Superior Court of Judicature for the Province of Maine, for killing his Negro woman,[91] the court holding that the slave's death was the result of " cruel beating and hard usage " by her master. Instead of being executed, however, Cane was fined " *five* pounds for the use of the county " and even the fine was " *not to be levyed till further order of the court.*" He was also assessed five pounds, ten shillings for costs of court and sentenced to be jailed until it was paid.[92]

Almost a quarter of a century later another master was tried and acquitted of killing his slave. In 1719 Samuel Smith of Sandwich, Massachusetts appeared before a Special Court of Assize and General Gaol Delivery held at Plymouth, on the

88 *Acts and Laws of His Majesty's Province of New Hampshire* (Portsmouth, 1771), p. 101.

89 *Ibid.*

90 The killing of a slave by his master was not punishable in the South at this time. Slaves were chattel and apparently masters had the power of life and death over them. McCord, *Statutes at Large of South Carolina,* VIII, 345 (Law of 1690). In Virginia in 1723, if a slave died under dismemberment or punishment, the owner was exempted from punishment. Manslaughter of a slave was not punishable and that was the only offense for which a master could be indicted and even then only upon the word of a creditable witness. Hening, *Statutes at Large of Virginia,* IV, 132-133.

91 *Correspondence Concerning Moore's Notes on The History of Slavery in Massachusetts* (New York, 1866), p. 7 n.

92 *Ibid.*

charge of beating to death his Negro slave, Futin.[93] He pleaded *not guilty.* At the trial, presided over by Justices Addington Davenport, Paul Dudley, and Edmund Quincy, the jury brought in a verdict of *not guilty.* Smith thereupon was discharged after paying costs of " five pounds one shilling and sixpence." [94] He was said to have acknowledged beating the slave, but he contended that the flogging was not the cause of the Negro's death. His contention was supported by a coroner's jury, which reported that " the slave died of suffocation having in yielding to his own ungovernable temper or in sleep subsequent upon it SWALLOWED HIS TONGUE." [95]

The case aroused considerable interest. Justice Addington Davenport, one of the trial judges, may have solicited Samuel Sewall's advice in the matter, for two days before the trial Sewall wrote Davenport asking indirectly that strict justice be meted out. Said he: the " poorest boys and girls in this province, such as are of the lowest condition, whether they be English, or Indians, or Ethiopians have the same right to religion and life, that the richest heirs have " and they who seek to " deprive them of this right . . . attempt the bombarding of HEAVEN, and the shells they throw will fall down upon their own heads." [96]

Sewall probably believed that Smith was guilty and that he should be punished for the crime, for he added: " Mr. Justice Davenport Sir, upon your desire, I have sent you these quotations, and my own sentiments. I pray GOD, the giver and guardian of life, to give his gracious direction to you, and the other justices . . ." [97]

93 This is the contention held by George T. Davis, who maintains that Smith was tried for the *alleged,* not the *actual,* killing of his slave. See letter to George H. Moore in *ibid.,* pp. 1-3.

94 *Ibid.,* pp. 4-9.

95 *Ibid.,* pp. 9-10.

96 *Ibid.,* p. 5.

97 *Ibid.*

Notwithstanding the appeal of Sewall and the apparent guilt of the prisoner, it was hardly probable that a jury of fellow-townsmen would recommend the death penalty for a master on trial for the killing of his slave, especially when, in a previous case, a master who beat his white indentured servant to death had escaped with a mere fine and whipping.[98] In theory the New England master did not have the right to take the life of his slave, but if he did so, a jury of his fellow citizens, as Moore pointed out, would hardly convict him of murder.[99] Withal, the knowledge that he could not escape the odium of a trial with its attendant inconveniences and costs, as well as public censure, acted as a powerful restraining force to deter the master from wanton killings. Furthermore, the possibility that a jury might recommend the death penalty naturally acted as a further deterrent to stay the hand of the master. For these reasons, together with the patriarchal attitude of many owners toward the slave, the deliberate killing of Negroes by New England owners was rare.

The Puritans manifested a liberal attitude toward the education of the slaves. No record exists of any statute denying or limiting their instruction. That no such prohibition existed may be ascribed in large measure to the social institutions of the Puritans, whose religion presupposed a personal knowledge of the Bible, a system wholly incompatible with ignorance. And slaves, as will be pointed out later, were potential church members. Moreover, the early and compulsory establishment of schools and colleges for their own children, and the active interest manifested by them in the education of the Indians would

[98] John Bates of Cambridge in 1652 beat Robert Knight his indentured servant with "a great plough staffe and also gave him severall Blowes w[th] ye great end of a Goad upon ye Back" from which Knight later died. Bates was sentenced to stand an hour before the gallows with a rope about his neck, to be whipped, pay a fine of £15, and Costs of Court and to be bound to good behavior for one year on a bond of 20 shillings. R. C. A., III, 24-25.

[99] Correspondence Concerning Moore's Notes on the History of Slavery in Massachusetts, p. 10.

have rendered it inconsistent for the Puritans legally to withhold similar instruction from their bondmen. Because of the complex character of Negro labor, already referred to, it was to the interest of the masters to impart to the slaves some of the rudiments of learning, for ignorant workmen, as previously indicated, were at a disadvantage in the diversified economy of New England. An intelligent slave, on the other hand, was a more valuable asset to his master. As a result many of the New England Negroes received elementary instruction in writing, reading, and arithmetic as well as industrial training. Their enlightenment was not the result of a general movement, but was fostered by kindly-disposed masters, members of the clergy, and by religious organizations.

Foremost among these agencies in the education of Negroes were the clergy. As early as 1674, John Eliot, the apostle to the Indians, interested himself in the education of the blacks. He deeply lamented the fact " that Christians should so much have the heart of demons in them, as to prevent and hinder the instruction of the poor blacks and confine the souls of their miserable slaves to a destroying ignorance, merely for fear of thereby loosing the benefit of their vassalage." [100] Eliot asked that masters within a radius of two or three miles send their slaves to him once a week for instruction, but he died before he could put this plan into execution. [101]

Eliot's work was continued by Cotton Mather, who not only favored but actually furthered the enlightenment of the slaves. He said, " I will put Bibles and other good and proper books into their hands; will allow them time to read and assure myself that they do not misspend this time." Mather also determined to act as censor to prevent undesirable literature from reaching the slaves. " If," he added, " I can discern any wicked books in their hands, I will take away those pestilential instruments of

100 Mather, *Life of John Eliot*, pp. 101-102.
101 *Ibid.*

wickedness."[102] He even contemplated employing those of his servants who were capable, to teach his own children and re- solved to " recompense them for so doing." [103] Mather not only enjoined other masters to enlighten their slaves, but in 1717, he set the example by opening a charity school for Indians and Negroes. The school was to remain open for two or three hours every night in order to instruct " Negroes, and Indians, in reading the Scriptures, and learning their Catechisms." This school was unfortunately shortlived. Whether attending school nightly after working hours proved too great a strain upon the slaves, whether the masters prevented them from attending, or whether the school was merely closed during the summer, re- mains a matter of conjecture. At any rate, on October 11, 1717, Mather expressed his determination to " revive the charity school for Negro's." [104]

In carrying out the intentions of John Eliot, Mather probably set a precedent in New England for the group education of slaves in classes, and his effort was the forerunner of schools for Negroes. His endeavors probably encouraged other masters to acquiesce in the instruction of their bondmen, for eleven years after the opening of Mather's school, one Nathaniel Pigott boldly announced the establishment of a school for Ne- gro servants and invited their masters to send them thither for instruction. His announcement read:

> Mr. Nath Pigott intends to open a School on Monday, next, for the Instruction of Negro's in Reading, Catechizing & Writing if required, if any are so well inclined as to send their Servants to said school near Mr. Checkley's Meeting House care will be taken for their Instruction as aforesaid.[105]

102 Cited in Carter G. Woodson, *Education of the Negro Prior to 1861* (Washington, 1919), p. 337.

103 " Diary ", *loc. cit.,* VIII, Part II, 422.

104 *Ibid.,* p. 478.

105 *New England Weekly Journal,* April 8, 1728.

Whether the school actually materialized is not known.[106]

Supplementing the work of individuals was the activity of religious societies. Prominent among them stood the Quakers, a sect notable for its endeavors in behalf of the slaves. As early as 1671 George Fox, one of the Quaker leaders, had spoken against slavery;[107] and Pastorius and his Germantown Quakers had published the first written protest against slavery in 1688.[108] By 1716 the New England Quakers had begun to question the justification of slavery.[109] At their Yearly Meeting in 1760 the Rhode Island Friends, after forbidding their brethren to engage in the slave trade, advised all Friends who held slaves to " treat them with tenderness and give those that are young, at least so much learning that they may be capable of reading."[110] Quaker influence, too, was largely responsible for the unique clause in the Rhode Island Emancipation Bill of 1784, making it compulsory that Negro children be taught to read and write.[111]

Operating on a continental scale was the Society for the Propagation of the Gospel, commonly known as the S.P.G., founded in London in 1701 and aided by philanthropic people of that city. Although primarily interested in the spiritual welfare of the slaves, the Society did not neglect their secular instruction. In his sermon before the Society in 1711, Bishop

106 Drake (*History and Antiquities of Boston,* II, 582), mentions Mr. Piggott's school near Rev. Checkley's meeting house, but throws no light upon its subsequent existence.

107 Locke, *op. cit.,* p. 21.

108 " Protest of Germantown Quakers against Slavery," *American History Told by Contemporaries,* ed. Albert B. Hart, II, 291.

109 Macy, *History of Nantucket,* p. 281; Locke, *op. cit.,* p. 35; Herbert Aptheker, " The Quakers and Negro Slavery," *Journal of Negro History,* XXV, 340.

110 *Book of Discipline agreed on by the Yearly Meeting of Friends in N. E.* (Providence, 1785), p. 101; Jones, *op. cit.,* pp. 162-163.

111 *Acts and Resolves of Rhode Island, Feb. 1784-Dec. 1786.* (Facsimile Reprints. Providence, n.d.), X, 7.

Fleetwood of St. Asaph, set the example by boldly declaring that the slaves were the moral and intellectual equals of their masters and urged that owners educate their Negroes. Throughout the colonial period other bishops followed his example.[111a] In 1727 Bishop Gibson of London, under whose direction the work of the Society fell, sent out ten thousand circular letters to all its missionaries as well as to masters and mistresses of slaves, impressing upon them the importance " as a religious duty to teach their slaves and domestics to read and write . . ." [112] These instructions, as will be shown later, were carried out by such ministers as the Reverend Mr. McSparran at Narragansett,[113] Dr. William Samuel Johnson at Stratford, and the Reverend Mr. J. Honeyman at Newport.[114] The Society also furnished schoolmasters to teach slave children, who sometimes attended the same classes with white pupils. This condition obtained in the case of Mr. Taylor, the Society's schoolmaster at Providence, who in 1774 " taught fourteen children, including one negro."[115] In 1762 the Associates of Dr. Bray maintained a school at Newport with thirty Negro children in attendance.[116]

In 1740 the S.P.G. was given £1000 to be applied to the instruction of Negroes in America, part of which was probably used for that purpose in New England.[117] Books and other materials for these schools were sent from the mother country. In

---

[111a] For best summary of efforts of the S.P.G. in colonial New York to educate Indians and slaves, *vide* Frank J. Klingberg, *Anglican Humanitarianism in Colonial New York* (Philadelphia, 1940), pp. 121-186. For Bishop Fleetwood's sermon, *vide ibid.*, pp. 197-212, esp. p. 203.

[112] Updike, *op. cit.*, I, 211.

[113] C. F. Pascoe, *Two Hundred Years of the S. P. G.*, p. 42; Updike, *op. cit.*, II, 200.

[114] Pasco, *op. cit.*, p. 47.

[115] Updike, *op. cit.*, III, 90.

[116] *An Account of the Associates of Dr. Bray* (London, 1766), p. 39.

[117] *Historical Collections Relating to the American Colonial Church*, ed. William Stevens Perry (Hartford, 1873), IV, 338.

1765 the Associates of Dr. Bray sent 1,032 pieces of literature to America for Negro schools maintained by the Society. Among them were " 248 Bibles, testaments, common prayers, psalters, spelling books and other bound books and 748 small tracts stitched." [118] In spite of the efforts of the Society to educate the slaves, its endeavors failed to enlist the necessary support of many masters, largely because of the prejudice of most New Englanders against the Episcopal Church and its activities. Although equipped with a qualified teacher, and capable of caring for thirty students, the school at Newport was on the point of closing in 1773 because it did not have enough Negro children to justify its continuance.[119]

The education of the slaves, meager as it was, increased the quality of service which they were equipped to render and thereby made them more valuable to their masters. Attention has already been directed to slaves who were trained in the skilled trades. Other slaves, among whom were Sharper, Mesheck, Lemuel Haynes and Pomp, managed farms, bought and sold goods, conducted stores, had charge of ships and warehouses and even practiced medicine for their masters.[120] Other slaves achieved some proficiency in writing. The education received in slavery equipped Prince Hall, Lancaster Hill and Felix Holbrook of Boston to help their more unfortunate fellows by drawing up several petitions between 1773 and 1778, which they sent to the legislature of Massachusetts, seeking the liberation of the slaves.[121] Nero Brewster, Pharaoh Moffat, Samuel Wentworth and others of New Hampshire did likewise in 1779. Some of these petitions compare favorably with contemporary ones and in style, logic, and grammar; the New Hampshire peti-

---

118 *An Account of the Associates of Dr. Bray*, p. 39; *cf.* Klingberg, *op. cit.*, p. 29.

119 *Newport Mercury,* April 12, 1773.

120 *Vide infra,* ch. iv.

121 For petition of 1773, original is in *The Appendix or Some Observations on The Expediency of the Petition of the Africans Living in Boston* (Boston, 1773), pp. 9-11; For others *vide Mass. Archives,* CCXII, 132; *Mass. Hist. Soc. Colls.,* Fifth Series, III, 432-433.

tion probably surpasses the average.[122] Newport Gardner, the slave of Caleb Gardner of Newport, Rhode Island, was given music lessons. He soon excelled his teacher and later opened a music school of his own on Pope Street where he taught both Negroes and white persons.[123]

A few Negroes attempted literary compositions. The aforementioned Newport Gardner is said to have written poetry as well as music.[124] Lucy Terry, the slave of Ensign Ebenezer Wells of Deerfield, Massachusetts, was probably the first American Negro to write poetry.[125] Her inspiration was the bloody Indian raid on Deerfield in 1746 and her poem describing that action preceded by a decade the writings of Jupiter Hammon, a New York slave who has been called the first Negro poet in America.[126] Lucy was not versed in syntax, but her poem gave a vivid picture of the massacre of the settlers by Indians on August 25, 1746. Despite the tragic theme, there was humor in it, not always intentional. According to Sheldon, the historian of Deerfield, Lucy's description of the Bars Fight [127] is the fullest and best contemporary version of that struggle now extant. The original has been lost but a " secondary " copy follows :

> August 'twas the twenty fifth
> Seventeen hundred forty-six
> The Indians did in ambush lay
> Some very valient men to slay
> The names of whom I'll not leave out
> Samuel Allen like a hero fout
> And though he was so brave and bold

122 *New Hampshire State Papers*, XVIII, 705-707.

123 Mason, *Reminiscences of Newport*, pp. 155-156.

124 *Ibid.*, p. 159.

125 Sheldon, *Negro Slavery in Old Deerfield*, p. 56.

126 Robert T. Kerlin, *Negro Poets and Their Poems* (Washington, 1923), pp. 20-23. Hammon was a New York slave who first began writing poetry about 1760. He has been heretofore considered the first Negro poet in America of whom there is any record. *Ibid.*, p. 20.

127 During King George's War, 1742-1748. Sheldon, *Negro Slavery in Old Deerfield*, p. 56.

His face no more shall we behold
Eleazer Hawks was killed outright
Before he had time to fight
Before he did the Indians see
Was shot and killed immediately.
Oliver Amsden he was slain
Which caused his friends much grief and pain.
Samuel Amsden they found dead
Not many rods off from his head.
Adonijah Gillet we do hear
Did lose his life which was so dear.
John Saddler fled across the water
And so excaped the dreadful slaughter
Eunice Allen see the Indians comeing
And hoped to save herself by running
And had not her petticoats stopt her
The awful creatures had not cotched her
And tommyhawked her on the head
And left her on the ground for dead.
Young Samuel Allen, Oh! lack a-day
Was taken and carried to Canada.[128]

Of much wider renown, Phillis Wheatley [129] stood forth as

128 *Ibid.*, p. 56.

129 Phillis Wheatley was the slave of Mr. and Mrs. John Wheatley of
Boston and was brought from Africa in 1761. Desiring a companion in her
old age, Mrs. Wheatley purchased the sickly looking girl. She taught her
to read and write and Phillis soon amazed Boston by her poetic talents. Her
accomplishments excited all the more attention, since she had never been
exposed to formal training. In addition to the volume of poetry published
in 1773, Phillis dedicated poems to Lady Huntington, Lord Dartmouth, a
Mr. Thornton, and others. She was taken to England by her mistress' son
where she was introduced to the aforementioned persons. Owing to the illness of Mrs. Wheatley in America, Phillis declined an urgent request to
remain in London until the opening of the Court in order that she might be
presented to the King, George III. In addition to dedicating a poem to
Washington, she also wrote one in honor of Major General Charles Lee.
Phillis' domestic life was unhappy. She married a Negro grocer named
Peters, a man otherwise unsuited to a person of her talents and temperament.
The marriage proved unsuccessful and Phillis died in 1784. Writing in
rhyming couplets, made famous by Pope and Cowper, she was as accomplished as any of the American poets of her time. Herbert G. Renfro, *Life*

the most famous Negro poet until the rise of Paul Laurence Dunbar more than a century later. Brought from Africa as a frail child of seven or eight, Phillis soon revealed such an astonishing capacity for learning that, twelve years after her arrival in America, her first volume of poetry appeared. Thereafter she gained an international reputation, including among her patrons several members of the English nobility and clergy. On October 26, 1775, Miss Wheatley wrote a panegyric of forty-two lines in rhyming couplets in honor of George Washington, a tribute which she sent to him shortly after he had assumed command of the American troops at Cambridge.[130] Washington, in acknowledging receipt of the poem on December 26, 1755, praised Miss Wheatley's poetical talents and extended her the following invitation to visit him at his headquarters: "If you ever come to Cambridge or near headquarters I shall be happy to see a person favored by the Muses and to whom nature has been so liberal and beneficent in her dispensations." [131] According to Lossing "Miss Phillis," as Washington addressed her, called upon the Commander-in-Chief of the American Armies at Cambridge and spent " half an hour with him, from whom and his officers, she received marked attention." [132] Although most of Phillis Wheatley's works are well known, the following poem, written when she was fifteen and which has not yet been published illustrates her literary talents:

and Works of Phillis Wheatley (Washington, 1916), passim; William C. Nell, Colored Patriots of the American Revolution (Boston, 1855), pp. 64-73; Mott, Biographies and Anecdotes (Second Edition, New York, 1837), pp. 10-12; Walter H. Mazyck, George Washington and the Negro (Washington, 1932), ch. vi.

130 Writings of George Washington, ed. Worthington C. Ford (14 vols., New York, 1889), III, 440; Writings of George Washington, ed. Jared Sparks (12 vols., New York, 1847), III, 297; Walter H. Mazyck, George Washington and the Negro (Washington, 1932), pp. 48-50.

131 Sparks, Writings of George Washington, III, 297-298; Ford, Writings of George Washington, III, 440; Mazyck, op. cit., p. 53.

132 Benjamin Lossing, Pictorial Field Book of the Revolution, 2 vols. (New York, 1860), I, 556; Mazyck, op. cit., p. 56.

## ON ATHEISM

Where now shall I begin this Spacious field
To tell what Curses—Unbelief doth Yield
Thou That Doest Daily feel his hand and rod
And Darst Deny the Essence of a God,
If There's No heaven—whither wilt thou go
Make thy Elysium in the Shades below
If There's No God,—from Whence did all things Spring
He made the Greatest, and Minutest Thing
With great Astonishment my Soul is struck
O Weakness great,—hast thou thy sense forsook?
Hast Thou forgot thy Preter perfect days,
They are recorded, in the Book of praise
It is not written with the hand of God,
Why is it Sealed with dear Imanuel's blood,
Now turn I pray thee, from ye dangerous road,
Rise from ye dust,—and See the Mighty God.[133]

Slave amusements were similar to many of those indulged in by white persons. Sports were not popular with the Puritan leaders of the seventeenth century and common present-day diversions, such as mixed dancing and card playing, were banned for a long period. These restrictions were relaxed somewhat in the eighteenth century as the grip of Calvinism upon New England was gradually loosened, but even then certain amusements, like the theatre, were prohibited. As late as 1762, Shakespeare's *Othello* could be presented in Newport, Rhode Island, only by advertising it as a " Moral Dialogue." Despite these restrictions there were many forms of diversion that were indulged in by New Englanders both in the seventeenth and eighteenth centuries. Slaves participated in the numerous house raisings, church raisings, apple parings, maple sugarings and corn huskings during which there was much social activity and much

133 This poem in manuscript is in possession of the Library Company of Philadelphia. The writer is indebted to one of his colleagues, Mr. T. Thomas Fletcher, Associate Professor of English at Lincoln University (Missouri) for a photostatic copy.

liquor consumed.[134] In the Narragansett Country, during harvest time the planters held great corn huskings followed by dancing, and the slaves who aided in the festivities enjoyed themselves in the kitchen.[135]

Slaves like other New Englanders also amused themselves by hunting, fishing, swimming, pitching quoits, riding horseback, running, jumping, wrestling, dancing and story telling.[136] On holidays Negroes also found opportunities for diversion. For example, Lecture Day, which usually fell on Thursday in Massachusetts, afforded the populace the satisfaction of seeing among other things malefactors sitting in the stocks, pilloried, beaten, hanged, or burned. Negroes were part of the curious crowds who listened to a sermon before a condemned person was punished [137] or heard wedding banns announced. Christmas, which did not become popular in most of New England until the nineteenth century, was a time of merriment for the slaves in the Narragansett Country where there was a considerable number of Episcopalians. At Yuletide the Negroes and their masters are said to have enjoyed two weeks of feasting and visiting.[138] Thanksgiving Day and Guy Fawkes Day also afforded opportunities for recreation; on the latter holiday huge bonfires were lighted and Negroes joined in the boisterous crowds that surged through the streets of Boston, much to the annoyance of pedestrians.[139]

134 Earle, *Customs and Fashions*, ch. x.

135 Updike, *op. cit.*, I, 224-225.

136 *Ibid.*, 213-214; Sheldon, *Negro Slavery in Old Deerfield*, pp. 55-56; *Boston Chronicle*, July 6, 1769; Esther Bernon Carpenter, *South Country Studies*, p. 81. In some of these diversions like horse-racing, the Negroes participated surreptitiously. For instance, while riding their masters' horses to the drinking ponds, the slaves often engaged slyly in racing. Sheldon tells a story of Cato, the slave of the Reverend Mr. Ashley of Deerfield, Massachusetts. Keen of wit, Cato, if caught in his favorite pastime, would protest vehemently that the horse ran away with him, concluding with, " Couldn't stop um no how massa." Sheldon, *Negro Slavery in Old Deerfield*, p. 55.

137 Earle, *Customs and Fashions*, pp. 236-273.

138 *Ibid.*, p. 216.

139 *Ibid.*, pp. 229-230.

Although the Sabbath was a holiday and work was forbidden, by the same token all play was also banned, a prohibition which extended to the slaves as well as to the freemen.[140] Sunday, the one day on which the slaves regularly were free from labor, was not to be profaned by their indulgence in sports or games so they usually spent this day either in a church,[141] at catechetical lectures after church,[142] or in attending services in their masters' homes.[143] Sometimes slaves, as well as white persons, were punished for Sabbath breaking. Hobart relates an anecdote of Negro Cuff, who was fined for such an offense by Judge Joseph Greenleaf of Abington, Massachusetts. After paying the fine, Cuff asked for a receipt. When the Judge inquired the reason Cuff answered, " By and by you die, and go to the bad place, and after a time, Cuff die, and go and knock at the good gate, and they say, ' What do you want, Cuff?' I says, ' I want to come in; ' they say I can't because I broke the Sabbath at such a time. I say, ' I paid for it.' They will say, ' Where is your receipt? ' Now, Mr. Judge, I shall have to go away down to a bad place to get a receipt of you before I can enter the good gate." [144]

Although Sunday amusements were forbidden, the slaves found other opportunities for diversion. Chief among these was Training Day when they gathered on the parade ground and watched the militia drill. On Election day when the new Governor was inaugurated slaves were often permitted to go to

140 The Rhode Island law of 1679 is a fair sample of such legislation. *Charter and Laws of Rhode Island and Providence Plantations*, 1719 (Providence, 1895), p. 32.

141 Pascoe, *op. cit.*, pp. 42, 47; Updike, *op. cit.*, III, 88; Sheldon, *op. cit.*, p. 456.

142 " It was even the custom in Puritan families to catechise the slaves Sunday noon regarding the sermon preached in the morning, a simple method by which many an ignorant black learned the fundamental truths of Christianity." *Connecticut Magazine* V, No. 6, pp. 321-322.

143 Lemuel Haynes received his inspiration to study for the ministry from such meetings.

144 Benjamin Hobart, *A History of Abington, Massachusetts* (Boston, 1866), p. 255.

town; [145] in Boston, it is said, they swarmed over the Common buying gingerbread and drinking beer.[146] However, when Gunpowder Day was observed in Boston on November 5, 1765, Negroes were barred from the Common.[147] On Artillery Election Day also, when the Ancient and Honorable Artillery Company held its formal parade and selected its new officers, who were then commissioned by the governor, it was said that no black face dared to be seen. The practice still obtained in 1817, when William Read, a Philadelphia Negro became so enraged because he could not accompany his white shipmates to see the celebration that he blew up a ship called the *Canton Packet* in Boston Harbor. For years thereafter it was said the white boys of Boston taunted Negroes with

> Who blew up the ship?
> Nigger, Why for
> 'Cause he couldn't go to 'Lection
> An' shake paw-paw.[148]

Many Negroes amused themselves and gratified their listeners by regaling them with stories of Africa, Lucy Terry built up an enviable reputation as a raconteur and her home, following her marriage to a free Negro, is said to have become a favorite gathering place for young people who found pleasure in her stories.[149] Most famous of all the Negro story tellers of the Narragansett section was Senegambia whose brand of tales, which are said to have been reminiscent of Aesop, are still familiar to South Country residents.[150]

145 " Diary of Mrs. Mary Vial Holyoke, 1760-1800," ed. George F. Dow (Salem, 1911), *Holyoke Diaries, 1709-1856.*

146 Earle, *Customs and Fashions in Old New England* (New York, 1896), p. 226.

147 Drake, *History of Boston,* II, 710.

148 " Paw-paw was a gambling game...played on the Common with four sea shells of the *Cyproen Monet.*" Earle, *op. cit.,* p. 226.

149 Sheldon, *Negro Slavery in Old Deerfield,* p. 56.

150 Carpenter, *op. cit.,* p. 81.

Fiddling and dancing were also favorite forms of diversion
for the slaves. Many of them played the violin with such ease
that numerous advertisements called attention to this talent.[151]
Polydor Gardiner of Narragansett was famous in that section
as a fiddler and was in demand at parties and balls.[152] So, too,
was Caesar, the slave fiddler of the Reverend Jonathan
Todd of East Guilford, Connecticut, who was such an accomplished performer that the minister used to call in the young
people to dance to his playing.[153] Zelah, a Negro of Groton,
Massachusetts, who later fought in the American Revolution,
became famous in his neighborhood as a musician.[154] Most
popular of all slave diversions, however, was dancing, an art
which the Negroes brought from Africa. Near Darien, Connecticut, it was reported that so frequently did the slaves in
the neighborhood dance at the nearby Middlesex Inn that " in
one room of the house the heavy hardwood floor is now thin in
places from the movement of the merry dancers." [155] Cato, the
slave of the Reverend Mr. Ashley of Deerfield, was so fond of
dancing that in his old age he used to whip his aged legs because
they no longer would enable him to dance " with the ease and
grace of his master's son." [156]

One form of diversion seems to have been peculiar to the
New England slaves: the celebrated " election " of Negro
" governors," which was followed by an elaborate inauguration
ceremony terminating in feasting and games.[157] Evidences of
the " election " of Negro " Governors," which seems to have

151 *Boston Weekly Post Boy,* Sept. 14, 1741; Boston News Letter,
August 4, 1768.

152 Carpenter, *op. cit.,* p. 218.

153 *Connecticut Magazine,* V, No. 6, p. 323.

154 Samuel Abbott Green, *Slavery in Groton, Massachusetts in Colonial
Times,* p. 6.

155 *The Colonial and Revolutionary Homes of Wilton, Norwalk, Westport, Darien and Vicinity,* p. 108.

156 Sheldon, *Negro Slavery in Old Deerfield, op. cit.,* p. 55.

157 Caulkins, *op. cit.,* p. 185; Updike, *op. cit.,* I, 213-215; Felt, *Annals of
Salem,* II, 419-420; Earle, *Customs and Fashions,* p. 227.

begun about the middle of the eighteenth century, have been found in all of the New England colonies. The " elections " varied as to time in the different colonies: in Massachusetts the slaves were allowed a vacation from the last Wednesday in May to the close of the week; [158] in Rhode Island, election day fell on the third Saturday of June,[159] while in Connecticut the slaves held " local elections " on the Saturday following the general election, and sent the results to Hartford.[160] Whether " kings " were elected as in New Hampshire,[161] or " Governors," as in the other colonies, it is probable that the master class supervised these celebrations.[162]

On " Lection Day," as they called it, the slaves were fitted out in their best clothing and, since the dress of the slave was held to reflect the opulence of his master, owners are said to have vied with one another to see whose slave would be the best attired. As a result, many Negroes were arrayed in all sorts of cast-off finery, even including pomaded wigs, and on this occasion some of them rode their masters' horses or even borrowed their owners' carriages. Following an elaborate reception, the election began about ten in the morning. Friends of each candidate then arranged themselves on either side of a line, with their favorite at the head, while votes for the rivals were cast. After a stated time all movement from one side of the line to the other was stopped, silence was enjoined, and the votes were counted by the chief marshal, who later announced the winner. The inauguration then followed; and the defeated candidate, after his introduction by the chief marshal, drank the first toast to his successful opponent. In the conviviality of the inaugural ban-

158 Earle, *op. cit.*, p. 226; Felt, *op. cit.*, II, 419; Stuart Scaeva, *History of Hartford in the Olden Time* (Hartford, 1853), pp. 37, 38.

159 Updike, *op. cit.*, pp. 213-215.

160 Orville H. Platt, " Negro Governors," *New Haven Historical Society Papers* (New Haven, 1900), VI, 319.

161 King Nero with his counsellors ordered a Negro delinquent to be whipped in New Hampshire. *Ibid.*, p. 321.

162 Scaeva, *op. cit.*, p. 37.

quent all animosities were forgotten. With the newly elected " governor " presiding, his lady on his left and the losing candidate on his right, the day ended merrily with dancing, games of quoits and other sports.[163]

But, these " elections " were sometimes criticized, for they were said to have had a demoralizing effect upon the slaves. Speaking of the elections in Norwich, Connecticut, Mrs. Caulkins marvels that they " should have been tolerated by the magistrates in a town so rigid in its code of morals." [164] According to a Massachusetts historian, the Negroes spent the rest of the week (from Wednesday) in amusements, " chiefly in dancing to the fiddle." " Such holidays were to them," he continued, " as those of Christmas have been to the blacks of our Southern States. The abuse of them led to immoralities which called for frequent admonitions." [165]

Sometimes these " elections " are said to have involved the masters in " heavy " expense, concerning which an anecdote is told of the Honorable E. R. Potter of Rhode Island, whose slave, John, was elected " governor " about 1800. Potter, who was probably unwilling to bear the costs incident to the inauguration, is said to have told the slave that one of them would have to quit politics or both would be ruined, whereupon " Governor " John retired to private life.[166]

Since these " elections " continued until about 1830, some of the names of the " governors " have been preserved. Among them were: Guy Watson of Rhode Island, who distinguished himself as a soldier during the Revolution, fought in the slave battalion of Rhode Island, and aided conspicuously in the capture of General Prescott.[167] Quaw, the slave of George Wyllys, Secretary of State of Connecticut was said to have enacted the

163 Updike, *ut supra;* for other accounts see Felt, *op. cit.,* II, 419-420; Platt, *op. cit.,* 324, 326, 331.

164 Caulkins, *op. cit.,* p. 185.

165 Felt, *op. cit.,* II, 420.

166 Updike, *op. cit.,* I, 214.

167 Platt, *op. cit.,* VI, 327-328.

role of governor to great satisfaction;[168] and Peleg Nott, the slave of Colonel Jeremiah Wadsworth of West Hartford, who drove a provision cart in the American Revolution, is said to have made a resplendent figure in his finery.[169] Cuff, who "appointed" John Anderson "Governor" of Connecticut in 1776, held office for ten years.[170] The first "governor" of Derby, Connecticut was Quosh, the slave of Agar Tomlinson of Derby Neck, where a branch of the Tomlinson family (1941) still resides. Tobias or Tobiah, a "governor" who was the slave of Captain Wooster of Derby, fought in the patriot army and his son, Eben Tobias, the property of Squire Bassett of Derby, also held the office. The son of Eben Tobias was the Honorable Eben D. Bassett, a well educated man who during the Civil War helped to enlist Negro soldiers for the Union Army, in recognition of which services President Grant appointed him Minister to Haiti, where he served creditably for eight years.[171]

On one occasion these elections provoked political repercussions—when John Anderson was elevated to the "governorship" of the Connecticut blacks in 1776. John was the slave of Governor Phillip Skene, a British officer on parole at Hartford for implication in a Negro plot.[172] In the midst of the excitement, suspicion, and unrest incident to the Revolution, the "election" of a Tory slave to the "control" of the Negroes in that State aroused grave apprehensions of an insurrection by the slaves. The Governor and Council met in special session and appointed a committee to investigate the election. Skene, upon questioning, denied any complicity in the elevation of his slave to the "gubernatorial" office. When Anderson was interrogated he confessed that he had bought the office, evidence that politics of that day, even among slaves, was not free from cor-

168 Scaeva, *op. cit.*, p. 39.

169 *Ibid.*, p. 40.

170 Platt, *op. cit.*, p. 327.

171 *Ibid.*, pp. 330, 331. His son, a Yale man, teaches at Dunbar High School in Washington, D. C.

172 *Continental Journal and Weekly Advertiser*, July 24, 1777.

ruption. According to Anderson, a Negro, named Sharper, induced him to run for the office, and being " desirous of the governorship," he " informed the Negroes that if they would elect him, he would treat them to the amount of $20." Although the subsequent entertainment cost him $25, Anderson nevertheless " declared that no regular officer or soldier had spoken to him on the subject, that there was no scheme or plot and that he had done it merely as a matter of sport." Anderson further disclaimed any intention of injuring the country, maintaining that he had acted only through the " curiosity of seeing an election," and having been told that the Negroes annually elected a " governor," he had determined to run for the office. Questioned as to how he secured the money he replied that he had earned it working on a vessel " where he had certain perquisites of his own."

When former " Governor " Cuff was interviewed, he told a different story. He not only declared that he had appointed Anderson to the office, but he also implicated some of the British regulars. According to Cuff " he had been advised to resign his office to Skene's negro by some of his black friends and some of the regulars." When the patriotic blacks refused to vote for a Tory " governor," Cuff, without the slightest semblance of an election, thereupon appointed Anderson to the office. Whether the British were really implicated in the appointment of Skene's Negro to the " governorship " is not definitely known. One incident, however, suggests that they were not wholly ignorant of the deal. Sometime after the installation of Anderson, a dance was given at Knox's tavern in Hartford and, although the expense involved amounted to fifty shillings, " Gov. Skene's negroes were not allowed to pay anything." The bill was paid by Majors French and Dermet of the British army.[173]

173 " These facts were stated to the Governor and Council by Jesse Root Esq., Chairman, May 22nd, 1776." According to Mr. James Brewster, Librarian of the Connecticut State Library at Hartford, the Journals of the Governor and Council of Connecticut are not extant from 1773 on, and the original sources for the above cannot be cited. For secondary accounts, *vide* R. R. Hinman, *A Historical Collection* (Revised Edition, 1842), pp. 31-33; *New Haven Colony Historical Society Papers*, VI, 326-329.

Just how much actual jurisdiction these Negro " governors " exercised over their constituencies cannot be stated with certainty.[174] To assume that they disposed of criminal cases where Negroes were concerned would be incorrect, for court records point abundantly to the contrary, yet these " governors " apparently did exercise considerable control over the blacks.[175] The Negro " government " had its " judges," " sheriffs," and " magistrates," and its " courts " probably tried trivial cases between Negroes, as well as petty cases brought by masters against their slaves. Platt cites the powers exercised by one of these Negro courts in Rhode Island:

> The judicial department consisted of the Governor, who sometimes sat in judgment in cases of appeal. The other magistrates and judges tried all charges brought against any negro, by another, or by a white person. Masters complained to the Governor and magistrates of the delinquencies of their slaves, who were tried, condemned and punished at the discretion of the court. The punishment was sometimes quite severe, and what made it the more effectual, was that it was the judgment of their peers, people of their own rank and color had condemned them, and not their masters, by an arbitrary mandate.[176]

The punishment is said to have usually consisted of a number of blows, well laid on " with a large cobbing board," the " high sheriff " or his " executioner " carrying out the sentence. According to Platt, the punishment was effective in restraining immorality, infidelity, petty larceny, or other delinquencies because offenders dreaded the " sneers and contempt of their equals." [177]

It is more probable that these punishments were simply carried out by the Negro executioner after the culprit had first

174 Scaeva relates that it is difficult to determine their actual jurisdiction. *Op. cit.,* p. 38.

175 Earle, *op. cit.,* p. 226.

176 Platt, *op. cit.,* p. 324.

177 *Ibid.*

been sentenced by a white magistrate. This was the case of a Connecticut thief whose sentence of thirty lashes was publicly administered by " Squire Nep," a Negro barber, on the town green. In addition, the humiliated slave was also forced for a stated period to give up his gun and tobacco.[178]

The mock Negro government with its elections and celebrations was in direct imitation of the master class, for Election Day with its " lection cake " and " lection beer " provided the biggest holiday in colonial New England.[179] Not only does the election of Negro " governors " reflect the gradual adoption of the masters' culture by the Negroes, but it also shows the paternalistic aspect of New England slavery. By the same token, the Negro " government " was a subtle form of slave control, for, by inducing the slaves to inform on and to punish their fellows, the threat to the masters' security was minimized. Psychologically, it served as an outlet for the pent-up ambitions of the more aggressive Negroes and their fellows and thereby tended to make the Negro more complacent in his bondage. Finally, it acted as a sort of political school wherein the slaves received the rudiments of a political education which could be drawn upon once they were enfranchised.

Masters who treated their slaves with kindness were frequently repaid by their Negroes. Several examples might be cited: in 1635 a Massachusetts Negro saved his mistress from being raped by one Dr. Richard Corden;[180] seventeen years

178 Roberts, *Historic Towns of the Connecticut Valley,* p. 218.

179 Earle, *Customs and Fashions,* p. 225.

180 Dr. Richard Corden was sentenced to prison until the meeting of the next session of the Quarterly Court for attempting to assault Mary, wife of John Roffe in the stable or corn house of her mother Mrs. Bishop. The doctor had attended the mother. When he asked for his horse in preparation to depart, Mary told him it was in the stable and went out with him. " In the stable he struck the candle out of her hand and she ran in front of the cows. He charged her to have a care for the cows, and she said she would as soon be gored by the cows as to be defiled by such a rogue as he, etc. She cried out to Sara (her sister) and she sent out the negro, and Corden threatened her if she told it." *E. C. C. R., 1627-1667* (Salem, 1913), III, 54-55.

later, another Negro rescued his mistress from a cruel beating by her drunken husband, the woman testifying that " if the negro had not taken him off, he would have killed her." [181] Peter, the slave of the famous Boston bookseller and printer, Thomas Fleet, was so attached to his master's children that, at his death, he bequeathed to them his life's savings of five pounds.[182] During the Indian attack on Deerfield in 1746, Parthenia and Frank, the slaves of the Reverend John Williams of Deerfield, Massachusetts, died in defense of the children committed to their care.[183]

Although the slaves were generally well treated in New England, slavery was so unbearable to some Negroes that, rather than remain in bondage, they committed suicide; others like the Negroes of Wait Winthrop and John Pynchon, merely threatened to take their lives.[184] Congo Pomp, who escaped from his master near Truro, Massachusetts, fled to Cape Cod and after placing at the foot of a tree a loaf of bread and a jug of water, hanged himself from one of its limbs.[185] Attention has already been directed to John, the slave of Henry Bartholomew of Providence, who shot himself to death in 1661.[186] Cato, the slave of Parson Williams of Longmeadow, Massachusetts, after being whipped repeatedly " for speaking out loud in meeting, [church] drinking too much cider, [and] going on a rampage ", finally drowned himself in a well.[187]

181 *Ibid.,* VII, 381-382.

182 For account of Fleet's slaves *vide* " Colonial Society of Massachusetts," *Transactions, 1922-1924,* XXV, 253-254.

183 Parthenia and Frank had been married by Rev. John Williams about 1703. Sheldon, *op. cit.,* pp. 50-51.

184 Waitstill Winthrop wrote thus to Fitz John Winthrop in 1682: " I fear Black Tom will do but little seruis. He usued to make a show of hangeing himselfe before folkes, but I believe he is not very nimble about it when he is alone. Tis good to have an eye to him & you think it not worth while to keep him eyether [either] sell him or send him to Virginia or the Barbadoes." Earle, *Customs and Fashions in Old New England,* p. 92.

185 *Ibid.*

186 *Vide supra,* p. 186.

187 Earle, *ut supra.*

# CHAPTER X

## SLAVERY AND CONVERSION

SECULAR education was supplemented and strongly influenced by the movement for the religious instruction of the New England slaves. In view of the Puritans' contention that slavery was a means of bringing the heathen to Christ, the conversion of the slaves should have been taken for granted,[1] and apparently, the early settlers felt that it was incumbent upon them to carry out this idea. Although Governor Bradstreet informed the British Committee of Trade and Plantations that no Negroes had been baptized in that colony up to 1680,[2] the first baptism of a New England slave is said to have occurred in 1641 only three years after Negroes had been enslaved there. In that year, according to John Winthrop, " a Negro woman belonging to Rev. Stoughton of Dorchester, Massachusetts, being well approved by divers years experience for sound knowledge and true godliness was received into the Church and baptized." [3]

Although other baptisms of slaves followed, relatively few Negroes were Christianized in the seventeenth century either in New England or elsewhere in colonial America. Economic, social, religious, and political obstacles constituted formidable barriers against conversion.[4] Baptism particularly was opposed on economic grounds. Many owners feared conversion might lessen the value of their chattels as laborers. Not only would

1 *Vide supra*, p. 62.

2 *Calendar of State Papers: Colonial, 1677-1680*, p. 530.

3 John Winthrop, *Journal*, ed. Savage, II, 26; Moore, *Notes on Slavery in Massachusetts*, p. 95 n; Theodore Lyman, Jr., " Free Negroes and Mulattoes," *Mass. Reports: House of Representatives*, Jan. 15, 1821 (Reprint, no title page), p. 4.

4 The best general summary of the efforts to convert the slaves in colonial America may be found in Marcus W. Jernegan, " Slavery and Conversion in the Colonies," *American Historical Review*, XXI, 504-527; *ibid.*, *Laboring and Dependent Classes in Colonial America, 1607-1783* (Chicago, 1931), ch. ii; Carter G. Woodson, *Education of the Negro Prior to 1861*, ch. i.

valuable time be lost in instructing them but, once converted, the Negroes would be compelled to attend church on Sunday. Prohibition of Sunday work by the slaves would increase maintenance costs, for in the plantation colonies, especially, the slaves raised part of their food on that day.[5] Although this obstacle did not loom so large in the minds of New England masters, where the Calvinistic theocracy forbade even the slaves to work on the Lord's Day, it had much significance in the tobacco and rice colonies where the economy was dependent upon the large numbers of slaves employed.

Besides the economic opposition, there were social objections to baptism of the Negroes. Conversion, in the opinion of many masters, would instill in the slaves notions of equality which would make them almost useless. In a system built upon the supremacy of the masters and the subordination of the slaves, many owners visualized the Christianized slaves as haughty, proud, intractable and rebellious.[6] This reasoning was apparent to Peter Kalm, the Swedish botanist, who travelled through the colonies in 1748. Deploring the general indifference of the planters to the spiritual welfare of the slaves, Kalm wrote:

> . . . they [the masters] are partly led by the conceit of its being shameful, to have a spiritual brother or sister among so despicable a people, partly by thinking that they should not be able to keep their Negroes so meanly afterwards; and partly through fear of the Negroes growing too proud, on seeing themselves upon a level with their masters in religious matters.[7]

The masters believed that the equalitarian gospel of Christianity, if put into practice, would utterly destroy slavery.

5 Dr. Humphreys, *An Account of the Endeavours of the Society for the Propagation of the Gospel to Instruct the Negro Slaves of New York* (London, 1730), pp. 4-5; Jernegan, *Laboring and Dependent Classes in Colonial America*, p. 35; *Ibid.*, " Slavery and Conversion in the Colonies," *loc. cit.*, p. 516.

6 Humphreys, *op. cit.*, pp. 26-27.

7 Peter Kalm, *Travels into North America*. Translated by John Reinhold Forster (3 vols., Warrington, 1770), I, 397.

Conversion of the Negroes was opposed also on religious grounds. The prevailing opinion among English settlers of America in the seventeenth century was that only heathen could be enslaved by Christians, and that once the slaves were Christianized, they automatically became free, for it was held that no Christian might hold another in bondage.[8] Although this principle had been repudiated by the Spanish, Portuguese, and French, both in Europe and in their American possessions,[9] many English settlers still adhered to it. Not only in New England, but especially in those colonies where slaves were numerous, owners feared that to allow conversion would deprive them of their property.[10] Sincere religious masters were in a quandary: to baptize the slave meant that they would lose him; to withhold conversion would retard the spread of Christianity.[11] Facing this dilemma, most masters let material motives outweigh moral and spiritual principles, and sought an expedient to preserve their slave property.

To achieve this end some owners went to the extreme of declaring that the Negro was not a man but a *beast,* and that he had no soul either to save or to lose.[12] " Talk to a *Planter* of the *Soul* of a *Negro,*" commented a writer in the *Athenian Oracle,*

8 Humphreys, *op. cit.,* p. 27; Jernegan, " Slavery and Conversion in the Colonies," *loc. cit.,* XXI, 505; *Ibid., Laboring and Dependent Classes in Colonial America,* p. 25; Woodson, *History of the Negro Church,* pp. 5-6; *vide* especially Klingberg, *op. cit.,* pp. 205, 217.

9 Donnan, *Docs.,* I, 18-41; Helps, *op. cit.,* I, 33; Johnston, *The Negro in the New World, passim;* Ramos, *The Negro in Brazil;* Stoddard, *The French Revolution in San Domingo,* ch. v.

10 *S. P. G. Transcripts,* Series B, I, Part II (1661-1778), 808. (Library Congress, pag. 597-598); Cotton Mather, *Life of John Eliot,* pp. 101-102; C. F. Pascoe, *Two Hundred Years of the S. P. G.,* p. 22; Jernegan, *Laboring and Dependent Classes,* pp. 25-26.

11 Jernegan, *op. cit.,* p. 26.

12 C. F. Pascoe, *Classified Digest of the Records of the Society for the Propagation of the Gospel in Foreign Parts, 1701-1892* (London, 1893), p. 15; Cotton Mather (*The Negro Christianized,* p. 23) sets forth clearly the attitude of those holding this view; *cf.* Updike, *History of the Narragansett Church,* I, pp. 212-213; Jernegan, *Laboring and Dependent Classes,* p. 35.

" and he'll be apt to tell ye (or at least his actions speak it loudly) that the body of one of them may be worth twenty pounds; but the souls of an hundred of them would not yield him one farthing." [13] Even in New England many masters regarded their Negroes as brutes. Referring to this attitude among Rhode Island slaveholders, Dean Berkeley in 1731 remarked that they considered " the blacks as creatures of another species, who had no right to be instructed or admitted to the sacraments." This, he added, is the main " obstacle to the conversion of these poor people.[14]

When humanitarians insisted that the Negroes were not *beasts* but men, many masters appealed to the colonial legislatures for legal assurance that Christianization would not result in manumission. Because of the close tie-up between property interests and colonial political institutions, six colonies between 1664 and 1706 passed laws of this nature. Maryland, Virginia, North Carolina, South Carolina, New York and New Jersey all formally renounced baptism as a means of emancipation, but the New England colonies, Georgia and Pennsylvania did not resort to such legislation.[15] Since the colonial acts did not carry sufficient assurance for some slaveholders, they sought the advice of the royal attorney-general and solicitor-general. The replies of these officials in 1729 reaffirmed the colonial statutes that baptism did not enfranchise the slaves.[16]

Ecclesiastical sanction still had to be obtained; but the Anglican Church did not oppose slavery and, as many of its ministers were slaveholders, it readily compromised with vested interests. Bishop Williams (1706), Bishop Fleetwood (1711), and in 1727 Bishop Gibson of London, who exercised considerable jurisdiction over the Anglican Church in America, threw the

13 *Athenian Oracle* (1705), II, 460-463, cited in Moore, *op. cit.*, p. 93; Jernegan, *Laboring and Dependent Classes,* pp. 34-35.

14 Updike, *op. cit.*, I, 212-213; *cf.* Pascoe, *Classified Digest of the Records of the Society for the Propagation of the Gospel in Foreign Parts,* p. 15.

15 Jernegan, *Laboring and Dependent Classes,* pp. 26-27.

16 Updike, *op. cit.*, I, 212-213; Jernegan, *Laboring and Dependent Classes,* p. 27.

vast weight of the Episcopacy in support of the propertied class. Said Gibson:

> Christianity and the embracing of the Gospel does not make the least alteration in Civil Property or in any of the duties which belong to civil Relations but . . . it continues Persons in the same State as it found them. The Freedom which Christianity gives, is a Freedom from the Bondage of Sin and Satan, and from the Dominion of Mens' Lusts and Passions and inordinate Desires; but as to their *outward* Condition, whatever that was before, whether bond or free; their being baptized and becoming Christians makes no manner of change in it . . .[17]

By this pronouncement the Episcopal Church accomplished a double purpose: it removed the hostility of many masters toward conversion and at the same time it encouraged the proselytizing of the slaves.[18]

In New England the political implications involved in baptism and church membership raised another temporary barrier. Some persons feared the political equality [19] which baptism would confer upon the slave, since the right to vote in Massachusetts between 1631 and 1664 was limited to church members.[20] Did the slave upon admittance to the church exercise this privilege by virtue of his becoming a freeman? Bancroft, answering in the affirmative, says: " The servant, the bondsman might be a member of the Church and therefore a freeman of the company." [21] Quincy says that slaves were admitted into

17 Humphreys, *op. cit.,* p. 27; see draft of Bill denying enfranchisement of slaves through Christianization in *Lambeth Palace Transcripts,* Vol. 941, No. 72 (Mss. in Library of Congress); for views of Bishops Williams and Fleetwood, *vide* Klingberg, *op. cit.,* pp. 15, 205-206.

18 Woodson, *Education of the Negro Prior to 1861,* p. 24.

19 Woodson, *History of the Negro Church,* p. 15.

20 " To the end that the body of freemen may be preserved of honest and good men, It is ordered that henceforth no man shall be admitted to the freedom of this Commonwealth but such as are members of some of the churches within this commonwealth." *Ancient Charters,* p. 17; cited in Moore, *Notes,* p. 95 n.

21 George Bancroft, *History of the United States,* I, 360.

the church when peculiar, political privileges were conferred upon church members.[22] Although church membership until 1664 theoretically made the Negro a member of the body politic, there is no evidence that this was actually the case. It is doubtful whether the General Court ever considered the Negro a member of the Company of the Massachusetts Bay, even though he were a communicant. To have done so would have been equivalent to a writ of emancipation. Furthermore, had such political privileges been accorded to the baptized slaves, an anomalous situation might have arisen in case the master were not a church member; for then, as Palfrey points out, the owner might be compelled to obey laws enacted in part by his chattels.[23] However, such a situation could hardly have existed for the Massachusetts election law making church membership the qualification for voting was in force only from 1631 to 1664. Furthermore, there were at that time so few Negroes in Massachusetts, and so little effort had been made to convert them, that the possibility of Christianized slaves voting is remote indeed.[24] In fact, there appears to be no record of Negroes voting at any time in colonial New England.[25]

Efforts to convert the bondmen met with less resistance in New England than elsewhere because less property in slaves was involved. Unlike the South, moreover, where the Anglican Church was directed from abroad, New England churches were overwhelmingly Congregational, therefore each church could act in an independent manner [26] in regard to baptizing the slaves.

These and other considerations checked somewhat the antagonism toward Christianizing the New England slaves. One of these factors was the attempt of the British Government to

22 *Reports,* p. 30 n; Moore, *op. cit.,* p. 94.

23 Palfrey, *History of New England,* II, 30 n.

24 Albert E. McKinley, *The Suffrage Franchise in the Thirteen English Colonies in America* (Philadelphia, 1905), p. 475.

25 *Vide, infra,* ch. xi.

26 Thomas Cuming Hall, *The Religious Background of American Culture* (Boston, 1930), p. 99 ff.; Jernegan in *American Historical Review,* XXI, 513.

spread the Protestant faith by competing with the Catholics in the conversion of Indians and Negroes. In 1660, King Charles II instructed the Council of Foreign Plantations to inquire

> how such of the Natives or such as are purchased by you from other parts to be your servants or slaves may be best invited to the Christian Faith, and be made capable of being baptized thereunto, it being to the honor of our Crowne and of the Protestant Religion that all persons in any of our Dominions should be taught the knowledge of God and be made acquainted with the misteries of Salvation.[27]

Queries of this nature frequently were sent by circular letter under *Heads of Inquiry* to the various governors.[28]

The effect of the royal concern for the spiritual welfare of the slaves cannot be evaluated, but it may have stimulated ministers to take the lead in advocating the Christianization of the Negroes. First to labor in their religious behalf was John Eliot. Deploring the fact that many masters treated their slaves like beasts, Eliot hoped that " the several planters that live upon the labours of their negroes, no more be guilty of such prodigious wickedness, as to deride, neglect, and oppose all due means of bringing their poor negroes unto the Lord . . ." He exhorted slaveholders to see that their Negroes like Abraham's servants were converted and not to " imagine that the Almighty God made so many thousands of reasonable creatures for nothing but to serve the lusts of epicures or the gains of mamonists . . ." He warned the masters not to neglect this duty, " lest the God of Heaven, out of mere pity, if not justice unto those unhappy blacks, be provoked unto a vengeance which may not without honor be thought upon."[29] Eliot offered to catechise and enlighten the Negroes if their masters would send them to him weekly.[30]

27 *Calendar of State Papers: Colonial, 1574-1660*, pp. 492-493.
28 *Ibid.* For other instructions, see *N. Y. Col. Docs.*, III, 374, 547.
29 Mather, *Life of John Eliot*, p. 109.
30 *Ibid.*, pp. 101-102.

Eliot's work was carried on by Cotton Mather, who was the most conspicuous Puritan advocate of the baptism of the slaves. In *The Negro Christianized,* Mather made an impassioned attack upon those who for various reasons refused to have their slaves baptized. Assailing those who claimed that the Negro had no soul, Mather exclaimed ". . . let that brutish insinuation be never whispered any more." Not only the slaves' speech shows that they have reason, he added, but " reason shows itself in the design which they daily act upon." The vast improvement that education has made in some slaves, argued Mather, shows " that there is a reasonable soul in all of them." To the theory that Negroes are barbarous, he replied : " So too were our own ancestors." He vigorously refuted the allegation that Negroes were beasts by reminding his fellows that the slaves were " men not beasts that you have bought and must be used accordingly." [31]

Directing attention to the charge that baptism would result in manumission and, therefore, in the loss of the masters' slaves, Mather sought a compromise by which the vested interests of the slaveholders might be protected and the slaves brought to salvation as well. Suppose baptism did give " a legal title to freedom." Could not the master prevent it " by sufficient indentures " ? But he maintained that no such expedient was necessary, since the belief that baptism frees the slave " is all a mistake." There was no basis for such apprehension, he asserted. " What *law* is it," he asked, " that sets the baptized *slave at liberty?* Not the *law* of *Christianity."* From Mather's point of view, Christianity and slavery were not antithetical; indeed Christianity recognized both bondmen and freemen.[32] Reassuring those who were apprehensive, Mather stated that neither under the canon law nor under the English constitution could baptism of the slave result in his emancipation. As proof of the former he cited the prevalence of slavery in all parts of Chris-

31 Mather, *The Negro Christianized,* p. 23.

32 *Ibid.,* p. 26.

tendom [33] and concluded that although " the baptised [slaves]
are not entitled unto their liberty," nevertheless, because of the
universal brotherhood of mankind,[34] they should be well treated.

Having overthrown the economic argument against baptism
to his evident satisfaction, Mather then made a special plea for
the baptism of slave children. He also expressed the hope that
adult slaves would not be forgotten and prayed that the " elder
servants as black as they are, will shortly be the candidates of
baptism." [35] To those who objected to the conversion of Negroes because of their color, he scornfully replied : " The whites
are the least part of mankind. God is no respecter of persons." [36]
He then placed the relationships of master and slave upon the
highest social and spiritual level. After quoting the Biblical precept " Thou shalt love thy neighbour," Mather warned the
slaveholders : " Thy Negro is thy neighbor . . . since . . .
God hath made of one blood, all nations of men, he is your
brother too." [37] How can the master, then, love his Negro and
see him under " the rage of sin and the wrath of God ? " [38] He
even suggested to the owners that the Negroes may be " the
Elect of God placed in their hands by Divine Providence," and
he pleaded with them " to treat not as *bruits* but as *men* those
rational creatures whom God has made your servants." [39]

Mather applied his precepts. In 1693 he made the first attempt
at group instruction of Negroes in spiritual things. In that
year, he organized a Society of Negroes and published a set of
rules for its guidance. Slaves who could obtain the permission
of their masters were invited to meet at his home every Sunday

33 *Ibid.,* p. 27; Mather was in error here for slavery had disappeared in
western Europe in the seventeenth century.

34 *Ibid.,* p. 28.

35 *Ibid.,* pp. 44-45.

36 *Ibid.,* p. 27.

37 *Ibid.,* pp. 5-6.

38 *Ibid.*

39 *Ibid.,* p. 4.

evening from seven to nine o'clock.[40] Here they would pray, sing, and listen to a sermon, which, upon questioning, they were to repeat.[41] The hours were so chosen that the slaves might not be *unseasonably absent* from their master's home.[42] Membership was to be carefully restricted to those slaves who desired to " avoid all wicked companies " and those " abstaining from all wickedness." Even these slaves were to be examined and passed upon by the minister before they might be accepted as members.[43] In order that the Negroes might not use such meetings for plotting against their masters, the gathering was to be supervised by " some wise and good man of the English and especially the officers of the Church." One of the prime purposes of the Society was to make the slaves exemplary servants, for any member " falling into the sin of drunkenness, or swearing or cursing, or lying or stealing or notorious disobedience or unfaithfulness " to his master was to be dropped for a fortnight. Unless the penitent returned " with great signs and hopes of his *repentance*," he was to be permanently dropped.[44] Any member guilty of fornication was to be suspended for six months and might be readmitted after that time only if he gave " exemplary testimonies " of repentance and proof of " his becoming a *new creature*." [45] All members were to learn the catechism and the slaves were to participate, for one was to ask questions while the others answered in order.[46] Mather proposed to use either the *New English Catechism,* the *Assemblies Catechism,* or the catechism in *The Negro Christianized* which he had prepared [47] especially for the slaves.

40 Cotton Mather, *Rules for the Society of Negroes* (1693), Boston, 1888, p. 6.

41 *Ibid.,* pp. 5-6.

42 *Ibid.,* p. 6.

43 *Ibid.,* pp. 6-7.

44 *Ibid.,* p. 7.

45 *Ibid.,* p. 8.

46 *Ibid.,* p. 9.

47 Mather, *The Negro Christianized,* pp. 28-31 ; 41-42.

Mather's efforts enlisted the support of other ministers. In 1694, a year after he published his *Rules for the Society of Negroes,* a group of Massachusetts ministers rallied to his support. Realizing that many slaveholders still feared their Negroes would become free as a result of baptism, the ministers petitioned the legislature for a law stating that baptism did not alter the slave status. The petition, tendered on May 30, 1694, and signed by ministers from all parts of the province, read:

> It is Desired That y$^e$ well knowne Discouragem$^t$ upon y$^e$ endeavors of many masters [to] Christianize their slaves may be removed by a Law which may take away all pre [text] to Release from just servitude, by receiving of Baptisme.[48]

The legislature apparently did not pass such a law, for no trace of it can be found. This was the first concerted effort of the Congregational ministry to effect a compromise similar to that adopted by the Anglican Church in the southern and middle colonies, whereby the soul of the slave might be saved and the slaveholder left in possession of his property. Failure to pass such a law rendered abortive all efforts to remove the economic obstacles to Christianizing the blacks in seventeenth century New England.

Nevertheless, the struggle to convert the slaves went on. In 1738 the General Association of the Colony of Connecticut opened the way for the baptism of infant slaves. Two questions were asked of the delegates: the first was "whether the infant slaves of Christian masters may be baptized in their master's right, provided they suitably promise and engage to bring them up in the ways of religion?" The meeting decided in the affirmative. To the second question: Whether masters were not bound to "offer such children" for baptism "and to promise as aforesaid?"—a similar reply was given.[49] The action of the church

48 *Mass. A. and R.,* VII, Appendix II, 537.

49 *Records of the General Ass'n. of Connecticut, 1738-1799,* I, p. 2.

at Medfield, Massachusetts, was apparently a result of these affirmations. After debating whether infant slaves might be baptized, even if their parents were not church members, the church voted that " if the masters think it their duty to bring such children, it [baptism] should not be denied them." [50]

During the period between 1730 and the Revolution, many Negroes were baptized and accepted into the churches of their masters. Since colonial New England was overwhelmingly Congregational, a majority of the slaves became members in the churches of that denomination. The records of the First Church of Salem, Massachusetts (Congregational) show that ten Negroes, including Rebecca, Titus, Judith, Pompey and others, were received as communicants between 1739-1758.[51] At Concord, New Hampshire, the Reverend Timothy Walker on September 28, 1746, baptized " Peter y^e son of George, Mr. Osgoods servant." Twenty years later he baptized Moses and Phebe, the slaves of Benjamin Fifield and Nathaniel Abbot, Jr., respectively.[52] Over a twelve-year period (between 1738 and 1750) six Negro children were baptized at the First Church in Plymouth, Massachusetts,[53] and according to Abram Brown, six Negroes—Ishmael, Qumbo, Toney, Hannah Drury, Lois Burdo and Abraham—were taken into the Church at Bedford, Massachusetts, between July 4, 1736 and March 11, 1753.[54] In 1772 the Reverend Chauncey Whittlesey of New Haven, Connecticut had from twenty to thirty Negroes in a total membership of

50 *History of the Town of Medfield, Massachusetts, 1650-1886,* ed. William S. Tilden (Boston, 1887), p. 134.

51 " Records of the First Church in Salem," ed. Henry Wheatland, *Essex Institute Historical Collections,* VIII, No. 3, pp. 152, 153.

52 *Diaries of the Reverend Timothy Walker,* ed. Joseph B. Walker (Concord, 1889), p. 18.

53 " Plymouth Church Records, 1620-1854," ed. Albert Mathews, *Colonial Society of Massachusetts, Collections,* 2 vols., XXII-XXIII (Boston, 1920-1923), II, 441-446.

54 Abram English Brown, *History of Bedford, Massachusetts* (Bedford, 1891), p. 31.

from 450 to 500. In Newport, Rhode Island, the Reverend Samuel Hopkins had six or seven Negro members in 1772 [55] and in the same town Ezra Stiles, pastor of the Second Congregational Church, reported " seventy blacks " and five hundred whites in his congregation. Of the Negroes were between fifty and fifty-five communicants.[56]

Supplementing the efforts of the Congregationalists to encourage the baptism of the slaves was the work carried on by two agencies of the Anglican Church. One of these was the Society of the Propagation of the Gospel in Foreign Parts,[57] whose activities in all the English colonies in America made it the most important single agency for the religious as well as secular instruction of the slaves. From 1702-1785 the Society sent missionaries, catechists and teachers to America, for the purpose of converting the Negroes; as well as thousands of printed copies of Annual Sermons, delivered before it, to slave owners in all the English colonies,[58] " exhorting them to encourage and promote the instruction of their Negroes in the Christian faith." Ten thousand copies of a letter of the Bishop of London were printed and circulated through the colonies in 1727. The Society also distributed catechisms, Common Prayer Books, thousands of Bibles, and other literature and set up schools for the special instruction of the Negroes.[59] Masters were urged by Bishop Gibson in his letter of May 19,

55 *Stiles, Literary Diary*, I, 293.

56 *Ibid.*, p. 33.

57 Humphreys, *op. cit., passim*; Pascoe, *Two Hundred Years of the S. P. G.*, p. 6; *vide supra*, p. 239 ff. For manuscript sources concerning the activities of the Society for the Propagation of the Gospel, see *Lambeth Palace Transcripts* and *Fulham Palace Transcripts*, in the Library of Congress. Hereinafter cited as S.P.G. or the Society.

58 *S. P. G., Lambeth Palace Transcripts*, 1123 I, No. 18 (May 6, 1740); Jernegan, *Laboring and Dependent Classes*, p. 29; Klingberg, *op. cit.*, pp. 20, 29, 63.

59 *Lambeth Palace Transcripts,* Series A, XXI, 403 (Library of Congress, pag. 303). Both Bishop Fleetwood (1711) and Bishop Gibson (1730) exhorted owners to Christianize their slaves. Humphreys, *op. cit.*, pp. 14, 15.

1727, to regard their Negroes " not merely as slaves upon the level with laboring beasts, but as *men* slaves and *women* slaves who have the same frame and faculties with yourselves and souls capable of being made eternally happy and reason and understanding to receive instruction . . ." [60] All missionaries were exhorted to use every endeavor to Christianize the blacks.[61]

Although the main activities of the *S.P.G.* were outside New England, its missionaries in the Puritan colonies endeavored to convert Negroes and Indians as well as to bring white members into the Anglican Church. Since the Puritans distrusted the Anglicans and feared the establishment of an English Episcopate in America,[62] they often hindered the Society's efforts to convert the Negroes. The Reverend J. Usher complained to the Secretary of the Society from Bristol, Rhode Island, in 1730 that although sundry Negroes had made application for baptism, he was forbidden by their masters to comply with their requests.[63] In like vein, Dr. Timothy Cutler wrote from Boston in 1740, saying that there was much indifference on the part of the masters to the conversion of their slaves.[64] At Newtown, Connecticut, the " Independents," as the Reverend J. Beach styled the Congregationalists, had stirred up the Indians against him, by telling them that the English Church was plotting to steal their lands. According to Beach the charge so infuriated

60 Humphreys, *op. cit.*, p. 29; *cf.* Updike, *op. cit.*, I, 210-211; Pasco, *op. cit.*, p. 47; Jernegan, *Laboring and Dependent Classes*, p. 29.

61 Humphreys, *op. cit.*, p. 4. The *S. P. G.* files of the *Lambeth Palace Transcripts* abound in such exhortations. (Mss. in Library of Congress).

62 Episcopalian missionaries and ministers in the colonies frequently stressed the need for an Anglican bishop in America. See *S. P. G. Transcripts*, Series B, I, Part II (1661-1778), pp. 469-472 (Library of Congress, pag. 370-375); *Ibid.*, pp. 533-536 (Library of Congress, pag. 415-416); *Ibid.*, 537-542 and *passim*.

63 *S. P. G. Transcripts;* Series A, XXIII, 125-126 (L. Congress, pag. 125-126); Pascoe, *Two Hundred Years of the S. P. G.*, p. 47.

64 Perry, *Historical Collections Relating to the American Colonial Church,* III, 231.

one of the chiefs that he threatened " if I came among them to shoot a bullet through my heart." Beach went, nevertheless, but the Indians regarded him with such sullenness that discretion overcame his religious zeal, and he withdrew, adding : " I feared if I had persisted in my discourse of religion they would have done me a mischief." [65]

In spite of these handicaps, Anglican ministers did succeed in converting a number of Indians and Negroes in New England. Hundreds of reports from missionaries in the different colonies to the Secretary of the *S.P.G.* in London confirm this statement. From Massachusetts several ministers sent accounts of their stewardship. On September 3, 1730, Dr. Timothy Cutler, stationed in Boston, wrote that during the past year he had " baptized 38 infant white children, 1 infant slave and 1 adult white." [66] Progress was slow for during a seven-month period, from December 26 to June 26, 1749-1750, he baptized twenty-six persons, only five of whom were Negro children and of these only one was a slave.[67] From Braintree the Reverend Ebenezer Miller informed his superior that within a year (March 25, 1738 to March 25, 1739) he had baptized eleven infants, one adult white person and one adult Negro.[68] For the year ending March 26, 1764, the Reverend Ebenezer Thompson of Scituate, Massachusetts, baptized " four white infants, one Negro and one Indian infant." [69]

Reports from Connecticut also showed that the Society's missionaries were making some progress among the slaves. On November 12, 1739, the Reverend Samuel Seabury of New London wrote the Secretary that during the last half year he had baptized eight adults, including a mulatto servant and fif-

65 Pascoe, *Two Hundred Years*, pp. 46-47.

66 *S. P. G. Transcripts*, Series A, XXIII, 131-132.

67 Perry, *op. cit.*, p. 439; *cf. ibid.*, p. 438 where, Cutler states " I have baptized 41 persons . . . 37 Infants 30 of which are Negro Slaves."

68 *S. P. G. Transcripts*, Series B, VII, Part I, 40 (Library of Congress, p. 39) ; Perry, *op. cit.*, p. 326.

69 *S. P. G. Transcripts*, Series B, I, Part II, 897-898 (Library of Congress, pp. 714-715).

teen children, among whom was a Negro child.[70] From New Haven the Reverend Theodore Morris, who also preached in Derby and Waterbury, reported that he had baptized eight infants and two adult Negroes.[71] Evidently Reverend Hubbard of Guilford found progress more difficult for, between 1764 and 1767, he had christened but two Negroes out of sixty or seventy converts.[72] From Stratford came a more favorable report: Reverend Samuel Johnson wrote to the Secretary on June 2, 1731, telling him that in the past six months he had baptized twenty persons, of whom one was " an adult Negro and two were mulatto children." [73] His report of May 26, 1729, showed that neither race nor nationality was a bar to his missionary zeal, for he wrote:

> I have baptized the Jew, Mr. Mordecai Marks, concerning whom I wrote you in my last, . . . two native Indians, both adults, two adult Negroes, and two Negro children all this last half year.[74]

Even more successful apparently was the Reverend Beach of Newtown, where more than half the population professed the Anglican faith. Beach, who had experienced trouble in trying to convert the Indians, reported that " after proper instruction " he had baptized most of the fifty Negroes in the town.[75]

In Rhode Island, which was noted for its liberalism in religion, the Society's agents found the slaves responsive. The Reverend John Checkley wrote to Dr. Bearcroft, Secretary of the S.P.G. in 1746, informing him that he had baptized four-

70 *Ibid.*, Series B, VIII, Part I, 61 (Library of Congress, pp. 64-65).

71 *Ibid.*, Series B, VII, Part II, 53-55 (Library of Congress, pp. 376-379).

72 Hawks and Stevens, *op. cit.,* 107.

73 *S. P. G. Transcripts,* Series A, XXIII, 247-249.

74 *Fulham Palace Transcripts: Connecticut,* No. 3, p. 7. Johnson later wrote that " as far as I can find, where the Dissenters have baptized one, we have baptized 2, if not 3 or 4 Negroes and Indians, and I have four or five communicants." Pascoe, *Two Hundred Years,* p. 47.

75 Hawks and Stevens, *op. cit.,* II, 133-134.

teen persons during the past year, two of whom were a Negro woman and her son.[76] Six years earlier he had baptized twenty-six persons, including a mulatto and two Negro boys.[77] Checkley was particularly proud of the fact that Governor Shirley of Rhode Island had sent him two Negroes to be brought up in the Anglican faith. One of these Negroes was evidently an Episcopalian, for Checkley added that the " Governor hath given me one to instruct the other." [78] More fruitful were the efforts of the pastors, Marmaduke Brown, James Honeyman and James McSparran. Brown, a Newport missionary, stating that between January 2 and July 1, 1766, he had baptized forty-three infants, two white and one black adults, also reported " one hundred and twenty communicants, seven of whom are blacks, who behave in a manner truly exemplary, and praise-worthy." [79] Dr. McSparran of Narragansett reported to the Secretary in September, 1941, that he had a class of fifty to sixty Negroes; [80] and the Reverend Mr. Honeyman of Newport who in the year ending July 15, 1740, had baptized seventy-seven persons, of whom three were blacks,[81] claimed that among his congregation on June 13, 1743, were more than " 100 Negroes who constantly attended the public worship." [82]

These Anglican ministers, like their Congregational fellow clergymen, did not stop at mere conversion of the slaves, but followed it up with catechetical lectures. Dr. McSparran cate-

76 " John Checkley or the Evolution of Religious Tolerance in Massachusetts Bay," *Prince Society Publications,* ed. Rev. Edmund F. Slater (2 vols.), II, 212. On May 1, 1750 Checkley wrote that he hoped to " christen the six children of a Negro woman." *Ibid.,* p. 216.

77 *S. P. G. Transcripts,* Series B, VII, Part II, 58 (Library of Congress, p. 381).

78 " John Checkley or the Evolution of Religious Tolerance in Massachusetts," *loc. cit.,* II, 202.

79 Updike, *op. cit.,* III, 88.

80 *S. P. G. Transcripts,* IX, Folio, p. 1 (Library of Congress, pp. 16-17) ; *Cf.* Updike, *op. cit.,* I, 522.

81 *Ibid.,* Series B, VII, Part II, 15 (Library of Congress, p. 331).

82 Pascoe, *Two Hundred Years,* p. 47.

chised his seventy Negro members before the Sunday morning service;[83] at Stratford, Connecticut, where the Reverend William Samuel Johnson held such lectures during the summer months, about eighty Indians, whites and Negroes attended,[84] and the Reverend John Usher of Bristol, Rhode Island, reported eighty slaves among his congregation in 1727.[85]

Closely allied with the work of the S.P.G. were the activities of another Anglican organization known as the Associates of Dr. Bray. Although this organization, as has been pointed out, did much for the secular enlightenment of the slaves, one of its chief objectives was to give them religious training. For this purpose the Associates not only supplied catechists, schools, missionaries and teachers, but also books, sermons, Bibles, prayer books and other literature.[86] The ministrations of the Associates of Dr. Bray and of the S.P.G. as well, were made easier by the pronouncement of the Bishop of London in 1727 to the effect that baptism did not confer freedom upon the slave.[87]

Also forwarding the work of converting the Negroes was the Society of Friends. Of all the religious denominations, the Quakers were to assume the most outspoken stand against slavery. Like other groups they first conformed to the spirit of the times and bought and sold slaves without scruple,[88]

83 *S. P. G. Transcripts*, IX, Folio, p. 1 (Library of Congress, p. 17).

84 Pascoe, *Two Hundred Years*, p. 47.

85 *S. P. G. Transcripts,* Series B, I, Part II (1661-1778), p. 808 (Library of Congress, pag. 597-598).

86 *Vide supra, An Account of the Associates of Dr. Bray*, p. 39; Perry, *Historical Collections Relating to the American Colonial Church*, IV, 338; Jernegan, *Laboring and Dependent Classes*, p. 30.

87 Humphreys, *op. cit.,* p. 27.

88 New England Quakers like Robert Hazard, Thomas Hazard, Jeremiah Austin and the Rodmans, all kept slaves. Jones, *The Quakers in the American Colonies* (London, 1911), p. 156; William Davis Miller, "The Narragansett Planters," *Proceedings of the American Antiquarian Society* (Worcester, 1934), p. 227.

but in 1773 they forbade their members to hold slaves.[89] Recalcitrant members were punished by dismissal from the Society.[90] The Quakers also favored the Christianization of the slaves, and as early as 1657 George Fox had entreated all Friends to give their slaves religious instruction.[91] In 1693 George Keith, leader of the Philadelphia Friends, advised the members not only to free their slaves, but to give them a Christian education.[92] In 1760 the Newport Friends enjoined all members who held slaves to impress God's fear in their minds and to see that they attended religious worship.[93] As a result of these efforts a number of Negroes were probably initiated into the Quaker faith.

Besides the efforts of the Quakers and the results attained by the Congregationalists and Anglicans, minor successes in Christianizing the Negroes were scored by the smaller denominational groups. In Rhode Island, which was a Baptist stronghold, Ezra Stiles reported in 1772 that there were seven Negro communicants in the Baptist churches of Newport.[94]

When the Great Awakening or New Light Movement,[95] inspired by Jonathan Edwards in 1735, inaugurated a series of revivals, which were destined to weaken the grip of Calvinism upon New England,[96] a great spiritual emotionalism stirred

89 *Book of Discipline Agreed on by the Yearly Meeting of Friends in New England* (Providence, 1785), p. 102; Jones, *The Quakers in the American Colonies,* p. 164.

90 Caroline Hazard, *Narragansett Friends Meeting,* pp. 145-147; Jones, *op. cit.,* pp. 164-165.

91 Jernegan, *op. cit.,* p. 31.

92 "An Exhortation and Caution to Friends Concerning Buying or Keeping of Negroes," *Pennsylvania Magazine of History and Biography* (Reprint, Philadelphia, 1884), p. 5.

93 Jones, *op. cit.,* p. 162.

94 *Literary Diary,* I, 213-214.

95 William Warren Sweet, *The Story of Religions in America* (New York and London, 1930), ch. ix., Hall, *Religious Background of American Culture,* ch. xii; Grover C. Loud, *Evangelized America* (New York, 1928), chs. iv, v.

96 Vernon Louis Parrington, "The Colonial Mind," *Main Currents in American Thought* (3 vols., complete in one), New York, I, 161.

whites and blacks alike. Roused to a crescendo of religious frenzy by the fiery sermons of Edwards, George Whitefield and John Wesley, hundreds of persons forsook the old formal Congregationalism for the new faith of " regeneration " and " conversion." So great was the excitement in Salem that the Reverend H. A. Brockwell, writing to the Secretary of the S.P.G., complained:

> So great has been the enthusiasm created by Wesley and Whitefield and Tenent that people talk of nothing but ' renovating regeneration, conviction and conversion . . .' Even children 8-13 assemble in bodies preaching and praying, nay the very Servants and Slaves pretend to extraordinary inspiration, and under the veil thereof cherish their idle dispositions and in lieu of dutifully minding their respective businesses run rambling about to utter enthusiastic nonsense.[97]

As the religious fervor spread, Negroes as well as whites, upon " conversion," were accepted into the churches. In Deerfield, for example, three slaves were admitted into the church and five adult Negroes were baptized. All of them belonged to the households of Justices Thomas and Jonathan Wells, whom Sheldon calls the aristocrats of Deerfield. Adam, a slave, " confessed [the] sin of lewdness " ; Peter, a more hardened transgressor, " confessed the sin of lewdness and drunkenness and stealing." Having purged their souls through open acknowledgment of their waywardness, the slaves were duly " received into charity with people; " [98] in other words, they were admitted into the church.

The quickening influence of the Great Awakening and the missionary efforts of the various churches did not constitute the only means by which Negroes were introduced to the Christian faith. The New England slaves, as has been repeatedly shown, were regarded as part of the master's family, and family worship was an important feature of the Puritan household.

97 Perry, *op. cit.*, III, 357.

98 Sheldon, *Negro Slavery in Old Deerfield*, pp. 52-53.

The day frequently began and ended with prayers.[99] On Saturday and Sunday evening, especially, the family gathered for Bible reading, instruction or prayers before the family hearth, and as part of the household, slaves and servants usually were included in these services. In Massachusetts, said Hawthorne, when the family " circle closed around the evening hearth, its blaze glowed on the dark shining faces intermixed familiarly with the master's children." [100] In Connecticut, according to Fowler, the slaves had to attend family prayers and hear the Scriptures read; [101] and Robert Warner in a recent study states that the slaves of New Haven took part in family prayers.[102] Not only were slaves participants in family worship, but in some Puritan households it was customary for the masters to question them on Sunday noon regarding the sermon which they had heard in the morning, " a simple method, it is said, by which many an ignorant black learned the fundamentals of Christianity." [103] It is impossible to estimate the number of slaves converted in this manner, but it is probable that most of the Christianized Negroes in colonial New England received their first religious impulse in the family worship of their masters' household.

The progress made in converting the New England slaves through the medium of family worship, as well as through the activities of the various sects, together with the revivalistic fervor imparted by the Great Awakening, probably helped to inspire an attempt to Christianize the Negroes in Africa.[104] The

99 Charles Atwater, *History of the Colony of New Haven* (Meriden, 1902), pp. 360-361.

100 Cited Calhoun, *op. cit.*, I, 82.

101 " Historical Status of the Negro in Connecticut," *loc. cit.*, p. 20.

102 *Negroes of New Haven*, p. 6.

103 *Connecticut Magazine*, V, No. 6, p. 88.

104 Stiles, *Literary Diary*, I, 364-365; Williston Walker, *Ten New England Leaders* (New York, 1901), p. 350. The Anglican Church had suggested such a plan as early as 1740. *Lambeth Palace Transcripts*, 1123 I, No. 18. (Ms. in Library of Congress). By 1773 Negroes had already been ordained as Episcopalian ministers to work among their own people in Africa. Stiles, *Literary Diary*, I, 364.

project was first conceived in 1773 by the Reverend Samuel
Hopkins, the theologian, whose church in Newport was located
in the chief slave mart of America. Hopkins planned to send
thirty or forty trained American Negroes as missionaries to
Africa to spread the Gospel among the natives. He believed that
if this number of qualified blacks would enter upon the work in
the spirit of martyrs, the souls of great numbers of Africans
might be saved.[105] Convinced, however, that the project should
be supported by a Society, he communicated his plan to a fellow
clergyman, Ezra Stiles, who at that time was also pastor of a
church at Newport. Stiles readily agreed to the proposal, but
he feared it would meet opposition from Episcopalian traders
in Africa because the English Church had already sent the
Reverend Quaquo, a Negro Episcopalian minister, as missionary to Africa.[106] Nevertheless, Hopkins and Stiles proceeded to
draw up concrete plans for the work and Hopkins selected two
Negro members of his church whom he believed best suited for
the task. One was Bristol Yamma, a slave, and the other, John
Quamino, a free black, both of whom were to be schooled in
" reading the Scriptures and Systematized Divinity." [107] Because Stiles feared that the Negroes would be unable to absorb
the involved theological system of Hopkins,[108] it was decided to
send them out of the colony for instruction.

105 Stiles, *op. cit.*, p. 364.

106 *Ibid.*

107 *Ibid.*, pp. 363-364. Hopkins favored Newport Gardner above Quamino
but Newport was a slave, though "a judicious steady good man who feels
greatly interested in promoting a Christian settlement in Africa and promoting Christianity there." Newport's master offered to free him and all his
children, except one, if Gardner would serve him two years at three dollars a
month. Mason, *Reminiscenses of Newport*, pp. 156-157. Newport did not
accept the offer and finally bought his freedom as a result of winning part
of $2000 in a lottery, with which he purchased the freedom of himself and
part of his family. His master liberated the others. Although he fervently
hoped to return to Africa, it was not until 1825 at the age of eighty-two that
Newport was at last able to sail to Liberia. He arrived February 6, 1825 but
died shortly afterwards. *Ibid.*, p. 159.

108 Stiles, *Literary Diary*, I, 365 n.

For this purpose an appeal for funds was made in 1773, and by 1776, more than £102 [109] had been collected, of which the Society of Edinburgh for Promoting Christian Knowledge had given at least £30.[110] Hopkins himself donated $100 which was said to have been the proceeds from the sale of a slave,[111] and in March, 1778, the Edinburgh Society promised another £100.[112] With these funds Hopkins and Stiles began to translate their plans into action. In 1774, the two Negroes, Yamma (whose freedom had been purchased) and Quamino, sailed from Newport enroute to Princeton, New Jersey, where they were to attend the College of New Jersey (now Princeton) under the tuition of President Witherspoon.[113]

Despite the auspicious beginning, however, the venture came to naught. The outbreak of the Revolutionary War in the following year interrupted the project; Quamino died [114] in 1779, so the plan was dropped.

It is clear that a number of Negro slaves were members of the various denominations in colonial New England, although it is not possible to say how numerous these communicants were. How were the slaves inducted? And once admitted, what was their status? They were generally prepared for church membership among both the Congregationalists and the Anglicans by a period of instruction in which they were given the rudiments of the Christian belief.[115] Among the Congregationalists the slaves must also pledge themselves to abide by the church covenant. A good example is given by the Reverend Daniel Wadsworth of Hartford, who noted in his diary for

109 Walker, *op. cit.*, p. 350.

110 Stiles, *Diary*, I, 450.

111 Walker, *ut supra*.

112 Stiles, *Diary*, III, 327.

113 *Ibid.*, I, 486.

114 *Ibid.*, III, 327 n; Walker, *op. cit.*, p. 351.

115 Mather, *Rules for the Society of Negroes*, pp. 8-9; "Diary of Cotton Mather," *loc. cit.*, VIII, Part II, 547-562; Stiles, *Literary Diary*, I, 521; Hawks and Stevens, *op. cit.*, II, 16; Perry, *op. cit.*, III, 231-439.

March 25, 1744: " Priscilla a negro woman made a publick confession & owned yᵉ covenant and was baptised." [116] With the advent of the evangelical faiths such as the Methodists, following the Great Awakening, Negro slaves like white persons, had to give evidence of a spiritual rebirth besides assenting to the articles of faith.[117]

Negroes were apparently baptized at the same time as white persons, though in what order it is not possible to say. Infants might be baptized in the name of the parents, as in the case of June, the infant daughter of Bastian (Sebastian) and his wife June.[118] Or they might be baptized in the name of the master as in the case of Esther, the mulatto slave of David and Sarah Glover, of Salem, who was baptized with Mrs. Glover acting as sponsor.[119] Upon baptism slaves occasionally had their classical or heathen names changed for Hebraic or Christian ones. For example, one Negro who was immersed as " Jupiter," emerged from the pool as " Jepthah." [120] Another, descending into the baptismal fount as " Cato," stepped forth as " Isaac." In the cases of Cato, Pompey and Titus, the masters were apparently satisfied to have the Christianized slaves still bear the classical names assigned them in their heathen state.[121]

What the exact status of the Negro became, once he was admitted into the church, is difficult to ascertain. It has been claimed that upon entering the Congregational churches the Negroes were received into full communion; that is, accorded

116 *Diary of the Rev. Daniel Wadsworth*, p. iii. Brown tells of four Negroes baptized and taken into the church at Bedford, Massachusetts after " owning the covenant." *History of the Town of Bedford, Massachusetts,* p. 31.

117 Sheldon, *Negro Slavery in Old Deerfield*, p. 52.

118 According to Samuel Sewall, " Bastian has a Daughter born . . . He calls her June." On November 2, 1701, " She is baptized by Mr. Allen. Bastian holds her up." " Diary of Samuel Sewall, 1674-1729," *loc. cit.*, VI, 46.

119 She was to be responsible for giving the child a Christian education. " Baptisms of the First Church in Salem," *loc. cit.*, VIII, 15.

120 *Ibid.*, p. 153.

121 *Ibid.*, pp. 158, 153, 209.

all the rights and privileges of white members. In regard to their status, Brown says that slaves were baptized and taken into membership upon owning the covenant;[122] Temple states that a Negro slave was accepted into the church at Hopkinton, Massachusetts ". . . in exactly the same condition and upon the same terms as others."[123] And the Reverend Ezra Stiles of Newport wrote in 1775: " I propounded my Negro servant Newport to be admitted into full communion in the church."[124]

It is apparently true that once admitted into membership, Negroes were accorded some of the privileges enjoyed by the general congregation. They took part in prayer and singing and also joined in the communion service.[125] Slaves, like other persons, might be transferred from one church to another[126] and were also liable to excommunication if they transgressed the church covenant or committed civil crimes. The case of Nero and Boston are examples in point.

> On February 2, 1743/4 The Pastor Stayed [held] the Chh. [church] after Lecture & the Chh. voted that Deacons Alwood & Terry Notify *Nero* a Negro man belonging to Mr. John Barnes and *Boston* a Negro man belonging to Mr. Thomas Foster that this Chh. suspend them from Communion at Present, they having been convicted of Scandalous offenses before the Civil Magistrate.[127]

122 Brown, *History of Bedford*, p. 31.

123 Temple, *History of Framingham, Mass.*, p. 237.

124 Stiles, *Literary Diary*, I, 521.

125 Pascoe, *op. cit.*, p. 47.

126 Nero, the slave of Rev. John Swift, pastor of the Church in Framingham, Massachusetts, was a member of Swift's Church until 1737. He was then transferred to the Church at Hopkinton. In 1746 he was admitted to Reverend Loring's Church at Sudbury, Massachusetts. Temple, *History of Framingham*, pp. 218, 236, 237. Nero, a Negro slave member of the First Church at Plymouth, Massachusetts was transferred to the First Church at Marshfield in the same colony whither he had moved. " Plymouth Church Records," *loc. cit.*, XXII, 297.

127 " Plymouth Church Records," *loc. cit.*, XXII, 295; *cf.* Steiner, *op. cit.*, p. 20; Sheldon, *Negro Slavery in Old Deerfield*, p. 53.

However, upon showing evidence of their reformation, the
excommunicated slaves might be restored to good standing.
Thus Peter, a member of the Church at Deerfield, Massachusetts, who was dropped from membership for various crimes,
confessed his " lewdness . . . excessive drinking & stealing &
was restored to charity " on October 2, 1738. Three years later
Adam " confessed the sin of Lying and was restored to Xtian
[Christian] watch." [128] On January 6, 1744, Boston, a Plymouth slave who had been expelled from the First Church for
civil crimes, " made public confession of his offense & was restored." [129]

Apparently, however, some discriminatory practices did exist.
For example, Negroes in " full communion " as members of
Congregational churches could not vote on church discipline
after 1743, if indeed they voted before that date. Referring to
this exclusion the Reverend Daniel Wadsworth, a sincere worker among the Negroes, says that at the meeting of the Association in Boston in 1743, the question was raised " whether males
under the age of twenty-one years and slaves that are members
in full communion with a church are to be allowed to give their
vote in matters of discipline in the church? " The answer was
" resolved in the negative." [130]

Not only were Negroes excluded from passing upon church
matters but they were also segregated in the church congregations. Although nearly every church made some provision for
Negroes, they were generally set apart from white members.
How much this arrangement was traceable to prejudice based
on color, or to class will perhaps never be known. Class dis-
tinctions segregated whites as well as Negroes in New England churches. The congregation was seated according to wealth
and position, sex and social status. So tender a point was the
place assigned persons in the church that pews were " digni-
fied " in order, as Alice Morse Earle says, to preserve the peace

128 Sheldon, *ut supra.*

129 " Plymouth Church Records," *loc. cit.,* XXII, 295.

130 *Diary of Rev. Daniel Wadsworth, 1737-1747,* p. 100 n.

and to assuage wounded pride.[131] Since Negroes were considered lowest in the economic and social order, the lowliest places in the meeting house would probably have been assigned to them, irrespective of their color. In some towns boys, the bane of most meeting houses, were classed with Negroes and seated with them.[132] Generally, however, there was an "African corner," [133] where Negroes either stood in the rear of the church or sat upon benches. [134] Sometimes they sat on the stairs. If the church had an upper story, the Negroes usually were asigned to a remote corner of the gallery, commonly referred to as the " Nigger Pew," [135] or " Nigger Heaven." According to Alice Morse Earle:

> Sometimes a little pew or short gallery was built high up among the beams and joists over the staircase, which led to the first gallery and was called the " swallows' nest " or the " roof pue " or the second gallery. It was reached by a steep ladder-like staircase and was often assigned to the Negroes and Indians of the congregation.[136]

Seating arrangements for Negroes varied in different churches: in Arlington, Massachusetts, Negroes had seats over the gallery stairs; [137] in the Reverend Chauncey Whittlesey's Church at New Haven, Connecticut, two sections of the galleries at the extreme ends of the building were allotted to Ne-

131 Mrs. Earle has an enlightening chapter on " Seating the Meeting " in her *The Sabbath in Puritan New England*, ch. v.

132 *Ibid.*, p. 62.

133 *Connecticut Magazine*, V, No. 6, 321-322.

134 Warner, *Negroes of New Haven*, pp. 6, 7.

135 Alice Earle tells of a Negro who carried liquor with him in order to keep warm in the freezing loft, but imbibed too freely of the stuff and fell asleep. His drunken snoring brought the dreaded tithing man who pulled him down the stairs and took him to a tavern to sleep off his potion. *Sabbath in Puritan New England*, p. 93.

136 *Ibid.*, p. 63.

137 Benjamin and William Cutter, *History of Arlington, Massachusetts, 1635-1819* (Boston, 1880), p. 35.

groes.[138] Slaves sat in the galleries in historic Old South Church in Boston,[139] and in Torrington, Connecticut, according to Steiner, the seats occupied by Negroes in the gallery " were boarded up so that the Negroes could see no one and be seen by none." [140] Even in the galleries Negroes were not always tolerated: The Corporation of Harvard College objected to their sitting in the gallery of the First Parish Church at Cambridge in 1756,[141] and the question of seating Negroes in the meeting house of Stoneham, Massachusetts in 1754 was the occasion for a special town meeting.[142]

Negroes were not only segregated in the churches but also in the graveyards, where usually a corner of the common cemetery was assigned to them.[143] However, in Boston evidently no definite place for the burial of Negroes had been designated up to 1744, for the grave diggers in that year petitioned the town to provide some place to " bury strangers and negroes." [144]

Speaking of Negro burials in Newport, Mason says that occasionally both whites and blacks mingled tears over the grave of the slaves.[145] Such scenes doubtless were common in New England for funerals were the occasion of considerable display among the eighteenth century Puritans; [146] and the slave in death sometimes received a recognition which was denied him in life. Samuel Sewall, upon the death of his Negro, Boston,

138 Stiles, *Literary Diary,* I, 283.

139 Personal interview with lady in charge, July 1934, at which time the Negro gallery was pointed out to the writer.

140 Steiner, *op. cit.,* p. 20.

141 Lucius R. Paige, *History of Cambridge, Massachusetts* (Boston, 1897), p. 292.

142 Samuel Drake, *History of Middlesex County, Massachusetts* (2 vols.), p. 343.

143 Brown, *History of Bedford, Massachusetts,* p. 32; Updike, *op. cit.,* I, 521-522.

144 *Boston Town Records, 1742-1757,* p. 53.

145 *Reminiscences of Newport,* pp. 106-107.

146 Earle, *Customs and Fashions in Colonial New England,* ch. xv.

" made a good fire, set chairs and gave sack " to those who came to mourn the dead slave.[147] Sometimes the funeral of a slave occasioned considerable notice in the community. In New Haven, where a slave was buried in 1770, Stiles says the church bells tolled and more than two hundred and fifty blacks followed the bier to the grave.[148] Greater honors were accorded a former slave in Boston in 1727, for in his funeral train were " 150 blacks and about 50 whites " among whom were " several magistrates, ministers, and gentlemen," [149] some of whom probably had owned or employed the Negro.

How many of these slaves had been converted is not known. The late Professor Jernegan believes that most of the Negroes in the American colonies died strangers to Christianity.[150] Although relatively larger numbers of slaves may have been Christianized in New England than in the plantation colonies, it is likely that at the end of the colonial era in 1776 a large proportion—possibly a majority—of the slaves in that section were still heathen.

Even when the slaves were exposed to Christian instruction, the interpretation placed upon the Scriptures would hardly have imbued the Negroes with a desire to take their masters' faith seriously. According to the racial philosophy of the Puritans, Negroes and Indians were an inferior race whom God had given them as part of their inheritance.[151] Not only was the Negro regarded as a sub-species, but as late as 1773 a member of the graduating class of Harvard University, debating the legality of enslaving the Africans, justified the institution partly on the ground that the Negro was " a conglomerate of child, idiot, and madman." [152] Religion, therefore, was largely em-

147 " Diary of Samuel Sewall," *loc. cit., Fifth Series,* VII, 394.

148 Stiles, *Literary Diary,* I, 52.

149 *New Weekly Journal,* September 8, 1729; cited in " Diary of Samuel Sewall," *loc. cit.,* VII, 394-395.

150 *Laboring and Dependent Classes,* pp. 41-42.

151 *Vide supra,* p. 61.

152 *A Forensic Dispute on the Legality of Enslaving the Africans.* By two candidates for the Bachelors Degree (Boston, 1773), p. 28.

ployed as a device for making the slave content and submissive in his bondage, thereby protecting the master in the retention of his property. This interpretation was first inculcated by Cotton Mather, who in his aforementioned *Rules for the Society of Negroes* in 1693, taught the slaves that they were the " miserable children of Adam and Noah," and exhorted them to be faithful to their masters. Slaves were instructed to inform upon each other, thus rendering easier control from above and affording greater security for the master in the continued possession of his chattels.[153] In the catechism prepared for the slaves to memorize, Mather taught the Negroes that they were enslaved because they had sinned against God and that God, not their masters had enslaved them.[154] Service to the master was identified with service to God and in the Ten Commandments, prepared by Mather for the slaves, submissiveness to and respect for the master were substituted for the similar deference which the owners gave to God. The Fifth Commandment (" Honor thy Father and Mother, . . .") was twisted to mean for the slave " I must show all due respect unto everyone and if I have a master or mistress, I must be very dutiful unto them." For the slave the Tenth Commandment (" Thou Shalt not Covet, . . .") was interpreted as " I must be patient and content with such a condition as God has ordered for me." [155] Mather then promised the slaves that if they were " faithful and honest servants," they would secure " rest from their labours " and, as a reward, God would " prepare a mansion in Heaven for them," where at last they would be " companions of angels in the glories of a Paradise." [156]

Mather's precepts set a precedent for using the religious indoctrination of the slaves as a subtle device for slave control and throughout the eighteenth century other ministers carried on the tradition. Notable among them were Ezra Stiles, Daniel

153 Mather, *The Negro Christianized*, pp. 5-8.

154 *Ibid.,* p. 32.

155 *Ibid.,* pp. 41-42.

156 *Ibid.,* p. 32.

Wadsworth of Hartford and Parson Ashley of Deerfield, Massachusetts.[157] The preachments of the Reverend Mr. Ashley were typical. In special sermons to the slaves he told those who might have had doubts upon the subject that Christianity permits of a master and servant relationship, and any insinuation " that they ought not to abide in ye place of servant . . . is to provoke God." Since they were slaves by divine dispensation, to run away or even to remain dissatisfied in their bondage would not only be to the " damage of their masters but would also be to the dishonor of religion and the reproach of Christianity." If the slaves complained of their hard lot on earth, Ashley consoled them with the assurance that they would enjoy in Heaven all " the great privileges " which freemen enjoyed " in the commonwealth." But the only sure road to salvation was to become Christ's freemen, and this status could be attained only by the slaves' remaining contented servants in this world. Otherwise they would become the " slaves of the devil," [158] and suffer eternal bondage.

The perverted form of Christianity with which the ministers indoctrinated the slaves probably made many Negroes less receptive to a genuine acceptance of the faith. Some slaves like Phillis Wheatley, who were special objects of the benign paternalism of their masters, not only saw no contradiction between Christianity and slavery, but Phillis could write:

'Twas mercy brought me from my pagan land,
Taught my benighted soul to understand,
That there's a God, there's a heaven too.[159]

---

157 The emphasis placed upon the slaves' being faithful or abstaining from theft or fornication, all of which were detrimental to the master class, loom conspicuous in the texts from which the sermons to the slaves were chosen: Luke, 14: 16-18; Rom. 5: 12; *Vide* Stiles, *Literary Diary*, I, 39 n., 91, 213; *passim*; *Diary of Rev. Daniel Wadsworth*, pp. 80, 86, 92, 93, 94; Sheldon, *History of Deerfield*, II, 901-902.

158 Sheldon, *History of Deerfield*, II, 901-902.

159 Renfro, *Life and Works of Phillis Wheatley*, p. 48.

Other Negroes, among whom were Prince Hall and Lancaster Hill, were more discerning. Thus when Hall and other free Negroes of Boston petitioned the Massachusetts legislature in 1773, praying for the liberation of the slaves, they pointed out the incompatibility between Christianity and slavery by stating that the bondmen were often compelled to obey " man in opposition to the laws of God." [160] In the following year, they complained in a similar petition that because of their condition the slaves were " rendered incapable of showing obedience to Almighty God." [161]

More outspoken even were several white ministers, one of whom was Elihu Coleman, a " minister " of the Society of Friends of Nantucket, Massachusetts. The hypocrisy of the Christians, said Coleman, makes the slaves hate the very name of Christian, for, he continued, " Christians tell the Negroes they must believe in Christ . . . receive the Sacrament, and be baptized, and so they do, but still they keep them [the Negroes] slaves for all this." [162] Instead of inculcating respect for Christianity in the Negroes, wrote the Reverend Samuel Hopkins of Newport in 1776, " their treatment by Christian masters " inflames them " with the deepest prejudices against the Christian religion." [163] This aversion did not apply to all the Negroes for one of them not only accepted the Christian faith but became an ordained minister. This was Lemuel Haynes, who later became the first Negro to preach regularly to white congregations in New England.

160 For petition *vide Mass. Hist. Colls.,* Fifth Series, III, 432-435.

161 *Ibid.,* pp. 432-433.

162 Elihu Coleman, *Testimony Against That Unchristian Practice of Making Slaves of Men* (1729), (Reprint Bedford, 1895), p. 18.

163 *Dialogue on the Slavery of the Africans* (1776), (New York, 1785), p. 20.

After more than a century of efforts to convert them, it is likely that when the colonial era ended in 1776, most of the Negroes in New England, as in the other American colonies, were still infidels.[164] Of those Negroes who had been converted the majority were probably nominal rather than genuine Christians. Nevertheless, the movement to Christianize the slaves was by no means a total failure, for the present-day Negro church in New England developed from the early religious zeal and activity of the converted blacks at the close of the colonial era.

164 Stiles, *Literary Diary,* I, 213-214.

# CHAPTER XI
## THE FREE NEGRO

In the foregoing pages attention has been centered largely upon the New England slaves. But side by side with the bondmen, existed another group of Negroes, whose status must now be briefly examined. These were the free Negroes. Just when this class was first liberated is not known, but the earliest mention of free Negroes in New England appears to have been in 1646, when Governor Theophilus Eaton of New Haven Colony freed John Wham and his wife and settled them on a farm.[1] The emancipation of these slaves was probably the beginning of private manumissions, through which a free Negro group was to arise in New England.

Freedom was gained in several ways. Some Negroes had never been actual slaves, that is, bound to service for life; they were indentured servants. Not being used to chattel slavery, English colonists in the seventeenth century, as repeatedly asserted, were not familiar with the law and practice of perpetual bondage. It has also been shown that to a great degree the New Englanders, influenced by the Mosaic Law, regarded the slave as synonymous with the Hebrew " servant," who was to serve for six years and then go free.[2] In fact, until almost the end of the seventeenth century the records refer to the Negroes as " servants " not as " slaves." [3] For some time no definite status could be assigned to incoming Negroes. Some were sold for a period of time only, and like the white indentured servant became free after their indenture. Others were probably emancipated because of the early inability of the colonists to decide upon the disposition of the children of slaves. Until 1670 slave offspring in Massachusetts were regarded as free, and only

[1] *Conn. Col. Recs.*, IV, 72 n; *Conn. Magazine*, V, No. 6, p. 323.

[2] Hurd, *op. cit.*, I, 179, 183, 225-226; *vide supra*, p. 167.

[3] *Conn. Col. Recs.*, I, 349; *Mass. A. and R.*, I, 154; *R. I. Col. Recs.*, III, 492-493; *R. I. Acts and Laws, 1636-1705*, p. 58.

after that date, as has been shown elsewhere,[4] were they legally enslaved. Just how many Negroes in New England were emancipated as a result of this uncertainty is not known, but the number could not have been large, for up to 1670 comparatively few Negroes had been imported.

Other Negroes were probably liberated through the application of the Rhode Island Law of 1652 which, as indicated, limited slavery to ten years.[5] Although openly violated, the law was never repealed, and, it is, therefore, possible that, under its provisions, a few slaves may have won their liberty.

Further additions to the free Negro group resulted from private agreements between master and slave, whereby the latter would be set free after serving his owner for a stated number of years from the date of purchase. The net result of such compacts was to convert the slave into an indentured servant. One of the earliest of these contracts was that between Judge John Saffin of Boston and his slave, Adam, in 1694, whereby the slave was to receive his freedom after six years of faithful service.[6] Five years later, William Hawkins of Providence, Rhode Island, agreed to emancipate his Negro, Jack, providing the latter served him dutifully for twenty-six years.[7] This practice continued into the eighteenth century. In 1723, Tolleration Harris, also of Providence, agreed to manumit her slave, Felix, if he faithfully " discharged his duties to her, her heirs, executors, administrators and assignees " for six years. Felix upon emancipation was to post a bond guaranteeing that he would not become a public charge; if unable to do so, he might gain his unconditional freedom by serving his master four years longer.[8]

Manumission of slaves by grateful masters in appreciation of faithful service increased the number of free blacks. Mention

4 *Cf. supra*, pp. 65-66. Virginia in 1662 declared all offspring of slave women were henceforth to be considered as slaves. Hurd, *op. cit.*, I, 231.

5 *Cf. supra*, p. 18.

6 *Mass. Archives*, IX, 153.

7 *Early Records of Providence*, IV, 71-72.

8 *Ibid.*, IX, 153.

has already been made of the slaves of Governor Eaton of
Connecticut.[9] In 1702 William Randall of Providence emancipated his slave, Peter Palmer, in return for the Negro's " good
and faithful service." [10] Two years later Dorothy Grecian, a
Boston widow, freed her slave woman, Betty,[11] and posted the
necessary bond of fifty pounds to insure the woman against
coming to want.[12] For a similar reason, Ann Bradstreet of
Salem, a relative of Governor Bradstreet, liberated her Negro
woman in 1713.[13] Four years later, William and Samuel Upton
of the same town manumitted their Negro, Thomas, in recognition of his devotion to their father.[14] Similarly motivated in
1718, Ezra Stiles, famous scholar, and " divine," freed Newport, whom he had purchased earlier for a hogshead of rum.[15]

The free Negro class also received accessions through the liberation of slaves whose emancipation had been provided for in
the wills of appreciative masters. Many examples can be cited:
Robert Dole of Newbury, Massachusetts, certified in his will of
1698 that his slave woman, Grace, could have her freedom " if
she will accept it." Another slave, Betty, was to be manumitted
after two additional years of service.[16] In like manner, Reverend
Timothy Walker of Concord, New Hampshire, liberated his
slave, Prince,[17] and Cotton Mather freed one of his slaves.[18]

Emancipated slaves did not always go forth empty-handed
from their masters' service. Some Negroes, like indentured

9 *Vide supra*, p. 195.

10 *Early Records of Providence*, III, 115-116.

11 *Mass. Archives*, IX, 154.

12 *Ibid.*, p. 154 a.

13 Felt, *Annals of Salem*, II, 415.

14 *Ibid.*

15 Stiles, *Literary Diary*, I, 521; II, 272; *Col. Soc. of Mass., Transactions, 1897-1898*, V, 238.

16 Cited Coffin, *Sketch of Newbury*, p. 336.

17 *Diaries of Reverend Timothy Walker, 1730-1782* (Concord, 1889), p. 25 n.

18 Stiles, *Literary Diary*, I, 521 n.

servants, were furnished with certain necessities for embarking upon their new life as freemen. In his will of 1708, Richard Arnold of Providence stipulated that when his slave, Toby, was freed at the age of twenty-five, he should be given " two suits . . . a good narrow axe, a broad hoe, and a sithe with tackling fitt for mowing and twenty shillings in money." [20] Upon freeing her slaves some time later, Lydia Plant of Newbury, Massachusetts, arranged in her will for the Negroes to have the use of her house and household goods for four years.[21] During the Revolution, Captain Samuel Smedley of Fairfield, Connecticut, not only freed Boston, but, before doing so, taught him a trade, gave him a workshop, established him in business as a shoemaker and also stipulated that his executors should give Boston a thousand dollars. To Boston's father, Smedley granted thirty dollars a year for the remainder of the Negro's life.[22]

The rise of the free Negro group was also facilitated through legal means. Aggressive Negroes, appealing to the Courts for their freedom, often received it. Impetus was given to such action during the constitutional controversy with Great Britain, when the bonds of slavery were gradually being dissolved by the revolutionary philosophy. Besides those already cited,[23] there was a suit brought by Jenny Slew of Ipswich, Massachusetts, in which the litigation is typical. On March 5, 1762, Jenny sued John Whipple, her master, charging that Whipple had unlawfully detained her in bondage from January 29, 1762 until March 5 of the same year. Jenny contended that she had been illegally deprived of her liberty, and that she also had suffered damages to her person in the amount of £25. This sum, together with costs of court, she sought to recover from Whipple. The master, countering with the sweeping claim that no such person as Jenny

19 *J. H. R. of Mass.*, XV, 174-175.

20 *Early Records of Providence*, VII, 5.

21 Cuvier, *History of Newbury*, p. 255.

22 Louis Middlebrook, *Maritime History of Connecticut During the American Revolution, 1775-1783* (Salem, 1925), I, 67-68.

23 *Vide supra*, pp. 182 ff.

Slew existed, further asked that he be granted " costs of court against the said Jenny." After several delays the Inferior Court decided in favor of Whipple, thereby remanding Jenny back into slavery. The slave then appealed to the Superior Court of Judicature for a reversal of the judgment and the Court at its session held at Salem in 1765 declared Jenny a freewoman and awarded her damages and costs amounting to more than £9.[24]

Through various means other Negroes joined the class of freedmen. A few slaves purchased their liberty. For example, in 1791, Newport Gardner of Rhode Island won two thousand dollars in a lottery, and immediately bought himself and most of his family.[25] Occasionally, free Negro men, like the aforesaid Scipio of Boston, and Abner of Wethersfield, Connecticut, purchased slave women as wives.[26] The free Negro group received additional members from the offspring of Negro slaves and Indian women, as such children were legally free.[27] Similarly, miscegenation of whites and Negroes added a number of legitimate, as well as illegitimate, mulattoes to the free Negro group.[28] White women who bore children to Negro slaves likewise contributed to the number of freemen.[29] Sometimes conscience-stricken masters, convinced of the injustice of slavery, set their slaves at liberty. One of the first to do so was Thomas Hazard, nicknamed " College Tom," of South Kingstown, Rhode Island, who freed his slaves in 1730; while Moses Brown, not only manumitted his Negroes, but became an ardent abolitionist.[30] Former Governor Robinson of Rhode Island is said to have bought up and manumitted the slaves he had previously imported and sold.[31] Negroes also earned their freedom by

24 The records of this case may be seen in Moore, *op. cit.,* pp. 113, 114.

25 Mason, *Reminiscences of Newport,* p. 157.

26 *Vide supra,* pp. 196 ff.

27 *Ibid.,* pp. 198 ff.

28 *Ibid.,* pp. 201 ff.

29 *Ibid.*

30 Jones, *The Quaker Colonies in America,* pp. 157-158.

31 Updike, *op. cit.,* I, 208.

serving in the colonial or revolutionary armies. Cambridge Moore, Caesar Prescott, Caesar Jones of Bedford, Massachusetts,[32] and Caesar of Griswold, Connecticut, won their freedom in this way.[33] Aged and decrepit slaves, turned adrift by callous masters who wanted to escape the responsibility of supporting their worn-out chattels, likewise helped to swell the number of freedmen.[34] Finally, during the Revolution, some Negroes, who comprised parts of confiscated Tory estates, were freed by the state.[35] Runaway slaves, like Crispus Attucks, were another source of the free Negro group, but how many won their freedom by this means will probably never be known.

For some slaves the transition from a slave status to one of freedom was accomplished only as a result of a struggle, especially in cases where the master refused to liberate the slave according to his promise or contract with his Negro. Barry tells of a master in Hanover, Massachusetts, who agreed to free his slave as soon as all the water in the North River had run by. The Negro thereafter, it is said, was frequently seen looking wistfully at the stream. Unhappily for the slave, death is reported to have ended his bondage.[36] There were others, however, who were more assertive; and aggrieved slaves sometimes appealed to the courts for redress against their owners. In 1735, James, the former slave of Samuel Burnell of Boston, brought

32 Brown, *History of Bedford, Massachusetts,* p. 32.

33 Steiner, *History of Slavery in Conn.,* p. 26; *vide* also Daniel, *op. cit.,* p. 7. A number of other Negroes were emancipated through the Connecticut law of 1777, which facilitated manumission. This law repealed an earlier law which had made the master responsible for the maintenance of the freedmen should they come to want. The purpose was ostensibly to secure additional recruits to the American army, necessitated by the British successes of the previous year. By promising emancipation to all Negroes who enlisted in the Rhode Island armies in 1778, the authorities of that state opened an avenue for the liberation of additional blacks.

34 This practice, as noted above, was curbed by laws requiring all masters to give bond before manumitting the slave in order to insure the Negro from becoming a town charge. *Vide supra,* pp. 138-139 ff.

35 Staples, *op. cit.,* pp. 236-237.

36 Barry, *History of Hanover, Massachusetts,* pp. 176-177.

suit against the son of his deceased master, claiming that his
late master, in four different wills, had assured him his freedom
upon the death of his [the master's] widow. When Mrs. Burnell
died, none of the wills could be found, and the son claimed James
as part of his inheritance. But the slave, contending that by the
will of his former owner he was a free man, brought suit
against his new master in 1735. The litigation was bitterly
fought out over a period of two years. During one of the trials,
the son disturbed the proceedings, and even threatened the life
of James. The Negro then petitioned the legislature for a writ
of protection, and after a two-year struggle, the legislature,
finally declared James a freeman, provided he could secure the
necessary guarantee of fifty pounds to insure against his becoming a burden upon the town.[37]

A more notable case was that of John Saffin and his Negro,
Adam.[38] Saffin, a Boston merchant and jurist, formally engaged
in 1694, to give Adam his liberty providing the Negro served
him faithfully for a period of seven years. Before Adam's term
had expired, however, Saffin bound him out to one of his tenants,
Thomas Shepard. At the close of his indenture, Adam requested
his freedom, but Saffin, contending that Adam instead of faithfully performing his duties, as he had agreed, had behaved
himself " turbulently, negligently, insolently and outrageously,"
refused to liberate him. Whereupon Adam appealed to the
courts. The result was a long litigation lasting from 1701 to
1703, during which time the case came before two sessions of
the inferior court and four sessions of the superior court. Legal
costs bore heavily upon Saffin and he complained to the legislature in November, 1703, that the trial had already cost him
" well above three score pounds." Seeking both relief from these
burdens and the custody of Adam, Saffin on two occasions in
1703 appealed to the legislature for redress. He further pleaded
that his life was in danger, that the Negro, now released from

37 *J. H. R. of Mass.*, XV, 172-175.
38 *Mass. Archives*, IX, 153.

prison,[39] was plotting revenge upon him. Adam had openly boasted, Saffin charged, that if he got the chance he would " twist or wring off the neck " of his master with as little compunction as he would that " of a snake." [40]

Saffin's fearful representations moved the House of Representatives on November 19th, 1703, to order the case reviewed at the next session of the superior court. In the meantime, Adam was to give bond for his good behavior. But the Council denied the master even this concession. Instead of concurring in the decision of the lower House, the Council in December of the same year vaguely referred the petitioner " to the law." [41] The action of the Council was probably influenced by Samuel Sewall, one of Saffin's co-jurists and his bitter enemy. Saffin had outraged Sewall's sense of legal decency by sitting in judgment upon Adam in one of the trials, and also by securing the appointment of one of his tenants to the jury that was to hear the case. For these breaches of legal and judicial etiquette, Sewall had caustically condemned him.[42] Saffin's efforts to recover his property were in vain, for Adam was subsequently set at liberty.[43]

Through these various means a free Negro group gradually came into being. How large this group was it is not possible to say, for the New England colonies did not classify Negroes as slave or free, and no tabulation of this nature appeared until the first federal census of 1790. At that time, as previously indicated, there were approximately 13,059 free Negroes in this

39 Adam had been sentenced to three months imprisonment for an attempt upon the life of the commanding officer of Castle William, the fort in Boston harbor. *Ibid.*, p. 152.

40 *Ibid.*, p. 153.

41 *Ibid.*

42 " Diary of Samuel Sewall," *loc. cit.*, VII, 79; *Col. Soc. of Mass., Transactions*, I, 90.

43 Thirteen years later he was listed among the free Negroes of Boston who were assigned work on the roads in lieu of militia duty. " Report of Record Commissioners of the City of Boston," *City Document*, 77 (Ms. in Antiquarian Society Library, Worcester, Mass.), p. 3.

section,[44] but the census returns of 1790 throw virtually no light upon the number of freedmen before 1775. The reason is obvious. By 1790, when the first attempt at classifying Negroes on a state-wide scale was begun, all of the New England states had abolished slavery as a permanent institution.[45] The numbers of Negroes freed between 1780, the year the movement began, and 1790 were naturally out of all proportion to those emancipated before that date, and much greater perhaps than the total number freed before 1775.

The status of the free Negroes has always varied according to time, place and the national groups among whom they have lived. For example, in Brazil, the slaves, once freed, were accorded every right and privilege enjoyed by free white persons. Every profession or opportunity was open to them; they might " enter the army or navy, become lawyers, doctors, professors, artists or clergymen." [46] Some of them during the Empire Period (1824-1889) were even " elected to the Chamber of Deputies and to the provincial assemblies." [47] In striking contrast, the freedmen of colonial America and those of the period before the Civil War faced discrimination and prejudice on every hand,[48] and whatever progress they made was achieved in spite of opposition.

The condition of the free Negroes in New England was probably no more favorable than elsewhere in colonial America. Strictly speaking, they were not free for they were proscribed politically, economically, and socially, while the white indentured servant, once freed, became a respected member of the com-

44 *Cf. supra*, p. 77 and note.

45 *Ibid.*

46 Herman James and Percy Martin, *The Republics of Latin America* (Revised Edition, 1924), pp. 123-124.

47 *Ibid.*, p. 124.

48 For general treatment of the difficulties of the free Negroes see Charles Wesley, *Negro Labor in the United States,* ch. ii; U. B. Phillips, *American Negro Slavery*, ch. xxi; especially, pp. 439-445; Carter G. Woodson, *Free Negro Heads of Families in the United States in 1830,* pp. xiv-xvi and *passim.*

munity, But the Negro, because of his color, continued in an inferior social status, even though he may have adopted the culture of his former master.[49] Legally, the freedmen held an intermediate status somewhat higher than that of the slaves, but palpably lower than that of free white persons. As evidence of their inferior standing, they were included with Negroes and Indians in the slave codes; they could not walk on the streets after nine o'clock at night without a pass, and they could use the ferries only under similar conditions. Without a pass, free Negroes could not go beyond the limits of the town wherein they resided and even in their homes they were circumscribed, for, unless permission of the masters had been obtained, free Negroes could not entertain Indian, Negro, or mulatto slaves. They could not own certain types of property. In South Kingstown, Rhode Island, free Negroes were not allowed to keep horses, sheep, or any other kind of domestic animals. In Boston they could not own swine, nor could any free person rent or lease them ground for such a purpose. No stick or cane might be carried by a Negro in Boston, unless needed for the actual support of the person.

Legal punishments for free Negroes, however, were the same as for free white persons. For less serious crimes they were fined and, if they were unable to pay, they might be whipped. For capital offenses the punishments were identical. A discriminating penalty was imposed upon free Negroes in Rhode Island, where the freedmen, if convicted of keeping a disorderly house, might be re-enslaved for a certain period.[50] Nowhere in New England could free Negroes serve on juries; otherwise

49 The lowly condition of the free Negro was commented upon by contemporaries both black and white; *vide,* Judge Winthrop's reply to Dr. Jeremy Belknap (1795) in *Mass. Hist. Soc. Colls.,* Fifth Series, III, 390; Brissot de Warville, *New Travells in North America, 1788* (Second Edition, 2 vols., London, 1794), I, 240; Prince Hall, "A Charge Delivered to the African Lodge June 24, 1797 at Menotony, Mass.," *Masonic Orders,* I (no pagination). See original in rare book room of New York Public Library.

50 *Vide supra,* ch. v.

they were accorded the same rights in the courts as free white men.

The inferior legal status of the free blacks was but one reflection of their lowly condition. Full citizenship was withheld from them, and although taxed as other free persons, they could not vote.[51] In some plantation colonies free Negroes enjoyed the franchise until 1754.[52] But in colonial New England there is no evidence that they ever were accorded this privilege. It has been claimed, nevertheless, that they could vote if they met the general tests. According to Emil Olbrich, Connecticut was the only New England colony or state to forbid Negro suffrage; and he says that this prohibition was contained in the Constitution of 1818.[53] Kirk Porter makes the same assertion regarding Rhode Island and adds that Connecticut excluded Negroes from the franchise in 1818.[54] Albert B. Hart is more sweeping in his assumptions. Of all the New England communities, he contends, Connecticut alone " has ever made any race distinction in its suffrage; Connecticut excluded Negroes in 1818 and kept it up until after the Civil War." [55]

The conclusions of these authorities, however, are not borne out by the facts. It is true, as Adams points out, that Connecticut did specifically disfranchise her Negro population in 1818,[56] but it is equally true that no record exists of Negroes voting either in Connecticut or elsewhere in New England during the

51 James Truslow Adams, " Disfranchisement of Negroes in New England," *American Historical Review*, XXX, 544; *Memoir of Paul Cuffee A Man of Color to Which is Subjoined the Epistle of the Society of Sierra Leone*, ed. W. Alexander (London, 1815), pp. 7-9.

52 According to McKinley, free Negroes voted in Virginia until 1723; in North Carolina till 1715; in South Carolina to 1701; and in Georgia till 1754. Albert E. McKinley, *Suffrage Franchise in the Thirteen English Colonies in America* (Philadelphia, 1905), pp. 36, 92, 137, 172.

53 *University of Wisconsin History Series, Bulletin,* II, No. 1, p. 24.

54 *History of Suffrage in the United States* (Chicago, 1918), p. 90 n., citing Weeks in *Pol. Sc. Quarterly*, X, 677.

55 *American Political Science Proceedings*, II, 150.

56 " Disfranchisement of Negroes in New England," *loc. cit.*, p. 544.

colonial period. The case of Massachusetts is typical. Not only were free Negroes denied the ballot before the Revolution, but even the equalitarian philosophy of that struggle did not prevent Negroes from being specifically barred from the suffrage in the rejected state constitution of 1778. Article V of this document expressly excluded Negroes, Indians and mulattoes from the ballot as follows:

> Every male inhabitant of any town in this state, being free, and twenty-one years of age excepting Negroes, Indians, and mulattoes, shall be entitled to vote for a Representative, as the case may be, in the town in which he is resident, provided he has paid taxes in said town (unless by law excused from taxes) and been resident therein one full year immediately preceding such voting, or that town has been his known and usual place of abode for that time, or that he is considered as an inhabitant thereof; and every such inhabitant qualified as above, and worth sixty-pounds clear of all charges therein, shall be entitled to put his vote for Governor, Lieutenant-Governor, Senators or Representatives, shall be by ballot and not otherwise.[57]

The exclusion of Negroes from the franchise did not go unchallenged, for a writer in the *Independent Chronicle,* after ridiculing the grounds upon which free Negroes were denied the suffrage, inquired with biting sarcasm:

> Would it not be ridiculous, inconsistent and unjust, to exclude freemen from voting for representatives and senators, though otherwise qualified, because their skins are black, tawny or reddish? Why not disqualified for being long-nosed, short-faced, or higher or lower than five feet nine? A black, tawny or reddish skin is not so unfavorable in hue to the genuine son of liberty, as a tory complection. Has any other state disqualified freemen for the colour of their skin? I do not recollect any, and if not, the disqualification militates with the proposal in the confederation, that the free inhabitants of each state

[57] *Constitution and Frame of Government for the State of Massachusetts Bay, 1778* (Boston, 1778), pp. 7-8.

shall, upon removing into any other state, enjoy all the privileges and immunities belonging to the free citizens of such state.[58]

If free Negroes voted during the colonial period, why did the citizens of Cambridge and Dartmouth in 1778 publicly admit that there was "no Negro, Indian or mulatto among their voters"?[59] Or, why should Paul and John Cuffee, Negro merchants of Westport, Massachusetts, petition the General Court of Massachusetts in February, 1780, praying for the right to vote in colonial and local affairs? Why also would they say that they had never exercised the suffrage themselves nor had they ever heard of any other person of color doing so?[60] Although the Massachusetts Constitution of 1780 did not discriminate against Negroes, custom and tradition apparently still barred them from exercising the franchise. As late as 1795, Judge James Winthrop and Thomas Pemberton of Boston, in answering a query of Dr. Jeremy Belknap, replied that Negroes could neither elect nor be elected to office in that state.[61]

Elsewhere in Revolutionary New England the political status of the Negroes was no more favorable. Both Vermont and New Hampshire continued the system under which the Negro was denied the vote, for neither mentioned race in setting forth qualifications for the suffrage in their constitutions of 1777 and 1784 respectively.[62] Connecticut and Rhode Island in the transition from colony to Commonwealth during the Revolution con-

58 January 8, 1776.

59 Moore, *op. cit.*, p. 196.

60 Paul Cuffee and his brother John objected to paying their personal tax on the grounds that taxation without representation was unconstitutional. They were jailed, paid the tax and later petitioned the legislature for the right to vote. The legislature is said to have enacted a law embodying Cuffee's demands. *Memoir of Paul Cuffee*, ed. Alexander, pp. 7-9; Sherwood, "Paul Cuffee," *Journal of Negro History*, VIII, 162-163.

61 *Mass. Hist. Soc. Colls.*, Fifth Series, III, 390.

62 *Vide* Benjamin Perley Poore, *Federal and State Constitutions*, II, 1280-1293, for New Hampshire; for Vermont, *ibid.*, pp. 1857-1865.

tinued with minor changes under their old charters.[63] Custom prevented the Negroes from voting in Connecticut before 1818, but the new constitution of that year expressly denied them the suffrage.[64] Not until after the Civil War was the ballot granted to them.[65] One effect of withholding the franchise from the free Negroes was to retard their assimilation into the society of colonial New England.

Exclusion from the militia further emphasized the subordinate position of the New England freedmen.[66] Free Negroes were forbidden to bear arms, yet in case of alarm all able-bodied " free male negro's or mulatto's sixteen years and upwards," in Massachusetts, were required in 1707 to report to the parade ground in their precinct. Here they were to perform any service assigned by the first commissioned officer so long as the company remained under arms. Failure to report was punishable by a fine of twenty shillings or by eighty days' labor.[67] As a substitute for militia service, free Negroes were compelled to work on the streets and highways. No specified number of days was required by the law itself, and length of service was left to the discretion of the selectmen of the various towns. These officials were to base the number of work days exacted of each Negro upon the time and services of the whites who served in the militia. Failure to report for duty carried a penalty of five shillings a day for every day the Negro did not put in an appearance.[68]

Pursuant to this law, the selectmen of the Town of Boston, on September 2, 1719, published the names of twenty-six Negroes, who were to report for work on the highways. The num-

63 *Ibid.*, see also *Public Laws of the State of Connecticut* (Hartford, 1821), pp. 28-29.

64 Efforts to grant the suffrage to Negroes in 1833 and 1847 were defeated by overwhelming majorities. Purcell, *Connecticut in Transition,* p. 399.

65 Adams, " Disfranchisement of Negroes in New England," *loc. cit.,* p. 66.

66 *Cf. supra,* ch. v.

67 *Mass. A. and R.,* I, 606-607; *cf. Conn. Acts and Laws, 1702* (Hartford, n. d.), p. 49.

68 " Report of the Record Commissioners of the City of Boston," *City Document,* 77 (1885), pp. 59-60.

ber of days each was to serve, varying from two to six, was placed opposite the name. Peter Quoquo and Tom Runny Marsh, for example, were to serve two days; Dick Dudley, Mingo Walker and Sebastian Levensworth, three days; Toney four; Tom Lawson, Boston Waite, Jo Jalla, Mingo Winthrop, Great John, and others were to serve six days. Dick Patience, though listed as dead, was also set down for six days' labor.[69]

The inferior political status of the free Negroes was further aggravated by economic proscription. Means of earning a livelihood were frequently closed to them because of their color. It was more difficult for the freedmen to find employment as freedmen than as slaves. When Negroes were the property of masters, the latter either furnished work for them or hired them out to someone else. As freemen, not only were the former slaves dependent upon themselves for the sale of their labor, but in addition they had to face the competition of white working men.[70] The latter not only resented the appropriation of available jobs by Negroes, but occasionally manifested their displeasure by violence. Especially during the hard times immediately preceding and following the Revolution, free Negroes were sometimes insulted, threatened and beaten by mobs of poor whites in the streets of Boston.[71] Frequently denied the opportunity of earning a living and forced into idleness as a consequence, free Negroes were to be later stigmatized as an idle, lazy and dissolute class.[72]

69 *Ibid.*

70 For discussion of the difficulties of the free Negro in the North in securing employment, *vide* Wesley, *op. cit.,* ch. ii; Greene and Woodson, *The Negro Wage Earner,* pp. 1-7.

71 Prince Hall, a prominent free Negro of Boston, recounts the treatment of Negroes in public places in Boston in 1797. Prince Hall, " A Charge Delivered to the African Lodge, June 24, 1797," *loc. cit.* (no pagination). Schomburg Collection, New York Public Library, New York City.

72 This charge according to Reverend Samuel Hopkins of Newport, Rhode Island, was used as a popular argument against freeing the slaves. *Dialogue on the Slavery of the Africans* (1776), pp. 50-51.

Whatever work the free Negroes secured was virtually identical with that done by the slaves, who, as previously shown, engaged in all types of labor. Freedom frequently wrought no change whatever in their labor status, for many remained with their former masters as hired servants.[73] This was true particularly where a close bond of attachment existed between the bondman and master, such as prevailed between Ezra Stiles and his slaves.[74] Some freedmen found work on the farms, but many upon liberation forsook the country and went to the towns, where more varied opportunities for employment attracted them. Here, however, they were confined mostly to domestic service. In this field of employment, according to contemporaries like Judge James Winthrop and travelers like Brissot de Warville, they encountered the least opposition.[75] Many were common laborers. Others worked at the trades or found employment on whaling[76] or coastal vessels.[77] Attractive as sea-faring occupations were to them, many free Negroes hesitated to venture on long voyages for fear of being kidnapped and sold into slavery in the tobacco colonies or in the West Indies.[78]

In spite of limited economic opportunities, some of the freedmen capitalized upon their training in slavery by establishing independent enterprises of their own. Through thrift and industry a few were able to save enough from their meagre wages to provide the necessary capital. Jim Riggs of Framingham, Massachusetts, was a jobber and basket maker and counted

73 *Mass. Hist. Soc. Colls.*, Fifth Series, III, 386.

74 *Cf. supra*, p. 221.

75 *Mass. Hist. Soc. Colls.*, Fifth Series, III, 400. According to De Warville they made " sober and industrious servants," *op. cit.*, p. 239; Brawley, *Early American Writers*, p. 4.

76 Temple, *op. cit.*, p. 237.

77 *Mass. Hist. Soc. Colls.*, Second Series, II, 29-30; De Warville, *op. cit.*, I, 238; *Memoir of Paul Cuffee*, p. 7; Brawley, *Negro Builders and Heroes*, p. 35.

78 *Ibid.* So flagrant did this crime become that all of the states were compelled to pass laws against it. *Vide supra*, pp. 128 ff.

among his patrons the Buckminster, Belknap, Horne, Howe, Eames and Haren families of that town. Riggs, who fought in the Revolution, died in 1828 at the age of ninety-two.[79] Cato Hanker, of the same town, the former slave of Joseph Haven, worked as a shoemaker after his liberation.[80] A Maine Negro is said to have made a living as a fortune teller,[81] and other Negroes like " Squire Nep " of Connecticut,[82] followed the barber's trade. Three of Salem's twelve barbers were Negroes.[83] In Newport, according to Mason, Negroes regularly served as undertakers among their own people.[84] The aforementioned Zelah of Groton, Massachusetts, a fifer in a Revolutionary regiment, is said to have been a famous musician,[85] while Newport Gardner, former slave of Cadet Gardner of Newport, Rhode Island, as already indicated, was a writer and teacher of music. He opened a music school and counted among his patrons whites as well as blacks; Mrs. Gardner, his former mistress, was one of his students.[86] John Peters, the husband of the poet, Phillis Wheatley, is said to have been alternately a baker, grocer, barber, physician and lawyer.[87]

Most outstanding of the free Negro group was Paul Cuffee, the seventh of eleven children of mixed Negro and Indian parentage. Starting as a sailor on a whaling vessel in 1776, Cuffee,

79 Temple, *op. cit.*, p. 238.

80 *Ibid.*, p. 237.

81 According to the Reverend Paul Coffin, a man who had lost a bar of iron suspected his neighbor, was given directions for locating it by a Negro " quack." " Memoir and Journals of the Reverend Paul Coffin, D.D.," *Maine Hist. Soc. Colls.*, IV (Portland, 1856), 291.

82 Roberts, *Historic Towns of the Connecticut Valley*, p. 218.

83 Felt, *Annals of Salem*, II, 154.

84 Champlin, *Reminiscences of Newport*, pp. 106-107.

85 Samuel Abbott Greene, *Slavery in Groton, Massachusetts in Provincial Times*, p. 6.

86 *Ibid.*, p. 155.

87 Brawley, *Negro Builders and Heroes*, p. 23.

during the latter part of the eighteenth and the first quarter of
the nineteenth century, was to become famous as a merchant,
philanthropist, and colonizer. At the height of his trading activities, he was master of a sixty-nine-ton schooner, the *Ranger*.
He also owned two brigs, several smaller vessels and considerable property in houses and lands. When the settlers themselves
refused to do so, he built a school in Westport, Massachusetts,
and gave it to the community. A staunch Quaker, Cuffee helped
in the building of a new meeting house for the Friends, and was
the first Negro to attempt the resettlement of the freedmen in
Africa. In connection with this work, Cuffee, in 1815, helped
found the *Friendly Society of Sierra Leone*. In the same year,
at a personal expenditure of $4,000, he took thirty-eight freed-
men to Liberia. In 1817 Cuffee died, leaving an estate estimated
at $20,000.[88]

In various occupations the freedmen applied the experience
they had gained in slavery. In no field was this better illustrated
than in catering and pastry making. " Duchess " Quamino of
Newport was extolled, says Weeden, as the " most celebrated
cake baker in Rhode Island." Popularly known as the
" Duchess," she conducted her business in a small house on
School Street, where annually she entertained three families
whom she had served before emancipation. The " Duchess," a
member of Dr. Patten's church, was buried in 1804 in a white
cemetery. So esteemed was she that the famous William Ellery
Channing (possibly one of her former owners) had a laudatory
verse carved upon her tombstone.[89] Another Negro pioneer in

88 For life of Paul Cuffee *vide, Memoir of Paul Cuffee a Man of Color
to Which is Subjoined the Epistle of the Society of Sierra Leone*, ed. William Alexander (London, 1811) ; Daniel Ricketson, *History of New Bedford, Bristol County, Massachusetts* (New Bedford, 1858), ch. xx; Paul
Sherwood, " Paul Cuffee," *Journal of Negro History*, VIII (1923), pp. 153-
232; also Reprint (1923) ; Benjamin Brawley, *Negro Builders and Heroes*
(Chapel Hill, 1937), pp. 35-39; Peter Williams, Jr., *A Discourse Delivered
on the Death of Captain Paul Cuffee Before the New York African Institution in the African Episcopal Zion Church*, Oct. 21, 1817, ed. W. Alexander.
(In Schomburg Collection, New York Public Library, West 135th St. Branch).

89 Channing, *Early Recollections of Newport*, p. 170.

business was Emanuel Manna Bernoon, who, in 1736, opened the first catering establishment in Providence.[90] So important did this enterprise become in the social life of the town that Weeden calls it " a way mark of civilization." Later Bernoon, and his wife, Mary, pooled their resources and opened an oyster house. Their business, says Weeden, far surpassed anything else in Providence and they numbered among their patrons the best people in that city. Bernoon's establishment served as a model for other Negro caterers who, before the Civil War, entered the business in such northern cities as Newport, New York and Philadelphia.[91]

Although these pioneer Negro merchants showed the way to their fellows, insufficient credit, lack of training and experience retarded the development of their enterprises. White persons generally regarded Negroes as poor business risks and consequently refused to extend them the credit necessary for the expansion of their business. These handicaps were well summed up by the French traveler, Brissot de Warville in 1788, who wrote:

> " Those Negroes who keep shops live moderately, and never augment their business beyond a certain point. The reason is obvious; the whites . . . like not to give them credit to enable them to undertake any extensive commerce nor even to give them the means of a common education by receiving them into their counting houses." [92]

Brissot was convinced that the failure of the freedmen to expand their business was due not so much to their incapacity as to the obstacles placed in their way by the master class.[93]

90 He was the former slave of Gabriel Bernoon and was freed in 1731. Weeden, *Early Rhode Island,* p. 224. Mary, before her marriage to Bernoon, is said to have made money from the illegal selling of liquor. *Ibid.*

91 Woodson, *Free Negro Heads of Families in 1830,* p. xxxviii; Wesley, *op. cit.,* p. 55; Woodson, *Negro in Our History,* p. 255.

92 J. P. Brissot de Warville, *op. cit.,* I, 239.

93 *Ibid.*

Some of the free Negroes, by acquiring a small amount of property, early demonstrated their ability to adjust themselves to their new status.[94] This was evident early in the seventeenth century. One of the first Negro land owners was Bostian Ken or " Bus Bus," of Dorchester, Massachusetts, who in 1656 not only owned a house and lot in that town but also four acres and a half of land planted in wheat.[95] Other property owners were Moninah and Munglay, mentioned above. In 1659, they sued Samuel Bennett of Lynn for the death of their mare, which had fallen into a pit left uncovered by Bennett.[96] When Angola, a Boston Negro, died in 1675, the Suffolk County Court decreed that his house and land should descend to his wife Elizabeth, and after her death to their children.[97] In 1694, Frank, a Providence Negro, owned a farm which he mortgaged in that year to a neighbor, Stephen Arnold. Frank vindicated Arnold's faith in his industry and integrity, for by 1706 he had discharged the mortgage to the full satisfaction of his creditor.[98]

In the eighteenth century free Negroes increased their holdings. Jack Howard of Providence, who died in 1745, left one hundred and forty-five pounds in colonial bills; John Read left one hundred pounds in 1753,[99] and Prince Vitto, former slave to the Reverend Oliver Peabody, owned five acres of land at Natick, Massachusetts in 1775.[100] At his death in 1757, Andrew Frank of Providence, a veteran of colonial wars, had personal property worth more than two hundred and twenty-nine pounds. In addition, he possessed a note of hand worth £60, wearing apparel, and an old Bible listed £20 and £2.10s respectively.

94 See Judge James Winthrop's letter to Dr. Belknap in 1795 in *Mass. Hist. Soc. Colls.*, Fifth Series, III, 390.

95 *Suffolk Deeds, 1629-1692,* Liber II, p. 297.

96 The suit was withdrawn. *E. C. C. R., 1656-1662,* II, 183.

97 *S. C. C. R., 1671-1680,* Liber XXX, Part II, 598. Whether the Court's ruling set a precedent for the inheritance of property by Negroes is not known.

98 *Early Records of the Town of Providence,* XX, 171-172.

99 Weeden, *Early Rhode Island,* p. 224.

100 *Mass. Archives; Domestic Relations, 1643-1774,* IX, 390-392.

Twenty-four hundred pounds of hay appraised at £17, a cow
and two calves, and a gun worth £16 completed the inventory.[101]
Cato Hanker, mentioned before, bought eleven square rods of
land in Framingham, Massachusetts, in 1751, and built a small
house upon it.[102] At his death in 1769 Emanuel Bernoon, the
Providence caterer, left a house and lot with personal property
to the value of £539.[103] A Rhode Island Negro and his wife are
said to have saved from £200 to £300 and to have sailed for
Africa.[104] When he died in 1772, Cuffee Slocum, the father of
Paul Cuffee, owned 100 acres of land at Cuttyhunk, Massachusetts.[105] Three of Slocum's sons, David, Jonathan and John,
cultivated their own lands,[106] while Paul Cuffee, another son, is
reported to have bought a farm worth $3,500.[107] One of the
largest Negro landowners was Abijah Prince, the former slave
of the Reverend Benjamin Doolittle of Wallingford, Connecticut, who in 1764 is said to have owned one hundred acres of
land in Guilford, Vermont. According to Sheldon, Prince was
also one of the original founders of Sunderland in the same
colony. As one of the first petitioners and grantees, Prince drew
an equal share of the lands in all six divisions of the new town-
ship.[108]

A few Negroes imitated the master class by becoming slave
owners. The first Negro, according to available New England
records, to buy a slave was " Bus Bus," or Bostian Ken. On
February 6, 1756, he mortgaged his house and land to Anna
Keayne of Boston in payment for Mrs. Keayne's Negro man,

101 Weeden, *Early Rhode Island*, p. 261.

102 Temple, *op. cit.*, p. 237.

103 Weeden, *ut supra*, pp. 224-225.

104 Weeden, *Economic and Social History of New England*, II, 451-452.

105 *Memoir of Paul Cuffee*, p. 6.

106 *Ibid.*

107 Brawley, *Negro Builders and Heroes*, p. 36.

108 *History of Deerfield*, II, 899.

Angola. The price was thirty-two pounds, sixteen of which "Bus Bus" agreed to pay "in wheat, peas and barley." The remaining sixteen pounds were to be discharged in two instalments: eight by the twenty-ninth of October of that year, and the balance within a year from that date. "Bus Bus" either liquidated his debt before the time expired or Mrs. Keayne, out of appreciation for his efforts to do so, cancelled the mortgage. At any rate, a brief statement in the court records, bearing date of December 24, 1656, tersely mentions that the "mortgage is cancelled by order of Mrs. Keayne."[109] Other Negroes evidently purchased slaves at a later date, for the first federal census of 1790 revealed that six Negro families in Connecticut held slaves.[110]

Notwithstanding these efforts at self improvement the freedmen were socially ostracized because of their color, and were forbidden to intermarry with whites in Massachusetts.[111] With few exceptions,[112] their children do not seem to have attended the public schools provided for white persons.[113] On certain public occasions, such as Gunpowder Day or Artillery Day, freedmen as well as slaves were forbidden to enter Boston Common.[114] Because of their low incomes and also because of the attitude of the majority group, they were frequently confined to most undesirable living quarters in the towns. In colonial New England, as in the country at large today, the Negroes generally lived near the docks, riverfronts or in alleys.[115] Upon venturing out of these areas, free Negroes were sometimes sub-

109 *Suffolk Records, 1629-1697*, Liber II, 297.

110 *A Century of Population Growth*, p. 222.

111 *Vide supra*, pp. 208-209.

112 Cooley, *op. cit.,* p. 36.

113 *Vide supra*, pp. 236 ff.

114 *Ibid.,* p. 248.

115 Negroes living in dilapidated tenant houses near Oliver's dock in Boston were among those routed in a great fire which destroyed a large part of that section in 1760. *Boston Weekly News Letter,* Friday, March 21, 1760.

jected to insults, maltreatment and indecencies at the hands of white mobs.[116] Like the slaves, freedmen were generally restricted to the galleries in the churches [117] and a specified restricted corner of the graveyard was reserved for the burial of their dead.[118]

Discrimination against the Negro reached its zenith in Connecticut, where legislative action prompted by citizens of New London threatened to make it impossible for free Negroes either to purchase property or to reside in the colony. In 1717 Robert Jacklin, a free Negro, attempted to buy a lot. Whereupon the citizens of New London on April 16, in town meeting assembled, voted to " utterly oppose and protest against Robert Jacklin . . . buying any land in this town." Furthermore, they objected to free Negroes living in the town, and they also went to the extremity of protesting against a Negro's right to hold " any possessions or freehold estate " within the colony.[119] Finally the townspeople instructed their deputies to have a law passed at the next meeting of the General Assembly [120] forbidding any Negro from owning any land within the colony.

The deputies evidently carried out their instructions, for the legislature passed a harsh law, which included all the demands of their constituency. Anticipating by over a hundred years similar enactments by some of the southern states, the assembly specifically prohibited any free Negro or mulatto from residing in any town in the colony.[121] Free Negroes were also forbidden to purchase land or to carry on any business, without first obtaining the consent of the town. Upon those Negroes who al-

116 Prince Hall, " A Charge Delivered to the African Lodge," *loc. cit.,* (no pagination).

117 *Vide supra*, pp. 282-284.

118 *Ibid.*, p. 284.

119 *Conn. Archives: Miscellaneous, 1662-1789,* Series II, Doc. 33.

120 *Ibid.*

121 *Ibid.*, First Series, II, Doc. 42. No date appears on the manuscript but the law was probably passed in May, 1717. *Cf. Conn. Magazine,* V, No. 6, p. 232.

ready resided or owned property in the colony, the law fell especially hard, for its provisions were retroactive. All purchases by them were to be considered null and void, and their residence within any town was to be deemed illegal. Enforcement was left to the selectmen who might peremptorily order " any free Negro to depart and leave " the town. Any Negro failing or refusing to obey such a mandate would be liable to prosecution.[122] Although the law was probably never enforced, its presence on the statute books and the possibility of its enforcement served further to impress upon the free blacks the insecurity of their existence.[123]

Less sweeping in its scope was the action of Massachusetts in a case which questioned the title to lands purchased by Negroes from Indian without licenses. On August 26, 1775, Prince Vitto, a free Negro, of Natick, petitioned the legislature to confirm him the possession of five acres of land which he had bought from John Cornecho, an Indian, who had been convicted and sentenced to jail for bastardy. Endeavoring to save her nephew from imprisonment, Cornecho's aunt transferred to him a deed to five acres of land which he was to sell in order to pay his fine. For this favor Cornecho bound himself to repay his aunt at the end of one year. He then sold the land to Vitto for " sixteen pounds, thirteen and four pence lawful money." With the proceeds, Cornecho secured his freedom, but instead of repaying his aunt he joined the British army.[124] The woman then sought to attach the land which had been sold to Vitto, on the ground that it had never belonged to her nephew. She also claimed that the sale itself was void, for no Negro might " purchase land from an Indian without a license." [125] On the other

122 *Ibid.*

123 With this law as a model, the plantation states, after 1830 were to pass similar enactments, which expatriated many free Negroes, and sent many of them seeking asylum in the northern states and Canada. For general accounts *vide* Woodson, *Free Negro Heads of Families in the U. S. in 1830,* pp. xxii, xxviii, xxx; Wesley, *op. cit.,* p. 81.

124 *Mass. Archives,* IX, 390.

125 *Ibid.,* p. 392.

hand, Vitto held that the Indian merely tried to take advantage of his ignorance of the law; that if the land were taken from him, he would lose not only his life's savings but the cost and labor of fencing the premises as well. Impressed by the Negro's plea, the legislature on December 27, 1755, confirmed Vitto in the possession of his land, by declaring that the Negro's deed was both legal and valid.[126]

Despite the handicaps under which they labored, the free Negroes of colonial New England were slowly shaping the foundation for the Negro families of the nineteenth and twentieth centuries. A number of them not only became leaders and spokesmen for their group but also received recognition from their former masters for demonstrating unusual abilities in their circumscribed condition.

Mention has already been made of such persons as Phillis Wheatley who became internationally famous for her poetry; Abijah Prince, a pioneer in the westward movement and one of the founders of Sunderland, Vermont; Lemuel Haynes, the gifted minister who served as the pastor of white congregations in Vermont and New York;[127] Captain Paul Cuffee, who was to become famous as merchant, philanthropist and colonizer; and Emanuel Bernoon, proprietor of the oyster house. Two other members of this class should be included, one of whom was Lucy Terry Prince, the first American Negro poet and a remarkable story teller. Possessed of unusual oratorical ability, she once used her eloquence in a three-hour attempt to persuade the Board of Trustees of Williams College to remove the color bar and to permit her son to enter the school.[128] On another occasion she is said to have carried a suit against Colonel Eli Bronson, her neighbor in Sunderland, Vermont, to the Supreme Court of the United States. Bronson claimed part of Lucy's land and even fenced off the disputed area within his own. Lucy sued Bronson. When the litigation reached the Supreme

126 *Ibid.*
127 *Vide supra*, pp. 241, 243 ff., 310.
128 Sheldon, *op. cit.,* II, 900-901.

Court of the United States, Lucy was represented by Isaac Ticknor, later Governor of Vermont. Opposing counsel were Stephen Bradley and Royall Tyler. When Ticknor's pleadings apparently failed to satisfy Lucy, she argued her own case before the Court. Later Justice Samuel Chase, who presided, is said to have remarked that Lucy's plea surpassed that of any Vermont lawyer he had ever heard.[129]

Even more important in the life of the Negro community in colonial and post-Revolutionary New England was Prince Hall. Born of an English father and a mulatto mother in Barbados in 1748, Hall came to Boston in 1765 in the midst of the controversy between England and the colonies over the Stamp Act. Little is known of his early life, but he worked for a time as steward on vessels plying between Boston and England. Distressed at the lowly condition of the Negroes in Boston, he sought means to improve their status, and, with other free Negroes, worked for the emancipation of the slaves in Massachusetts.

After vainly seeking admission in 1775 to the St. Andrew Lodge of white Masons, headed by Joseph Warren, Hall and fourteen other Negroes were initiated into the British Army Lodge of a regiment stationed near Boston. In 1784, after the white Masons, headed by Joseph Warren, in 1775, Hall and Negro brethren, Hall applied to the Grand Lodge of England for a warrant to set up an independent Negro Lodge. The warrant was granted in September of the same year but was not received until 1787. The Lodge, which was to be known as the African Lodge No. 459, marks the beginning of Negro Masonry in the United States. Hall later became a Methodist minister, and in this capacity he worked faithfully to improve the economic, social and spiritual condition of the New England freedman.[130]

129 *Ibid.*, 900.

130 For Prince Hall *vide* Prince Hall, "A Charge Delivered to the African Lodge, June 24, 1797 at Menotomy, Massachusetts," *Masonic Orders,* I (no pagination); Benjamin Brawley, *Early American Writers,* p. 96; John Bruce, "Prince Hall, the Pioneer of American Masonry," *Masonic Orders, II* (New York, 1921), pp. 1-8 especially.

# CHAPTER XII

## SUMMARY

In the foregoing pages an attempt has been made to inquire into the condition of the Negro in colonial New England. During the approximate century and a half embraced in the limits of this study, Negro slaves were brought into the region in such numbers that they influenced in many ways the economic, political, social and religious institutions of their masters.

Negro slavery in New England was inextricably bound up with the slave trade. Geographic conditions forced the early settlers to seek economic opportunities in fishing, whaling, shipbuilding, general commerce and particularly the slave trade. In 1638, Puritan merchants began the New England slave trade by bringing in Negroes from the West Indies; and in 1644 they started to import Negroes from Africa. The demand for slaves —almost insatiable in the British and foreign West Indies and in the plantation colonies of the South—meant high profits for the traders. By the end of the seventeenth century, Massachusetts merchants were not only selling slaves in the West Indies and the South, but also were supplying their neighbors in New England. The total New England slave trade, however, was small in the seventeenth century and was confined almost wholly to Massachusetts. Puritan merchants had neither the capital nor the physical force to match the powerful Dutch West India or the English Royal African Company whose monopolies, covering the entire West African Coast, legally excluded all private traders from the main source of slaves.

Probably less than a thousand Negroes had been brought to New England by 1700. The hey-day of the trade came a generation later, when the Puritan colonies ranked as the greatest slave-carrying section in the New World. Aided by the revocation in 1696 of the monopoly formerly held by the Royal African Company and by the British contract received under the terms of the Treaty of Utrecht (1713) for supplying the

Spanish American colonies with 4,800 slaves a year, the eighteenth century slave trade developed into New England's
greatest industry. The famous triangular slave commerce was
based upon the economic interdependence of New England,
Africa and the West Indies. The Caribbean islands, although
producing vast amounts of sugar, molasses, rum and other sub-
tropical products, could not supply their inhabitants and, therefore, needed the surplus food, fish, lumber and manufactured
goods of New England, which in turn was dependent upon the
West Indies for rum, molasses, and sugar. Africa, the third
partner in the trade, used great quantities of New England rum,
trinkets, and bar iron for which the slaves, so sorely needed in
the West Indies and the plantation colonies, were exchanged.

Rum was the principal staple of the slave trade and a great
distilling industry, manufacturing millions of gallons of cheap
rum, sprang up in New England. This was carried to Africa in
small ships ranging from forty to two hundred tons and manned
by crews rarely exceeding eighteen men and a boy. Crammed
between decks, spoon-fashion, in a space three feet ten inches
high, slaves suffered cruelly in the Middle Passage, as the leg of
the journey from Africa to America was called.

The greatest slave-trading colonies were Massachusetts and
Rhode Island; Connecticut and New Hampshire played lesser
roles. Vermont—at that time part of New York—had no share
in this traffic. Boston and Newport were the leading slave ports
but Salem, Kittery, Providence, Bristol, Charlestown, Middletown and New London—in fact, nearly all the seaports in New
England—were connected with the trade in Negroes. Exploit-
ing this commercial opportunity were slave merchants like the
Fanueils, Pepperells, Royalls of Massachusetts; the Wantons,
Browns, and Champlins of Rhode Island, the Whipples of New
Hampshire, and the Eastons of Connecticut.

Although slave merchants sold most of their Negroes in the
West Indies, where the greatest profits were to be made, the
smaller New England market was not neglected. Newspapers,
which first appeared regularly in 1704, provided the means for

the dealers to enlarge their clientele; and the newspaper columns from the time of their establishment were widely used for the advertisement of slaves, together with other goods and chattels. Most of the Negroes seem to have been brought from Africa, although nearly all had first been taken to the West Indies. In general, New England received second-rate Negroes, prime slaves being sold in the West Indies and southern colonies. Merchants resorted to high pressure salesmanship in disposing of their wares, playing up both the physical and the moral qualities of the slaves. Merchants handled Negroes, Indians and whites indiscriminately, sometimes selling them from the same auction block. All three races were commonly listed by traders with miscellaneous goods like butter, beef, cheese, wine and iron. A local trade in Negroes went on, introduced by persons who, for various reasons, desired to dispose of their chattels. Compared with the internal slave trade of the antebellum South, however, it was small and was marked neither by the drama nor the cruelty associated with the latter.

Fluctuations of colonial currencies, and absence of prices in newspaper advertisements, make it difficult to state with accuracy the prices paid for slaves. There were many factors involved: age, sex, quality, skill, demand and the haggling power of the buyer. The average price for a slave in the seventeenth century was probably £20-£30 sterling; for the eighteenth century prices were higher. Depreciated currency late in the eighteenth century caused slaves to bring as high as £1200 in Rhode Island money; but the average price of a slave on the eve of the Revolution may have been £40 or £50 sterling. Slave transactions were usually executed by deed, though some Negroes are said to have passed from hand to hand without this formality. Slaves were sold for "cash" or on "credit." Because of the scarcity of hard money they were sometimes paid for partly in cash and partly in goods. Installment buying was common, but merchants were frequently forced to resort to court action in order to collect unpaid balances. Dealers often misrepresented their chattels, and the courts, upon appeal in such cases, granted

redress to the aggrieved purchasers. Fraudulent selling of Negroes was common in New England, but Massachusetts alone
(1767) passed a law to stop the practice. At least two New England colonies, Massachusetts (1705-06) and Rhode Island
(1711), derived a revenue from the slave trade by levying duties
upon imported Negroes. However, these duties were loosely
administered and were finally disallowed by the British Parliament in 1732.

The effects of the New England slave trade were momentous.
It was one of the foundations of New England's economic
structure; it created a wealthy class of slave-trading merchants,
while the profits derived from this commerce stimulated cultural development and philanthropy. At the same time the slave
trade helped to destroy flourishing African civilizations, contributed to the depopulation of Africa, and introduced an alien
race into New England.

On the basis of none too reliable census returns, it would
seem that the Negroes constituted a small minority in New
England's population, although few estimates for the section
as a whole are available. The Negro population grew slowly in
the seventeenth century, and by 1700 there were probably not
more than a thousand blacks in the entire section. Increasing
well-being in the colonies, together with a demand for labor and
the consequent rise in importations of slaves, caused a more
rapid growth in the Negro population during the eighteenth
century. In 1715 it was estimated at 4,150 out of a total of
158,000; sixty years later there were approximately 16,034 Negroes in a total population of about 659,446. When the first
federal census was taken in 1790, only 16,822 Negroes were
returned for New England out of 1,009,206 inhabitants.

Massachusetts contained the largest number of Negroes until
1774, when she was outstripped by Connecticut, which in that
year reported 6,464 blacks, or more than one-third of New England's Negro population. The largest number recorded for
colonial Massachusetts (including Maine) was 5,249 in 1776;
for New Hampshire 674 in 1773; and for Rhode Island, 4,697

in 1755, which gave that colony one Negro for every nine inhabitants. In no other colony did the ratio exceed that of Connecticut in 1761, one in thirty-three.

Distribution of Negroes within the various colonies was not uniform. Commerce, handicrafts and large-scale agriculture determined the concentration. For this reason, counties like Rockingham in New Hampshire; Essex and Suffolk in Massachusetts; New London, Hartford and Fairfield in Connecticut, and Newport and Washington Counties of Rhode Island had the largest number of black inhabitants. In these countries, important trading and manufacturing towns like Boston and Salem in Massachusetts; Portsmouth, New Hampshire; Newport, South Kingstown and Jamestown, Rhode Island; and New London, Fairfield and Hartford, Connecticut reported the highest ratios of Negroes to whites. Of these towns, Boston with 1,541 Negroes in 1752 and Newport with 1,234 in 1755 contained the largest number of slaves. Relatively few families seem to have owned slaves. Out of the 40,876 families in Massachusetts in 1764, only one-eighth owned the colony's 5,235 slaves. No other figures were available until the federal census of 1790, but the abolition of slavery in all the New England states before that date renders the first national enumeration of little value for the period under consideration. The number of slaves per family ranged from one to sixty, but the average number was about two to a household. That slaveholding was a class rather than a racial institution is suggested by the fact that at least one Negro family owned slaves in colonial New England, while six Negro slaveholders were reported from Connecticut in 1790.

In short, Negroes were not important numerically in New England and whatever influence they exerted upon the institutions of that section must be based upon other than numerical considerations. The failure of the Indian as a laborer and the limited tenure of the white indentured servants created a demand for additional workers in New England's fields, forests, shipyards, small manufactories and households. The role of the slaves was determined by the complex economy of the section and by the interests of the masters. Since those interests were diverse and complicated, the slaves had to be better trained and more versatile than the plantation Negro in the South and the West Indies, if he were to be an economic asset. Investigation into the work performed by slaves shows that they were generally trained to follow whatever calling their masters pursued. The time-honored theory that the New England slave was wholly or mainly a house servant no longer seems tenable for, from the seventeenth century on, Negroes were associated with every form of New England's economic life. They worked on the farms, raising a variety of food products, forage crops, flax, tobacco, cattle and sheep. The wealth of the " Narragansett Planters " of Rhode Island and of the large farmers in eastern Connecticut was derived from slave labor, a few farms having as many as forty or sixty black workers. In the homes Negroes served as cooks, maids, nurses, valets, butlers, coachmen and attendants. In New England's great maritime industries they worked as sailors and in other capacities on whaling, fishing and trading vessels, and even on slave ships and privateers. As skilled workers Negro men were employed as sawyers, carpenters, shipwrights, butchers, iron workers, rope makers, tailors, distillers, printers, bakers and blacksmiths; slave women as spinners, sewers and weavers. Many Negroes worked as common laborers, ditch diggers, chimney sweeps, teamsters, errand boys and porters.

Some slaves discharged their tasks so well that they held responsible positions as managers of farms, warehouses and ships or as storekeepers, peddlers, keepers of menageries and even assistants to physicians. Many Negro slaves were " handy " men, that is, they were able to discharge a variety of tasks. This type of slave was perhaps the delight of the Yankee master, who often had to be a " jack of all trades." Most of the slaves may actually have belonged to this class, as such talents were conspicuously " played up " in the eighteenth century newspapers. White laborers resented the intrusion of Negro labor in the skilled trades but the only legal attempt to bar Negroes from such employment in colonial New England occurred in Boston, when a statute, passed either in 1661 or earlier, forbade the working of Negroes as artisans. This prohibition, however, was subsequently ignored and New England masters, like those in other colonies, trained their Negroes in whatever calling was necessary to their own affairs. With their masters to provide work for them, during the slave era, the type of employment open to New England Negroes was higher than at any time since the period under discussion. Faced with the powerful opposition of the master class, the white workmen manifested a sullen antagonism to the slaves which, as John Adams remarked in 1795, might have resulted in their destroying slavery, had it not been abolished earlier by statute. The Negro, then, was an integral and important factor in the economy of colonial New England.

Controls were necessary to regulate the behavior of the slaves in order to preserve the safety, supremacy and property of the master. There were two kinds of controls: public and private. Public control was evident in special laws, called slave codes, for which the Barbadian legislation of 1644 served as a model. The codes arose out of the necessity of the moment, rather than as a result of conscious planning. Massachusetts first legalized slavery in 1641 and in 1670 revised her law to permit the enslavement of the offspring of slaves. The other New England colonies followed her example. By custom in New England, rather than by positive law as in the plantation colonies, slave children were given the status of the mother.

In the main, the slave codes were similar in wording and intent and aimed to protect the masters' property and the community. Specific provisions were designed to prevent running away, theft, drunkenness, damage to public property, assault upon a white person, defamation of a white person, disturbances of the peace, riots, and insurrections. Other laws purported to protect indigent or superannuated slaves, or to save the town expense, by forcing masters to post bonds to guarantee that the

slave, if set free, would not become a public charge. The scope
of the codes was wide; they were applied to Indian slaves, frequently to white indentured servants and free Negroes, and
occasionally to free white minors. The severity of slave legislation was determined by the potential threat to the master class
inherent in the density of the slave population in a given locality. Thus the code of Rhode Island, which had the largest proportion of blacks, was the harshest in New England, and supplementary legislation in Boston and the Narragansett Country,
where large numbers of slaves were concentrated, was especially
severe. All the codes, however, were much milder than those of
the plantation colonies. For example, a slave found abroad after
nine o'clock was punished in New England by ten or fifteen
stripes; for the same offense in Virginia (1723) he might be
dismembered.[1] A slave striking a white person was to be
whipped with thirty stripes, in Connecticut (1708) and at the
discretion of the trial justices in Massachusetts (1705-06). In
South Carolina a slave who offered to strike a white person was
to be severely whipped; for the second offense he was to be
severely whipped, have his nose slit, and be burnt in the face;
for the third offense he was to suffer death.[2]

Slave controls, however, were not always effective and the
laws were not rigorously enforced. Some, like the exclusion
from the armed forces, were waived in time of emergency;
masters often concealed the crimes of their slaves in order to
escape paying their fines or losing their property; and the slaves
themselves weakened the controls by violating them and committing many crimes and misdemeanors. Hundreds of slaves
ran away; how many were caught is not known. A list of slave
crimes includes theft, drunkenness, mutilation, rape, counter-
feiting, duelling, arson, murder, and insurrections. Some of
these crimes, like running away, arson, murder and insurrection
were probably directed against the master class as a protest
against slavery. Legal punishments in the main were the same

1 Hening, *Statutes at Large of Virginia*, IV, 132.
2 McCord, *Statutes at Large of South Carolina*, VII, 343.

for whites: fines or whipping, and hanging for capital crimes. Barbaric sentences, such as burning at the stake and hanging in chains were occasionally meted out to slaves for arson and murder in order to deter others from similar crimes.

Legally, the New England slave held a position somewhere between that of a plantation slave and an indentured servant. This was due to the influence of Jewish slavery after which the Puritans patterned their system of involuntary servitude. The New England slave was in a measure a member of his master's family and, following the Hebraic tradition, was usually refered to as " servant," rarely as slave. Holding this intermediate status, Negroes were considered both as property and as persons before the law; hence their legal status was never rigidly fixed. As property, Negroes were bought, sold, transferred, included in wills, inventories and deeds, and other personal estate. They were escheated to the town if the master died intestate and without heirs. Slaves might also be seized or sold to satisfy legal claims brought against themselves or their masters. Slaves were at the same time considered to be persons and as such could acquire, receive, hold, administer and transfer property. They could also sue and be sued and they had the right of appeal to the highest colonial courts. As persons, moreover, they enjoyed virtually the same rights before the courts as did free white persons. They possessed the right of trial both by the grand and petit juries; they could pass upon their trial jurors, and could offer testimony against white persons in the courts in cases not involving Negroes. This was quite different from the plantation colonies where Negroes could testify only for or against each other, and in Virginia (1732) only in case of a slave being tried for a capital offense.[3] In New York (1706) no slave could testify for or against a freeman in any case, be it civil or criminal.[4] As persons, moreover, New England slaves had a right

3 Hening, *op. cit.*, IV, 327.

4 *New York Colonial Laws,* I, 598. For summary of slave legislation in colonial New York, *vide* Samuel McKee, Jr., *Labor in Colonial New York, 1664-1776,* pp. 141-155.

to life. The killing of a slave by the master—at least in theory
—was a capital offense, although no master appears to have
paid the extreme penalty for such a crime. In the plantation
colonies the killing of a slave under correction was not a crime
punishable at law.[5] As persons, Negroes fought in the land and
sea forces of all the New England colonies during the colonial
and Revolutionary wars. On the other hand, slaves could not
vote or serve on juries, but neither was a slave woman compelled to testify against her husband. Withal, the status of the
slaves in New England approximated that of the indentured
servant and was perhaps unique in colonial America.

The New England slaves, however, were forced to conform
to the domestic institutions of their masters. The New England
family was the fundamental unit, economically, spiritually and
socially, and its preservation was deemed essential to the perpet-
uation of the Puritan way of life. Therefore marriage and the
family were jealously guarded, and sexual irregularities either
before or after marriage were relentlessly hunted down and
severely punished. The family, following the Hebraic model,
was largely patriarchal and most of the control of the household
fell to the father who as head of the family exerted dominion
over all who dwelt under his roof. As part of the household,
the slaves were subject to the same community controls governing marriage and the family as were free white persons. The
sexual promiscuity so common among the plantation slaves was
not tolerated in New England. Slaves had to marry and their
" intentions to marry " or " banns " had to be publicly posted or
read before the wedding could take place. Slave marriages
were numerous and were duly inscribed upon the records. Marriages took place between Negro slaves, Negro slaves and free
Negroes, Negroes and Indians—free and slave—and Negroes
and whites. The shortage of black women acted as a spur to the
crossing of Negroes with whites and Indians. Moreover, the
children resulting from such unions were free. Most marriages

5 Hening, *op. cit.,* IV, 132-133; McCord, *op. cit.,* VII, 345.

between whites and Negroes seem to have taken place between white women and Negro men. Despite stringent public controls, sexual promiscuity was common to all races and classes, resulting in a long series of court actions for fornication, bastardy or both. Illicit relationships were common between Negro women and the males of the master class, but whether they were motivated by mutual attraction, physical compulsion, or by the prestige of the master class is not known. There were numerous paternity cases involving Negro women and white men in which the courts sometimes named the man as the father of the child, and even occasionally ordered him to maintain his offspring. Adultery caused the break-up of both white and black families. Miscegenation between whites and blacks resulted in a considerable mulatto element by 1700 and prompted Massachusetts to pass a law (1705-06) which proscribed intermarriage as well as illicit intercourse between whites and Negroes. Although Massachusetts was the only New England colony to take this step, the law was as ineffectual then in curbing miscegenation as later legislation has proved to be elsewhere.

Family life among the slaves was open to certain demoralizing influences. Marriage did not give the psychological feeling of oneness, because slaves assumed no surname upon marrying. They could not exercise full marital or parental rights for they still remained the property of their masters. Sexual immorality, adultery, separation of parents by sale, separation of the children from their parents, and infanticide all tended to break up the slave family. In contrast to the situation in the South, slave breeding does not seem to have been practiced generally, and records of but two cases have been found. New England slave women were not esteemed for their breeding qualities, for the economy of New England could not absorb unlimited numbers of slaves; hence, slave women were occasionally sold because they were too prolific. With all their defects, the marital relationships of slaves in New England were doubtless on a higher plane than elsewhere in colonial America, and when freedom came after the American Revolution, the Negro family of New

England did not experience the profound shock of adjustment to the domestic mores of the general community such as the Southern Negroes suffered after the Civil War.

Slaves were treated more kindly in New England than elsewhere in colonial America. Because of economic and political conditions peculiar to the section, together with the Puritans' patriarchal conception of slavery based upon the Old Testament, the Negroes were often considered a part of the family in which they lived. As a result strong bonds of affection frequently developed between master and slave. The slaves seem to have been well fed and sufficiently clad to endure the severe New England weather. In case of illness, they were cared for either by their mistresses or by the family physician; during epidemics like the smallpox, they were often inoculated and confined in the same hospital as the whites. Slave mortality, in comparison with the general death rate, however, was high. Although there was no general movement to educate the Negroes, no statute prohibited their instruction. Furthermore, the Puritan religion was founded on a personal knowledge of the Bible, and if the souls of slaves were to be saved, the Negroes must be taught to read. As a result, many masters, either through kindness or self-interest, gave their slaves instruction in reading, writing and the trades. Members of the Congregational clergy, like Cotton Mather and John Eliot, also pioneered in the secular instruction of the slaves. Performing a similar service, were such organizations as the Quakers, the Society for the Propagation of the Gospel, and the Associates of Dr. Bray. The two latter organizations, which were connected with the Anglican Church, not only provided missionaries, books, Bibles, and other materials for the Negroes but also opened schools for them. Education made the slaves more valuable assets to their owners. Many Negroes were thus equipped to discharge skilled or responsible tasks for their masters. Some slaves helped manage or even conducted business for their owners. Many Negroes like Newport Gardner, Lemuel Haynes, and Lucy Terry, by virtue of such instruction, became useful members of their communities, while Phillis Wheatley, the poetess, achieved international fame.

Private control of the slave by the master, which was based upon coercion, sometimes resulted in excessive flogging of slaves and servants of all races. The colonial era was a brutal age in which persons of all sexes and races, both free and slave, were often cruelly punished. Court records reveal many cases of the inhuman beatings administered to indentured servants but they are generally silent on similar whippings of Negroes. However, slaves were sometimes brutally flogged and occasionally died under the lash, but no cases of private mutilations are recorded. Slaves like other persons were forbidden to work or play on Sunday. They amused themselves by participating in such social gatherings of their masters as corn-huskings, house-raisings, church-raisings, attending elections, watching the militia parade, and in swimming, horse racing, pitching quoits, fiddling, story telling and dancing; but in Boston on certain occasions they were barred from celebrations. Unique to the New England slaves was the election of Negro " Governors ", a practice carried out in mimicry of white elections which served not only to give the slaves political experience, but more important, to render them more tractable. As such it served as a subtle means of slave control. Those slaves who were the object of especially kind treatment by their owners manifested their gratitude even to the extent of giving their lives in protection of their masters' children. However, in spite of the mildness of New England slavery, there were Negroes who found their bondage so intolerable that they committed suicide.

Some New England slaves were converted to Christianity and admitted into Church membership during the colonial era. The first recorded instance of a slave baptism occurred in 1644. However, the baptism of Negroes came only as the result of a long struggle, for conversion of the slaves was opposed in New England, as in other colonies, on economic, social, and religious grounds. Some masters feared that conversion would lessen the value of their Negroes as laborers. Others, probably realizing that the equalitarian spirit of Christianity was unalterably opposed to slavery, believed that the social consequences of baptism would actually destroy the institution. In order to avoid these consequences, it was claimed that the Negro was a *beast* not a *human being*. As damaging from the master's point of view were the potential effects of the unwritten law of Christianity which—as the English settlers understood it—made the baptized subject unfit for slavery. Therefore, apprehensive that conversion would automatically work manumission, many masters refused to permit the Christianization of their slaves.

In New England, as in the other colonies, conversion was effected in part by a compromise between religious and ethical principles and property interests. While in New York (1706) and in the plantation colonies the legislatures repudiated the idea that baptism meant liberation from bondage,[6] custom accomplished the same end in New England. Religious denominations likewise bowed to the interests of property. The Bishop of London, speaking for the Anglican Church, and Cotton Mather, as spokesman for the Congregationalists (1706), both denounced the theory that slavery and Christianity were incompatible. Christianity, according to the Bishop of London, (1727) conferred a spiritual, not a civil freedom, and baptism in no way altered the slave status. With this assurance many New England masters permitted their slaves to be baptized. Some of the Negroes were formally prepared for church membership by the various denominations; a larger number probably received religious instruction in the families to which they belonged. Once converted, the slave usually became a member of the church which his master attended.

As church members, Negroes seem to have enjoyed many of the rights of free white communicants. They joined in the singing and praying, could be transferred from one church to another, might be excommunicated and also might be restored to

6 *N. Y. Col. Laws,* I, 597-598; McCord, *op. cit.,* VII, 343.

membership upon evidence of their repentance. They also participated in the communion service, though probably they were the last to be served. Upon baptism, their classical or heathen names were sometimes changed to Christian or Hebraic ones. However, some discrimination was practiced against them. For example, Negroes, along with free white minors, were not permitted to vote on Church discipline and they were usually segregated in the galleries or in the rear of the churches, but whether this was motivated primarily by class or racial consideration cannot be determined, although it is possible that race was a factor. Slaves were given Christian burials and sometimes both whites and blacks followed the bier. Usually a corner of the graveyard was reserved for slaves and appreciative masters sometimes marked their graves by tombstones.

The number of slaves Christianized is not known, and it is possible that not many of them had been formally converted at the end of the colonial period. Most masters were probably more concerned with material things than with religion. Moreover, the manner in which Christianity was interpreted to Negroes tended to set up within them a cultural resistance to the religion of their masters. Religion was prostituted as a means of conserving the master's property by rendering the slave meek and complacent in his bondage. Negroes were taught that God had enslaved them and Cotton Mather, for example, embodied this idea in his catechism and in the ten commandments which he wrote for the slaves in 1706. Ministers like Mather, Ezra Stiles, Daniel Wadsworth and Parson Ashley, all exhorted the Negroes to be good and faithful servants in their bondage if they would enjoy the " great privileges " of heaven.

A few Negroes like Phillis Wheatley and Lemuel Haynes readily accepted this form of Christianity, Haynes later becoming a Congregational minister and preaching to white congregations, but others, like Prince Hall and Lancaster Hill, saw through the duplicity of the ministers. It was this hypocrisy, according to the Quaker minister, Benjamin Coleman of Nantucket, Massachusetts, that made the Negro hate the name of

Christian. It is probable that many Negroes were little disposed to accept a religion that sanctioned their bondage. At any rate, at the end of the colonial era, although some Negroes had been converted and admitted into New England Churches, it is probable that most of them were still strangers to the Christian faith. Nevertheless, the movement to convert the slaves had not been in vain, for out of the baptism of the blacks of the colonial era was to emerge the Negro church of post-Revolutionary New England.

A number of Negroes in New England, as in the other colonies, held the status of freedmen, a group whose origin probably dates from 1646. Freedom was gained in many ways. Some Negroes were probably never slaves but, because of the early unfamiliarity of the Puritans with slavery, were really indentured servants and went free at the end of their period of servitude. Others may have been liberated by the Rhode Island law of 1652, which limited involuntary service to ten years. In some cases Negroes won their freedom by entering into formal contracts with their masters to serve them for a period of years in return for their freedom. Some slaves were manumitted for faithful service; others through the wills of their owners. Aggressive Negroes sometimes won their liberation by appealing to the courts; others purchased themselves or their loved ones, while still others were freed as a result of service in the colonial or Revolutionary wars. Freedom in many instances was probably gained by running away, but of the hundreds of Negroes who absconded no estimate of those who made good their escape is available. Decrepit slaves, freed by masters in order to avoid supporting them, for a time swelled the list of free Negroes, but this practice was checked by laws forcing the master to post a bond before liberating his chattel. Other slaves were emancipated by conscience-stricken masters who had been tardily convinced of the injustice of slavery. There were no censuses of the free Negro population of colonial New England; hence, no estimate of their numbers is possible. Judging from the literature of the period, however, and in view of the relative ease with which freedom was obtained, a considerable number of Negroes must have been free. The listing of 13,059 New England Negroes as free in the first federal census of 1790 is not indicative of the colonial situation, since by that date slavery and the slave trade had been abolished in that section.

The freedmen in New England, as in other English colonies, occupied an intermediate and inferior status, somewhat between that of a free white person and an indentured servant. This was in marked contrast to the free Negroes of colonial Brazil who, once liberated, are said to have been accorded social, and political rights enjoyed by other free persons. The status of the New England freedmen was much less favorable. Legally, their condition did not differ much from that of the slaves and they were usually included in the slave codes with Indian and Negro slaves. They could not vote, although they were taxed, could not serve on juries and were excluded from the militia in peace time. In lieu of military service they were compelled in Massachusetts (1707) to perform menial service on the parade ground or to labor on the roads. Legal punishments for free Negroes, however, were virtually the same as those for free white persons.

Economically the status of the free Negroes was inferior to that of the slaves. Whereas in slavery every type of employment was open to them, in freedom, faced with the combined competition of slaves, indentured servants and free white workmen, the freedmen were confined by circumstances largely to domestic service. Prejudice also contributed to their economic difficulties. A few Negroes found work on the farms, on trading and whaling vessels or in menial employments but only in the face of mounting hostility on the part of white workmen, who after the Revolution often manifested their antagonism by insulting and beating Negroes and in riots against them. Frequently forced into idleness because of their inability to find work, the freedmen were often stigmatized as a lazy and dissolute class. Socially, the freedmen were also faced with discrimination. In the towns they were confined largely to the alleys, near the docks or along the river fronts; they were not generally permitted to send their children to the public schools and on certain occasions were forbidden to appear in public places. Like the slaves, they were segregated in the churches and were buried in a separate corner of the graveyard.

In spite of these difficulties, many of the freedmen demonstrated their ability to adjust themselves to their new status by accumulating a certain amount of property. Some owned farms; others real estate in the towns. A number of freedmen capitalized upon their experience and training in slavery by becoming proprietors of small businesses; others even practiced as physicians. A few Negroes, because of unusual talents, not only were regarded as spokesmen by their own group, but were recognized as such by the general community. Among these were Phillis Wheatley, the poetess; Lemuel Haynes, who became pastor of a white congregation; Abijah Prince, one of the founders of Sunderland, Vermont, and Prince Hall, the founder of Negro Masonry in the United States. Not only were some of the freedmen concerned with improving their own lot, but Prince Hall, Abijah Prince, Lucy Terry, Lancaster Hill and others were assiduous in working for the freedom of the enslaved blacks.

In spite of the handicaps under which they labored, the free Negroes by the end of the colonial period had given evidence of their ability to assimilate the ways of their former masters and, had not full integration in the community been denied them because of their color, they might have achieved a more enviable status before the Revolution. But, the efforts of the colonial freedmen at the opening of the American Revolution had laid the economic and social foundations for the present Negro population of New England.

The condition of the Negro, then, in colonial New England was primarily that of a chattel. But slavery was so conditioned and modified by the social and religious philosophy of the Puritans, that, in reality, it was an admixture of bondage and indentured service. The bonds of slavery in New England were never tightly drawn and it required only the impact of humanitarian dogma to break the fetters of the slaves. That philosophy was already at work at the close of the colonial period in the " rights of man " theory of the American Revolution, and the application of this principle was destined to sweep away the already weakened structure of slavery in New England.

# APPENDICES

APPENDICES

# APPENDIX A

## Distribution of Negroes in Massachusetts by Counties in 1776 [1]

| Counties | Whites | Negroes | Total | Per Cent Negro |
|---|---|---|---|---|
| Suffolk ............. | 27,419 | 682 | 28,101 | 2.4 |
| Essex ............... | 50,903 | 1,049 | 51,952 | 2.0 |
| Middlesex ......... | 40,119 | 702 | 40,821 | 1.7 |
| Hampshire ........ | 34,315 | 245 | 34,560 | 0.7 |
| Plymouth ......... | 26,906 | 487 | 27,393 | 1.7 |
| Barnstable ........ | 15,344 | 171 | 15,515 | 1.1 |
| Bristol ............ | 26,656 | 583 | 27,241 | 2.1 |
| York ............... | 17,593 | 241 | 17,834 | 1.3 |
| Dukes ............. | 2,822 | 59 | 2,881 | 2.0 |
| Nantucket ........ | 4,412 | 133 | 4,545 | 2.9 |
| Worcester ......... | 46,331 | 432 | 46,763 | 0.9 |
| Cumberland ....... | 13,910 | 162 | 14,072 | 1.1 |
| Lincoln ............ | 18,563 | 85 | 18,648 | 0.5 |
| Berkshire .......... | 18,552 | 216 | 18,768 | 1.1 |
| Total ........ | 343,845 | 5,249 | 349,094 | 1.5 |

[1] *Journals of the Provincial Congress of Massachusetts in 1774 and 1775* (Boston, 1838), p. 755; cf. *A Century of Population Growth, 1790-1900*, pp. 158-161.

# APPENDIX B

## Negroes in Boston by Wards, in 1742 [1]

| Wards | Population | Houses | Ware-houses | Negroes | Horses | Cows |
|---|---|---|---|---|---|---|
| 1 ....... | 1,028 | 106 | 4 | 44 | 8 | 7 |
| 2 ....... | 1,483 | 147 | | 76 | 5 | 5 |
| 3 ....... | 1.255 | 127 | 11 | 105 | 16 | 4 |
| 4 ....... | 1,135 | 110 | | 84 | 21 | 4 |
| 5 ....... | 1,328 | 132 | 12 | 109 | 31 | 4 |
| 6 ....... | 1,363 | 142 | 15 | 115 | 31 | 5 |
| 7 ....... | 1,204 | 127 | 8 | 124 | 37 | 21 |
| 8 ....... | 1,216 | 146 | 99 | 135 | 45 | 7 |
| 9 ....... | 1,264 | 139 | 8 | 166 | 47 | 9 |
| 10 ....... | 1,857 | 195 | 4 | 167 | 61 | 26 |
| 11 ....... | 1,365 | 138 | 5 | 115 | 40 | 15 |
| 12 ....... | 1,884 | 208 | | 134 | 76 | 36 |
| Totals.... | 16,382 | 1,717 | 166 | 1,374 | 418 | 141 |

1 *Mass. Hist. Soc. Colls.*, Second Series, III, 95.

# APPENDIX C

## Distribution of Negroes by Sex and Towns in Massachusetts in 1754-1755 [1]

| County and Towns | Males | Females | Total |
|---|---|---|---|
| Suffolk | | | |
| Boston ................ | 647 | 342 | 989 |
| Dorchester ............. | 18 | 13 | 31 |
| Roxbury ............... | 38 | 15 | 53 |
| Weymouth ............ | 12 | 11 | 23 |
| Hingham .............. | | | |
| Dedham ............... | | | 17 |
| Braintree .............. | 20 | 16 | 36 |
| Hull .................. | 7 | 4 | 11 |
| Medfield .............. | 3 | 1 | 4 |
| Milton ................ | 15 | 4 | 19 |
| Wrentham ............. | 13 | 3 | 16 |
| Brookline ............. | 10 | 7 | 17 |
| Needham .............. | 1 | 0 | 1 |
| Medway ............... | 4 | 3 | 7 |
| Bellingham ............ | 1 | 1 | 2 |
| Walpole .............. | 0 | 1 | 1 |
| Stoughton ............. | 6 | 2 | 8 |
| Chelsea ............... | | | 35 |
| Middlesex | | | |
| Charlestown ........... | | | |
| Watertown ............ | 7 | 5 | 12 |
| Medford .............. | 33 | 7 | 34 |
| Cambridge ............ | 33 | 23 | 56 |
| Concord .............. | 10 | 5 | 15 |
| Sudbury .............. | 9 | 5 | 14 |
| Woburn ............... | 9 | 8 | 17 |
| Reading .............. | 14 | 6 | 20 |
| Malden ............... | 16 | 5 | 21 |
| Groton ............... | 7 | 7 | 14 |
| Billerica .............. | 3 | 5 | 8 |
| Chelmsford ............ | | | 8 |
| Marlborough .......... | 3 | 3 | 6 |
| Dunstable ............. | | | |
| Sherburne ............. | 3 | 0 | 3 |
| Stowe ................. | | | |
| Newtown .............. | 10 | 3 | 13 |
| Framingham .......... | | | |
| Dracut ................ | | | |

1 *Mass. Hist. Soc. Colls.*, Second Series, III, 95-97.

## APPENDIX C—*Continued*

| County and Towns | Males | Females | Total |
|---|---|---|---|
| **Middlesex** (continued) | | | |
| Weston ............... | 8 | 2 | 10 |
| Lexington ............ | 13 | 11 | 24 |
| Littleton .............. | 3 | 5 | 8 |
| Hopkinton ............ | | | 15 |
| Holliston ............. | | | |
| Stoneham ............ | 6 | 2 | 8 |
| Wastford ............. | | | 5 |
| Bedford .............. | 2 | 4 | 6 |
| Wilmington .......... | 4 | 3 | 7 |
| Townsend ............ | 2 | 1 | 3 |
| Towksbury ........... | 1 | 1 | 2 |
| Acton ................ | 1 | 0 | 1 |
| Waltham ............. | 2 | 2 | 4 |
| Shirley ............... | 1 | 0 | 1 |
| Pepperell ............ | | | |
| Natick ............... | 0 | 3 | 3 |
| Lincoln .............. | 16 | 7 | 23 |
| **Essex** | | | |
| Salem ................ | 47 | 36 | 83 |
| Ipswich .............. | | 62 | |
| Newbury ............. | 34 | 16 | 50 |
| Lynn ................. | | | |
| Gloucester ........... | | | 61 |
| Rowley .............. | 10 | 2 | 12 |
| Salisbury ............ | 6 | 1 | 7 |
| Wanham ............. | | | 16 |
| Manchester .......... | 1 | 5 | 6 |
| Haverhill ............ | 8 | 8 | 16 |
| Andover ............. | 28 | 14 | 42 |
| Marblehead .......... | | | |
| Fopsfield ............ | 4 | 1 | 5 |
| Amesbury ............ | 3 | 2 | 5 |
| Beverly .............. | 12 | 16 | 28 |
| Bradford ............. | 3 | 2 | 5 |
| Boxford .............. | 4 | 4 | 8 |
| Middleton ........... | 9 | 3 | 12 |
| Danvers ............. | 9 | 12 | 21 |
| **Worcester** | | | |
| Lancaster ............ | 4 | 1 | 5 |
| Mendon .............. | | | |
| Brookfield ........... | | | 8 |

# APPENDIX C—*Continued*

| County and Towns | Males | Females | Total |
|---|---|---|---|
| Worcester (continued) | | | |
| Oxford | 3 | 1 | 4 |
| Worcester | 4 | 4 | 8 |
| Leicester | 5 | 1 | 6 |
| Rutland | 1 | 2 | 3 |
| Sutton | | | 3 |
| Westborough | 4 | 2 | 6 |
| Uxbridge | | | 7 |
| Southborough | 0 | 1 | 1 |
| Shrewsbury | 3 | 1 | 4 |
| Lunenburgh | 6 | 2 | 8 |
| Dudley | 1 | 1 | 2 |
| Harvard | | | |
| Grafton | | | 6 |
| Upton | | | |
| Hardwick | | | |
| Bolton | 2 | 1 | 3 |
| Sturbridge | 2 | 2 | 4 |
| Holden | | | |
| Western | 2 | 1 | 3 |
| Douglas | | | |
| N. Braintree | | | |
| Spencer | 2 | 1 | 3 |
| Leominster | 1 | 1 | 2 |
| Rutland-Dist. | | | 2 |
| Hampshire | | | |
| Springfield | 22 | 5 | 27 |
| Hadley | 13 | 5 | 18 |
| Westfield | 15 | 4 | 19 |
| Hatfield | 5 | 4 | 9 |
| Deerfield | | | |
| Northampton | | | |
| Northfield | | | |
| Sunderland | | | |
| Brinfield | | | |
| Blandford | | | |
| Pelham | | | |
| Palmer | 1 | 0 | 1 |
| Southampton | | | |
| South Hadley | | | |
| Greenfield | | | |
| New Salem | | | |
| Montague | | | |

# APPENDIX C—*Continued*

| County and Towns | Males | Females | Total |
|---|---|---|---|
| Hampshire (continued) | | | |
|   Granville | | | |
|   Greenwich | | | |
|   Sheffield | | | |
|   Stockbridge | | | |
| Plymouth | | | |
|   Plymouth | 22 | 21 | 43 |
|   Scituate | | | |
|   Duxborough | | | |
|   Marshfield | 17 | 8 | 25 |
|   Bridgewater | | | |
|   Middleboro | | | 12 |
|   Rochester | | | |
|   Plymton | 6 | 3 | 9 |
|   Pembroke | 6 | 4 | 10 |
|   Abington | 5 | 2 | 7 |
|   Kingston | 3 | 3 | 6 |
|   Hanover | 8 | 9 | 17 |
|   Halifax | 2 | 2 | 4 |
|   Wareham | | | |
| Bristol | | | |
|   Taunton | | | 27 |
|   Rehoboth | | | |
|   Dartmouth | | | 34 |
|   Swanzey | | | |
|   Freetown | 14 | 7 | 21 |
|   Attleborough | 7 | 3 | 10 |
|   Norton | | | |
|   Dighton | 9 | 9 | 18 |
|   Easton | 2 | 1 | 3 |
|   Raynham | | | |
|   Berkeley | 7 | 2 | 9 |
| Barnstable | | | |
|   Barnstable | 18 | 15 | 33 |
|   Sandwich | 4 | 4 | 8 |
|   Yarmouth | | | |
|   Eastham | 6 | 5 | 11 |
|   Falmouth | | | 10 |
|   Chatham | | | |
|   Truro | | | |
|   Provincetown | | | |
|   Harwich | 8 | 6 | 14 |

# APPENDIX C—*Concluded*

| County and Towns | Males | Females | Total |
|---|---|---|---|
| **Dukes** | | | |
| Edgarton .............. | | | |
| Tisbury .............. | | | |
| Chilmark .............. | 3 | 4 | 7 |
| **Nantucket** | | | |
| Sherburne ............. | | | |
| **York** | | | |
| York .................. | | | 24 |
| Kittery .............. | 18 | 17 | 35 |
| Wells ................ | 12 | 4 | 16 |
| Falmouth ............. | 16 | 5 | 21 |
| Scarborough .......... | 7 | 4 | 11 |
| Berwick .............. | 14 | 8 | 22 |
| Biddleford ............ | | | |
| Arundel .............. | 2 | 1 | 3 |
| N. Yarmouth .......... | 2 | 1 | 3 |
| Brunswick ............ | 2 | 1 | 3 |
| Georgeton ............ | | | 7 |
| Newcastle ............ | | | |
| Gorhamtown .......... | 2 | 0 | 2 |

# APPENDIX D

## Distribution of Negroes in Rhode Island by Towns, 1748-1749 [1]

| Townships | Whites | Negroes | Indians |
|---|---|---|---|
| Newport ..................... | 5,335 | 110 | 68 |
| Providence ................. | 3,177 | 225 | 50 |
| Portsmouth ................. | 807 | 134 | 51 |
| Warwick .................... | 1,513 | 176 | 93 |
| Westerly ................... | 1,701 | 59 | 49 |
| New Shoreham .............. | 260 | 20 | 20 |
| North Kingstown ........... | 1,665 | 184 | 86 |
| South Kingstown ........... | 1,405 | 380 | 193 |
| Greenwich ................. | 956 | 61 | 27 |
| Jamestown ................. | 284 | 110 | 26 |
| Smithfield ................. | 400 | 30 | 20 |
| Scituate ................... | 1,210 | 16 | 6 |
| Gloucester ................. | 1,194 | 8 | |
| Charlestown ............... | 641 | 58 | 303 |
| West Greenwich ............ | 757 | 8 | 1 |
| Coventry .................. | 769 | 16 | 7 |
| Exeter .................... | 1,103 | 63 | 8 |
| Middletown ................ | 586 | 76 | 18 |
| Bristol ................... | 928 | 128 | 13 |
| Tiverton .................. | 842 | 99 | 99 |
| Little Compton ............ | 1,004 | 62 | 86 |
| Warren ................... | 600 | 50 | 30 |
| Cumberland ............... | 802 | 4 | |
| Richmond ................. | 500 | 5 | 3 |
| Total ................ | 28,439 | 3,077 | 1,257 |

1 *R. I. Col. Recs.*, I, 271.

# APPENDIX E

## Distribution of Negroes in Connecticut, by Towns, in 1774 [1]

| Counties | Towns | White | Black |
|----------|-------|-------|-------|
| Hartford | Bolton ................... | 994 | 7 |
| | Chatham ................ | 2,369 | 28 |
| | Golchester ............. | 3,057 | 201 |
| | East Haddam .......... | 2,743 | 65 |
| | East Windsor .......... | 2,961 | 38 |
| | Enfield ................ | 1,353 | 7 |
| | Farmington ............. | 5,963 | 106 |
| | Glastenbury ............ | 1,992 | 79 |
| | Haddam ................ | 1,713 | 13 |
| | Hartford ................ | 4,881 | 150 |
| | Hebron ................ | 2,285 | 52 |
| | Middletown ............. | 4,680 | 198 |
| | Simsbury .............. | 3,671 | 29 |
| | Somers ................ | 1,024 | 3 |
| | Stafford ................ | 1,333 | 1 |
| | Suffield ................ | 1,980 | 37 |
| | Tolland ................ | 1,247 | 15 |
| | Wethersfield ............ | 3,347 | 142 |
| | Willington ............. | 1,000 | 1 |
| | Windsor ................ | 2,082 | 43 |
| New Haven | Branford ................ | 1,938 | 113 |
| | Derby .................. | 1,819 | 70 |
| | Durham ................ | 1,031 | 45 |
| | Guilford ................ | 2,846 | 84 |
| | Milford ................ | 1,965 | 162 |
| | New Haven ............. | 8,022 | 273 |
| | Wallingford ............. | 4,777 | 138 |
| | Waterbury .............. | 3,498 | 38 |
| New London | Groton ................ | 3,488 | 360 |
| | Lyme ................... | 3,860 | 228 |
| | Killingsworth ........... | 1,957 | 33 |
| | New London ............ | 5,366 | 522 |
| | Norwich ................ | 7,032 | 295 |
| | Preston ................ | 2,255 | 83 |
| | Saybrook .............. | 2,628 | 59 |
| | Stonington ............. | 4,956 | 456 |

1 *Conn. Col. Recs.*, XIV, 485-491.

# APPENDIX E—*Concluded*

| Counties | Towns | White | Black |
|---|---|---|---|
| Fairfield | Danbury | 2,473 | 53 |
| | Fairfield | 4,544 | 319 |
| | Greenwich | 2,654 | 122 |
| | New Fairfield | 1,288 | 20 |
| | Newtown | 2,168 | 61 |
| | Norwalk | 2,243 | 145 |
| | Redding | 1,189 | 45 |
| | Ridgefield | 1,673 | 35 |
| | Stamford | 3,503 | 60 |
| | Stratford | 5,201 | 354 |
| Windham | Canterbury | 2,392 | 52 |
| | Coventry | 2,032 | 24 |
| | Pomfret | 2,241 | 65 |
| | Killingly | 3,439 | 47 |
| | Lebanon | 3,841 | 119 |
| | Mansfield | 2,443 | 23 |
| | Plainfield | 1,479 | 83 |
| | Ashford | 2,228 | 13 |
| | Voluntown | 1,476 | 35 |
| | Union | 512 | 2 |
| | Windham | 3,437 | 91 |
| | Woodstock | 1,974 | 80 |
| Litchfield | Barkhemsted | 250 | 62 |
| | Canaan | 1,573 | |
| | Colebrook | 150 | |
| | Cornwall | 957 | 17 |
| | Goshen | 1,098 | 13 |
| | Hartland | 500 | |
| | Harwinton | 1,015 | 3 |
| | Kent | 1,922 | 74 |
| | Litchfield | 2,509 | 45 |
| | New Hartford | 985 | 16 |
| | New Milford | 2,742 | 34 |
| | Norfolk | 966 | 3 |
| | Salisbury | 1,936 | 44 |
| | Sharon | 1,986 | 26 |
| | Torrington | 843 | 2 |
| | Westmoreland | 1,922 | |
| | Winchester | 327 | 12 |
| | Woodbury | 5,224 | 89 |
| | Total | 191,392 | 6,464 |

# APPENDIX F

## Preponderance of Males among Negro Population in Massachusetts by Counties, in 1764 [1]

| County | Total Population | NEGROES AND MULATTOES | | | INDIANS | | |
|---|---|---|---|---|---|---|---|
| | | Male | Female | Total | Male | Female | Total |
| Suffolk ....... | 36,410 | 814 | 537 | 1,351 | 38 | 34 | 72 |
| Essex ........ | 43,751 | 624 | 446 | 1,070 | 5 | 3 | 8 |
| Middlesex .... | 33,732 | 485 | 375 | 860 | 16 | 29 | |
| Hampshire ... | 17,245 | 121 | 73 | 194 | | | |
| Worcester .... | 30,412 | 138 | 114 | 252 | 15 | 19 | |
| Plymouth .... | 22,256 | 243 | 219 | 462 | 75 | 148 | |
| Barnstable ... | 12,464 | 135 | 96 | 231 | 223 | 293 | |
| Bristol ....... | 18,076 | 165 | 128 | 293 | 41 | 59 | |
| York ........ | 10,739 | 120 | 105 | 225 | 95 | | |
| Cumberland .. | 7,474 | 55 | 40 | 95 | | | |
| Lincoln ...... | 3,644 | 17 | 7 | 24 | | | |
| Dukes ....... | 2,719 | 25 | 21 | 46 | 124 | 189 | |
| Nantucket ... | 3,526 | 24 | 20 | 44 | 83 | 66 | |
| Berks ........ | 3,250 | 50 | 38 | 88 | 108 | 113 | |
| Total ..... | 223,841 | 3,016 | 2,219 | 5,235 | 728 | 953 | 80 |

1 United States Department of Commerce, Bureau of the Census, *A Century of Population Growth*, pp. 158-161.

# APPENDIX G

## Burials and Baptisms in Boston, 1701-1752 [1]

| Year | Whites | Blacks | Total | Baptisms |
|---|---|---|---|---|
| 1701 ............. | 146 | a | 146 | |
| 1702 b ............ | 441 | | 441 | |
| 1703 ............. | 159 | | 159 | |
| 1704 ............. | 203 | 17 | 220 | |
| 1705 ............. | 238 | 44 | 282 | |
| 1706 ............. | 216 | 45 | 261 | |
| 1707 ............. | 225 | 38 | 263 | |
| 1708 ............. | 245 | 46 | 291 | |
| 1709 ............. | 295 | 82 | 377 | |
| 1710 ............. | 248 | 47 | 295 | |
| 1711 ............. | 305 | 58 | 363 | |
| 1712 ............. | 270 | 46 | 316 | |
| 1713 ............. | 380 | 100 | 480 | |
| 1714 ............. | 340 | 73 | 413 | |
| 1715 ............. | 281 | 55 | 336 | |
| 1716 ............. | 284 | 71 | 355 | |
| 1717 ............. | 371 | 80 | 451 | |
| 1718 ............. | 334 | 46 | 380 | |
| 1719 ............. | 253 | 51 | 304 | |
| 1720 ............. | 261 | 68 | 329 | |
| 1721 c ............ | 968 | 134 | 1102 | |
| 1722 ............. | 240 | 33 | 273 | |
| 1723 ............. | 342 | 71 | 413 | |
| 1724 ............. | 360 | 47 | 407 | |
| 1725 ............. | 268 | 56 | 324 | |
| 1726 ............. | 290 | 53 | 343 | |
| 1727 ............. | 373 | 106 | 479 | |
| 1728 ............. | 385 | 113 | 498 | |
| Total ........ | 8,721 | 1,580 | 10,301 | |

a No estimate " published of the Number of Blacks 'till the year 1704."

b " This year the Small Pox went thro' the town."

c " This year the Town was visited with the Small Pox, and 844 died of that Distemper."

1 *Boston Gazette and Weekly Advertiser*, January 23, 1753.

# APPENDIX G—*Concluded*

| Year | Whites | Blacks | Total | Baptisms |
|------|--------|--------|-------|----------|
| 1729 d ............ | 471 | 99 | 570 | |
| 1730 e ............ | 749 | 160 | 909 | |
| 1731 ............ | 318 | 90 | 408 | 563 |
| 1732 ............ | 400 | 99 | 499 | 526 |
| 1733 ............ | 374 | 84 | 458 | 526 |
| 1734 ............ | 440 | 88 | 528 | 536 |
| 1735 ............ | 370 | 85 | 455 | 579 |
| 1736 ............ | 532 | 85 | 617 | 514 |
| 1737 ............ | 516 | 91 | 607 | 519 |
| 1738 ............ | 476 | 100 | 576 | 530 |
| 1739 ............ | 468 | 86 | 554 | 499 |
| 1740 ............ | 568 | 136 | 704 | 591 |
| 1741 ............ | 455 | 100 | 555 | 680 |
| 1742 ............ | 455 | 72 | 517 | 716 |
| 1743 ............ | 536 | 84 | 620 | 585 |
| 1744 ............ | 425 | 72 | 497 | 566 |
| 1745 ............ | 706 | 74 | 780 | 573 |
| 1746 f ............ | 479 | 99 | 578 | 480 |
| 1747 ............ | 710 | 67 | 777 | 492 |
| 1748 ............ | 626 | 114 | 740 | 504 |
| 1749 ............ | 581 | 96 | 677 | 493 |
| 1750 ............ | 507 | 97 | 604 | 533 |
| 1751 ............ | 548 | 76 | 624 | 488 |
| 1752 g ............ | 893 | 116 | 1,009 | 357 |
| Total ........ | 12,593 | 2,270 | 14,863 | 11,850 |

d "The measles spread through the Town this year, which was exceedingly favorable, few dying of the same."

e "The Small Pox spreads in the Town this year, and 400-odd die of the same."

f "About this time an epidemical Fever prevails, brought from *Cape-Breton*, which proved very mortal."

g "This year the Small Pox spread thro' the Town, 7669 had it, of which died 569."

N. B. "By the above list of Baptisms for 21 years past, the Burials have exceeded by one thousand five hundred and thirty-four."

# APPENDIX H

## List of 162 leading slave-holding families in colonial New England

### (colony of Connecticut)

| Name | Town |
|------|------|
| 1. Hoadley, William. | Branford |
| 2. Buell, N. | Coventry |
| 3. Buell, Peter. | Coventry |
| 4. Bassett (Squire). | Derby |
| 5. Tomlinson, Agar. | Derby |
| 6. Wooster, Colonel. | Derby |
| 7. Chauncey, Reverend Nathaniel. | Durham |
| 8. Todd, Reverend Jonathan. | East Guilford |
| 9. Elliot, Reverend Joseph. | Guilford |
| 10. Edwards, Reverend Jonathan. | Hartford |
| 11. Hopkins, Edward (Governor). | Hartford |
| 12. Pantry, John. | Hartford |
| 13. Richard, Captain Thomas. | Hartford |
| 14. Tolcott, John. | Hartford |
| 15. Woodbridge, Timothy. | Hartford |
| 16. Wyllys, George. | Hartford |

---

1 *Conn. Archives: Court Papers, 1700-1705*, I, 373.

2 Dimock, *op. cit.*, p. 120.

3 *Ibid.*

4 Platt, *op. cit.*, p. 331.

5 *Ibid.*, p. 330.

6 *Ibid.*, p. 331.

7 *Connecticut Magazine*, V, No. VI, p. 320.

8 *Ibid.*, p. 323.

9 *Ibid.*, p. 320.

10 Earle, *Customs and Fashions in Colonial New England*, p. 91.

11 *Conn. Magazine*, V, 320.

12 Steiner, *op. cit.*, p. 20.

13 *Conn. Col. Recs.*, IV, 471 ; Steiner, *op. cit.*, pp. 17-18.

14 *Conn. Magazine*, V, 320.

15 *Ibid.*

16 "Wyllys Papers," *Conn. His. Soc. Colls.*, XXI, 456.

## APPENDIX H—*Continued*

### (colony of Connecticut)

| *Name* | *Town* |
|---|---|
| 1. Elliott, Reverend Jared. | Killingsworth |
| 2. Marsh, Colonel Ebenezer. | Litchfield |
| 3. Talmadge, Colonel Benjamin. | Litchfield |
| 4. Wolcott, Oliver. | Litchfield |
| 5. Stocking, Joseph. | Middletown |
| 6. Andrews, Ephraim. | New Hartford |
| 7. Davenport, John. | New Haven |
| 8. Eaton, Theophilus. | New Haven |
| 9. Ingersoll, Jared. | New Haven |
| 10. Stiles, Reverend Ezra. | New Haven |
| 11. Rogers, James. | New London |
| 13. Walworth, John. | New London |
| 14. Whiting, John. | New London |
| 15. Thatcher, Partridge. | New London |
| 16. Huntington, Nathaniel. | Norwich |
| 17. Lothrops (The). | Norwich |

1 *Conn. Magazine*, V, 323.

2 White, *History of Litchfield*, p. 152.

3 *Ibid.*

4 *Ibid.*

5 "Wyllys Papers," *loc. cit.*, XXI, 456.

6 *Conn. Archives: Crimes and Misdemeanors, 1737-1755*, IV, 71-73.

7 *Conn. Magazine*, V, 320.

8 *Conn. Col. Recs.*, IV, 77n..

9 "Ingersoll Papers," *New Haven Historical Society Papers*, IX, 221.

10 Stiles, *Literary Diary*, II, 272; *Col. Soc. of Mass., Transactions, 1897-1898* (Boston, 1902), V, 238.

11 Steiner, *op. cit.*, p. 19.

12 *Conn. Magazine*, V, 321.

13 Weeden, *Economic and Social History of New England*, II, 690-691.

14 *New London Gazette*, Friday, December 2, 1768.

15 *Two Centuries of New Milford, Connecticut*, pp. 102-103.

16 *Conn. Archives*, CXXXV, Doc. 31, p. 30.

17 Caulkins, *op. cit.*, p. 185.

## APPENDIX H—*Continued*

### (colony of Connecticut)

| *Name* | *Town* |
|---|---|
| 1. Isaacs, Benjamin. | Norwalk |
| 2. Worthington, Reverend William. | Saybrook |
| 3. Huntington, Samuel. | Warwick |
| 4. Clark, Deacon. | Waterbury |
| 5. Wadsworth, Colonel Jeremiah. | West Hartford |
| 6. Griswold, Jacob. | Weathersfield |
| 7. Wolcott, Samuel. | Weathersfield |
| 8. Malbone, John. | Windham |
| 9. Chapman, Samuel. | Windsor |
| 10. Wolcott, Henry, Jr. | Windsor |

1 National Society of the Daughters of the American Revolution, *The Colonial and Revolutionary Homes of Wilton, Norwalk*, etc., p. 45.

2 *Conn. Magazine*, V, 320.

3 Caulkins, *op. cit.*, 185.

4 Bronson, *History of Waterbury, Connecticut*, p. 323.

5 Scaeva, *op. cit.*, p. 40.

6 Steiner, *op. cit.*, p. 26.

7 *Col. Soc. of Mass., Transactions*, VI, 324.

8 Preston, *op. cit.*, p. 116.

9 *Conn. Col. Recs.*, VIII, 246.

10 Steiner, *op. cit.*, p. 20.

## APPENDIX H—*Continued*

(colony of Massachusetts)

| Name | Town |
|---|---|
| 1. Greenleaf, Joseph. | Abington |
| 2. Beauchamp, Magdalene. | Boston |
| 3. Bowdoin, James. | Boston |
| 4. Boyleston, Dr. Zabdiel. | Boston |
| 5. Bromfield, Colonel Henry. | Boston |
| 6. Carver, Henry. | Boston |
| 7. Cheever, Joshua. | Boston |
| 8. Cobbett, Dr. John. | Boston |
| 9. Coleman, John. | Boston |
| 10. Cunningham, Nathaniel. | Boston |
| 11. Dean, Thomas. | Boston |
| 12. Fanueil, Andrew. | Boston |
| 13. Fanueil, Peter (his nephew). | Boston |
| 14. Fleet, Thomas. | Boston |
| 15. Foster, Miles. | Boston |
| 16. Gardner, Samuel. | Boston |
| 17. Hobby, Sir Charles. | Boston |

1 Hobart, *A History of Abington, Massachusetts*, p. 255.

2 *J. H. R. of Mass., 1715-1770*, I, 52.

3 "Bowdoin and Temple Papers," *Mass. Hist. Soc. Colls.*, Sixth Series, IV, 393-394.

4 Drake, *History and Antiquities of Boston*, II, 562.

5 Brown, *John Hancock*, pp. 111-112.

6 *Mass. Hist. Soc. Colls., Proceedings, 1875-1876*, XIV, 101.

7 *Boston Weekly Post Boy*, June 26, 1749.

8 *Continental Journal and Weekly Advertiser*, March 12, 1777.

9 *Col. Soc. of Mass., Transactions, 1899-1900*, VI, 86-87.

10 *Mass. Archives: Domestic Relations, 1643-1774*, IX, 451-452.

11 *Boston Town Records, 1660-1701*, p. 5.

12 *New England Weekly Journal*, Feb. 14, 1738.

13 *Col. Soc. of Mass., Transactions*, I, 367-368.

14 *Ibid., Transactions, 1922-1924*, XXV, 253-254.

15 *E. C. C. R.*, VII, 368.

16 *Ibid.*, p. 410.

17 *Col. Soc. of Mass., Transactions, 1666-1717*, III, 151-152n.

## APPENDIX H—*Continued*

### (colony of Massachusetts)

| *Name* | *Town* |
|---|---|
| 1. Hancock, John. | Boston |
| 2. Hatch, Jabez. | Boston |
| 3. Holyoke, Reverend Edward. | Boston |
| 4. Hutchinson, Thomas. | Boston |
| 5. Mather, Cotton. | Boston |
| 6. Mather, Increase. | Boston |
| 7. Otis, James. | Boston |
| 8. Pemberton, Thomas. | Boston |
| 9. Rowe, John. | Boston |
| 10. Royall, Isaac. | Boston |
| 11. Saffin, John. | Boston |
| 12. Sewall, Samuel. | Boston |
| 13. Staniford, John. | Boston |
| 14. Thair, Deborah. | Boston |
| 15. Vassal, Leonard. | Boston |

1 Brown, *John Hancock*, pp. 111-112.

2 *Boston Weekly News Letter*, Aug. 4, 1768.

3 "Diary of Reverend Edward Holyoke, 1709-1768," *Holyoke Diaries, 1709-1856*, pp. 17, 18, 21-22, 23.

4 *Mass. Archives*, VI, 308.

5 "Diary of Cotton Mather," *Mass. Hist. Soc. Coll.*, Seventh Series, VIII, Pt. II, pp. 547-562.

6 Murdock, *Increase Mather*, p. 384.

7 *Boston Town Records*, XXX, 90.

8 *Col. Soc. of Mass., Transactions*, III, 154-155.

9 Brown, *op. cit.*, p. 55.

10 *J. H. R. of Mass.*, XV, 225.

11 *Mass. Archives*, IX, 153.

12 "Diary of Samuel Sewall," *Mass. Hist. Soc. Colls.*, VI, 296, 394.

13 *Boston Gazette and Weekly Advertiser*, April 9, 1754.

14 "Diary of Samuel Sewall," VI, 22.

15 *J. H. R. of Mass.*, IV, 139-140; Winsor, *Memorial History of Boston*, II, 594.

# APPENDIX H—*Continued*

## (colony of Massachusetts)

| *Name* | *Town* |
|---|---|
| 1. Wadsworth, Benjamin. | Boston |
| 2. Warren, Joseph. | Boston |
| 3. Warren, Major Joseph. | Boston |
| 4. Webb, John. | Boston |
| 5. Winthrop, Adam. | Boston |
| 6. Winthrop, Waite. | Boston |
| 7. Codman, John. | Charlestown |
| 8. Slocum, John. | Dartmouth |
| 9. Childs, Timothy. | Deerfield. |
| 10. Hinsdale, Colonel Ebenezer. | Deerfield |
| 11. Oxenbridge, Reverend John. | Deerfield |
| 12. Wells, Ebenezer. | Deerfield |
| 13. Wells, Justice John. | Deerfield |
| 14. Wells, Justice Thomas. | Deerfield |
| 15. Hutchinson, Richard. | Essex County |
| 16. Price, Theodore. | Essex County |
| 17. Price, Walter. | Essex County |
| 18. Whipple, John. | Ipswich |

1 *Harvard College Records*, III, 461.
2 "Wyllys Papers," *loc. cit.*, XXI, 456.
3 *Boston Town Records*, XXVIII, 2.
4 *Suffolk Deeds*, XIV, Liber I, 262.
5 *Boston Town Records*, XXVIII, 31.
6 *Mass. Hist. Soc. Colls.*, Second Series, II, 166n.
7 *Journal of Negro History*, VII, 154.
8 Sheldon, George, *Negro Slavery in Old Deerfield*, p. 53.
9 Sheldon, *op. cit.*, p. 51.
10 *Ibid.*, p. 49.
11 *Ibid.*, p. 53.
12 *Ibid.*
13 *Ibid.*, p. 52.
14 *Ibid.*
15 *E. C. C. R.*, VIII, 434.
16 *Ibid.*, V, 65.
17 *Ibid.*, p. 167.
18 Moore, *op. cit.*, pp. 113-114.

## APPENDIX H—*Continued*

### (colony of Massachusetts)

| *Name* | *Town* |
| --- | --- |
| 1. Johnson, Samuel. | Kittery |
| 2. Muzzey, Benjamin. | Lexington |
| 3. Pepperell, Sir William. | Lexington |
| 4. Brown, Enoch. | Middleboro |
| 5. Coffin, Joseph. | Newbury |
| 6. Coffin, Nathaniel. | Newbury |
| 7. Gerrish, Moses. | Newbury |
| 8. Greenleaf, Richard. | Newbury |
| 9. Mogridge, Samuel. | Newbury |
| 10. Rolfe, Henry. | Newbury |
| 11. Short, Henry. | Newbury |
| 12. Maverick, Samuel. | Noddles Island |
| 13. Edwards, Rev. Jonathan. | Northampton |
| 14. Ann "relict" [relative] of Governor Bradstreet | Salem |
| 15. Dole, Richard. | Salem |
| 16. Greene, Reverend Joseph. | Salem |
| 17. Putnam, Nathaniel. | Salem |
| 18. Wolcott, Josiah. | Salem |
| 19. Prout, John. | Salem |
| 20. Alden, John. | Salem |
| 21. Webb, Reverend Nathan. | Uxbridge |

---

1 *Boston Weekly Post Boy*, Sept. 18, 25; Oct. 2, 9, 16, 1749.

2 Drake, *History and Antiquities of Boston*, II, 574n.

3 Parsons, *Life of Sir William Pepperell*, p. 28.

4 "Bowdoin and Temple Papers," *loc. cit.*, Sixth Series, IV, 393-394.

5 Coffin, *Sketch of Newbury*, p. 337.

6 *Ibid.*    7 *Ibid.*, p. 188.

8 *Ibid.*, p. 241.    9 *Ibid.*

10 *Ibid.*    11 *E. C. C. R.*, V, 431.

12 *Mass. Hist. Soc. Colls.*, Third Series, III, 237.

13 Earle, *Customs and Fashions*, p. 91.

14 Felt, *Annals of Salem*, II, 415.

15 *E. C. C. R.*, V, 316.

16 "Diary of Rev. Joseph Greene of Salem Village, 1700-1715," *Essex Institute Collections*, p. 79.

17 Felt, *Salem*, II, 476.

18 *Ibid.*, p. 480.

19 Moore, *Notes*, p. 185.

20 *Mass. Archives. Domestic Relations, 1643-1774*, IX, 448-450.

21 *Ibid.*

# APPENDIX H—*Continued*

## (colony of Rhode Island)

| *Name* | *Town* |
|---|---|
| 1. Northrup, Immanuel. | East Greenwich |
| 2. Pierce, William. | East Greenwich |
| 3. Potter, E. R. | East Greenwich |
| 4. Wells, James, Jr. | Hopkinton |
| 5. Hazard, Colonel Thomas. | Narragansett |
| 6. McSparran, Reverend James. | Narragansett |
| 7. Coddington, John. | Newport |
| 8. Hazard, Robert. | Newport |
| 9. Hopkins, Rev. Samuel. | Newport |
| 10. Hopkins, Stephen. | Newport |
| 11. Malbone, Godfrey. | Newport |
| 12. Redwood, Abraham. | Newport |
| 13. Wanton, Governor Joseph. | Newport |
| 14. Jones, Daniel. | North Kingstown |
| 15. Gardner, Christopher. | North Kingstown |
| 16. Hammond, William. | North Kingstown |
| 17. Updike, Lodowich. | North Kingstown |
| 18. Updike, Colonel. | North Kingstown |
| 19. Angel, John. | Providence |
| 20. Bent, John. | Providence |
| 21. Bowen, Jabez. | Providence |

1 Updike, *op. cit.*, I, 214.          2 *Ibid.*

3 *Ibid.*

4 *Correspondence of the Colonial Governors of R. I.*, I, xxxvii; *Rhode Island Historical Tracts*, No. 10, pp. 73-74.

5 Updike, *op. cit.*, I, 208.          6 *Ibid.*, II, 182-183.

7 *R. I. Hist. Tracts*, No. 10, pp. 73-74.

8 Updike, *op. cit.*, I, 527, 528.

9 Walker, *Ten New England Leaders*, p. 350.

10 Jones, Rufus, *op. cit.*, p. 165 (note 2).

11 *R. I. Hist. Soc. Coll.*, XVI, 116.

12 Donnan, III, 118-131n., 140n.; *D. A. B.*, XV, 444-445.

13 *Corresp. of the Col. Govs. of R. I.*, I, xxvii.

14 Jones, *op. cit.*, p. 158n.

15 *Ibid.*          16 *Ibid.*

17 *R. I. Hist. Tracts*, No. 10, pp. 73-74.

18 Updike, *op. cit.*, I, 216.

19 *Early Records of the Town of Providence: Will Book*, No. 2, XVI, 163.

20 *R. I. Hist. Tracts, ut supra.*

21 *Early Records of the Town of Providence*, IX, 65.

# APPENDIX H—*Continued*

(colony of Rhode Island)

| *Name* | *Town* |
|---|---|
| 1. Brown, James. | Providence |
| 2. Brown, John. | Providence |
| 3. Brown, Joseph. | Providence |
| 4. Brown, Moses. | Providence |
| 5. Brown, Nicholas. | Providence |
| 6. Brown, Obadiah. | Providence |
| 7. Burke, James. | Providence |
| 8. Crawford, Gideon. | Providence |
| 9. Crawford, William. | Providence |
| 10. Mathewson, John. | Providence |
| 11. Robinson, William. | Providence |
| 12. Shoemaker, Jacob. | Providence |
| 13. Talbot, Silas, Esq. | Providence |
| 14. Carpenter, Ann (Heirs of). | South Kensington |
| 15. Champlain, Robert. | South Kensington |
| 16. Cooke, Governor. | South Kensington |
| 17. Gardener, Benjamin. | South Kensington |

---

1 *Letter Book of James Brown*, p. xi.

2 Jones, *op. cit.*, p. 165n.

3 *Letter Book of James Brown*, p. xi.

4 Jones, Augustine, " Moses Brown," *R. I. Hist. Soc. Papers*, pp. 14-15.

5 *Letter Book of James Brown*, p. xi.

6 *Ibid.*; Weeden, *Early Rhode Island*, p. 263.

7 *Early Records of the Town of Providence*, VI, 270-271, 272.

8 *Ibid.*

9 *Ibid.*; *Will Book*, No. 2, XVI, 154.

10 *Early Records of the Town of Providence*, XVI, 10, 11.

11 Updike, *op. cit.*, I, 216.

12 Staples, *Annals of Providence*, pp. 236-237.

13 Updike, *ut supra*.

14 *Early Records of the Town of Providence*, VI, 270, 271, 272.

15 *Ibid.*

16 *Ibid.*

17 Jones, Rufus, *op. cit.*, p. 158 (note 2).

## APPENDIX H—*Concluded*

### (colony of Rhode Island)

| *Name* | *Town* |
|---|---|
| 1. Hazard, " College Tom ". | South Kingstown |
| 2. Rhodes, Nehemiah. | South Kingstown |
| 3. Saltonstall, Dudley. | South Kingstown |
| 4. Greene, William. | Warwick |
| 5. Austen, Jeremiah. | Westerley |
| 6. Babcock, Hezekiah. | Westerley |
| 7. Babcock, James. | Westerley |
| 8. Hazard, Robert. | West Greenwich |
| 9. Tillinghast, Benjamin. | West Greenwich |

1 Jones, Rufus, *ut supra.*

2 *R. I. Hist. Tracts*, No. 10, pp. 73-74.

3 Kimball, *Corresp. of the Col. Govs. of R. I.*, I, xxxvii.

4 Jones, Rufus, *ut supra.*

5 *Ibid.*

6 Updike, *op. cit.*, I, 216-217.

7 *Ibid.*, I, 216.

8 *Ibid.*, I, 527-528.

9 *Corresp. of the Col. Govs. of R. I.*, I, xxxvii.

# BIBLIOGRAPHY

## I. Primary Sources

### A. MANUSCRIPTS

*Connecticut Archives: Crimes and Misdemeanors, 1720-1773.* Vols. II-V invaluable for cases of fraud, rape and other crimes committed by and against Negroes. Mss. in State Library, Hartford, Connecticut.

——, *Court Papers, 1700-1705,* I. Mss. in State Library, Hartford.

——, *Miscellaneous, 1635-1789,* II. Mss. in State Library, Hartford, Connecticut. An indispensable repository of data of a social and legal nature respecting Negroes in Connecticut.

*Massachusetts Archives,* Vol. 142, p. 58. Important for Bill of 1777 for emancipation of the Negroes in Massachusetts. Ms. in Archives Division of State Library, Boston.

——, Vol. 212, pp. 130-131 contains the bill introduced to free slaves in Massachusetts in 1777. Pp. 132-133 contains the improved petition of Lancaster Hill, Prince Hall and other Negroes to the legislature in 1777. Mss. in State Library, Archives Department, Boston.

——, *Colonial 1774-1775.* Vol. VI.

——, *Domestic Relations, 1643-1774.* Vol. IX. Whole volume of great value for cases governing the Negro from civil point of view. Pp. 457-459 important for bill for abolition of slave trade in 1774.

——, *Hutchinson's Correspondence, 1770-1774.* Vol. XXVII, pp. 159-160 particularly important for Hutchinson's official views on slavery and his attitude toward abolition of the slave trade.

——, *Estates, etc., 1697-1742.* Vol. XVII. Ms. in State Library, Boston. Contains data on bequeathing of Negroes in wills.

——, *Witchcraft, 1656-1750.* Vol. 135. Important for witchcraft documents, especially Doc. 20, p. 78, giving testimony of Mary Black, a slave woman accused of witchcraft.

——, *Revolutionary Letters* (1778). Vol. 199, pp. 82-84, important for act of Rhode Island Legislature of 1778.

*Petition of John Winslow to the Governor and Council Sitting at Boston,* June, 1680. Photostat of Ms. in Library of Massachusetts Historical Society, Boston.

*Records of the General Court of Massachusetts, 1773-1774.* Ms. in State Library, Boston.

*Records of the General Association of Connecticut, 1738-1799.* I, pp. 1-2. Ms. property of Congregational House, Hartford, Connecticut. Photostat copy by Connecticut State Library.

*Society for the Propagation of the Gospel: Lambeth Palace Transcripts,* Series A, VII, VIII, XXI, XXII, XXIII, XXIV. Mss. L. C.

*Society for the Propagation of the Gospel: Lambeth Palace Transcripts, 1661-1778,* Series B, I, VII, VIII, IX, XVII, XX, XXIV, XXV. Mss. L. C.

Wheatley, Phillis. *On Atheism*. Unpublished Poem presented by Phillis
    Wheatley to Dr. Benjamin Rush of Philadelphia. Ms in Library Com-
    pany of Philadelphia.

B. NEWSPAPERS AND PERIODICALS

*Boston Chronicle* (1767-1770). Scattering issues.
*Boston Evening Post* (1735-1775). Scattering issues.
*Boston Exchange Advertiser.*
*Boston Gazette* (*1719-1798*), 1757-1759, 1769.
*Boston Gazette and Country Journal*, 1769-1771.
*Boston News Letter* (1704-1763). Photostatic copies to 1716.
*The Boston News Letter and the New England Chronicle* (1763).
*Boston Weekly Post Boy* (April, 1749-April, 1775). Scattering copies.
*Connecticut Courant and Weekly Intelligencer*. (Hartford, Connecticut)
    1775-1780. Scattering copies in New York Public Library.
*Connecticut Gazette.*
*Connecticut Gazette and Universal Intelligencer* (1776).
*Continental Journal and Weekly Advertiser*. (Boston) 1776-1779, 1780-1784.
*Essex Gazette* (Salem, Massachusetts) 1769-1771, Boston Public Library.
*New England Chronicle* or the *Essex Gazette:* changed to *New England
    Chronicle* (April, 1776) ; *New England Chronicle* and *The Universal
    Advertiser*.
*New England Weekly Journal* (1727-1738), New York Historical Society
    has scattering copies from January 4, 1731 to December 26, 1738.
*New Hampshire Gazette* (1756-1774).
*The New Hampshire Gazette or Historical Chronicle* (Portsmouth). Valu-
    able for slave advertisements, slave accidents, crimes, and advertisements
    showing preference for white apprentices.
*New London Gazette* (1768-1772). Scattering copies.
*Newport Mercury* (Newport, Rhode Island).

C. PUBLIC DOCUMENTS

1. *Connecticut*

*Acts and Charters of Connecticut*. New London: Timothy Greene, 1728.
*Acts and Laws of His Majesties Colony of Connecticut in New England*.
    Boston: Printed by Bartholemew Green and John Allen, 1702. Printed
    in 1702 and now first reissued. Hartford Press, n. d.
*Acts and Laws of His Majesties Colony of Connecticut in New England*.
    Reprinted and sold by Timothy Greene, Printer to his Honour the Gov-
    vernour and Council ... New London, 1729.
*Acts and Laws of the State Connecticut in America*. New London: Timothy
    Greene, 1784, pp. 144-145, 233, 368, 369.
*Acts and Laws of the State of Connecticut in America*. Hartford: Elisha
    Babcock, 1786.
*Acts and Laws of the State of Connecticut in America*. Hartford: Hudson
    and Goodwin, 1796. Contains all laws bearing upon slavery and slave
    trade in Connecticut down to 1792 but does not give date until 1788.

Bailey, Frederick W. ed. "Early Connecticut Marriages as found on Ancient Church Records Prior to 1800," *Published by Bureau of American Ancestry*, New Haven, 1896-1906, 7 books. Extremely valuable for marriage of slaves and free Negroes, also inter-marriage of Negroes with Indians and whites.

*Public Records of the Colony of Connecticut*, 1636-1776, 15 vols., Hartford, 1850-1890.

*Public Records of the State of Connecticut from October, 1776, to February, 1778, inclusive.* With the Journal of the Council of Safety from October 11, 1776 to May 6, 1778, inclusive and an appendix. Hartford, edited by Charles J. Hoadley, 1894, 1895, 1922.

*Public Statutes and Laws of the State of Connecticut as revised and enacted by the General Assembly in May, 1821.* Hartford: Goodrich, Huntington & Hopkins, 1821.

"Records of the Particular Court of Connecticut, 1639-1663," *Connecticut Historical Society Collections*, XII, Hartford, 1928.

"Roles of Connecticut Men in the French and Indian Wars, 1755-1762," *Connecticut Historical Society Collections*, 2 vols., IX, X. Hartford: 1903-1905.

### 2. *Great Britain*

Great Britain. *Acts of the Privy Council: Colonial Series*, 6 vols., London, 1908-1912. Of great value for official instructions to and reports of colonial governors and other officials concerning slavery as well as information on every phase of colonial life.

Great Britain. *Calendar of State Papers: Colonial Series*, ed W. N. Saintsbury, et al., 38 vols., London, 1860-1939.

### 3. *Massachusetts*

*Acts and Resolves, Public and Private, of the Massachusetts Bay.* To which are prefixed the charters of the Province with Historical and explanatory notes, and an appendix published under Chapter 87 of the Resolves of the General Court of the Commonwealth for the year 1867. 5 vols. Boston: Wright and Potter, 1869-1886. Volumes from 1692 to 1780 indispensable for laws governing Negroes in Massachusetts.

*Acts and Laws of the Commonwealth of Massachusetts.* Boston: Printed by Adams and Nourse, Printers to the Honorable General Court, 1786. Reprinted by Wright and Potter, State Printers, 1893. Valuable for law prohibiting slave trade and kidnapping of Negroes as well as for mention of letter giving account of Negro slaves carried from Massachusetts by the British.

*Charters and General Laws of the Colony and Province of Massachusetts Bay, The.* Carefully collected from the Public Records and Ancient Printed Books to which is added an Appendix. Tending to explain the spirit, progress, and History of the Jurisprudence of the State, especially in a moral and political view. Published by order of the General Court. Boston: T. B. Wait Co., 1814, pp. 368, 384, 746, 748, 749.

*Colonial Laws of Massachusetts, The.* Reprinted from the Edition of 1660 with the supplements to 1672. Containing also the Body of Liberties, 1641. Published by Order of the City Council of Boston under the supervision of William H. Whitmore, Record Commissioner. With a complete Index. Boston, 1899, pp. 84, 85, 87, 88, 91.

*Colonial Laws of Massachusetts, 1672-1686, The.* Printed from the Edition of 1672 with supplements through 1686. Together with the Body of Liberties of 1641 and the Records of the Court of Assistants, 1641-1644. Ed. William H. Whitmore, Boston: Rockwell and Churchill, 1890. Important for first law legalizing slavery in English America.

Dane, Nathan. *A General Abridgement and Digest of American Law with Occasional Notes and Comments,* 9 vols., Boston: Cummings, 1825-1829.

*General Laws and Liberties of the Massachusetts Colony.* Revised and Reprinted by Order of the General Court Holden at Boston, May 15, 1672. Cambridge: Samuel Greene for John Usher of Boston, 1672. Valuable for laws governing Indians.

*Journals of the House of Representatives of Massachusetts, 1715-1740.* 17 vols., Cambridge: The Massachusetts Historical Society, 1919-1940. Of great assistance in throwing light upon imposts on Negroes imported into Massachusetts, petitions for drawbacks, and legislative reaction thereto.

*Journal of the Honourable House of Representatives of his Majesty's Province of the Massachusetts Bay in New England.* Begun and held at Boston, in the County of Suffolk, on Wednesday the Twenty-Eighth day of May, Annoque Domini, 1766 to March 20, 1767. Boston: Printed by Green and Russell. Printers to the Honourable House of Representatives, 1766 and 1767.

*Journal of the Honourable House of Representatives of His Majesty's Province of the Massachusetts Bay in New England.* Begun and Held at Harvard College in Cambridge, in the County of Middlesex on Wednesday, the Twenty-seventh day of May, Annoque Domini, 1772. Also for 1773. Both in one volume. Boston: Printed by Edes and Gill, Printers for the Honourable House of Representatives, 1772, 1773.

*Journal of the Honourable House of Representatives of His Majesty's Province of the Massachusetts Bay in New England.* Begun and held at Boston in the County of Suffolk, on Wednesday, the Twenty-sixth day of May, Annoque Domini, 1773. March 8, 1774. Two volumes in one: Printed by Edes and Gill, Printers to the Honourable House of Representatives, 1773-1774. Useful for efforts to abolish Massachusetts slave trade.

*Journals of Each Provincial Congress of Massachusetts in 1774 and 1775 and of The Committee of Safety,* with an Appendix containing the Proceedings of the County Conventions, Narratives of the Events of the Nineteenth of April, 1775—Papers relating to Ticonderoga and Crown Point and Other Documents illustrative of the History of the American Revolution. Published agreeable to a Resolve Passed March 10, 1837. William Lincoln, editor, Boston: Dutton & Wentworth, 1838. Contains census of Massachusetts for 1776.

*Journal of the Honourable House of Representatives of the Colony of the Massachusetts Bay in New England.* Begun and held at the Meeting House in Watertown, in the County of Middlesex, on Wednesday, the Twenty-ninth Day of May being the last Wednesday in said month, A. D., 1776, Contains proceedings from Wednesday, May 29, 1776 — Thursday, April 3, 1777, n. d. Incomplete photostat in State Library, Boston.

*Journal of the Honourable House of Representatives of the State of Massachusetts Bay in New England.* Begun and held at Boston, in the County of Suffolk, on Wednesday the Twenty-eighth Day of May, A. D., 1771 to May 1, 1778. Boston: Thomas and John Fleet, Printers to the Honourable House of Representatives, 1777.

*Massachusetts Soldiers and Sailors in the War of the Revolution.* 17 vols. Boston: Wright and Potter, 1896-1908.

*Muddy River and Brookline Records, 1634-1838.* Brookline: J. E. Farwell, 1875.

Quincy, Josiah, Jr. *Reports of Cases Argued and Adjudged in the Superior Court of Judicature of the Province of the Massachusetts Bay Between 1761 and 1772.* Printed from His Original Manuscripts in the possession of His son, Josiah Quincy, and edited by His Great-Grandson, Samuel M. Quincy with an Appendix upon the Writs of Assistance. Boston: Little, Brown, 1865. Contains cases involving freedom suits by Negroes.

*Records and Files of the Quarterly Courts of Essex County, Massachusetts, 1636-1692.* 8 vols. George Francis Dow, editor. Salem: Essex Institute, 1911. Indispensable for crimes and misdemeanors of slaves.

*Records of the Governor and Company of the Massachusetts Bay in New England, 1628-1674.* 4 vols. Nathaniel B. Shurtleff, M. D., editor. Printed by order of the Legislature. Boston: William White, 1853-1854. Valuable for instances of whites condemned to slavery, and early reaction of Massachusetts to slavery and the slave trade.

*Records of the Courts of Assistants of the Massachusetts Bay, 1630-1692.* 3 vols. John Noble, supervisor. Boston. Published by Suffolk County, 1901-1904.

"Records of the Suffolk County Court, 1671-1680." 2 vols. *Colonial Society of Massachusetts Publications.* Boston: Published by the Society, 1933. Contains records of crimes and punishments of Negroes.

*Records of the Town of Plymouth, Massachusetts, 1636-1742.* 2 vols. Plymouth: Avery and Doten, 1892.

*Reports on Cases Argued and Determined in the Supreme Judicial Court of the Commonwealth of Massachusetts.* Dudley Atkins Tyng, editor, IV, Part I. Exeter: Charles Morris, 1809.

*Reports of the Record Commissioners of Boston, Massachusetts.* 31 vols. Boston, 1881-1909. The following have been particularly helpful:
Volumes VII-VIII  "Boston Records, 1660-1728."
    "     IX           "Boston Births, Baptisms, Marriages, 1630-1699."
    "     XI           "Boston Records, Selectmen, 1701-1715."

Volumes XII        "Boston Records, 1729-1742."
   " XIII        "Records of Boston Selectmen, 1716-1736."
   " XIV         "Boston Records, 1742-1757."
   " XV          "Records of Boston Selectmen, 1736-1742."
   " XVI         "Boston Records, 1770-1774."
   " XIX         "Selectmen's Minutes, 1754-1763."
   " XX          "Selectmen's Minutes, 1764-1768."
   " XXVIII      "Boston Marriages, 1700-1809."

State of Massachusetts. *Constitution and form of Government for the State of Massachusetts-Bay. Agreed upon by the convention of said State, February 28, 1778, to be laid before the several towns and Plantations in said State, for the Approbation or Disapprobation.* Boston: J. Gill, 1778.

State of Massachusetts. *A Constitution or Frame of Government, Agreed upon by the Delegates of the People of the State of Massachusetts-Bay in convention Begun and Held in Cambridge on the first of September, 1779 and continued by Adjournment to the second of March, 1780, etc.* Boston: Benjamin Edes & Sons, 1780.

*Suffolk County Deeds, 1629-1697.* 14 vols. Boston: Rockwell and Churchill, 1880-1906.

*Temporary Acts and Laws of His Majesty's Province of the Massachusetts-Bay in New England.* Boston: Printed by and sold by Samuel Kneeland and Timothy Green, by Order of His Excellency the Governor, Council and House of Representatives, 1742, p. 15. Important for laws to prevent smuggling of Negroes.

*Temporary Acts and Laws of His Majesty's Province of the Massachusetts-Bay in New England.* Printed by order of his Excellency the Governor, Council and House of Representatives. Boston: Printed and Sold by Kneeland in Queen-street, 1755, p. 142. Valuable for laws against selling Negroes strong drink.

Washburne, Emory. *Sketches of the Judicial History of Massachusetts from 1630 to the Revolution of 1775.* Boston: Little, Brown, 1840.

#### 4. New Hampshire

*Acts and Laws of his Majesty's Province of New Hampshire in New England with Sundry Acts of Parliament.* By order of the General Assembly. To which is prefixed the Commissions of President John Cuttes, Esq. and His Excellency John Wentworth, Esq., Portsmouth: Printed by Daniel and Robert Fowle and sold at their office near the State House, 1771, pp. 57, 101.

*Provincial Papers, Documents and Records Relative to the Province of New Hampshire from the Earliest Period of its Settlement, 1623-1786.* 33 vols. Nathaniel Bouton, D. D., compiler and editor. Published by the Authority of the Legislature of New Hampshire, Concord and Nashua, 1867-1877.

## 5. *New York*

*Colonial Laws of New York, (The) from the year 1664 to the Revolution, 1691-1775.* 5 vols. Albany: J. B. Lyon, 1894.

O'Callaghan, Edmund Bailey, editor. *Documentary History of the State of New York.* 4 vols. Albany: Weed, Parsons, 1849-1851.

## 6. *Rhode Island*

*Acts and Laws of His Majesty's Colony of Rhode Island and Providence Plantations in America.* Newport: James Franklin, 1730.

*Acts and Laws of His Majesty's Colony of Rhode Island and Providence Plantations in New England from Anno 1745, to Anno 1752.* Newport: James Franklin, 1752. Valuable for aspect of slave codes.

*Acts and Resolves Passed by the General Assembly of the State of Rhode Island and Providence Plantations.* Facsimile Reprints. Providence: Oxford Press, 1801-1940. Vols. V and X especially helpful for laws regarding slavery.

*Charter and the Acts and Laws of His Majesty's Colony of Rhode Island and Providence Plantations in America, The* (1719). A Facsimile. Reprints, with bibliographical and historical introduction by Sidney S. Rider. Providence: Sidney S. Rider and Burnett Rider, 1895. Valuable for laws dealing with control of Negroes.

*Early Records of the Town of Portsmouth, Rhode Island.* Providence: E. L. Freeman and Sons, 1901.

*Early Records of the Town of Providence.* 20 vols. Being Part of the Third Book of the town of Providence Otherwise called the Book with Brass Clasps. Printed under authority of the City Council of Providence by Horatio Rogers, George Moulton Carpenter and Edward Field, Record Commissioners. Providence: Snow & Fornbrow, 1892-1909. Contains much information on private manumissions, bequeathing of slaves in wills, inquests, and holding of property by slaves and free Negroes.

*Laws and Acts Made from the First Settlement of Her Majesties Colony of Rhode Island and Providence Plantations* by the General Assembly of Said Colony and Confirmed by Authority thereof according to His Majesty's Gracious Charter. Granted to said Colony in The Fifteenth Year of His Reign Anno Domini, 1663. Providence: 1705. Contains laws regulating slaves.

*Marriages of Charlestowne, Rhode Island.* James Arnold, editor, *Narragansett Historical Register.*

*Nine Muster Rolls of Rhode Island Troops Enlisted During the Old French war to which is Added the Journal of Captain William Rice in the Expedition of 1746.* Issued at the Annual Court of the Society of Colonial Wars in the State of Rhode Island and Providence Plantations, by its Governor, George Leander Shepley, Esq., and the Council of the Society. Providence: Standard, 1915. Valuable for information on Negro soldiers in colonial wars.

*Records of the Colony of Rhode Island and Providence Plantations in New England, 1636-1792.* 10 vols. John Russell Bartlett, editor. Printed by the order of the General Assembly. Providence: Providence Press, 1856-1865. Very helpful for deeds, indentures, and other documents concerning slaves and free Negroes in Rhode Island.

*Three Muster Rolls of Companies Enlisted by the Colony of Rhode Island in May, 1746 for an Expedition Against Canada Proposed by Great Britain.* Society of the Colonial Wars in the State of Rhode Island and Providence Plantations. Providence: Standard, 1915.

### 7. South Carolina

*Statutes at Large of South Carolina.* 13 vols. T. Cooper and David J. McCord, editors. Columbia, 1846-1866.

### 8. Vermont

*Records of the Council of Safety and Council of the State of Vermont.* To which are prefixed the Records of the General Conventions from July, 1775 to December, 1777. 8 vols., E. P. Walton, editor. Montpelier: Poland Press, 1873. Vol. I. Valuable for clause in constitution abolishing slavery.

### 9. Virginia

Hening, William Waller, editor. *The Statutes at Large: being a collection of all the Laws of Virginia from the First Session of the Legislature in the Year 1619 to 1792.* 13 vols. Richmond, 1819-1823.

### 10. General

*The Federal and State Constitution, Colonial Charters and Other Laws of the United States.* 2 vols. Benjamin Perley Poore, compiler. Second edition. Washington, D. C.: Government Printing Office, 1887.

*United States Department of Commerce, Bureau of the Census, Negro Population Growth, 1790-1909.* Washington, D. C.: Government Printing Office, 1909.

*United States Department of Commerce, Bureau of the Census, A Century of Population Growth, 1790-1909.* Washington, D. C.: Government Printing Office, 1909.

*United States Department of Commerce, Bureau of the Census, Negro Population in the United States, 1790-1915.* Washington, D. C.: Government Printing Office, 1918.

#### D. OTHER PRIMARY SOURCES

*Transcripts, Broadsides, Church and College Records, Diaries, Letters, Memoirs, Pamphlets, Travels, etc.*

*Account of the Designes of the Associates of the Late Dr. Bray with an Abstract of their Proceedings.* London, 1766. Valuable for secular and religious instruction of Negroes and Indians by Episcopalian missionaries especially in Rhode Island.

Adams, Charles Francis, editor. *The works of John Adams.* 10 vols.
Boston: Little, Brown and Co., 1850-1856.

Adams, Hannah, *History of New England.* Dedham, 1799.

Appendix, (The): *Or Some Observations on the Expediency of the Petition
of the Africans, living in Boston, & lately presented to the General Assembly of this Province to which is Annexed, the Petition referred to
Likewise Thoughts on Slavery with a Useful extract from the Massachusetts Spy, of January 28, 1773, by way of an Address to the Members
of the Assembly.* By a lover of constitutional liberty. Boston: Printed
and sold by E. Russell, 1773.

Arthur: *The Life and Dying Speech of Arthur, a Negro Man, who was
Executed at Worcester, October 20, 1768, for a rape committed on the
Body of one Deborah Metcalfe.* Printed and sold in Milk street. Dated
at Worcester Gaol, October 18, 1763. Boston, 1768. Broadside, American
Antiquarian Society Library, Worcester, Mass.

"Aspinwall Papers", *Massachusetts Historical Society Collections.* 2 vols.
Ninth Series, X. Boston: The Society, 1871.

*Athenian Oracle, The*: Being an Entire Collection of all the Valuable Questions and Answers in the old Athenian Mercury Intermixed with many
cases in Divinity, History, Philosophy, Mathematics, Love, Poetry.
Never before Published. Third Edition. 4 vols. London, 1728. A
miscellany. Vol. II. Valuable for observation on Christianizing Negroes.

" Belcher (Jonathan) Papers ", 2 vols. *Massachusetts Historical Society
Collections.* Sixth Series, VI-VII. Boston: The Society, 1893-1894.

" Belknap (Jeremy) Papers ". 3 vols. *Massachusetts Historical Society
Collections.* Fifth Series, II, III. Boston: The Society, 1877-1891.

" Bowdoin and Temple Papers ". *Massachusetts Historical Society Collections.* 2 vols. Sixth Series, IX, Seventh Series, VI. Boston: The
Society, 1907.

Bradford, William. "A History of Plymouth Plantations, 1620-1647 ".
*Massachusetts Historical Society Collections.* Charles Deane, editor.
Fourth Series, III. Boston: The Society, 1856.

Browne, James. *The Letter Book of James Browne of Providence: Merchant, 1735-1738.* From the original manuscript in the library of the
Rhode Island Historical Society with an introduction by George Philip
Kropp, Ph. D., Professor of English in Columbia University and a
biographical sketch by John Carter Brown Woods. Providence: Printed
for the Rhode Island Historical Society, 1929. Valuable for light thrown
on opening of Providence slave trade and general commercial business
of eighteenth century.

Burnaby, Rev. Andrew, D. D. *Travels Through the Middle Settlements in
the years 1759 and 1760; with Observations upon the state of the Colonies
by Rev. Andrew Burnaby, D. D., Archdeacon of Leicester and Vicar of
Greenwich.* Third Edition. London: T. Payne, 1798.

Catterall, Helen T., editor. *Judicial Cases Concerning American Slavery
and the Negro.* 5 vols. Washington: Carnegie Institution, 1926-1937.
Incomparable source for the Negro before the law.

Coleman, Elihu. *A Testimony Against that Anti-Christian Practice of Making Slaves of Men wherein it is Shewed to be contrary to the Dispensation of the Law and Time of the Gospel, and very opposite both to Grace and Nature.* Printed in the year 1773. Reprinted for Abraham Shearman. New Bedford, June, 1825.

*Constitution of the Providence Society for Abolishing the Slave Trade with several acts of the Legislature of the States of Massachusetts, Connecticut and Rhode Island, for that Purpose.* Providence: John Carter, 1789.

Cooper, Rev. William. *One Shall be Taken and Another Left: A Sermon Preach'd to the Old South Church in Boston, May 22, 1740-1741.* A Season wherein there was a remarkable Display of the Sovereign Grace of God in the work of CONVERSION. Boston, 1741.

Donnan, Elizabeth, editor. *Documents Illustrative of the Slave Trade to America.* 3 vols. Washington, D. C.: Carnegie Institution of Washington, 1930-1935. By far the best and most abundant source of first hand information on American slave trade. Vol. III indispensable for New England slave traffic.

Dexter, Franklin B., editor. *Extracts from the Itineraries and other Miscellanies of Ezra Stiles, D.D., LL.D., 1755-1794 with a Selection from his Correspondence.* New Haven: Yale University Press, 1916.

——, *The Literary Diary of Ezra Stiles, D.D., LL.D.* 2 vols. New York: Charles Scribners Sons, 1901. Vol. I interesting for sidelights on various aspects of Negro life in New England by a sympathetic and competent observer, especially on religious instruction of Negroes and for Negro members of Congregational Churches in New England. Also for proposed plan to convert the Negroes of Africa.

Dow, George Francis, editor. *The Holyoke Diaries, 1709-1856*: Salem: Essex Institute, 1913.

Felt, Joseph B. "Statistics of Population in Massachusetts", *American Statistical Association Collections*, I, 121-316. Boston, 1897.

"Fitch (Governor Thomas) Papers, Correspondence and Documents, 1754-1766", *Connecticut Historical Society Collections.* 2 vols., XVII-XVIII. Hartford, 1918-1920.

Greene, Rev. Joseph. "Diary of Rev. Joseph Greene of Salem Village, 1700-1714", *Essex Institute Historical Collections*, VIII, No. 4 (Salem, 1868).

Gardner, Samuel. "Diary for the Year 1759. Kept by Samuel Gardner of Salem", *Essex Institute Historical Collection*, XLIX. Salem, 1913.

Hall, Prince. "A Charge Delivered to the African Lodge June 25, 1797" in *Masonic Orders*, I.

Hart, Albert Bushnell, editor. *American History Told by Contemporaries.* 5 vols., New York: Macmillan, 1897-1929.

——. *Hamilton's Itinerarium. Being a Narrative of a Journey from Annapolis, Maryland through Delaware, Pennsylvania, New York, New Jersey, Connecticut, Rhode Island, Massachusetts and New Hampshire from May to September 1744 by Doctor Alexander Hamilton.* Private distribution by William K. Bixby. St. Louis: Bixby Press, 1907.

"Harvard College Records, 1636-1750," *Publications of the Colonial Society of Massachusetts*, 2 vols., XV, XVI. Boston: The Society, 1925.

Hawks, Francis L. and Perry, William Stevens, et al., editors. *Documentary History of the Protestant Episcopal Church of the United States of America. Containing Numerous Hitherto Unpublished Documents Concerning the Church in Connecticut*, 2 vols., New York: James Pott, 1863.

Hazard, Thomas. *Nailer Tom's Diary Otherwise the Journal of Thomas B. Hazard of Kingstown, Rhode Island, 1778-1840 which includes Observations on the weather, Records of Births, Marriage, and Deaths. Transactions by Barter and Money of Varying Value. Preaching Friends and Neighboring Gossip.* Printed as written and introduced by Caroline Hazard. Boston: Merrymount Press, 1930.

Hopkins, Samuel. *A Dialogue Concerning the Slavery of the Africans.* Showing it to be the duty and interest of the American States to emancipate all their Negroes. With an Address to the owners of such Slaves. Dedicated to the Honourable the Continental Congress To which is prefixed the Constitution of the Society in New York, for promoting the Manumission of slaves, and protecting such of them as have been, or may be liberated. Norwich: Printed by Judah P. Spooner, 1776. Reprinted by Robert Hodge, New York, 1785.

Hubbard, William A. *Narrative of Indian Wars in New England.* From the First Planting thereof in the year 1607 to the year 1677 containing a relation of the occasional rise and progress of the war with the Indians in the southern, eastern, and northern parts of the country. Worcester: Greenleaf, 1801.

Humphreys, Dr. *An Account of the Endeavors used by the Society for the Propagation of the Gospel in Foreign Parts to Instruct the Negroes in New York.* Together with two of Bishop Gibson's Letters on that Subject. Being an Abstract from Dr. Humphrey's *Historical Account of the Incorporated Society for the Propagation of the Gospel in Foreign Parts from its Foundation to the Year 1728.* London, 1730. Of inestimable value for controversy over conversion of Negroes in Colonial America and efforts of this Episcopalian Society to effect Christianization of them.

Jameson, John F., editor. *Privateering and Piracy in the Colonial Period: Illustrative Documents.* New York: Macmillan, 1923.

Josselyn, John. "An Account of Two Voyages to New England, made during the years 1638, 1663." *Massachusetts Historical Society Collections.* Third Series. Boston, 1833.

Kalm, Peter. *Travels into North America, 1748-1751 containing its Natural History, and a circumstantial Account of its Plantations and agriculture in general, with the Civil, Ecclesiastical and Commercial State of the Country* ... By Peter Kalm. 3 vols. Warrington and London: William Eyres, 1770-1771.

Keith, George. *An Exhortation and Caution to Friends Concerning Buying or Keeping of Negroes.* New York: William Bradford, 1693. Reprinted from the *Pennsylvania Magazine of History and Biography* with a foreword by George H. Moore. Philadelphia, 1889. The first written protest, against slavery in America.

Kimball, Gertrude, editor. "Commerce of Rhode Island, 1723-1800." 2 vols. *Massachusetts Historical Society Collections*, Seventh Series. Of prime importance for official information of Rhode Island slave merchants and slavery.

Knight, Sarah. *A Journal of Madame Knight on a Journey from Boston to New York in the year 1704.* New York, 1825. An account of early eighteenth century New England life by an observant traveller.

*Life and Confession of Johnson Green (The), Who is to be Executed this day, August 17th, 1786, for the Atrocious Crime of Burglary: Together with his LAST AND DYING WORDS.* Worcester: Isaiah Thomas, 1786. Broadside. Dated Worcester Gaol, August 16, 1786.

Martin, Eveline, editor. *Nicholas Owen: Journal of a Slave Trader.* A view of some remarkable accidents in the life of Nicholas Owen on the coast of Africa from the year 1746 to the year 1757. London: G. Routledge and Sons, Ltd., 1930. Depicts horror of slave trade.

Mathews, Albert, editor. *Diary of the Reverend Thomas Prince, 1737.* Reprinted from *Colonial Society of Massachusetts, Publications*, XIX, pp. 331-364, Boston, 1917.

——. "Plymouth Church Records, 1620-1864," *Colonial Society of Massachusetts Collections*. 2 vols., XXII, XXIII. Boston: The Society, 1920-1923. Gives list of Negroes baptized and received into church during colonial period. Also contains information on church discipline.

Mather, Cotton. *Magnalia Christi Americana or the Ecclesiastical History of New England from its First Planting in the year 1620, unto the Year 1698.* In seven books. 2 vols. Boston, 1820. First American edition from London edition of 1702. Hartford: Roberts and Bros., 1820.

——. *The Life of the Rev. John Eliot The First Missionary to the Indians of North America.* New Edition, London, 1820.

——. *The Negro Christianized, An Essay to Excite and Assist that Good Work, The Instruction of Negro Servants in Christianity.* Boston: B. Green, 1706.

——. *Rules for the Society of Negroes, 1693.* New York: Reprinted by George H. Moore, 1888. Original in M. H. S. L.

——. "Diary of Cotton Mather." 2 vols. *Massachusetts Historical Society Collections.* Seventh Series, VIII, Parts I and II. Important for Mather's attitude toward slavery and part played in converting slaves.

*Memoir of Paul Cuffee A Man of Colour to which is Subjoined the Epistle of the Society of Sierra Leone.* W. Alexander, editor. London: Peacock, 1811. Treats of Massachusetts free Negro who became merchant, ship owner and philanthropist.

*Memoir and Poems of Phillis Wheatley a native African and a slave: also Poems by a slave.* Third edition. Boston: Isaac Knapp, 1823.

Niles, Nathaniel, M. A. *Two Discourses on Liberty.* Delivered at the North Church in Newbury-port on Lords Day, June 5, 1771 and published at the general desire of the hearers. Newburyport: Tinges, 1774.

Warren, Charles, editor. *Jacobin and Junto or Early American Politics as Viewed in the Diary of Dr. Nathaniel Ames, 1758-1872.* Cambridge: Harvard University Press, 1931.

Patten, Matthew, editor. *Diary of Matthew Patten of Bedford, New Hampshire from Seventeen Hundred fifty-four to Seventeen Hundred eighty-eight*: Published by the town. Concord: Rumford, 1903.

Perry, William Stevens, editor. *Historical Collections Relating to the American Colonial Church.* Hartford: Church Press, 1873.

Peters, Rev. Samuel. *A General History of Connecticut from its First Settlement under George Fenwick, esq., to its Last Period of Amity with Great Britain including a Description of the country and many Curious and Interesting Anecdotes.* London: J. Bew, 1781.

" Pitkin (Governor William) Papers, Correspondence, and Documents, 1766-1769," *Connecticut Historical Society Collections,* XIX. Hartford, 1921.

Robertson, Douglas, editor. *Joseph Hadfield: An Englishman in America, 1785.* Being the diary of Joseph Hadfield. Toronto: Hunter, Rose, Ltd., 1933.

Rowe, John. *Letters and Diaries of John Rowe, Boston Merchant, 1759-1762, 1764-1779.* Ann Howe Cunningham, editor. Boston: W. B. Clarke, 1903.

Sewall, Samuel. " Sewall's Letter Book, 1686-1729 ". 2 vols. *Massachusetts Historical Society Collections,* Sixth Series, I, II. Boston: The Society, 1886-1888.

——. " Diary of Samuel Sewall ". 3 vols. *Massachusetts Historical Society Collections,* Fifth Series, V-VII. Boston, Published by the Society, 1878-1882.

Sherill, Charles H. *French Memoirs of Eighteenth Century America.* Illustrated. New York, 1915.

Sparks, Jared, editor. *The Writings of George Washington.* 12 vols. New York, 1847-1852. Volume three contains Washington's acknowledgment of poem written and sent to him by Phillis Wheatley, the slave poet.

Swan, James. *A Dissuasion to Great Britain and the Colonies from the Slave Trade to Africa, shewing the injustice thereof, &c.* Revised and abridged. Boston: Printed for J. Greenleaf, 1773.

" Talcott (Governor Jonathan) Papers, Correspondence and Documents, 1724-1741." 2 vols. *Connecticut Historical Society Collections,* IV, V. Hartford, 1892-1896.

Tudor, John. *Deacon Tudor's Diary or Memorandums from 1709 & by John Tudor to 1775 & 1778, 1780 and 1793. A Record of More or Less Important Events in Boston, From 1737 to 1739, by an Eye Witness.* William Tudor, A. B., editor. Boston: Wallace Spooner Press, 1896.

" Walcott (Governor Roger) Papers, Correspondence and Documents, 1750-1754 ", *Connecticut Historical Society Collections,* XVI. Hartford, 1916.

Walker, Joseph B., editor. *Diaries of the Reverend Timothy Walker. The First and Only Minister of Concord, New Hampshire. From His Ordination November 18, 1730 to September 1, 1782.* Concord: Ira Evans Press, 1889.

Weeks, Lyman Horace and Brown, Edwin M. *An Historical Digest of the Provincial Press.* Being a collation of all items of Personal and Historical Reference Relating to American Affairs Printed in the Newspapers of the Provincial Period, Beginning with the Appearance of the Present State of the New English Affairs 1689, Public Occurrences 1690 and the First Issue of the *Boston News Letter* 1704 and Ending with the Close of the Revolution 1783. Illustrated. Boston: Society for Americana, 1911.

Wesley, John, A. M. *Thoughts Upon Slavery.* London: R. Hawes (No. 34), 1774.

Wheatley, Phillis. *Poems of Phillis Wheatley.* Reprinted from original London edition of 1773, Philadelphia: R. R. and C. C. Wright, 1909.

Winthrop, John. *History of New England, 1630-1649.* James Kendall Hosmer, editor. 2 vols. New York, 1908. Important for beginnings of slavery in New England.

——. *History of New England from 1630-1649.* James Savage, editor. 2 vols. Boston, 1853.

" Winthrop Papers, The ", *Massachusetts Historical Society Collections.* 6 vols. Fourth Series, VI, VII. Fifth Series, I, VIII. Sixth Series, III, V. Boston: The Society, 1863-1892.

Williams, Peter, Jr. *A Discourse Delivered on the Death of Captain Paul Cuffee Before the New York African Society in the African Methodist Episcopal Zion Church.* October 21, 1817. New York: W. Alexander, 1818.

" Wyllys Papers, Correspondence and Documents, Chiefly of Descendants of Governor George Wyllys, 1590-1796 ", *Connecticut Historical Society Collections*, XXI. Hartford, 1924.

## II. Secondary Sources

### A. LOCAL AND STATE HISTORIES

Andrews, Charles McLean. *Connecticut's Place in Colonial History.* New Haven: Yale University Press, 1924.

Atwater, Edward E. *The History of New Haven Colony to its Absorption into Connecticut.* Second Edition. Boston: Rand Avery, 1902.

Baylies, Francis. *An Historical Memoir of Plymouth Plantation.* 2 vols. Boston: Wiggins and Lunt, 1866.

Belknap, Jeremy. *History of New Hampshire.* John Farmer, editor. Dover, New Hampshire, 1862.

Bicknell, Thomas Williams. *The History of the State of Rhode Island and Providence Plantations.* 3 vols. New York: American Historical Society, 1920.

Brewster, Charles. *Rambles about Portsmouth, New Hampshire.* 2 vols. Portsmouth, 1859.

Bronson, Henry, M. D. *History of Waterbury, Connecticut.* Waterbury, 1858.

Barber, John Warner. *History and Antiquities of Every Town in Connecticut.* Improved edition. New Haven, 1838.

Barry, John S. *History of Hanover, Massachusetts.* Boston, 1853.

Brown, Abram English. *History of the Town of Bedford, Middlesex County, Massachusetts from its earliest Settlement to the year of our Lord, 1891.* An account of Indian claims and Troubles; Colonial Grants, sketches of its Heroes; its part in the Struggle for Independence and the War for Nationality; Its Burial Grounds and Epitaphs, Its Industrial Success, and a Record of its whole Progress. Bedford: Published by the Author, 1891.

Cahoone, S. S. *Sketches of Newport and its Vicinity with Notices Respecting the History, Settlement and Geography of Rhode Island.* Illustrated with engravings. New York: John S. Taylor, 1842.

Caulkins, Francis M. *History of Norwich, Connecticut.* Norwich, 1845.

Coffin, Joshua. *Sketch of Newbury, etc.* Boston, 1845.

Cutter, Benjamin and William. *History of the Town of Arlington, Massachusetts Formerly the Second precinct in Cambridge or district of Meontomy, afterward The Town of Cambridge 1635-1879 with a Genealogical Register of the Inhabitants of the Precinct.* Boston: David Clapp, 188r

Cuvier, John J. *History of Newbury, Massachusetts, 1635-1902.* Boston: Damsell & Upham, 1902.

Channing, George A. *Early Recollections of Newport, Rhode Island from the year 1793 to 1811.* Boston: A. J. Ward and Charles E. Hammett, Jr., 1868.

Clarke, George L. *A History of Connecticut, its People and Institutions.* Second Edition. New York and London: Putnam, 1914.

DeForest, Heman Packard and Bates, Edward Craig. *The History of Westborough, Massachusetts.* Westborough: Published by the Town, 1891.

Denison, Rev. Frederick. *Westerly (Rhode Island) and its Witnesses, 1626-1875.* Providence: J. A. & R. A. Reid, 1878.

Drake, Samuel G., A.M. *The History and Antiquities of Boston, the Capital of Massachusetts and Metropolis of New England from its Settlement in 1630, to ... 1770. With Notes and Critical and Illustrative material.* 2 vols. Boston: Luther Stevens, 1856.

Dunlap, William. *History of New York.* 2 vols. New York, 1839.

Felt, Joseph B. *Annals of Salem.* Second edition. 2 vols. Salem, 1845, 1849.

Hobart, Benjamin, A. M. *A History of the Town of Abington, Massachusetts from its First Settlement.* Boston: T. A. Carter and Sons, 1866. Not scientifically done. Anecdotes, etc.

Hudson, Charles. *History of the Town of Lexington, Middlesex County, Massachusetts from its First Settlement to 1868.* 2 vols. Revised and continued to 1912 by the Lexington Historical Society. Boston and New York: Houghton Mifflin, 1913. Second volume largely genealogy. Not scientific.

Hurd, Hamilton D. *History of Essex County, Massachusetts.* 1888.

Jones, Mott Bushnell. *Vermont in the Making.* Cambridge: Harvard University Press, 1939.

Kimball, Gertrude S., editor. *Pictures of Rhode Island in the Past 1642-1833 by Travellers and Observers.* Providence: Preston & Rounds, 1900. Valuable for light thrown on religious training of Negroes by Anglicans.

Livermore, Rev. S. T., A. M. *A History of Block Island from its Discovery in 1514 to the Present Time, 1876.* Hartford: Case Lockwood and Brainard, 1877.

Larned, Ellen D. *History of Windham County, Connecticut.* 2 vols. Worcester, 1874.

Love, Rev. William de Loss. *The Colonial History of Hartford.* Hartford, 1914.

Mason, George Champlin. *Reminiscences of Newport.* Illustrated. Newport: Charles E. Hammett, Jr., 1884.

Mayo, Lawrence Shaw, editor. *The History of the Colony and Province of the Massachusetts Bay.* 3 vols. Cambridge: Harvard University Press, 1936.

Osgood, Charles S. and Batchelder, H. M. *Historical Sketch of Salem, 1626-1879.* Salem: Essex Institute, 1879, pp. 182-7.

McCrady, Edward. *History of South Carolina under the Proprietary Government, 1670-1719.* New York, 1907.

Paige, Lucius R. *History of Cambridge, Massachusetts, 1630-1877.* With a genealogical register. Boston, 1877.

Peterson, Edward. *History of Rhode Island and Newport in the Past.* New York, 1853.

Pierce, John. "Historical Sketch of Charlestowne, Massachusetts," *Massachusetts Historical Society Collections.* Boston: The Society, 1814.

Richman, Irving B. *Rhode Island: A Study in Separatism.* Boston and New York: Houghton Mifflin, 1905.

Ricketson, Daniel. *New History of New Bedford, Bristol County Massachusetts.* New Bedford: Published by the author, 1858. Ch. xx, valuable for life of Paul Cuffee.

Schenck, Elizabeth H. *The History of Fairfield, Fairfield County, Connecticut from the Settlement of the Town in 1639 to 1818.* New York: Published by the author, 1889-1905.

Sheldon, George A. *A History of Deerfield, Massachusetts.* The Times when and the People by Whom it was Settled, Unsettled, and Resettled, with a special Study of the Indian Wars in the Connecticut Valley with Genealogical tables. 2 vols. Deerfield, 1895.

Shurtleff, Nathaniel B. *A Topographical and Historical Description of Boston.* Third edition. Second impression. Published by order of the Common Council. Boston: Rockwell and Churchill, City Printers, pp. 46-49. See pp. 453-55 for blowing up of Canton Packet in Boston Harbor by a Negro, William Read, on Artillery Election Day 1817 as protest against discrimination against Negroes in public places.

Staples, William R. *Annals of the Town of Providence.* Providence: 1843.

Sumner, William H. *A History of East Boston, with Biographical Sketches of its early Proprietors and an Appendix.* Boston: J. E. Tilton, 1858, pp. 90-93. Apologetic toward Massachusetts.

Stiles, Henry R., A.M., M.D. *The History and Genealogies of Ancient Windsor, Connecticut including East Windsor, South Windsor, Bloomfield, Windsor Locks, and Ellington, 1635-1891.* 2 vols. Hartford: Case, Lockwood and Brainard, 1891-1892. Ch. x, treats of slaves as members of churches.

Temple, Josiah H. *History of Framingham, Massachusetts Early Known as Danforth's Farms, 1640-1880 with a Genealogical Register.* Published by the town of Framingham, 1887. Interesting for anecdotes of slaves. Pp. 254-255 gives intimate and favorable account of Crispus Attucks.

Tilden, William S., editor. *History of the Town of Medfield, Massachusetts, 1850-1886.* With genealogies of the families that held real estate or made any considerable stay in the town during the first two centuries. Illustrated with Portraits and engravings after drawings by John A. S. Monks. Boston: George Ellis, 1887.

Wells, Daniel White, and Field, Reuben. *A History of Hatfield, Massachusetts.* Springfield: F. C. Gibbons, 1910, pp. 116-129, 169, 196, 248, 279, 281, 284, 285, 312, 320. Apologetic toward slavery in Massachusetts.

White, Alain C. "The History of the Town of Litchfield, Connecticut," Litchfield: *Litchfield Historical Society,* 1920.

Williamson, William D. A. *A History of the State of Maine from its Discovery, A. D. 1602 to the Separation, A. D. 1826, Inclusive.* 2 vols. Hallowell, Glazier, Masters, 1832. Prejudiced toward Negroes.

Winsor, Justin. *Memorial History of Boston.* 3 vols. Boston, 1881.

Wheatland, Dr. Henry. *Standard History of Essex County.* Boston, 1818.

### B. OTHER SECONDARY SOURCES

Adams, James Truslow. *Founding of New England.* Boston: Atlantic Monthly Press, 1921.

Andrews, Charles M. *Colonial Folkways.* New Haven: Yale University Press, 1921.

Anonymous. *Slavery Among the Puritans: A Letter to the Rev. Moses Stuart.* Boston: Little, Brown, 1850.

Baldwin, Alice M. *The New England Clergy and the American Revolution.* Durham: Duke University Press, 1928.

Ballagh, James Curtis. "White Servitude in the Colony of Virginia", *Johns Hopkins University Studies in Historical and Political Science*, XIII. Baltimore: Johns Hopkins University Press, 1895.

Bancroft, Frederic. *Slave Trading in the Old South.* Baltimore, 1931.

Baron, Salo. *A Social and Religious History of the Jews.* 3 vols. New York: Columbia University Press, 1937.

Batchelder, Samuel. "Col. Henry Vassall and His Wife Penelope Vassall with Some Account of His Slaves," *Cambridge Historical Society Publications: Proceedings*, X, January 26, 1915. Cambridge, 1917.

Battle, Charles A. *Negroes on the Island of Rhode Island.* Newport: n. p., 1932. Interesting for aspects of Negro life in Rhode Island from earliest times to present. Written by Negro. Value lessened by lack of documentation.

Bigelow, Bruce M. "Aaron Lopez, Colonial Merchant of Newport", *New England Quarterly*, IV (October, 1930).

Blake, W. O. *History of Slavery and the Slave Trade.* Columbus, 1857.

Bourne, Edward G. "Spain in America," *American Nation Series*, I. New York: Harper and Brothers, 1904.

Brawley, Benjamin. *A Short History of the American Negro.* New York: Macmillan, 1913.

——. *A Short History of the American Negro.* Revised edition. New York: Macmillan, 1919. Also revised fourth edition of 1939.

——. *A Social History of the American Negro.* New York: Macmillan, 1921.

——. *Early Negro American Writers.* Chapel Hill: University of North Carolina Press, 1935.

——. *Negro Builders and Heroes.* Chapel Hill: University of North Carolina Press, 1937.

Brown, D. E. *Fanueil Hall and Fanueil Hall Market.* Boston, 1901.

Bruce, John. "Prince Hall, The Pioneer of Negro Masonry" in *Masonic Orders*, II. S. C. N. Y. P. L.

Burnett, Edmund C. *Letters of the Members of the Continental Congress.* 8 vols. Washington, D. C., 1921-36.

Buxton, Thomas Folwell, Esq. *The African Slave Trade and Its Remedy.* London: John Murray, 1840.

Calhoun, Arthur W. *A Social History of the American Family.* 3 vols. Cleveland, 1917-1919.

Campbell, Douglas. *The Puritans in Holland, England and America: An Introduction to American History.* New York and London: Harper, 1899.

Channing, Edward. "The Narragansett Planters: A Study of Causes", *Johns Hopkins University Studies in Historical and Political Science*, Fourth Series, III. Baltimore: Johns Hopkins Press, 1886.

——. *History of the United States.* 6 vols. New York: Macmillan, 1912-1925.

Chapin, Howard. *Privateer Ships and Sailors: The First Century of American Colonial Privateering, 1625-1725.* Toulon: Mouton, 1926.

——. *Privateering in King George's War, 1739-1748.* Providence: Johnson, 1928.

——. *Rhode Island in the Colonial Wars: A List of Rhode Island Soldiers And Sailors in the Old French and Indian War, 1755-62.* Providence: Rhode Island Historical Society, 1918.

Chapman, Charles Edward. *Republic Hispanic America: A History.* New York: Macmillan, 1937.

Chickering, Jesse. *Statistical View of the Population of Massachusetts from 1765-1840.* Boston, 1846.

Cobb, Thomas R. *An Inquiry into the Law of Negro Slavery in the United States of America.* To which is affixed an historical sketch of slavery. Philadelphia and Savannah: Johnson and Williams, 1858.

Coffin, Joshua. *An Account of some of the Principal Slave Insurrections.* And others which have occurred or been attempted in the United States and elsewhere during the last Two Centuries. Collected from Various Sources by Joshua Coffin. New York: American Anti-Slavery Society, 1860.

Cooley, Timothy Mather, D.D. Sketches of the Life and Character of the Rev. Lemuel Haynes, A.M., for many years Pastor of a Church in Rutland, Vt. and late in Granville, New York. New York: Published by John S. Taylor, 1839. Treatment of a Negro who became pastor of white churches in New England.

Delafosse, Maurice. *The Negroes of Africa: History and Culture.* Washington: The Associated Publishers, 1931.

Dexter, Franklin Bowditch. " Estimates of Population in the American Colonies ", *The New Haven Historical Society Papers.* New Haven, 1918.

Donnan, Elizabeth. " The New England Slave Trade after the Revolution." *New England Quarterly,* III (April, 1930). Deals in scholarly way with New England slave trade from close of Revolution till prohibition of trade in 1808.

Dow, George Francis. " Slave Ships and Slaving," *Marine Research Society,* no. XV. Salem, 1927. Valuable for contemporary accounts of slave ships and especially for first hand account of R. I. slavers.

—— and Edmond, John Henry. *Pirates of the New England Coast, 1630-1730.* Salem: Marine Research Society, 1923.

——. " The Sailing Ships of New England ", *Marine Research Society Publications,* Series III. Salem, 1928, pp. 1-45. Gives valuable summary of shipbuilding in Massachusetts.

Du Bois, William B. *The Negro.* New York: Holt, 1915.

——. " The Negro Artisans ", *Atlanta University Publications,* no. 7. Atlanta, 1902.

——. " The Suppression of the African Slave Trade to the United States of America, 1868-1870," *Harvard Historical Studies,* I. New York:

Longmans Green, 1896. Still the standard work on this subject. Chs. iv and v especially valuable.

Earle, Alice Morse. *Customs and Fashions in Old New England.* New York: Scribners, 1896. Invaluable for social and religious customs 'of Puritans.

Edward, Bryan, F. R. S. S. A., *The History Civil and Commercial of the British Colonies in the West Indies.* To which is added a general description of the Bahama Island. 4 vols. Philadelphia, 1805.

Felt, Joseph B. *The Ecclesiastical History of New England, including not only Religious, But also Moral and Other Relations.* 2 vols. Boston: Published by the Congregational Library Association and by the Congregational Board of Publication, 1862.

——. " Statistics of Towns in Massachusetts ", *American Statistical Association: Collections.* Boston. Printed for the Association by T. R. Marvin, 1847.

Fowler, William G. " Historical Status of the Negro in Connecticut ". *Year Book of Charlestown, South Carolina,* 1900.

Frazier, E. Franklin. *The Negro Family in the United States.* Chicago: Chicago University Press, 1939.

Green, Samuel Abbott. *Slavery in Groton Massachusetts in Provincial Times.* Cambridge: John Wilson Press, 1919.

Greene, Evarts B. and Harrington, Virginia D. *American Population before the Federal Census of 1790.* New York, 1932.

Greene, Lorenzo J. and Woodson, Carter G. *The Negro Wage Earner.* Washington: Association for the study of Negro Life and History, 1930.

Hall, Thomas Cuming. *The Religious Background of American Culture.* Boston: Little, Brown, 1930.

Hazard, Caroline. *The Narragansett Friends Meeting in the XVIII Century.* With a chapter on Quaker Beginnings in Rhode Island. Cambridge: Houghton Mifflin, 1900. Valuable for light thrown on attitude of Quakers toward Negro slavery.

Helps, Sir Arthur. *The Spanish Conquest in America.* 4 vols. New York: 1900.

Horsmanden, Daniel, Esq. *The Negro Conspiracy or a History of the Negro Plot with the Journal of the Proceedings against the conspirators at New York in the Years 1741-1742.* New York, 1810.

Howard, George Elliot. *A History of Matrimonial Institutions.* 3 vols. Chicago and London: University of Chicago Press, 1904.

Hurd, John Codman. *Law of Freedom and Bondage.* 2 vols. New York, 1858.

Jernegan, Marcus W. *Laboring and Dependent Classes in Colonial America, 1607-1783.* Chicago: University of Chicago Press, 1931. Excellent.

——. " Slavery and Conversion in the Colonies ", *American Historical Review,* XXI, pp. 504-527. Valuable for data on Christianization of Negroes before Revolution. Deals mostly with Negroes in South.

Jones, Abram English. *John Hancock: His Book.* Boston, 1898.

Johnston, Sir Harry H. *The Negro in the New World*. New York: Macmillan, 1910.

Johnston, William. *Slavery in Rhode Island, 1755-1776*. Reprinted from Publications of the Rhode Island Historical Society. Providence, 1894.

*Journal of Negro History*, 25 vols. ed. Carter G. Woodson. Washington, D. C. Published by The Association for the Study of Negro Life and History, 1916-1940. The following articles have been helpful:

Greene, Lorenzo J. " Slaveholding New England and Its Awakening ". XIII, No. 4 (October, 1928), pp. 492-533.

Hartgrove, W. B. " The Negro Soldier in the American Revolution ", No. 2 (April, 1916), pp. 110-132.

" Notes on Connecticut as a Slave State ", II, No. 1 (January, 1920), 79-82.

Woodson, Carter G. " The Beginnings of the Miscegenation of the Whites and Blacks ", III, No. 4 (October, 1918), pp. 335-354.

——. " The Relations of Negroes and Indians in Massachusetts ", IV, No. 1 (January, 1920), pp. 44-58.

Kerlin, Robert T. *Negro Poets and Their Poems*. Washington: Associated Publishers, 1923.

Klingberg, Frank J. "Anglican Humanitarianism in Colonial New York", *Church Historical Society*, Publication No. 11. Philadelphia: The Society, 1940.

Lauber, Almon Wheeler. *Indian Slavery in Colonial Times*. New York, 1913. Best study of Indian slavery before the Revolution.

Lawrence, Henry. *The Not Quite Puritans: Some Genial Follies and Peculiar Frailties of our Revered New England Ancestors*. Boston: Little, Brown, 1928. Delightful account of social customs in New England.

Lawrence, Robert Means, M.D. *New England Colonial Life*, Cambridge: Cambridge Press, 1927.

Loud, Grover C. *Evangelized America*. New York and Toronto: Deal Press, 1928.

Mason, George C. " The African Slave Trade in Colonial Times," *American Historical Record*. Philadelphia: John E. Potter and Co., 1873, I, no. 1, pp. 312-319; I, no. 8, 338-345. Important for short secondary account of New England slave trade. Does not spare New England.

Matthews, Albert. " Hired Man and Help ", *Colonial Society of Massachusetts Transactions, 1897-1898*. Vols. 225-256. Boston: The Society, 1902.

McKee, Samuel, Jr. *Labor in Colonial New York, 1664-1776*. New York: Columbia University Press, 1935.

McKinley, Albert Edward. " The Suffrage Franchise in the Thirteen English Colonies in America ", *Publications of the University of Pennsylvania Series in History*, no. 2. Philadelphia, 1905. Helpful for information on elective status of Negroes in colonial America.

Mendelsohn, Isaac. *Legal Aspects of Slavery in Babylonia, Assyria, and Palestine, 3000-500 B. C.* Williamsport, 1932.

Moore, George H. *Notes on Slavery in Massachusetts.* New York, 1866. Contains a large amount of documentary material on Negro slavery in Massachusetts from 17th century down to 1800. The author is biased against the Puritans.

Morris, Richard B. *Studies in the History of American Law.* New York: Columbia University Press, 1930.

Mott, Alexander. *Biographical Sketches and Interesting Anecdotes of Persons of Colour to which is added a Selection of Pieces in Poetry.* Second edition, New York: Mahlon Day, 1837, pp. 10-12. Interesting for early account of Phillis Wheatley. Short, uncritical.

Murdock, Kenneth Ballard. *Increase Mather: The Foremost American Puritan.* Cambridge: Harvard University Press, 1925.

Murray, Thomas B. *Irish Rhode Islanders in the American Revolution.* Providence, 1903.

Nell, William C. *The Colored Patriots of the American Revolution.* With Sketches of several distinguished Colored Persons to which is added a Brief Survey of the Conditions and Progress of Colored Americans. Boston: Published by Robert F. Wallcut, 1886. Valuable but uncritical series of sketches of Negroes during colonial, revolutionary and later periods.

Palfrey, John Gorham. *History of New England.* 5 vols. Boston: Little, Brown, 1859-1890.

Phillips, Ulrich B. *American Negro Slavery.* New York and London: D. Appleton and Co., 1918.

——. *Life and Labor in the Old South.* Boston: Little, Brown, 1929.

Platt, Orville H. "Negro Governors", *New Haven Historical Society Papers,* VI. New Haven, 1900.

Porter, Kirk. *A History of Suffrage in the United States.* Chicago: University of Chicago Press, 1918.

Powell, Chilton L. "Marriage in Early New England", *New England Quarterly,* I (1926).

Ramos, Arthur. *The Negro in Brazil.* Washington, 1939.

Rantoul, Robert, Sr. "Negro Slavery in Massachusetts", *Essex Institute Historical Collections,* XXIV, No. 4., Salem, 1888, pp. 81-108. Leans to defense of Massachusetts slave trade. Compare with Weeden or Moore. Not accurate on number of slaves per family.

Reeves, Tapping. *The Law of Baron and Femme; of Parent and Child; of Guardian and Ward; of Master and Servant; and of the Powers of the Court of Chancery with an Essay on the Terms Heir, Heirs of the Body.* New Haven: Oliver Steele, 1816.

Shattuck, Lemuel. *Report to the Committee of the City Council Appointed to Obtain the Census of Boston for the year 1845 Embracing Collateral facts and Statistical Researches Illustrating the History and Condition of the Population and the Means of Progress and Prosperity*, Boston: John Eastbrun, City Printer, 1864. Valuable for estimates of Negro Population before 1790.

Davis, George T. and Moore, George H., Esq. *Slavery in Massachusetts.* Two Letters from the Historical Magazine, September and October, 1866. New York, 1866.

Stark, James. *The Loyalists of Massachusetts.* Boston, 1910.

Steiner, Bernard C. "History of Slavery in Connecticut," *Johns Hopkins University Studies in Historical and Political Science.* Eleventh Series, IX-X. Herbert B. Adams, editor. Baltimore: The Johns Hopkins Press, 1893. Mainly legalistic in treatment of slavery in Connecticut.

Swift, Zephaniah. *A System of Laws of the State of Connecticut.* 2 vols. Windham: John Byrne, 1796. Valuable for digest of relations between master and servant.

Turner, Lorenzo Dow. *Antislavery Sentiment in American Literature Prior to 1865.* Washington: The Association for the Study of Negro Life and History, 1929.

Warner, Robert Austin. *New Haven Negroes: A Social Study.* New Haven: Yale University Press, 1940.

Washburne, Emory. *Slavery as it once Existed in Massachusetts.* Boston: John Wilson and Son Press, 1869.

——. "Extinction of Slavery in Massachusetts," *Massachusetts Historical Society Collections.* Fourth Series. IV. Boston: Little, Brown, Publishers for the Society, 1858.

Weatherford, W. D. *The Negro from Africa to America.* New York: George H. Doran Company, 1924. See chapters iv and v for horrors of Middle Passage and treatment of slaves in West Indies.

Weeden, William B. "The Early African Slave Trade in New England," *Proceedings of the American Antiquarian Society.* New Series, V. Worcester: The Society, 1889. Hostile to New England's attitude and participation in slave trade.

Wells, William Vincent. *Life and Public Services of Samuel Adams.* 3 vols. Boston: Little, Brown, 1865.

Wesley, Charles H. *Negro Labor in the United States, 1850-1925.* New York: Vanguard Press, 1927. Pioneer study in this field.

Wilson, Henry. *Rise and Fall of the Slave Power in America.* 2 vols. Boston, 1872.

Woodson, Carter G. *The African Background Outlined.* Washington, D. C.: The Association for the Study of Negro Life and History, 1936.

——. *The Negro in Our History.* Sixth Edition, Washington: The Association for the Study of Negro Life and History, 1932.

——. *History of the Negro Church,* Washington: The Association for the Study of Negro Life and History, 1921.

——. *Free Negro Heads of Families in the United States in 1830*. With a brief treatment of the Negro. Washington, D. C.: The Association for the Study of Negro Life and History, 1925. Indispensable for statistical account of free Negroes and for general discussion of their economic, social, and political status.

——. *The Education of the Negro Prior to 1881*. New York: Putnam, 1915. The standard work on this subject.

Wyndam, Hon. H. A. "The Atlantic and Slavery," *Problems of Imperial Trusteeship*. London: Oxford University Press, 1935.

Zook, George F. *The Company of Royal Adventurers Trading Into Africa*. Reprinted from *Journal of Negro History*, IV, No. 2 (April, 1919). Lancaster: New Era Printing Company, 1919.

# INDEX

Abda, mulatto slave, sues for freedom, 182-183

Abner, free Negro, buys wife, 196, 294

Abraham, slave, testifies in *Chapman* vs. *Anderson*, 181-182

Adam, Negro soldier, 187

Adam, slave, sues master, wins freedom, 183

Adams, Abigail, wife of John Adams, 163

Adams, John, aversion to slavery, 109-110, 110n., abolition of slavery in Massachusetts largely economic, 113, 322

Adams, Rev. Eliphalet, marries Negroes, 201

Adultery, 191; between blacks and whites, 206, 207

Aesop, 248

Africa, plan to Christianize Negroes in, 278-279; dropped, 279

African Lodge, 315

Alden, John, slaveholder, 228, 356

Alford, James, slave merchant, 33

Alford, John, slave merchant, 33

Allis, Rev. Samuel, 145

Allyn, Jonathan, slaveholder, 155

Amalgamation, of Negroes and Indians in New England, 96, 198-202; of Negroes and white persons, 202-210; see also Miscegenation, Marriages, Slave Marriages

Ames, Nathaniel, 221

Anderson, John, slave "governor", 252-253

Andrews, Ephraim, 351

Andrews, William, sentenced to slavery, 19n.

Andros, Sir Edmund, Governor of Dominion of New England, estimates Negro population of Massachusetts, 80; instructions to, 233

Angel, John, slaveholder, 357

Anglican Church, not hostile to slavery, 260, 329

Anna, slave, 214

Appendices, 337-358

Arlington, Massachusetts, 283

Armies, Negroes in colonial, 187-190; in American Revolutionary, 190

Arson, Negroes to be punished for, 135

Arthur, Negro criminal, 158-159

Artisans, Negroes employed as, 111-114; *see also*, Slave Labor

Ashley, Parson, of Deerfield, Mass., taught Negroes God had enslaved them, 287, 330

Assiento, of 1713, terms of, 23n.; importance of, 23

Associates of Dr. Bray, efforts to educate slaves, 241; to Christianize them, 274

Athenian Oracle, 529

Attucks, Crispus, Negro, marries Indian woman, 200; runaway, 295; employed on ship, 116

Austin, George Lowell, 66

Babcock, Hezekiah, slaveholder, 106

Babcock, James, slaveholder, 106 and n.

Bagley, Joshua, Sr., gives land to Negro servant, 179

Bagley, Josiah, slave merchant, 33

Bailey, Frederick C., 195n.

Bancroft, Frederick, 216n., 261, 261n.

Banishment, of slaves to West Indies, 131

Bannister, John, slave merchant, 33

Banns, posting or reading of, required of all persons in New England, 192; by slaves, 194-195

Baptism, of slaves, opposition to, in colonial America, on economic grounds, 257-258; on social grounds, 258; on religious grounds, 259; on political grounds in New England, 261-262; less opposition to in New England, 262; does not work manumission, 261-262, 264, 267; in New England, 268-269, 280; names changed after, 280; in Boston, 348-349

Baptists, 275

Barbadian legislation, 322

Barbados, Negroes brought to, 21; slave code of, 124

Barjonah, Isaiah, Negro Minuteman, 190

Barney, slave, 155-156

Barnstable Bay, 150

Bartholomew, Henry, slaveholder, 186

Bartholomew, Henry, slaveholder, 256

Bassett, Eben D., Negro Minister to Haiti, 252

Bassett, Squire, slaveholder, 252, 350

Divorce, granted husband because of wife's adultery with slave, 206-207; granted Negro slave because of wife's adultery with white man, 207

Dodge, Caleb, slaveholder, 183

Dole, Richard, slaveholder, 356

Dole, Robert, frees slaves in will, 292

Domestic servants, Negro slaves employed as, 108-111; free Negroes employed as, 305

Don, Ebenezer, 133

Donnan, Elizabeth, 17, 18n., 20n., 23n., 24,, *passim*

Dow, Henry, slave merchant, 20n.

Dowd, Jerome, 102 and n.

Downing, Emanuel, considers Negro slaves essential to New England, 60

Dudley, Governor, of Massachusetts, reports Negro population of colony, 80; climate minimizes value of slaves in New England, 101

Dudley, Justice Paul, 235

Duke County, Mass., Negroes in, 82

Dunbar, Paul Laurence, 244

Dutch, brutality toward slaves, 218

Dutch West India Co., 21, 316

Duties on imported Negroes, £4 in Massachusetts, 50; £3 in Rhode Island, 50; Virginia, 56; none levied by Connecticut or New Hampshire, 50; purpose of, apparently for revenue in Massachusetts, 56; to pave and repair streets of Newport and to maintain bridges in Rhode Island, 56; evasion of, in Massachusetts, 52; in Rhode Island, 52; petitions for refund of, 54-55; petitions granted, 54; petitions denied, 55; supplementary legislation to enforce payment of, in Massachusetts, 52-53; in Rhode Island, 52-53; failure of, to end slave trade or slavery, 51-52, 55-56; ordered repealed by British Parliament in 1732, 56

Earle, Alice, 118-119

East Guilford, Conn., 249

Eaton, Governor Theophilus, frees slaves, 290

Edgehill, Captain Simon, 190

Education, of slaves, *see* Slaves

Edwards, Rev. Jonathan, 276; slaveholder, 350, 356

Eggleston, Edward, 102

Eliot, John, furthers Indian and Negro education, 237; advocates conversion of Negroes, 263; offers to instruct Negroes, 237, 327

Ellery, William, slave merchant, Lieutenant-Governor of Rhode Island, 58

Elliott, Rev. Jared, slaveholder, 351

Elliot, Rev. Joseph, slaveholder, 350

Endicott, John, slave dealer, 22

Episcopal Church, 261; see Conversion, Christianization

Essex County, Mass., slave concentration in, 81-82; Quarterly Courts of, 151, and *passim*

Exeter, New Hampshire, number of Negroes in, 78-79

Faireweather, John, slaveholder, 185

Family, importance of, among Puritans, 191; slaves regarded as members of master's, 168; slaves compelled to adopt mores of master's, 192; slaves worship with master's, 277

Fanueil, Andrew, 28; Boston slave merchant, 28n., 42, 70; uncle of Peter Fanueil, 28n.; sold slaves in home, 42

Fanueil, Peter, 28; Boston slave merchant, 28n., 36-37, 59, 70; philanthropist, 59; slaveholder, 353

Farmington, Conn., Negro population of, 92

Farms, slave labor on, 103-108; slaves and masters work together on small, 104; large numbers of slaves employed on Narragansett and eastern Connecticut, 104-108

Father, importance of, in New England family, 191

Ferrymen, 128, 129

Festus, free Negro, 202

Fidella, free Negro, 202

Fitch, Governor Thomas, statement to Board of Trade by, 103n., 166

Fleet, Thomas, Boston bookseller, printer and slaveholder, 256, 353

Fleetwood, Bishop of St. Asaph, declares Negroes moral and intellectual equals of masters, 240; denies incompatibility of Christianity and slavery, 260

Flora, a slave, 226

Fornication, Negroes punished for, 203-204; whites punished for, 204, 206; *see also* Crimes

*Lorenzo Johnston Greene*

Professor Greene's professional career began as Research
Assistant to Dr. Carter G. Woodson, founder and director of
the Association for the Study of Negro Life and History. His
active interest in Negro history and Negro welfare he attrib-
utes to his association with Woodson, who recommended him
for a position at Lincoln University, where he is now Professor of History. Dr. Greene is a member of the American Historical Association, the Organization of American Historians,
the Association for the Study of Negro Life and History, the
Southern Historical Society, and the Missouri State Historical Society. He is author (with Carter G. Woodson) of *The
Negro Wage Earner* (1931) ; (with Mary Colson Callis)
of *Negro Employment in the District of Columbia* (1932) ;
(with Charles Johnson and others) of *Negro Housing* (1933) ;
and *The Negro in Colonial New England*. He is a member of
the NAACP, the Missouri Advisory Committee to the United
States Civil Rights Commission, and was a delegate to President Johnson's conference on "To Fulfill These Rights" in
1966.

# *Atheneum Paperbacks*

## HISTORY—AMERICAN—1900 TO THE PRESENT

# *Atheneum Paperbacks*

## HISTORY

## HISTORY—ASIA

# *Atheneum Paperbacks*

## STUDIES IN AMERICAN NEGRO LIFE

# Atheneum Paperbacks

## LAW AND GOVERNMENT

## DIPLOMACY AND INTERNATIONAL RELATIONS

# Atheneum Paperbacks

## STUDIES IN AMERICAN NEGRO LIFE

## Atheneum Paperbacks

# Atheneum Paperbacks

# Atheneum Paperbacks

## THE WORLDS OF NATURE AND MAN

## LITERATURE AND THE ARTS